FOOD FOR THOUGHT

FOOD FOR THOUGHT

Understanding Older Adult Food Insecurity

**Colleen M. Heflin and
Madonna Harrington Meyer**

Russell Sage Foundation • New York

The Russell Sage Foundation

The Russell Sage Foundation, one of the oldest of America's general purpose foundations, was established in 1907 by Mrs. Margaret Olivia Sage for "the improvement of social and living conditions in the United States." The foundation seeks to fulfill this mandate by fostering the development and dissemination of knowledge about the country's political, social, and economic problems. While the foundation endeavors to assure the accuracy and objectivity of each book it publishes, the conclusions and interpretations in Russell Sage Foundation publications are those of the authors and not of the foundation, its trustees, or its staff. Publication by Russell Sage, therefore, does not imply foundation endorsement.

BOARD OF TRUSTEES
Jennifer Richeson, Chair

Marianne Bertrand
Cathy J. Cohen
James N. Druckman
Jason Furman
Michael Jones-Correa

David Laibson
David Leonhardt
Earl Lewis
Hazel Rose Markus

Tracey L. Meares
Thomas J. Sugrue
Celeste Watkins-Hayes
Bruce Western

ROR: https://ror.org/02yh9se80
DOI: https://doi.org/10.7758/rzos2617

Library of Congress Cataloging-in-Publication Data

Names: Heflin, Colleen, author. | Harrington Meyer, Madonna, 1959- author.
Title: Food for thought : understanding older adult food insecurity / Colleen M. Heflin and Madonna Harrington Meyer.
Description: New York : Russell Sage, [2025] | Includes bibliographical references and index. | Summary: "The U.S. Department of Agriculture measures food insecurity by focusing on whether households have enough money to purchase food during the last twelve months. Among households containing adults sixty and older in 2022, 8.7 percent were classified as food insecure, and this proportion rises to 29.7 percent when the focus is on adults ages sixty and older living below the federal poverty line. When the authors consider the risk of food insecurity over a longer time frame than twelve months, 22 percent of older adults experienced food insecurity at some point in their sixties and seventies. This means that the cumulative risk of food insecurity is quite high across older ages. Food insecurity is not concentrated within a small subset of the population. Instead, a significant portion of older adults currently face economic constraints in their ability to afford food. This book starts with two basic questions: Why does the measured risk of food insecurity go down in older age, and why are levels of participation in the Supplemental Nutrition Assistance Program so much lower for older adults than they are for prime-aged households? The answers to these two basic questions, and the others that they lead to, are critical to understand if we want to ensure that our public policies and programs support the needs of older adults. Motivated by their own desire to dig into the data and lived experience of older adults, the authors aim to create a better understanding of the issues around food insecurity for older adults with the goal of influencing public policy"—Provided by publisher.
Identifiers: LCCN 2024049485 (print) | LCCN 2024049486 (ebook) | ISBN 9780871548580 (paperback) | ISBN 9781610449397 (ebook)
Subjects: LCSH: Food security. | Older people–Social conditions. | Older people–Economic conditions.
Classification: LCC HD9000.5 .H453 2025 (print) | LCC HD9000.5 (ebook) | DDC 338.1/9–dc23/eng/20250402
LC record available at https://lccn.loc.gov/2024049485
LC ebook record available at https://lccn.loc.gov/2024049486

Copyright © 2025 by Russell Sage Foundation. All rights reserved. Printed in the United States of America. No part of this publication may be reproduced, stored in a retrieval system, or transmitted in any form or by any means, electronic, mechanical, photocopying, recording, or otherwise, without the prior written permission of the publisher. Permission is not granted for large language model training. Reproduction by the United States Government in whole or in part is permitted for any purpose.

The paper used in this publication meets the minimum requirements of American National Standard for Information Sciences—Permanence of Paper for Printed Library Materials. ANSI Z39.48-1992.

Text design by Genna Patacsil. Front matter DOI: https://doi.org/10.7758/rzos2617.2205

RUSSELL SAGE FOUNDATION
112 East 64th Street, New York, New York 10065
10 9 8 7 6 5 4 3 2 1

To the older adults in our lives and in this book

CONTENTS

	List of Illustrations	ix
	About the Authors	xi
	Acknowledgments	xiii
	Introduction: The Need to Address Older Adult Food Insecurity	1
Chapter 1	Measuring Old Age Food Insecurity in the United States	13
Chapter 2	The Economic Roots of Old Age Food Insecurity	40
Chapter 3	Beyond Income: Compounding Problems for Food Insecurity	65
Chapter 4	Understanding the Limits of SNAP	88
Chapter 5	Understanding the Limits of Community-Based Free and Subsidized Food Programs	125
Chapter 6	Policy Recommendations to Address Old Age Food Insecurity	167
	Appendix	183
	Notes	217
	References	235
	Index	277

ILLUSTRATIONS

FIGURES

Figure 1.1	Adults Age Sixty and Older Who Are Food Insecure, 2001–2023	15
Figure 1.2	Food Insecurity Rate by Characteristics of Adults Age Sixty and Older, 2023	25
Figure 1.3	Percent Who Are Food Insecure by Age, 2021–2023	29
Figure 1.4	Adults Age Sixty and Older with Household Incomes Below 185 Percent of the Federal Poverty Line Who Need to Spend More to Meet Household Food Needs, 2001–2023	34
Figure 2.1	Adults Age Sixty and Older in Poverty Who Were Unable to Cover Essential Expenses	46
Figure 2.2	Trade-Offs Between Food and Other Expenses Within the Last Month (Adults Age Fifty and Older)	48
Figure 3.1	Factors That Negatively Impacted Respondents' Access to Food in the Prior Two Weeks, by Age	68
Figure 4.1	Total SNAP Caseload, Fiscal Years 1969–2024	93
Figure 4.2	Sources of Income for Adults Age Sixty and Older on SNAP, Fiscal Year 2022	98
Figure 4.3	Demographic Characteristics of Adults Age Sixty and Older in SNAP Households, Fiscal Year 2022	99
Figure 4.4	SNAP Recipients Age Sixty and Older, 1994–2022	100
Figure 4.5	Trends in Estimated SNAP Eligibility Rate by Age, 2002–2018	101

Figure 4.6	Trends in SNAP Uptake Rate by Age, 2002–2018	102
Figure 4.7	Older Adult Uptake in SNAP by State, Fiscal Year 2018	120
Figure 5.1	Nonprofit Programs That Mainly Provide Nutritional Assistance to Older Adults, 2000–2021	131
Figure 5.2	Adults Age Sixty and Older with Household Income Below 185 Percent of the Federal Poverty Line Reporting Having Eaten Prepared Meals at a Community Program or Senior Center in the Previous Thirty Days, 2001–2021	134
Figure 5.3	Number of Nonprofit Organizations That Mainly Provide Congregate Meals to Older Adults by State, 2000 and 2021	136
Figure 5.4	Adults Age Sixty and Older with Household Income Below 185 Percent of the Federal Poverty Line Reporting That They Have Received Home-Delivered Meals in the Previous Thirty Days, 2001–2021	145
Figure 5.5	Number of Nonprofit Organizations That Mainly Provided Home-Delivered Meals by State, 2000 and 2021	146
Figure 5.6	Adults Age Sixty and Older with Household Income Below 185 Percent of the Federal Poverty Line Reporting That They Received Food from a Food Pantry in the Last Twelve Months, 2001–2021	150
Figure 5.7	Number of Nonprofit Organizations That Mainly Provide Food Pantries by State, 2000 and 2021	152
Figure A.1	State Food Insecurity for Adults Sixty and Older, 2023	183
Figure B.1	Qualitative Sample Characteristics Compared with Nationally Representative Poor and Food Insecure Adults Age Sixty and Older	196

TABLES

Table 1.1	Two Perspectives for Understanding the Risk of Older Adult Food Insecurity	21
Table A.1	Major Food Programs Available to Older Adults in the United States	184
Table A.2	Various Measures of Food Hardship	190
Table B.1	Qualitative Sample Characteristics	192
Table B.2	Individual Characteristics	197

ABOUT THE AUTHORS

Colleen M. Heflin is professor of public administration and international affairs at Syracuse University. She is senior research associate at the Center for Policy Research, faculty affiliate at the Aging Studies Institute, and faculty research affiliate at the Lerner Center.

Madonna Harrington Meyer is university professor at Syracuse University. She is Meredith Professor of Teaching Excellence, senior research associate at the Center for Policy Research, faculty affiliate at the Aging Studies Institute, and faculty research affiliate at the Lerner Center.

ACKNOWLEDGMENTS

This work was supported in part by Grant #1908-17412 to Madonna Harrington Meyer and Grant #1905-15081 to Colleen Heflin from the Russell Sage Foundation. Any opinions expressed are those of the principal investigator(s) alone and should not be construed as representing the opinions of the foundation. Our thanks to Claire Pendergrast, Sarah Reilly, Winston Scott, and Rebecca Wang for assistance with conducting interviews; Shanel Khaliq for assistance with data management and literature reviews; Anna Delapaz for editorial assistance; and Gabriella Alphonso, Camille Barbin, Clay Fannin, Hyeryung Jo, Siobhan O'Keefe, Hyojeong Kim, Julia Stafford, Xiaohan Sun, Lauryn Quick, Yuwei Zhang, and Dongmei Zuo for data and research assistance. Our thanks to Suzanne Nichols, our editors at the Russell Sage Foundation, and our anonymous reviewers.

Introduction: The Need to Address Older Adult Food Insecurity

> Sometimes when I look in the fridge and it's pretty bare, and I'm going, hmm, I worked for fifty years and my life's going to end up like this.
>
> —Alex, age sixty-five, with low food security

Most of the people that we interviewed for this book did not expect to be food insecure as older adults. Alex and his wife never gave it a thought as they raised four children and welcomed seven grandchildren. Until they experienced it for themselves, they never imagined they would join the 7.4 million others age sixty and older in 2023 who are food insecure.[1]

Throughout Alex's life, his family had a stable, middle-class lifestyle. He had steady manufacturing work and his wife mostly stayed home with the children. They had plenty of food. Alex used a small inheritance to purchase their current mobile home and save for their retirement. His family's trajectory began to change when he was injured while lifting heavy equipment at work. His unemployment insurance counselor told him he was eligible for Social Security Disability Insurance (SSDI) benefits, but the paperwork and rules proved too formidable, and he never received it.

Alex's troubles intensified when he was fifty-eight. The machine shop closed, he was not in good health, and he could not find work. "I think it's age discrimination. I just couldn't get . . . any interviews hardly at all. And when

https://doi.org/10.7758/rzos2617.2917

I did I'd get a face-to-face, and first thing I could see they'd look at my gray whiskers and go . . . 'Well, you're so close to retirement.'" For two years, he delivered pizzas. Then, because of chronic back pain and a bout with cancer, he was no longer able to work. His wife could not work either. She has psoriatic arthritis and glaucoma, as well as anxiety and other health problems, is unable to drive, and faces serious mobility challenges. During their futile attempts to obtain SSDI, they spent most of their retirement savings. "I kept slowly eating away at my savings, because I was making about a third of what I was. . . . You know, basically just a couple of years ago all the money ran out. . . . I don't have any emergency money anymore."

Out of options, he retired early at age sixty-two. Now sixty-five, he and his wife receive $16,000 annually from Social Security. Like many of the sixty-three low-income older adults we interviewed for this book, they do not always have enough money for food, medical costs, or household bills. "Trying to stay on budget is the big problem. . . . Like we'll go to the grocery store, and you get some groceries . . . that'll last us until payday. And then it doesn't. It just doesn't." They live from month to month. Sometimes from day to day. "Money for us is the problem. We're just really strapped for cash. . . . I don't have any emergency money anymore. . . . I ended up spending a lot of it on medical bills for my wife. Yeah, we're one step away from disaster."

Alex and his wife continually make budget trade-offs. He tries to pay for medications during the weeks he can go to the food bank. If not, the family will run short on food. "I usually get ninety days on my medicine . . . but sometimes you got to buy two or three prescriptions that week, and then that kind of puts a big hole. . . . If that's the week I don't go to the food bank, we might be a little slim that week."

He drives a fifteen-year-old car and must frequently evaluate whether he can afford to get an oil change and still have enough money for food. If his car stops working, he will not have a way to get groceries.

> We don't have public transportation here. . . . I drive [an old] car with 234,000 miles on it . . . and the air conditioning does not work. . . . I'm going like $50 to get an oil change or do I go to the store and get some milk and bread? You know. I'm kind of thinking well, we're not driving that much. We can make it a little bit more.

The couple often needs personal and cleaning supplies but spends their limited money on food. "You put off, you say well, we'll get soap in a couple of days, let's buy some food now. . . . There's been budget trade-offs, for sure. We spend $20 here and there for soap and groceries. Then if we spend it all at once then we wouldn't have any money."

For a while, Alex and his wife received $33 a month from the Supplemental Nutrition Assistance Program (SNAP). But their benefits were small, the amounts kept changing, and the administrative burdens were difficult to navigate, so they did not renew them.

> And then it come up for renewal I had to—I don't know, send in some paperwork, my medical stuff, my paperwork and everything . . . and we go down there to the office. . . . Finally get up to the window. And then she just points at a computer in the hallway and said "You need to use this." I had all this medical expenses paperwork for nothing? And so I just gave up . . . I don't know how anybody gets through the system.

Now they rely on food pantries. Asking for help can be stigmatizing and humiliating, especially at an age when most adults already have spent a lifetime caring for others, but Alex has little choice because he needs groceries.

> It was pretty tough at first for me to do, but I got to looking at the food and I'm going, well, you know, they're giving it away. And you're going they're either going to throw it away or they're going to give it away. . . . But it helps a lot, and I really appreciate it.

When he can afford gas to drive, he gets as much food as the food pantry permits, but often leaves without the components of a well-rounded diet, which further jeopardizes his health. "Seems like meat's been in short supply. . . . Last week when I went to the—both food pantries, I didn't get meat from either one." Inability to obtain nutritious food is further jeopardizing their health. Much of the food he receives is near or past its expiration date.

> They [food pantries] always have a lot of produce, you know. . . . Sometimes it's on the verge of going bad and you don't get much out of it. . . . It really used to bother me to throw out that much food, and I'm going, well, we were the last stop before the trash can anyway.

Alex buys a lot of his food at the Dollar Store, where the prices are low, but so is the nutritional quality.

> We got $20. . . . We go down to the Dollar General, because it's cheap. Get a loaf of bread, pack of baloney and a pack of cheese, pork and beans. . . . I don't think that's—I'm sure it'll keep you alive, but I don't know if that's 100 percent nutritional. . . . It's not real chicken breasts and roasted vegetables that we should be eating. Sometimes we get inexpensive microwave dinners and just eat those. Between Dollar General and Dollar Tree, and going to the food pantries, that's how we do it. That's how we get by.

Alex and his wife's struggle with food security limits the time that they spend with their grandchildren.

> Because, you know, the grandkids or something, they all want to go out and eat and everything, and . . . I'm just going, "We really can't afford it." We have to turn down stuff, you know, if we know that we're going to have to pony up financially. . . . Yeah, I'd like to be able to take the grandkids out for ice cream.

Food insecurity in old age is somewhat invisible at the societal level, but as Alex notes, his food insecurity is very visible to his grandchildren. "It's kind of embarrassing, actually, sometimes. The grandkids come over and they go look in the fridge, And they're like 'Hey. There's no food over here.'"

Alex's struggles with food insecurity are linked to disadvantages that began to accumulate in middle age, including disabilities, layoffs, and difficulty obtaining work. They are also linked to limitations in both federal and community-based programs.

Food insecurity among households with children often makes the headlines. A quieter issue that receives much less attention is the food insecurity faced by households with people age sixty and older. The U.S. Department of Agriculture defines food security as "access by all people at all times to enough food for an active, healthy life."[2] It measures food insecurity more narrowly, based on whether households had problems affording food during the last twelve months. In 2023, 9.2 percent of households with adults age sixty and older met this classification, as did 20.5 percent of households with adults age sixty and older living below 185 percent of the federal poverty line.[3] When we measure beyond the twelve-month time frame, 22 percent of older adults experienced food insecurity at some point in their sixties and seventies.[4] This means that the cumulative risk of food insecurity is quite high across old age. It is not concentrated within a small subset of the population. Instead, a significant portion of older adults face economic constraints in their ability to afford food.

This book focuses on a single dimension of well-being among adults age sixty and above—food insecurity—that connects to nearly all other dimensions of well-being. Though food insecurity often plays out in the privacy of one's own home, it is a social issue, not just a personal one. Food insecurity affects dietary quantity and quality and therefore is particularly problematic for older adults who have unique dietary and nutritional needs.[5] While adults age sixty and older have lower caloric needs compared to younger adults, they have similar or higher nutrient requirements as a result of changes in metabolism, age-related loss of bone and muscle mass, and less physical activity.[6] Older adults have less acute senses of taste and smell, which can lead to a reduction in appetite and make it harder to consume the recommended levels of protein, calcium, vitamin D, and vitamin B—nutrients that reduce frailty and morbidity. Difficulty chewing and swallowing can also make eating difficult.[7] In addition, as adults age, they are increasingly likely to develop difficulties with mobility and stamina that make it more difficult to procure and prepare food, contributing to food insecurity.[8] Thus, older adults face unique challenges to meeting their dietary needs.

Food insecurity is associated with a wide array of negative health outcomes for older adults. Given the connection between diet, nutrition, and health, inconsistent access to affordable and healthy foods is a widespread problem that only becomes more urgent as one ages. Because health disadvantages accumulate over one's lifetime, adults are likely to enter older age with physical disabilities and chronic health conditions that are sensitive to diet and nutrition, such as mid-life diabetes and hypertension.[9] Currently, more than 95 percent of Americans age sixty and older have at least one chronic health condition, and more than 80 percent have two or more.[10] Additionally, a rising share of older adults will experience the later onset of diabetes, hypertension, congestive heart failure, physical disabilities, functional limitations, dementia, and limitations to activities of daily living (such as feeding oneself) that place them at higher risk of food insecurity.[11] The likelihood of acute, episodic illnesses such as cancer, broken hips, and pneumonia also increases with age, which may also contribute to food insecurity among older adults.

Eating is not only a biological necessity. It is also central to social life, and social isolation is a key risk factor for nutritional deficiency in older adults.[12] Eating alone is associated with a reduction in the quantity and quality of food intake, greater rates of depression, and factors related to the gradual loss of oral function, including loss of teeth and inadequate dentures among older adults.[13] Food insecurity can compound issues that affect older adults' mental, cognitive, and social well-being.[14] These include higher rates of depression, anxiety, isolation, and loneliness, as well as lack of social support.[15]

When limited economic resources force older adults to choose between essential expenses, such as food and heat or prescription drugs, health is further impacted.[16] These trade-offs may then lead to avoidable health-care utilization and out-of-pocket medical expenses, further reducing the economic resources available for food. What follows is a cycle in which food insecurity increases the risk of poorer health outcomes, more health-care spending, and more food insecurity.[17] This cycle imposes costs at both the individual and the societal level. Most health-care costs for low-income and older adults are covered by the state or federal government, and food insecurity increases these costs.[18] Put differently, not addressing food insecurity directly will come at a shared societal cost. In the coming decades, we all as taxpayers will bear many of the costs of the negative health consequences.

Older adult food insecurity is an issue that everyone has a stake in—we all have older adults in our lives, including grandparents, parents, other family members, and friends, and will become older adults ourselves, if we have not already. Food insecurity in old age is not limited to those who are chronically poor their entire lives. It also touches the lives of people like Alex, whose life trajectories change in middle age or during retirement, particularly if they live in an area without an infrastructure to support older adult food security.

ADDRESSING OLDER ADULT FOOD INSECURITY

Understanding and addressing the everyday realities of food insecurity in old age is increasingly important in the United States, because a growing proportion of the population is older than sixty-five. Not only are the baby boomers, who were born after World War II and now range in age from sixty-one to seventy-nine, aging, but U.S. fertility and migration are at historic lows and improvements in health-care technology continue to extend life expectancy. Consequently, the number of adults sixty-five and older is projected to exceed the number of children younger than eighteen in the United States for the first time in history by 2034 and will continue to rise over time. By 2060, nearly one in four Americans will be older than sixty-five and just one in five will be eighteen or younger.[19] This increase in the size and proportion of the older adult population will be accompanied by a changing demand for services and governmental programs across a range of areas, including food and nutrition assistance.[20] Looking ahead, concern about food insecurity in old age will grow without substantial policy intervention.

Tomorrow's older adult population will not look the same as yesterday's. On one hand, older adults will be more racially and ethnically diverse, fewer will be married, and more will live alone or with grandchildren—all of which are risk factors for food insecurity.[21] Additionally, fewer older adults will have served in the military and received veterans' benefits than in the past.[22]

On the other hand, three factors will moderate the rise in levels of food insecurity.[23] First, education levels among older adults will be higher than in prior years. Second, more older adults will live in metropolitan areas. Finally, the average age of retirement will likely increase as people remain in the work force longer. Employment, education levels, and metropolitan area residence are all factors that are associated with reductions in food insecurity.[24] However, our analysis of changes in demographic characteristics suggests that, without significant policy intervention, future levels of food insecurity among older adults will be higher than they are today. The United States should rethink its approach to addressing food insecurity to prepare for tomorrow's older adults.

It is well understood that employment declines with age and that the accompanying reductions in income can make it more difficult to afford a nutritious diet. Only one in five adults age sixty-five and older is employed today, including 9 percent of adults age seventy-five and older. However, the U.S. Bureau of Labor Statistics projects the share of adults age sixty-five and older to grow from 6.6 percent of the labor force in 2022 to 8.6 percent by 2032.[25] The increase in employment among older adults, which may work to moderate food insecurity, is attributed to a number of factors, including policy changes that discourage early retirement, the changing nature of jobs that are less physically taxing, an overall improvement in the health of older adults, and higher average education levels, which are associated with later retirement. Nonetheless, the link between employment and food insecurity remains a concern, because adults age sixty-five and older who work earn, on average, just 80 percent of what workers between the ages of twenty-five to sixty-four earn, and only 62 percent of adult workers age sixty-five and older work full time.[26]

However, working longer is not feasible for all older adults. Less-educated and lower-income adults have experienced smaller gains in life expectancy and have fewer productive years in which to work relative to higher educated and higher income adults.[27] Among all people who retire, 46 percent cite health problems, the need to take care of others, or the inability to find a job as the reason for retirement.[28] Among adults age sixty-five and older, 25 percent of men and 16 percent of women are employed. Levels of employment among older adults vary by race and ethnicity—ranging from 25.7 percent among Asian men to a low of 19.5 percent among Black men and 17.7 percent among Asian women to a low of 14.3 among Latinas.[29] While age discrimination laws theoretically create an even playing field, U.S. employers are more likely to offer job interviews to younger applicants with the same qualifications.[30] In addition, older workers are more likely to be laid off or let go.[31] Each of these factors make it harder for older adults to work longer and may contribute to food insecurity.

Nearly all older Americans eventually receive Social Security benefits. Social Security provides continuous income support for workers after retirement and is widely considered the most effective anti-poverty program in the United States.[32] Though Social Security benefits are nearly universal among older adults, they are, for many people, relatively modest. The average benefit for workers who are retired or have disabilities and older widows and widowers (the three largest groups of beneficiaries) is just $1,788 a month or $21,455 a year in 2023.[33] Among people who worked and received average earnings, those who begin to withdraw from Social Security at age sixty-five find that benefits replace just 37 percent of past earnings. Those who begin to withdraw from Social Security at age sixty-two receive 30 percent smaller benefits for the remainder of their lives than those who begin at sixty-five. They receive 45 percent smaller benefits than those who wait to withdraw until age seventy, when the largest benefits become available.[34]

Further, for a large portion of retirees, Social Security comprises the bulk of their income. One in two older adults receive half their income from Social Security, and for one in four older adult households, Social Security income comprises 90 percent of total household income.[35] For households that rely heavily on these benefits, incomes are often fixed and not necessarily able to absorb health or other economic shocks. Currently, Social Security faces a manageable shortfall. However, without action at the federal level, benefit reductions will be necessary, which would further reduce the ability of low-income households that rely solely on Social Security to meet their essential needs.

The Social Security program is often credited with keeping levels of food insecurity and poverty for older adults below those for other age groups, including children, but it is inadequate by itself to address the unique barriers to older adult food security.[36] Our own analysis of Current Population Survey data reveals that among households with annual household incomes below 185 percent of the federal poverty line, 20.5 percent of households with adults age sixty and older report that they did not have enough money for food in 2023. The Supplemental Poverty Measure shows that older adults are the age group most likely to be poor in the United States. The Supplemental Poverty Measure is the preferred measure of poverty because it incorporates the value of social welfare programs (such as SNAP), as well as nondiscretionary spending for items such as out-of-pocket medical expenses, which are much higher for older adults than other age groups. According to the Supplemental Poverty Measure, 14.2 percent of adults age sixty-five and older were poor in 2023, compared to 13.7 percent of children younger than age eighteen and 12.2 percent of adults age eighteen to sixty-four.[37] The fixed monthly income provided by Social Security is insufficient to assure food security for all older adults, but affordability is not the only barrier for older adults.

TIME TO RETHINK OUR APPROACH TO OLDER ADULT FOOD INSECURITY

The United States should rethink its approach to older adult food insecurity. Federal food and nutrition policies play an important role in addressing food insecurity across the life course, but few programs are designed to support adults age sixty and older. While programs available from the U.S. Department of Agriculture reach one in four Americans annually, very little of this support reaches older adults. Food and nutrition programs are a patchwork, and the support that is available differs dramatically by age group, household type, and location within United States, sometimes by design and sometimes by accident.

Early childhood is targeted by the Special Supplemental Nutrition Program for Women, Infants, and Children, which currently covers half of all U.S. infants at birth. Once children enter school, they are eligible to participate in the School Breakfast Program and National School Lunch Program.[38] In addition, after-school snacks and sometimes dinner are available through the Child and Adult Care Food Program. During the transition to adulthood, however, the patchwork becomes thin.

SNAP is the largest food and nutrition program in the United States. It is available to all adults who meet the income requirements, and for those who have disabilities, have dependent children in the home, or are age sixty and older, there are no limits on the number of months that a person can receive benefits over their lifetime.[39] However, in 2022, SNAP uptake for adults age sixty and older was roughly 63 percent that of the general population; only 55 percent of eligible older adults, compared to 88 percent of the total eligible population, received SNAP.[40] In this book we look at why.

Older adults are served by a complicated web of community-based free and subsidized food programs funded in part by the U.S. Department of Agriculture, the Older Americans Act, and charitable donations. Programs include community-based group meals such as congregate meals and soup kitchens, home-delivered meals such as Meals on Wheels, and food to be prepared at home available through food pantries and farmers market coupons. However, the availability and structure of these programs vary substantially throughout the country, in part because federal and charitable funds are administered by local governments and community organizations. Appendix table A.1 summarizes these programs. In this book, we describe meaningful barriers to participation among these food resources—including those specifically designed for older adults—that limit programs' ability to meet the food needs of older adults, and we suggest ways to ease access to these important components of the older adult food system.

Few people we interviewed expected to be food insecure in old age. The twists and turns of Alex's life exemplify how the difficulties linked to food insecurity in old age can accumulate over time from factors such as changing economic opportunities, declining physical health, the high cost of food and medicine, and the declining state of motor vehicles. His story demonstrates how food insecurity is at the nexus of other social problems. Food insecurity is correlated with an inability to meet basic needs such as medical care, housing, energy, and transportation. It is also linked to declining physical, cognitive, and mental health. Therefore, many solutions to food insecurity may lie outside the food system, and efforts to address food insecurity could benefit other important social policy objectives.

This is not a new issue for either of us. Madonna has completed more than 150 qualitative interviews on topics important to older adults, in which people brought up food insecurity without prompting. Colleen has studied food and nutritional assistance programs and food insecurity using a variety of public surveys and administrative data sources since the Department of Agriculture's measure of food insecurity was created in 1996. Working together at Syracuse University provided an opportunity to identify new puzzles that each of us explored in different ways.

We started with two basic questions: First, why does the measured risk of food insecurity go down in older age? And second, why are levels of SNAP participation so much lower for household with older adults than they are for other households? Understanding the answers to these questions, and the others that they led us to, is critical to ensure that our public policies and programs support the needs of older adults. Motivated by our own desire to dig into the data and lived experience of this group, we came together to create a better understanding of the issues around food insecurity for older adults with a goal of influencing public policy.

We started this project just before COVID, and our interviews and policy discussions speak to what happened during and since 2020. The pandemic provides an interesting test case for how low-income older adults are affected by social and economic downturns, as well as for how quickly policy can change when the political will to respond to urgent needs exists. In addition, the differential experience across America during COVID reveals how the advantages and disadvantages of individual life trajectories are shaped and reshaped by local programs and policies.

Our qualitative interviews helped us identify the weaknesses of the current food security measure. We learned that for older adults who do not have enough money to cover all their essential needs, food often ranks below or competes with housing, utilities, transportation, medical care, prescription drugs, and personal and cleaning supplies. The U.S. Department of Agriculture's food security measure is effective at identifying these people as food insecure. However, food insecurity in old age is also linked to nonfinancial factors including poor physical health and mobility; cognitive and mental health issues, including depression, anxiety, and loneliness; lack of access to healthy food; and transportation challenges. The formal measure of food security is not designed to identify older adults who may have sufficient money yet suffer from these nonfinancial problems as food insecure, even though they lack access to enough food for a healthy, active lifestyle.[41]

The emergency food and nutrition assistance system in the United States is not well designed for older adults. SNAP and the web of community-based free and subsidized food programs frequently require transportation or computer and internet service and involve administrative processes that may be difficult for older adults and people with disabilities to complete. Where one lives shapes access to services that address food insecurity, such as the application process for SNAP, and the quantity and quality of available community-based free and subsidized food programs.

Food insecurity is not evenly distributed across the population of older adults. Women, Black and Hispanic people, those with disabilities or lower levels of education, and single-person and multigenerational households are more likely to be food insecure in old age. Yet these groups are also less likely to participate in programs designed to alleviate this issue.

At the individual level, food insecurity in old age undermines physical, emotional, cognitive, social, and financial well-being. At the societal level, it undermines the social fabric of our families, communities, and health-care systems. This book is about how we can and must shore up food security among older Americans.

Addressing the issue of food insecurity in this country is gaining policy momentum. In September 2022, the Biden administration released a National Strategy on Hunger, Nutrition and Health, with a call to end hunger (or very low food security) in the United States by 2030.[42] Increasingly, the idea that food is medicine is leading to pilot interventions that provide nutritiously dense food to patient groups with specific disease disorders sensitive to nutritional intake.[43] However, it is too soon to determine whether these studies will lead to broadscale change in the food consumption of older adults. As we go to press, it is also too soon to know what actions the Trump administration will take and their consequences for older adult food insecurity. We want to make sure that the everyday experiences of food insecure older adults are woven into the fabric of any new policy efforts. Food insecurity among older adults is an issue where substantial progress can be made in a short period of time. We see a policy window that we hope to influence.

CHAPTER 1

Measuring Old Age Food Insecurity in the United States

> Food security for a household means access by all members at all times to enough food for an active, healthy life.
> —United States Department of Agriculture[1]

In 2023, 9.2 percent of U.S. adults age sixty and older—7.4 million people—were food insecure.[2] Unlike other parts of the world, the United States rarely suffers from true food shortages, such as those experienced during COVID.[3] While most Americans do not eat the recommended number of servings of fruits and vegetables to support a healthy lifestyle, it is not because there is a national shortage of fruits and vegetables.

The formal U.S. Department of Agriculture definition goes on to indicate that at a minimum food security includes: "the ready availability of nutritionally adequate and safe foods" and "the assured ability to acquire acceptable foods in socially acceptable ways (that is without resorting to emergency food supplies, scavenging, stealing, or other coping strategies)."[4] While the U.S. Department of Agriculture's definition embraces a wide understanding of the issues related to food insecurity, its formal measure does not include these holistic ideas.[5] Instead, the measure focuses on affordability constraints alone.

The risk of food insecurity in old age is determined by both advantages and disadvantages accrued earlier in life (known as life course theory) and where one lives (known as social ecological theory). This risk falls along other axes of inequality and is higher among women, Black and Hispanic people, those without a college degree, and those with a disability. While the risk of food insecurity declines as one grows older, the level of food insecurity in older age is increasing over time. Finally, rising food prices has limited older adults' ability to access healthy foods.

LEVELS OF FOOD SECURITY

Researchers and policymakers identify four levels of food security, based on responses to a questionnaire designed by the U.S. Department of Agriculture known as the Food Security Scale. When there are children present in the household, respondents answer up to eighteen questions about the extent to which their ability to afford food limits their access to food. When no children are present, respondents answer up to ten questions.[6] For example, one question asks how often during the last twelve months "we worried whether our food would run out before we got money to buy more."

Respondents are then categorized into four levels of food security. First, those who respond no to all the questions are considered food secure. Second, respondents who reply yes to one or two questions have marginal food security. Typically, they report anxiety over food sufficiency or shortages of food in the house, but there is little or no indication of changes in diets or food intake. Third, those who answer yes to three to five questions (or three to seven if children are present in the household) have low food security. Such respondents report reducing the quality, variety, or desirability of what they eat, but with little or no indication of reduced food intake. Fourth, those who answer yes to more than five of the questions (seven if children are present) have very low food security.[7] This is the most severe level of food security and includes multiple indications of disrupted eating patterns including reduced food intake. Very low food security is the level closest to the colloquial term "hungry."

In figure 1.1, we show how the percentage of adults age sixty and older who suffer from each of the three levels of intensity of food insecurity changed between 2001 and 2023. The share of older adults who were categorized as having marginal food security, low food security, or very low food security has fluctuated over the last twenty years, with the marginal food insecurity rate showing the most change and the very low food security rate remaining the most consistent. Marginal food security and low food security have risen steadily between 2020 and 2023. These changes in the levels and depths of food insecurity suggest that experiences, mechanisms, and consequences of food insecurity

Figure 1.1 Adults Age Sixty and Older Who Are Food Insecure, 2001–2023

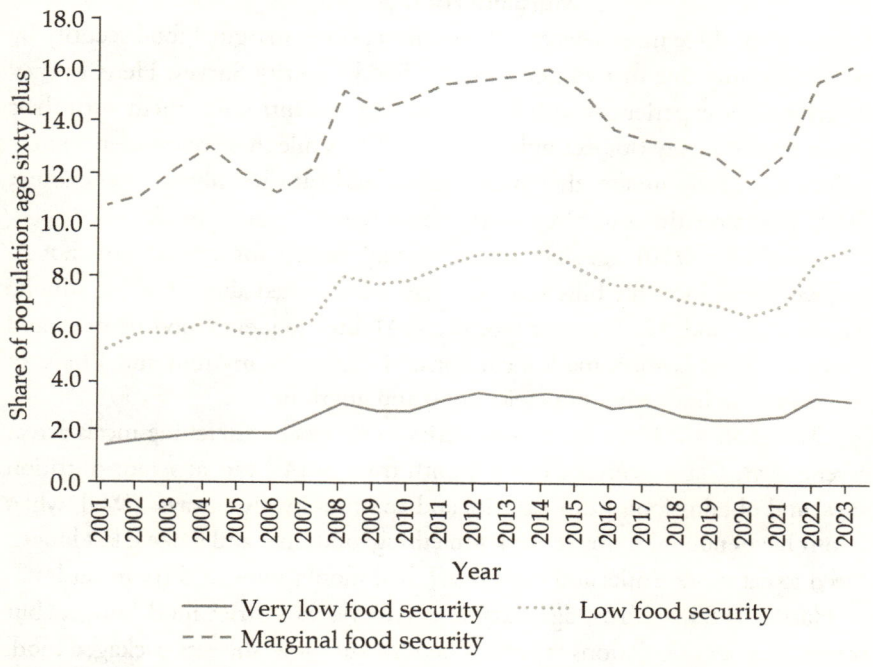

Source: Authors' calculations based on the official U.S. Department of Agriculture food security measure and the 2001–2023 Current Population Survey (Flood et al. 2024).
Note: Marginal food security includes those with low and very low food security.

during older ages are also likely not constant but changing over time, particularly after COVID.

As the older population increases in size, so does the raw number of older adults who are experiencing food insecurity. From 2001 to 2023, the number of adults age sixty and older who had very low food security quadrupled (from 0.6 million to 2.6 million), the number who had low food security more than quadrupled (from 1.7 million to 7.4 million), and the number who had marginal food security (but not low or very low food security) more than doubled (from 2.4 million to 5.4 million).[8] Altogether, this continued increase over time in the number of older adults who meet the criteria for some level of food insecurity means that more people will have family members who experience some level of food insecurity, and that health-care providers will be more likely to see patients who experience food insecurity.

Marginal Food Security

Of our sixty-three interviewees, 19 percent reported marginal food security by endorsing only one or two items on the Food Security Survey. Here, as they describe their experiences with food insecurity, we introduce them with their scores on the survey (for example, FSS = 1/10). While these respondents rarely reduce their food intake, they must budget and eat carefully to have enough food. They sometimes or often worry about having enough food.

Nick (FSS = 1/10), age sixty-six, has enough money for rent but not enough to cover other monthly bills and food. He is concerned about making sure he has enough food. He does not receive SNAP but frequents food pantries and uses subsidized farmers market coupons. "I can make my rent and I have to really work at budgeting to pay for food and anything else."

Clara (FSS = 2/10), age sixty-two, tries to eat less by stretching meals across several days. Clara receives $114 a month from SNAP, eats at senior nutrition sites, and obtains food from pantries and commodity give aways. "Well, when I don't have enough, trying to cook something for dinner and make it last longer. Need to eat more [fruits and vegetables]. Just money wise . . . I try to eat less."

Harriet (FSS = 2/10), age sixty-five, adheres to a strict food budget, but sometimes her calculations are off. When she runs low, she eats packaged food. "I worry about when I'll be able to get more food and stuff. That's why I started stocking up on the ramen noodles."

Low Food Security

Respondents with low food security answered yes to three to five out of ten Food Security Survey questions (or three to seven out of eighteen questions for households with children); 27 percent of our interviewees met this classification. People with low food security rarely skip meals or reduce their caloric intake, but they change the types of foods that they eat and worry about having enough food to eat. However, during interviews, Carmen and Julie, who both had low food security, talked about skipping meals. They often do not know where their next meals will come from and expend time and energy trying to budget and stretch their food dollars so that they have enough food to get to the end of the day, week, and month. As Carmen (FSS = 4/10), age sixty-five, nears the end of the month she eats less and less. She receives $234 a month from SNAP and eats congregate meals. But when her cash is gone, she turns to bread and mayonnaise.

Sometimes, like the end of the month, I don't have much to eat. . . . Oh, yeah, I eat less. I cut down a lot. . . . Really it's not enough. It's not enough. So then comes the food. . . . I try to stretch it as much as I can. . . . I'm going to tell you the truth. It's hard. Because at the end of the month, I don't have a penny to my name. Right now I've got $14 in the bank until I get paid again.

Julie (FSS = 7/18), age sixty-two, lives with her grandson in a household of four and receives $66 a month from SNAP. She stretches her budget by eating just one or two meals a day. While breakfast and lunch are infrequent, she tries to make dinner a constant. "I normally eat two meals a day. It just depends. I might eat breakfast or I might not. I might eat lunch or might not. But it's usually at night."

Very Low Food Security

Respondents with very low food security answered yes to six to ten Food Security Survey questions for households without children or eight to eighteen questions for households with children; 22 percent of our interviewees met this classification. People with very low food security run out of food and are hungry at times. Some older adults described sporadic very low food security, including skipped meals, mainly as food ran out at the end of the month. Others described chronic very low food security, including systematic reductions in food intake throughout the month, such as skipping one meal each day to stretch food longer across the month. They described this reduction as a daily habit to reduce food consumption—not as a response to a specific short-term need but a long-term strategy. Both sporadic and chronic very low food security are at odds with general social expectations. For people with chronic conditions such as diabetes or hyperglycemia, who need to keep their blood sugar levels at a consistent level, skipping meals may endanger their health and well-being.

Older adults with sporadic very low food security tend to skip meals more at the end of the month as income, SNAP benefits, and food supplies are exhausted. For Kenneth (FSS = 6/10), age sixty-two, very low food security is sporadic. He receives $210 a month from SNAP and frequents food pantries. He explained just how long a month can seem when there are other younger household members to feed first. "I would not eat so that they could eat. . . . You don't have the money to get food. . . . You live from paycheck to paycheck. . . . I've got my self-pride but, you know I don't like to ask for food."

For Nancy (FSS = 8/10), age seventy-one, very low food security is episodic. It hits hard at the end of the month, when she is often nearly out of food. She receives $186 a month from SNAP, eats home-delivered meals, and obtains food from pantries. She tries to stretch meals out over several days. "Just at the end of the month, when I've just run out of money and didn't have any to get anything. Yeah, the last few days. I just scrounge up and deal with what I got in the house."

People with chronic very low food security tend to skip meals systematically across the month to ensure they will still have food at the end of the month. Meredith (FSS = 6/10), age sixty, adheres to a strict grocery list to stretch her food across the month. She does not receive SNAP but goes to food pantries to obtain food.

> I have drastically less than what I need. I have less than half of what I need. . . . I don't get everything I want. I get it because it's cheap. . . . My finances work so I can pay the electric, pay the water and garbage—pay that. And there was probably about $50 or $60 for the food.

Ruth (FSS = 10/10), age sixty, always stretches meals for an additional day. Ruth used to receive $40 a month in SNAP benefits, until she was removed from SNAP because she began to receive Social Security widow benefits. She was trying to reenroll in SNAP when we spoke to her. In the meantime, she relies heavily on the food pantry at her church and a home-delivered senior food box. There is very little fresh produce; much of the food is expired or turning, and she has to throw it out. She struggles to pay her household bills and frequently runs out of food. She has trained her body to become used to just one or two meals a day.

> You learn to keep a little for—or you eat less one day so you can make it two or three days or you spread it out. You know? I mean you just have to learn to adjust. . . . When food is short you know your body don't . . . your body's used to what it's used to.

Ginny (FSS = 7/10), age sixty-two, experiences chronic food insecurity. She stretches food by eating only one or two meals a day so that she will have food for the month. "I have breakfast regularly, and dinner is sporadic. Lunch I eat sporadically."

A BRIEF HISTORY OF THE MEASUREMENT OF FOOD SECURITY

In the 1990s, the U.S. Department of Agriculture developed the Food Security Supplement to measure food security, food expenditures, and participation in food and nutrition programs. This official food security measure, developed under the leadership of Mark Nord at the department's Economic Research Service, was included in the Current Population Survey, an annual survey of a national representative sample of U.S. households conducted by the U.S. Census Bureau since 1995. The Food Security Supplement questions focus exclusively on identifying food limitations that occur because "there wasn't enough money for food." Individuals who restrict their intake voluntarily, such as dieters, or those who face other barriers to meeting their food needs, such as physical access or transportation barriers, are excluded by design through the word choice of each question. Appendix A provides the full eighteen-item Food Security Scale.[9] The U.S. Department of Agriculture releases annual estimates each fall for food insecurity levels in the prior year.

Over time, the U.S. Department of Agriculture has created six- and ten-item versions of the eighteen-item scale, as well as a thirty-day measure of food security. Additionally, a two-item measure, the Hunger Vital Sign, based on the Food Security Scale, is now used in a variety of public and private clinical settings, including those operated by the Veteran's Health Administration. The two items are, first, "within the past 12 months we worried whether our food would run out before we got money to buy more," and second, "within the past 12 months the food we bought just didn't last and we didn't have money to get more." Respondents are given the choice to answer whether these statements are often true, sometimes true, or never true. Those who answer sometimes or often true are screened as food insecure. This measure has been validated for clinical use among older adults, as well as other age groups.[10] The level of food insecurity varies depending on how food security is defined, the length of the reference period, and the specific details of the survey, including how it is administered (online or in person); the income, age, and geography of the target population; the size of the sample; and the time of year it is fielded.

The term "food insecurity" is used informally in the United States by the public and media in a variety of ways. In this book, we use the formal U.S. Department of Agriculture measure whenever possible and state clearly when we use a different measure that is the best information available. For example, the Health and Retirement Study uses a single-item report of whether households have not always had enough money to buy the food that they needed within the last two years. While food insecurity is sometimes used as a synonym for the term hunger, a 2006 Committee on National Statistics of the National Academies report drew a clear distinction between food insecurity and hunger. Based on this report, we do not use the term hunger, though some of our respondents did so.

Food insufficiency is an alternative measure of food adequacy that is assessed with a single item measuring whether households "sometimes or often do not have enough to eat." During COVID, the Household PULSE Survey used this single-item measure to assess food insufficiency within the last seven days to track rapid changes over time. Food insufficiency is measured across a twelve-month reference period in the U.S. Department of Agriculture's Food Security Supplement as a screener question. Comparisons of the two measures indicate that the population classified as food secure and food sufficient are quite similar, although levels of food insufficiency are generally much lower than those for food insecurity.[11] In 2019, 2.8 percent of adults age sixty and older were classified as food insufficient. During COVID, food insufficiency rose to 4.9 percent in July 2020.[12]

THE DIFFERENCE BETWEEN FOOD INSECURITY AND POVERTY

A common misconception about food insecurity is that it captures the same general experience as the poverty measure and that the population that is food insecure is basically the same as the population that is poor. This view is both a simplification of the underlying reasons for food insecurity and not empirically true. While food insecurity and poverty are clearly related, the two measures are quite distinct.[13] Sometimes, this difference is described conceptually as one in which food security is an intrinsic need, or a resource required for survival, while having enough income to avoid poverty is an instrumental need, or a resource that allows one to obtain other resources needed for survival.[14]

According to the 2023 Current Population Survey data, 38.7 percent of households with household incomes below the federal poverty line were food insecure.[15] One implication of this statistic is that most poor households managed to avoid experiencing food insecurity in 2023, perhaps in part due

Table 1.1 Two Perspectives for Understanding the Risk of Older Adult Food Insecurity

		Life Course Perspective	
		Low advantage in earlier life	High advantage in earlier life
Social Ecological Model	Low resources	High risk of food insecurity	Moderate risk of food insecurity
	High resources	Moderate risk of food insecurity	Low risk of food insecurity

Source: Authors' representation of conceptual framework.

to the support of food and nutritional assistance programs. Furthermore, although food insecurity is more common among low-income households, it is not limited to them: 7.4 percent of households with household incomes greater than 185 percent of the federal poverty line, or $57,165 for a family of four, were food insecure in 2023, with 2.6 percent reporting very low food security.[16]

Finally, the design of the U.S. social welfare system prioritizes food insecurity over other social outcomes, such as income poverty. Policymakers typically design policies to address basic needs, and SNAP is one of the largest social welfare programs in the United States (see chapter 4). Given this policy emphasis, it is important to understand the extent to which food insecurity and poverty provide different metrics of success for the social welfare system. Scholars on both the left and right of the political spectrum are interested in using direct measures of well-being, such as food insecurity, as a means of measuring progress toward social and economic goals.[17]

OUR CONCEPTUAL MODEL OF THE RISK OF OLD AGE FOOD INSECURITY

While food insecurity may have a simple definition, the forces that lead to food insecurity in old age are complex. Understanding food insecurity among older adults requires viewing the issue through the intersection of two different perspectives simultaneously: the life course perspective and the social ecological model, as shown in table 1.1.

The life course perspective emphasizes the extent to which people reach older adulthood with the cumulative advantages or disadvantages that they have built up earlier in life.[18] At the core are the beliefs that the timing and location of events matter, that humans continue to develop throughout their life span, that people make decisions based on the context of their lives, and that social relationships with family and friends influence how one experiences events. Life course theory recognizes the importance of access to healthy food at every age across the entire life course. People arrive at old age with different levels of resources across a range of factors that influence the individual risk of food insecurity, such as health conditions, economic resources, social networks, and knowledge of and attitudes toward social welfare programs. Each of these factors, in different ways, together capture the individual-level resources and constraints older people face when pursuing access to a sufficient supply of healthy food.[19]

The social ecological model emphasizes the extent to which food insecurity in old age is linked to variation in interpersonal, institutional, community, social, political, and economic factors.[20] It suggests that many of the causes of, and solutions to, food insecurity lay outside the food system. Compounding factors such as poor health and mobility, mental health challenges including anxiety and depression, lack of access to healthy food, and inadequate transportation increase the risk of food insecurity.[21] The neighborhood in which one lives may either raise or reduce the risk of food insecurity. If the local community provides reliable transportation, excellent grocery stores, and a wide array of free and subsidized food options, the risk of food insecurity may lower. If it does not offer such resources, the risk of food insecurity may increase.

Together, these two perspectives help explain the differences in the lived experiences of two of the older adults we interviewed. One of our respondents, Deb, is a sixty-two-year-old widowed Hispanic woman who lives with her forty-year-old daughter with a disability. She receives $16,000 a year from a Social Security widow pension and a private widow pension. Her daughter receives about $6,000 a year in Supplemental Security Income (SSI) and SNAP, bringing the household total to $22,000. Though her household budget is tight, Deb is food secure and can pay her bills in full each month. By contrast, Gerald is a sixty-seven-year-old divorced Black man who lives with his fifty-year-old stepson with a disability. Gerald receives $19,000 a year in Social Security and $16 a month from SNAP. Gerald's household budget is very tight. He has very low food security and frequently needs to trade between paying for food and paying for other household necessities.

Given the similarities in their household composition and budgets, why are Deb's and Gerald's levels of food insecurity so different? In part, the difference is attributable to the differences in their life course trajectories. As life course theory points out, over their lifetimes, some people accumulate more advantages and others accumulate more disadvantages. Deb was married for thirty years and accumulated certain advantages. She earned a four-year college degree and worked as a government official in a job that now provides her with health and dental insurance and a pension. She is in good health, despite asthma, high cholesterol, and a stent. She can walk to the grocery store and push the cart full of groceries home. She often volunteers, enjoys spending time with her sisters, and attends extended family celebrations.

By contrast, Gerald was married for fifteen years before his divorce and accumulated certain disadvantages. He has a GED and rents a second-floor apartment with his son-in-law. Both men's disabilities make it very difficult for them to navigate the steps to their home. Gerald's disability from a back injury makes it difficult for him to walk and impossible for him to take public transportation. He has end-stage kidney disease, diabetes, and high blood pressure. He needs a kidney transplant. He has no contact with his two adult children or any of his grandchildren, because he is angry that they refuse to test whether they are eligible to donate a kidney to him. He does not own a car and is mostly housebound unless he can pay a friend for a ride.

In part, the difference in food security between Deb and Gerald is attributable to the magnitude of the resources in the neighborhoods where they live. As social ecological theory suggests, the types of social programs available, and the scale of those programs, vary markedly by state, county, and even neighborhood. Residents living in some areas have access to numerous programs that are open many hours and offer a wide variety of goods and services, while residents living in other areas have access to fewer programs with narrower hours and sparse goods and services.

Deb regularly eats meals with other older adults at her local senior nutrition site. When those meals were discontinued during COVID, the center delivered boxes of food to her home. Whenever she is running short of food, she can visit a food pantry and get what she needs. She receives farmers market vouchers for fresh produce. She said members of her community look out for each other to make sure they all know where to find free and subsidized food.

Her car is not working well, and she cannot afford to fix it, but transportation is easily accessible where she lives. When she needs groceries, she takes the train, walks, or calls a friend for a ride.

Gerald also eats meals with other older adults at his local senior nutrition site, but only when he can afford to pay a cab or a friend for a ride. He is permitted to bring home one box of food per month, but he has difficulty getting it home and up the steps in his building. Moreover, the box of free food is typically filled with processed food that he cannot eat. Because he lacks access to fresh produce, most of his fruits and vegetables come from cans. His girlfriend occasionally visits and brings food for him but he sees no family members. He lives near a grocery store, but it is too far for him to walk, so he can only get groceries when he has a ride and when someone can carry his grocery bags up the steps. When he is short on food, he tries to eat at soup kitchens, but they are far from his home and the rides are usually too expensive. He used to tend a garden that was overflowing with his favorite produce, but during COVID the landlord closed that garden. He sometimes skips meals, eats meals that are not properly balanced, or makes budget trade-offs between paying for food and paying for transportation, clothing, household supplies, or medical care. He needs dental care, but because Medicare only covers prevention, he is delaying care until he can afford to pay out of pocket.

Deb is an example of the intersection shown in the bottom right box of table 1.1, with a low risk of food insecurity; Gerald would fit into the top left gray box, with a high risk of food insecurity. This simplified typology provides an overview of our conceptual model to explain why there is so much variation in older adult food insecurity, how much of the risk is related to earlier life advantage and disadvantage, and why levels of food insecurity differ by geographic area. Life course and social ecological factors operate on a three-dimensional continuum and vary over time. Much like Deb and Gerald, most individuals experience both positive and negative aspects in their life course and their environment. For any individual, both dimensions shape the everyday reality of food insecurity.

RISK FACTORS FOR FOOD INSECURITY

The risk of food insecurity is not equally shared among all older adults in the United States. In 2023, 9.2 percent of adults age sixty and older met the criteria for food insecurity (3.2 percent were classified as having very low food security). Figure 1.2 shows who is more likely to be food insecure in old age.

Figure 1.2 Food Insecurity Rate by Characteristics of Adults Age Sixty and Older, 2023

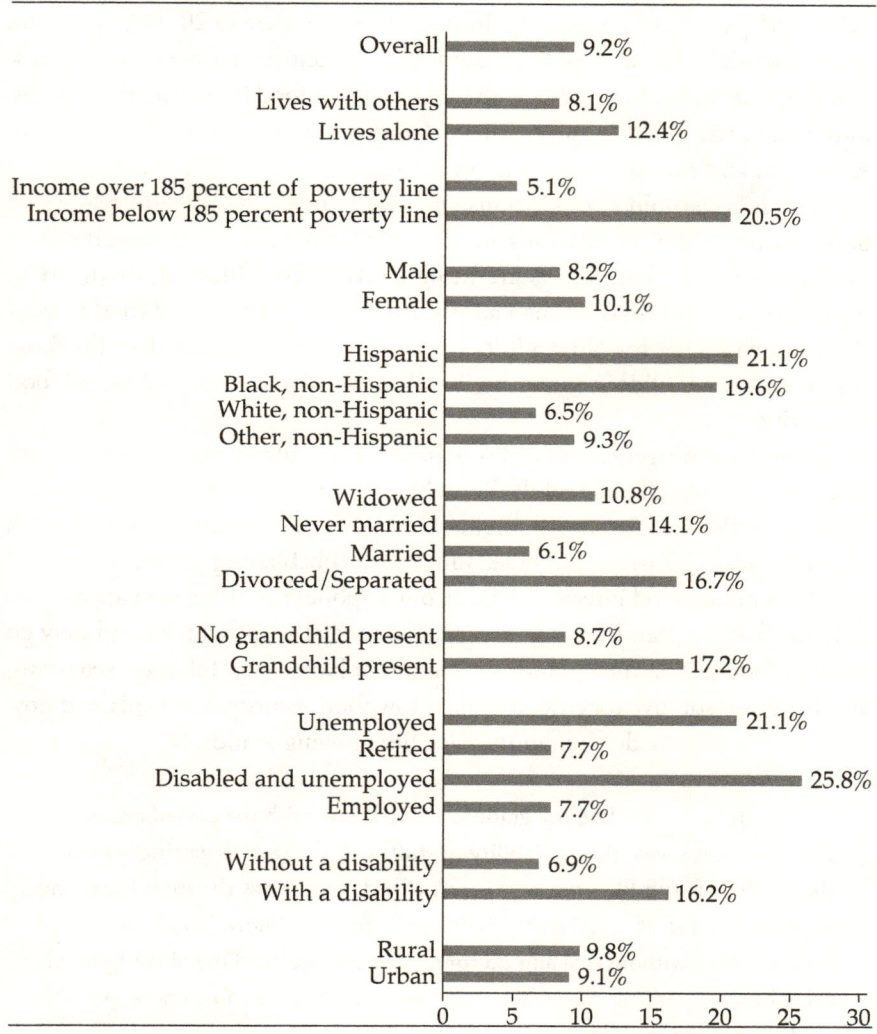

Overall	9.2%
Lives with others	8.1%
Lives alone	12.4%
Income over 185 percent of poverty line	5.1%
Income below 185 percent poverty line	20.5%
Male	8.2%
Female	10.1%
Hispanic	21.1%
Black, non-Hispanic	19.6%
White, non-Hispanic	6.5%
Other, non-Hispanic	9.3%
Widowed	10.8%
Never married	14.1%
Married	6.1%
Divorced/Separated	16.7%
No grandchild present	8.7%
Grandchild present	17.2%
Unemployed	21.1%
Retired	7.7%
Disabled and unemployed	25.8%
Employed	7.7%
Without a disability	6.9%
With a disability	16.2%
Rural	9.8%
Urban	9.1%

Source: Authors' calculations based on the official U.S. Department of Agriculture food security measure and 2023 Current Population Survey (U.S. Census Bureau 2024).

The ratio of household incomes to the poverty line is strongly related to food insecurity. One in five older adults living in households with incomes below 185 percent of the poverty line were food insecure in 2023. Women are at a higher risk than men of older adult food insecurity. Non-Hispanic Black and Hispanic individuals face much higher rates of food insecurity than White individuals, with "Other, non-Hispanic" individuals (including Asian, Native American, and mixed-race people) in between.

Certain household compositions and family types that are more likely to occur among older populations are also associated with an increased risk of food insecurity. Older adults are more likely to be widowed, divorced or separated, or never married than adults age 25–64.[22] The risk of food insecurity is much higher for older adults with these marital statuses than for those who are married. Older adults who live alone are also at increased risk of food insecurity.

Living in multigenerational households, particularly skipped-generation households in which older adults live with and are responsible for their grandchildren, is also associated with higher levels of food insecurity.[23] As figure 1.2 demonstrates, 17.2 percent of older adults with cohabitating grandchildren and grandparents are food insecure. Among our respondents, those who are responsible for feeding grandchildren described a special set of worries and may go without food so that their grandchildren might have more. Julie, age sixty-two, and her grandson live together and have low food security. She explained how difficult it is to provide enough milk for her growing grandson.

> I worry about . . . feeding my grandson. You know, with the cost of everything and the—you know, the availability of stuff with the world's getting—I worry about a lot of stuff like that. . . . I can't afford, you know, the fresh fruits and vegetables and stuff. . . . Again, it's like milk and you know, like the meat and stuff. I may go without that and eat something else because I'm going to provide it for him. . . . It's the vegetables and fruit and the milk. You know, essential needs of a growing child.

Another key risk factor for food insecurity is living with a disability.[24] In 2023, 29 percent of households that included adults with disabilities were food insecure (34 percent of households that included an adult out of the labor force because of disability).[25] The relationship between food insecurity and disability is so strong that among all food insecure households, one in two contain an adult with a work-limiting disability.[26] In 2023, one in five adults age sixty and older who are out of the labor force due to unemployment and one in four due to disability are food insecure, compared to 7.7 percent of older adults who are retired or employed. Among all disabled adults age sixty and older, 16.2 percent were food insecure in 2023.

Adults with work-related disabilities may reduce food insecurity by qualifying for SSDI support until the Social Security age of retirement, as well as SSI. For example, Russell, age sixty-four, had to leave the labor force after he could no longer complete the lifting his job required. "Worked in the grocery store . . . I worked in produce. It was a lot of lifting and rotating and dating stuff and kind of messed my back up doing that. . . . I couldn't lift. I couldn't lift no more." Yet he has remained food secure, because he now receives SNAP benefits of $194 a month, SSI, and SSDI.

In contrast, Julie, age sixty-two with low food security, has numerous health conditions that made working difficult, but she never qualified for SSDI. She lives with her grandson in a household of four and receives $66 a month from SNAP. She has low food security and frequently obtains food at pantries.

> I haven't worked in ten years. . . . I have a lot of disabilities. . . . I'm diabetic. . . . I have thyroid issues. I have high blood pressure issues. I have cholesterol issues . . . PTSD, severe depression, severe anxiety . . . the last ten years have been due to illness and stuff. I just finally got widow's benefits when I turned sixty. So I had no income for like ten years. . . . Some months, you know, there's not enough for food or I have to switch things up because of the other things I have to pay.

Health issues experienced earlier in life, particularly those that impact the type and amount of work that people can perform, can increase the risk of food insecurity in older age by reducing the ability to work during prime adulthood. This connection between earlier health and employment status and later life food security status is one example of how early life course events can increase the risk of food insecurity in old age.

Disability-related programs are among the hardest types of income support programs to access. Applicants often wait over a year from the point of application to the start of benefits, and more often than not, their applications end in denial. SSDI requires a five-month waiting period before benefits can begin, and the current website indicates that applicants can expect to wait six to eight months for an initial decision.[27] Only 20 percent of initial claims were awarded in 2019, with another three percent or so being awarded on appeal (on average, 67 percent of claims are denied).[28] Between 2019 and 2021, 57 percent of adults with disabilities who applied for SSI were also denied benefits.[29] Since benefits are tied to the amount of income earned while working, SSDI tends to pay out higher benefits than SSI, which only provides cash income to low-income individuals. Additionally, because of the difficulty accessing disability income support programs, adults who enter old age with preexisting disabilities are more likely to have already experienced changes in nutritional intake.[30] In chapter 3, we discuss the other ways in which poor health can act as a barrier to food insecurity by making it difficult to access, prepare, and eat healthy and nutritious food.

Finally, as the social ecological model predicts, the risk of food insecurity also varies substantially by geography. Where one lives is an important determinant of food insecurity that reflects differences in economic conditions and access to transportation and food, variations in state policies governing eligibility and generosity of social welfare programs, and the availability of local sources of support such as churches, nonprofit organizations, and senior supportive services. There are some clear and consistent patterns. Generally, food insecurity levels are higher among residents of rural areas relative to urban residents (see figure 1.2).

At a regional level, food insecurity is generally higher in the South because of state policy differences. In fact, in 2023, seven of the ten states with the highest levels of older adult food insecurity were in the South. The level of food insecurity among older adults varies by state, from 3.3 percent in Nebraska to 16.0 percent in Texas.[31] (We include a map of state food insecurity levels for adults age sixty and older in the appendix; see figure A.1.) We address the reasons for these systematic differences by region and state more fully in chapters 4 and 5, in which we discuss the extent to which access to food and nutritional services varies by state.

The risk of food insecurity changes as one ages. It is highest during childhood; after age eighteen, the risk declines steadily to midlife, when it remains relatively stable. The risk falls again after age sixty, because of the availability of income support through Social Security and the different eligibility criteria for SNAP (see figure 1.3). Using Current Population Survey data from 2021 to 2023, we plot the risk of food insecurity by age and show that the percentage

Figure 1.3   Percent Who Are Food Insecure by Age, 2021–2023

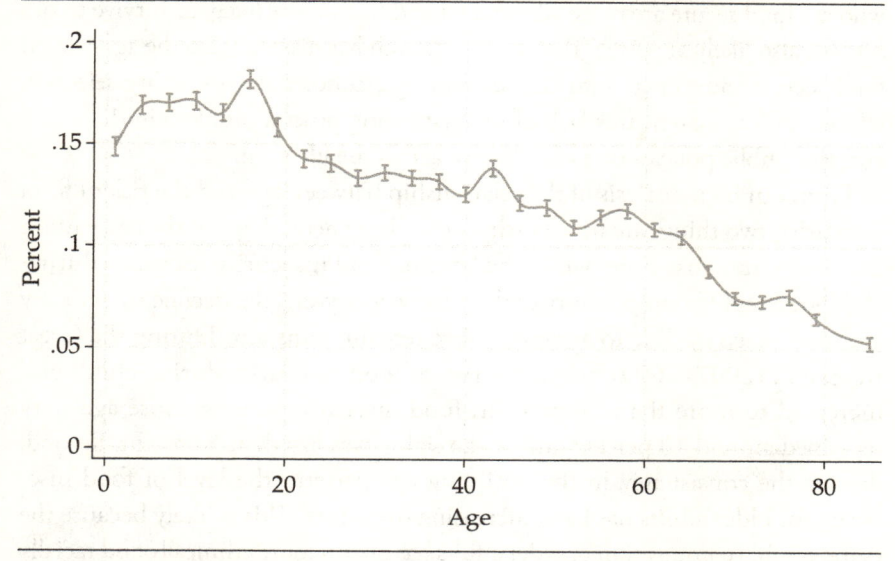

Source: Authors' calculations using a three-year moving average of the official U.S. Department of Agriculture food security measure and the 2021–2023 Current Population Survey (U.S. Census Bureau 2024).
Note: Whiskers indicate the standard error around the mean.

of people who are food insecure is 6.9 percent at age eighty, 11.4 percent at age sixty, and 19.1 percent below age eighteen.

What explains the age-related pattern? Is declining food insecurity in old age related to age effects (due to factors related to age), cohort effects (due to shared experiences across those born in the same decade), or selection bias (due to who survives to old age)? We do not know; we do not have consistent data over time using this standard measure to help us answer these important questions. Age effects might be driven by age-related increases in informal and formal support (such as access to Social Security benefits and more lenient SNAP policies) or moves into living arrangements with shared meals, both of which reduce food insecurity. On the other hand, cohort effects might be the result of unique characteristics of Baby Boomers that reflect their differential exposure to adverse social and economic conditions; compositional differences in demographic characteristics, human capital, and family structures; and access to different health technologies—all of which are associated with food insecurity. Finally, mortality-related selection—the fact that individuals who are food secure are more advantaged and thus, more likely to survive to old age—is also likely at play.[32] To date, no research has disentangled the age-related food security advantage into the relevant age, cohort, and mortality selection effects. Unfortunately, this lack of understanding poses a problem in designing effective public policies that are effective across the life span.

From our own analysis of the relationship between age and the risk of food insecurity, two things are noteworthy. First, the general shape of the age pattern is consistent across time: while the level of food insecurity increases during childhood at different points over the past twenty years, the decline by age sixty and then steep decline to age eighty-five remains constant. During the Great Recession (2007–2009), when the risk of food insecurity during childhood increased to more than 20 percent, food insecurity among those age sixty remained around 10 percent and at age eighty was less than 5 percent. Second, despite the consistency in the declining age pattern, the level of food insecurity for older adults has been increasing over time. This is likely because the demographic composition of older adults has grown more ethnically and racially diverse, with a wider income distribution and more variation in health than early cohorts. Given that these patterns are projected to continue, without policy change, we expect to see increases in older adult food insecurity in the future.

LIMITATIONS OF THE U.S. DEPARTMENT OF AGRICULTURE FOOD SECURITY MEASURE

This book focuses squarely on older adult food insecurity, which is officially measured using the eighteen-question U.S. Department of Agriculture Food Security Survey. In addition to the narrow focus on economic barriers to food insecurity, this formal measure of food insecurity has at least three other potential sources of error. Each of them may lead to the undercounting of the number of older adults who are unable to access enough food for an active, healthy lifestyle at all times.

First, many older adults live in nursing homes, group homes, and other residential care facilities. These places are classified as "group quarters" and are not sampled by nationally representative surveys such as the Current Population Survey, the main source of national data on food insecurity.[33] As a result, the experiences of older adults in these living situations are not included in the official measure. However, many residential care facilities do not provide three meals a day, seven days a week. Older adults may not be able to afford the charge associated with purchasing extra meals and may be eligible for SNAP even though they do not receive it. Many older adults receive residential care because of their physical limitations, which may prevent them from obtaining food and cooking it on their own. Finally, because it is a twelve-month measure, the official count of food insecurity does not include reports of food insecurity that occurred before people moved into a residential care facility. This issue is not easily addressed because it reflects the sampling frame of the Current Population Survey, but it should be acknowledged.

Second, the Food Security Survey assumes that household food is only consumed by household members. As a result, older adults who do not live with their grandchildren are only given the opportunity to answer ten items on the survey, not the full set of eighteen that relate to childhood food insecurity. From previous research, Madonna Harrington Meyer noted that many grandparents who do not live with their grandchildren still feed them regularly and may be food insecure as a result. In one study, for example, Jamica frequently fed grandchildren who did not live with her. She did not have enough money to fix her car and lost substantial weight—six dress sizes—walking to her housecleaning jobs.[34] She had not been to the doctor or dentist in eight years. Another grandmother, Candi, paid for her grandchildren's formula and diapers instead of putting gas in her car. She described feeding the grandchildren before herself: "I don't eat, money is tight. I let the kids eat first and if there is not enough food I don't eat."[35]

Similarly, Theo and his wife do not live with their grandchildren but care for them five days a week. Their food insecurity is compounded by how often they feed their grandchildren. At age sixty-six, they answered yes to all ten questions, making their official FSS score 10/10. They often go without meals, something Theo said he was growing used to. Because his grandchildren do not live in his household, the U.S. Department of Agriculture asks him only ten of the eighteen questions. But we incorrectly asked him all eighteen questions because Theo talked about feeding his grandchildren routinely. He answered yes to three of the questions about children, making his unofficial FSS score 13/18.

Many grandparents who do not live with their grandchildren, particularly those who help with childcare, routinely feed their grandchildren. This can exacerbate food insecurity in a way that is currently undetected by the

U.S. Department of Agriculture measure. Theo scraps metal to buy milk for his one-year-old grandchild and gas for the car. He and his wife often forgo eating so that their grandchildren have enough food.

> I made that money this morning and then it goes to my sister. I can get a carton of milk for him . . . if we don't have the egg or bread or something like that. I just don't eat anyway. . . . Two or three times a month . . . I would do without it myself to give them some food. . . . As long as my family gets something to eat, I'm all right.

An August 2024 survey found that 20 percent of grandparents provide weekly or near-weekly care for grandchildren under age 18, with 8 percent providing daily or near-daily care. Perhaps most important, 47 percent of grandparents report cooking for their grandchildren within the last month with an equal share reporting buying food for their grandchildren.[36] Asking the full set of eighteen questions to all grandparents who regularly feed their grandchildren, regardless of residency, would help to capture more of the existing food insecurity in old age but would require an additional screener question and a change to the survey administration protocol.

Finally, the current U.S. Department of Agriculture food security measure focuses on the quantity of food consumed and not its dietary quality. Only one item taps into food quality—a question about balanced meals. Given older adults' reduced caloric requirements, food secure older adults may still lack nutritional security. Researchers and practitioners now recognize food security as a social determinant of health;[37] the connection between diet and health has led to a movement for a measure of nutritional security. Many of our respondents discussed how difficult it was to afford nutritious food. Shocked by how little he could buy with $40, Bobby, age sixty-two with marginal food security, reluctantly turns to peanut butter and jelly sandwiches.

> I only eat like twice a day. . . . When I go down to the store downstairs I can spend $40 and have five items. . . . Everything was just jacked up and like I said, you go to the store four or five times a month, you're left with $20. . . . I might just eat like a peanut butter and jelly or something instead of cooking.

Scarlett, age sixty-seven with very low food security, noted how rising gas prices are taking a bite out of her food budget.

If gas prices keep going up, I'll say I have less than I need. . . . I can go through a tank of gas a week, all the driving I have to do. Lack of money, the cost of food so outrageous now. But as I say, lot of the cans is the cheap one. It's not the best choice, though.

SHORT OF MONEY FOR FOOD

As COVID waned in 2021 and 2022, inflation surged. For the first time in thirty-five years, stores such as Dollar Trees raised their standard price on items to more than a dollar, due to decreased sales, higher costs, and supply-chain shortages.[38] The increases in food prices in 2020 and 2021 (3.4 and 3.9 percent, respectively) were moderate relative to the record 9.9 percent price increase in 2022. However, food price growth slowed in 2023 to 5.8 percent, as supply-chain issues and inflationary pressures eased, with the estimated level for 2024 at 2.3 and the predicted level for 2025 at 1.9 as of the beginning of 2025.[39]

The nationally representative Current Population Survey asks respondents if they would need to spend more money "to buy just enough food to meet the needs of your household," and if so, how much they need. About 50 percent more older adults as those who are considered food insecure, or 15.1 percent of all adults age 60 and older, answered that they needed to spend more money in 2023 according to our calculations. Figure 1.4 shows the share of the adult population age sixty and older with household incomes below 185 percent of the federal poverty who report needing more money. At different points over the last twenty years, including between 2021 to 2023, the share rises to approximately one in four low-income older adults. Our own analysis shows that women and Black and Hispanic adults are more likely to report being short of money for food. The risk of being short of money for food decreases steadily with age and income. The risk is lower for married individuals and older adults residing in metropolitan rather than rural counties.

Among low-income older adults who report needing more money for food, how much more do they need to spend on food to meet weekly basic household needs? According to our calculations, in 2023, the average amount was about $78 weekly or $312 per month. Hispanic and non-Hispanic Black low-income older adults who are short on money for food require about $90 weekly, while non-Hispanic White households need $69 weekly. To put this amount in context, the majority of SNAP older adult households are single-person households, for which the minimum SNAP benefit for fiscal year 2025

Figure 1.4 Adults Age Sixty and Older with Household Incomes Below 185 Percent of the Federal Poverty Line Who Need to Spend More to Meet Household Food Needs, 2001–2023

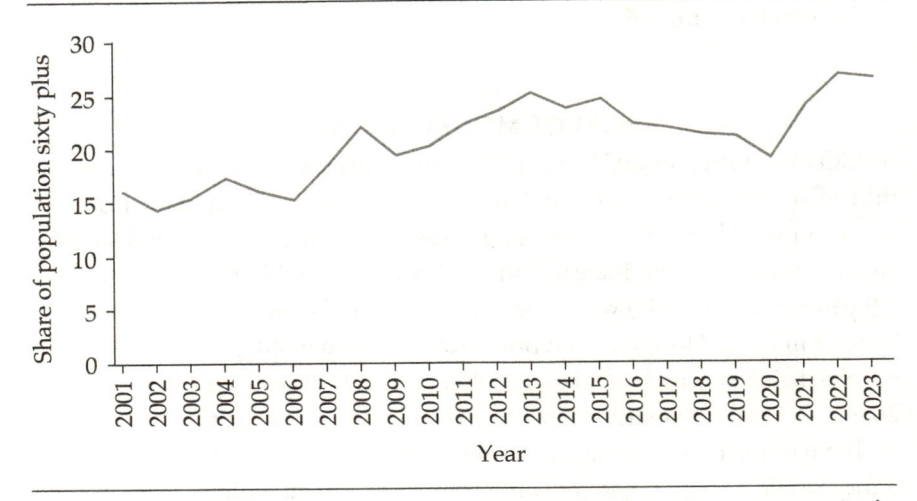

Source: Authors' calculations based on 2001–2023 Current Population Survey responses to the question: "In order to buy just enough food to meet the needs of your household, would you need to spend more than you do now, or could you spend less?" (Flood et al. 2024).

is $23 per month and the maximum benefit is $292.[40] The average per person benefit in fiscal year 2024 was $188.[41]

Rising food costs continue to be a problem according to a study by researchers at AARP. In December 2022, although many older adults did not meet the definition of being food insecure, 51 percent of adults age fifty and older cited rising food prices as the top factor negatively impacting their ability to access food in the last two weeks. When asked how increasing grocery prices changed how they shop for food, 53 percent indicated that they spent more money or bought cheaper foods, 47 percent bought cheaper alternative items, and 38 percent shopped more frequently at discount stores. In addition, 37 percent bought less food, 34 percent shopped less often, 23 percent bought less fresh fruit and vegetables, and 16 percent bought less healthy food items. Only 10 percent of all adults age fifty and older indicated that rising food prices had not changed how they shop.[42]

Lack of money for food is a serious issue, but it is not the only challenge to food insecurity faced by many older adult households. In December 2022, the same AARP study reported that 19 percent of adults age fifty and older reported that a physical disability negatively impacted their access to food, and 15 percent cited the physical distance to a store or limited transportation as a challenge.[43] As subsequent chapters show, the inability to cover other household and daily expenses, coupled with individual physical, cognitive, and emotional health problems and poor access to transportation and nutritious food, compound the daily realities of food insecurity in old age.

A NOTE ON THE EVIDENCE USED FOR THIS BOOK

Our analysis relies on a wide range of nationally representative quantitative surveys, including the Current Population Survey, the Survey of Income and Program Participation, the Health and Retirement Study, and the Household PULSE Survey. Each of these surveys uses a different measure of food insecurity, which we detail in appendix table A.2. Each figure in the book notes the source of data used to calculate the figure.

We also collected qualitative data consisting of in-depth interviews with sixty-three adults age sixty and older with incomes less than 130 percent of the federal poverty line. We conducted phone interviews from March to November 2021; COVID rates were high, but vaccines were becoming more readily available. Recruitment was tricky because many of the places where we would have recruited low-income older people were closed due to the pandemic. Thus, we used a variety of methods to recruit interviewees, including mailing flyers to food distribution centers and subsidized housing locations, placing Facebook ads, and asking for volunteers. Everyone who completed an interview received a $50 cash card as an honorarium.

Our sample is a convenience sample; it is national in scope but not nationally representative. The sample is described in detail in appendix table B.1. When compared to the general population of people who are poor or people who are food insecure, as shown in figure B.1, our sample has higher proportions who are female, have a disability, are single, have some college, and are Black. Basic sociodemographic information about each respondent is provided in appendix table B.2. In general, 76 percent of our respondents are female, 51 percent are Black, 44 percent are white, 63 percent have at least some college, 12 percent are married, 49 percent are food insecure, 5 percent have residential grandchildren, 70 percent have a person in their household with a disability, 78 percent receive SNAP, 43 percent live in subsidized housing, and 79 percent use food pantries. The sample is diverse in terms of representing a wide variety of lived experiences demonstrating the causes and consequences of poverty and food insecurity.

Our goal with the qualitative data is not to show how common any particular event is but to provide a rich description of how older adults experience food insecurity on a day-to-day basis in the United States, and in turn, to help design better public policy.[44] Some members of our sample have almost always been poor and are very familiar with food insecurity. They started life with few resources and accumulated more disadvantages than advantages throughout their life course. Others have only recently become poor and are new to the challenges of food insecurity.

Our sixty-three respondents described how living with food insecurity changed during COVID. In many ways, conditions during the pandemic improved. Some respondents had received economic stimulus checks and used them to stock their pantries. Thus, at the time of the interviews, some had more food than usual. Others had used stimulus checks to fix cars, making it easier to obtain groceries. Some were paying more toward food and less toward rent because evictions were prohibited during the pandemic, while others were paying less toward utilities because providers were prohibited from cutting off power during the pandemic. Several respondents who received SNAP benefits reported that recertifications had been delayed, simplified, or moved online. From March 2020 until February 2023, states were allowed to provide households increased SNAP benefits, known as emergency allotments, up to the maximum benefit amount for the household size. Some respondents were still receiving higher SNAP benefits at the time of the interview and described how the larger benefits eased budgetary tensions. However, others had just reverted to their earlier benefit levels and told us about their difficulties without the emergency allotments. In addition, in October 2021, the Biden administration increased SNAP benefits for all households by 22.5 percent through a combination of a revaluation of the Thrifty Food Plan and a cost-of-living increase. The October 2022 cost-of-living increase resulted in a further 12.5 percent benefit increase for all households. However, the end to this policy in March 2023 may have increased food insecurity rates.[45]

In other ways, COVID made conditions more difficult. During the pandemic, many community-based sources of free and subsidized food were closed. Those that remained open limited their hours or pivoted from pickup to delivery to reduce the health risks for clients and workers. Several respondents reported that senior centers or food pantries dropped off boxes of food at their subsidized housing units, which made obtaining food easier than usual, but the boxes rarely contained fresh produce and often included food they could not use. When group meal sites and food pantries were open, many had very long lines or ran out of food. Some respondents received food vouchers for farmers markets and appreciated the chance to purchase fresh produce, but needed transportation to pick up the coupons and then go to the farmers market, where the risk of exposure to COVID could be high. Others told us that public transportation was particularly challenging during the pandemic and that buses would drive right by them as they waited for a ride to the grocery store. In many parts of the country, buses had to comply with social distancing regulations and could only take a few passengers at a time. Respondents described how they were unable to see family and friends during the pandemic; some ate too little when their social lives diminished, while others ate too much given their reduced physical activity. Finally, as the grip of the pandemic weakened, the grip of inflation strengthened, driving food prices up and tightening already strained budgets.[46]

OVERVIEW OF THE BOOK

In this book, we examine the measurement of and response to food insecurity for low-income older adults to identify policy changes that would better meet their needs. In this chapter, we defined food security and described how the day-to-day experience varies for people who are food secure, marginally food secure, low food secure, and very low food secure using the official U.S. Department of Agriculture definition. In 2023, 9.2 percent of adults age sixty and older, or 7.4 million adults, were classified as food insecure. We presented the risk factors for food insecurity in old age and showed how the risk of food insecurity varies over the life span. Life course theory, which focuses on individual and household-level risk factors, and social ecological theory, which concentrates on the geographic variation in access to resources, together explain the wide variation in the lived experience of food insecure older adults. The U.S. Department of Agriculture measure of food insecurity is designed to identify changes to eating patterns and consumption related to affordability issues alone. Lack of income is indeed the greatest challenge, but it is not the only one. By focusing exclusively on whether respondents have enough money for food, the current measure of food insecurity provides an incomplete description of the challenges older adults face in securing access to healthy food. The remaining chapters in the book focus on these additional challenges, as well as policy solutions.

In chapter 2, we show how food insecurity in old age is linked to economic insecurity. Despite Social Security benefits, household incomes of adults age sixty and older are not always sufficient to cover monthly essential expenses, especially with the rising cost of food. Older adults report making budget trade-offs between food and medical costs, housing, utilities, transportation, personal and cleaning supplies, and phone and internet services. They tend to prioritize paying for some of these household expenses, particularly housing and utilities, before food. Such trade-offs contribute to food insecurity. Solutions to address older adult food insecurity must therefore include dimensions beyond the realm of food; programs that support out-of-pocket medical expenses, housing, utilities, and transportation would likely reduce food insecurity in old age.

In chapter 3, we show how nonfinancial factors make it difficult for low-income older adults to obtain, prepare, and consume healthy, nutritious meals. Food insecurity in old age is often linked to nonfinancial factors, including poor physical, cognitive, and mental health; lack of access to healthy food; and transportation challenges. We emphasize the interactive nature of these challenges for older adults. For example, given that many older adults have chronic health conditions that require daily management, a poor diet may interfere with disease-management protocols such as taking medicine with food or following a low-sugar diet. Lack of access to healthy food may lead to poorer health, higher health-care bills, difficulty with stairs or using public transportation, or increased depression and anxiety. Each of these in turn may make it more difficult to obtain healthy, nutritious meals. People working with older populations must regularly screen for nonfood causes of food insecurity and evaluate how food insecurity may be impacting health.

In chapter 4, we discuss the most effective U.S. policy to address food insecurity—SNAP. Despite SNAP's benefits in supporting healthy aging and decreasing health-care costs, as well as the 88 percent level of participation among the total eligible population, roughly 55 percent of eligible adults age sixty and older participate.[47] We examine the history and program structure of SNAP, as well as the process that applicants must go through to access benefits, which is particularly burdensome for older adults. SNAP benefits may be quite low and difficult to redeem for older adults who have physical disabilities or transportation problems. Finally, geographic variation in how the SNAP program operates at the state and sometimes county level creates spatial inequality in terms of who participates and the size of benefits. SNAP uptake among older adults who are eligible ranges from just 22 percent in Wyoming to 78 percent in Rhode Island.[48] Such variations in SNAP uptake makes geographic location a key axis of inequality for older adults.

In chapter 5, we explore the availability and limitations of community-based free and subsidized food. We assess the impact on food insecurity of community-based group meals, such as congregate meals and soup kitchens; home-delivered meals, such as Meals on Wheels; and food to be prepared at home, such as food pantries and farmers market coupons. Older adults with physical disabilities, cognitive decline, and transportation problems, as well as those who live far from services, find it more difficult to participate in the patchwork of free and subsidized food programs that rely on public and private nonprofit partnerships to provide food. Community-based food programs typically require an application process to determine eligibility; they may also require recipients to be physically present on-site during narrow service windows and may require monetary donations or charge fees. Whether they are funded though the Older Adults Act Title III(C) Nutritional Service programs, or through the U.S. Department of Agriculture's emergency food programs, community-based free and subsidized food programs are not widely or consistently available. Where one lives determines the quantity and quality of free and subsidized food programs available.

In chapter 6, we lay out our five main suggestions for improving the United States' response to old age food insecurity. Policymakers must measure food insecurity in multidimensional ways, treat food insecurity as a health issue, encourage states to increase the benefits and older adult uptake of SNAP, connect food assistance programs with other social welfare programs, and increase income supports for older adults. Without these changes, stories like Alex, from the introduction of this book, may become increasingly familiar. We believe that the United States is up for the challenge.

CHAPTER 2

The Economic Roots of Old Age Food Insecurity

Food insecurity often occurs within a web of other economic insecurities and hardships. People who have accumulated disadvantages over their life course or who live in resource-poor communities face difficulties meeting basic needs on a fixed monthly income. Our respondents described how stretching resources across a month can make the month seem long, especially if unexpected expenses arise. So they trade off between paying for food and other expenses such as medical costs, housing, energy, transportation, personal supplies, and phone and internet.

Barbara, age sixty-eight, has difficulty juggling her household bills and money for food. She is a retired, single mother of five and grandmother of 22 who lives alone in an apartment. She lives on $8,000 a year from Social Security and $16 a month from SNAP.[1] Her life course began promisingly; she has a BA in theology. Then, as a single mom, she worked in numerous fields including cosmetology and hospitality. She was diagnosed with an autoimmune disease at age thirty-nine but continued to work as much as her disease permitted. A car accident at age sixty-three, and then a serious fall, left her with a disability and unable to work. Now she has limited use of her left leg and gets around using a walker or a scooter.

Barbara has very low food security and a great deal of trouble paying her bills. She carefully avoids answering calls from collection agencies. Barbara augments her food supply by eating at congregate dining sites. She used to receive home-delivered meals but stopped doing so because of the poor quality of the food; she obtains food at the pantry but cannot eat most of it because

https://doi.org/10.7758/rzos2617.4805

it is largely processed. She is not able to store fresh produce for long, so she makes soups. But sometimes even the soup runs out.

> I try to buy stuff that I can make a meal that will at least last more than a day, but sometimes you might do that there and I think I made enough and it seems like it doesn't last. Maybe I should measure it out to a cup and I just fix regular plates, and then I had more than a cup or I might eat it more than twice in that day so that shortens me.

When the soup is running low, she eats just once a day before she goes to sleep so she does not have to think about her hunger at night. When the soup is gone, she relies on oatmeal until her check arrives at the end of the month.

> I had made a soup and stew with potatoes and cabbage and I thought, so that will hold me a little while and when I looked around it didn't do that. I was out.... Last night I ate the last part of it and that was that.... I'll just wait until next month or something like that or I'll look and [see] if I have some oatmeal. I can probably do something with that but like what I normally would eat is gone.

Barbara told us she receives both Medicare and Medicaid. Though traditional Medicare does not cover prescriptions, Medicaid typically does. It is possible that she is not receiving Medicaid, however, because she also told us that she often delays filling her prescriptions and stretches her medicines farther than recommended so that she has money left for food.

> If I'm really hungry then I guess I just won't get my medicines.... Instead of taking it like it's prescribed, I may only take it at night and just hope that that will suffice, and I hope I don't get enough pain or get that pain that will cause me to have to take more.... That way I don't have to buy next month's supply. I can use that money for something else.

On a monthly basis, Barbara must also choose between buying food and personal and cleaning supplies. "Probably every month about—every month, I have to choose whether I buy disposables [adult diapers] for myself or dish liquid for my dishes. If I have enough at least you can go to the dollar store to get it, dish liquid and stuff, body soaps, you know?"

She makes trade-offs between paying for transportation and paying for food. She owns a car but cannot drive because she cannot afford the registration and tags. She has had to choose between buying food and attending to her car. "That's why my car is sitting there with no tags and no registration because that is a little bit too much right now. I have to put it aside or wait until I can or something else comes along." When her car is not operable, she uses public transportation and pays for rides, but doing so reduces her food budget. She often stays home to limit her transportation costs and reserve money for food.

Barbara's food insecurity is linked to a combination of disadvantages she has accrued over her life course, including being a single mother, having a chronic condition, and being involved in several accidents. Her food insecurity is also influenced by the limited support she receives from social programs, notably the lack of accommodative, affordable transportation, the poor quality of free and subsidized food, and the modest size of her SNAP benefits.

The challenges low-income older adults such as Barbara face in stretching their household incomes to meet their monthly expenses are different from those of younger adults. When older adults do not have enough money to cover all their basic needs, they make trade-offs between food and nonfood expenses.[2] Our qualitative interviews describe how they balance food and other expenses such as medical costs, housing, energy costs, transportation, clothing, personal and cleaning supplies, and phone and internet coverage. The choices that they make are often connected to the financial and health advantages and disadvantages that they have accumulated throughout their life, as well as the availability of formal and informal sources of support where they live.

CHALLENGES OF BUDGETING ON A FIXED INCOME FOR OLDER ADULTS

Most people who live in low-income households have gone through periods when the expenses that need to be paid are greater than the resources available to pay them—often referred to as having "more month than money."[3] Older adults are no exception.

For people younger than age sixty, higher instability in living arrangements, housing, employment status, and other key factors corresponds with higher food insecurity. By contrast, for people age sixty and older, higher stability in income streams, living arrangements, housing, and employment status often corresponds with higher food insecurity. While younger people may have fortuitous events in their future, such as new jobs, partners, or roommates who can help offset expenses, older people are substantially less likely to experience such positive life events. Hence, younger people tend to move from mishap to windfall, while older people, typically constrained by fixed incomes, tend to continuously live on the edge of mishap. When fixed incomes are stretched to the brink, it may be impossible to absorb another shock such as a broken hip, car, or lease and remain food secure. In old age, income stability, which may appear to be a blessing, may at times be a curse. This is particularly likely, as social ecological theory points out, for people who live in areas that are resource poor.

For adults age sixty and older in the United States, food insecurity is often connected to retirement insecurity. Most older adults receive income through the federal Social Security program; they can do so as young as age sixty-two, when early retirement becomes an option. Social Security plays a crucial role in keeping the total household income above the federal poverty line for 19.5 million adults age sixty-five and older.[4] But those benefits do not necessarily stretch far enough to cover food costs, in addition to medical care, prescription drugs, rent, utilities, and other household expenses.

The retirement system in the United States results in the highest level of old-age poverty among the richest countries in the world and exacerbates gender and racial income and wealth disparities.[5] Even with Social Security, approximately one in ten adults older than sixty-five in the United States lives in a household with income below the official federal poverty line.[6] For 50 percent of older adults, Social Security constitutes half of their household income; for 25 percent of older adults, it makes up 90 percent of their income.[7] For families with a head of household age 50–64 in 2013, the median retirement savings account balance was $0 for the bottom 50 percent of the income distribution.[8] Households that rely heavily on Social Security benefits as their main source of income have fixed incomes that increase only when benefits are annually adjusted for inflation and are less able to respond to sudden changes in household expenses.

Older adults spend their money differently than other adults. These differences are captured in the Supplemental Poverty Measure, which adjusts income for expenses such as childcare, out-of-pocket medical expenditures, and housing. According to this measure, in 2023, 14.2 percent of adults age sixty-five and older were poor.[9]

Most U.S. families rely on one of three strategies to get by when household expenses are greater than the resources available to pay for them: they either work more, tap into savings, or go into debt. The availability of each of these options in old age is shaped by factors that develop much earlier in the life course.

First, families may try to increase household income by working more, either by picking up extra hours at their current job or by holding multiple jobs. Doing so is difficult for low-income older adults who may face age discrimination or physical limitations. The Bureau of Labor Statistics projects that the share of adults age sixty-five and older in the workforce will grow from 6.7 percent of the labor force in 2023 to 8.6 percent by 2033.[10] However, older workers are more likely to be laid off or let go.[11] Many middle-age people who have disabilities accrued them in previous jobs. This is particularly true for workers in physically demanding jobs—notably construction, cleaning, and delivery—who are in worse health than other workers.[12] Many of the food-insecure individuals we spoke with have disabilities and, at the time of the interview, had been out of the workforce for several years.

Second, to minimize budget trade-offs, households may draw from their savings. However, one in ten U.S. households, and one in four Black U.S. households, has no wealth or negative net worth.[13] Though older adults tend to have more wealth than younger adults, much of their wealth is not held as liquid assets but tied up in their homes, which cannot easily be tapped to assist with rising food costs.[14] Older Black and Hispanic households have much lower levels of wealth than White households, particularly liquid assets that could be used for basic needs such as food consumption.[15]

Third, as a last resort to minimize budget trade-offs, low-income households may go into debt. However, as adults age, they are less likely to hold debt, given their fixed incomes. In 2019, half of adults age seventy-five or older had no debt. Further, like net worth, debt is more likely to be held as housing debt. According to the Survey of Consumer Finance, the percentage of all older adults with any household debt has grown over time, but the size of that debt has decreased.[16] Low-income older adults on fixed incomes may be reluctant to take on debt because they see little opportunity to pay it back.

If sufficient economic resources are not available through earnings, savings, or debt, younger households may make ends meet by reorganizing expenditures or juggling bills. For example, a household may decide to pay its utility bill after the due date to cover the cost of another week of food. However, expenditures on essential expenses decrease as people near retirement age in the United States. According to our analysis of the Consumer Expenditure Survey data from 2021, average expenditures on housing, food, transportation, and utilities all significantly decreased after age fifty-five. The only area in which expenses increased after age fifty-five was that of health care. While other households may be able to juggle bills to get by for a month, low-income older adults are less likely to have slack in their budgets that they can move to other areas without experiencing negative consequences such as delaying medical procedures, not taking prescribed medicine, being evicted, or having utilities disconnected.

Finally, while younger households may be able to avoid budget trade-offs by rearranging their household composition to share housing and other expenses, older households are less likely to be able to do so. The average U.S. household size has been declining over the past century (although, since 2010, there are signs of reversal, particularly in multigenerational households).[17] For older adults, additional household members may bring new resources with them—financial, instrumental, social, or emotional—but they may also bring new demands on household economic resources. For example, rates of food insecurity in households with a grandchild present are more than twice as high as households without a grandchild present.[18]

Married households have a significant advantage in terms of food security in older age relative to multigenerational, single-adult, or nonfamily households.[19] But rates of marriage in the United States are at historical lows and decline quickly with advancing age, particularly for women.[20] Living alone increases the risk of food insecurity for both men and women, yet recent research finds that a move to a multigenerational household did not diminish the risk of food insecurity.[21] So, while changing household living arrangements may be an effective strategy at younger ages, it does not seem to reduce the risk of food insecurity for older adults, for whom the options vary depending on their connections and geographic proximity—consistent with life course theory—to other family members.

When all the standard approaches to increasing household resources and reducing expenses are not enough, people in low-income households are forced to make difficult choices. Often this involves deciding which bill and basic need will be met this month and which one will not be fully covered. In the triage of paying bills, where do food expenses fall? Our respondents tend to prioritize housing and utilities before food; they can survive without a meal

Figure 2.1   Adults Age Sixty and Older in Poverty Who Were Unable to Cover Essential Expenses

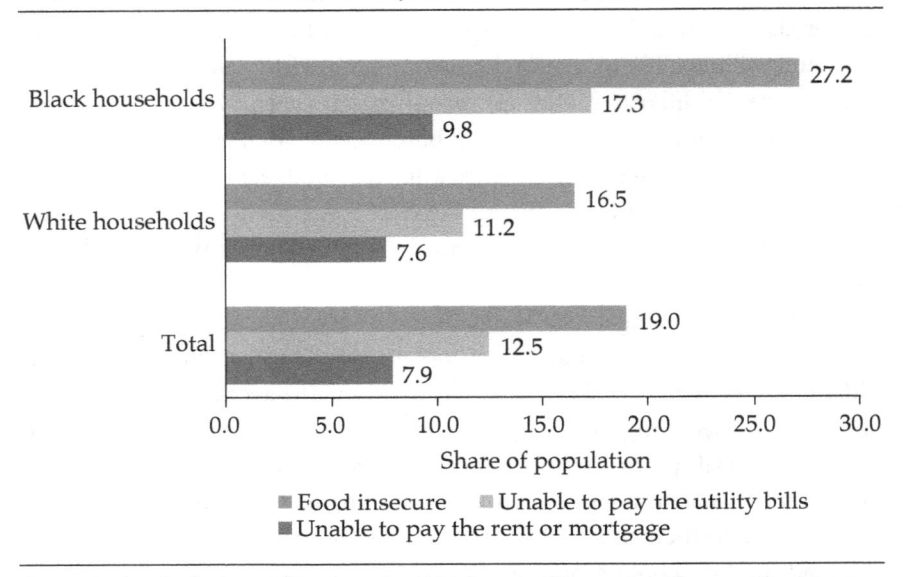

Black households: 27.2 / 17.3 / 9.8
White households: 16.5 / 11.2 / 7.6
Total: 19.0 / 12.5 / 7.9

Share of population (0.0–30.0)

■ Food insecure   ■ Unable to pay the utility bills
■ Unable to pay the rent or mortgage

Source: Authors' calculations based on the 2021 Survey of Income and Program Participation.

but not without a home or electricity. Other household expenses, including medical care, transportation, personal and cleaning supplies, and telephone and internet, tend to compete with food, with the ranking of priorities shifting across respondents and across months. One priority that does not shift is the need to avoid going into debt, particularly for older adults living on fixed budgets with no windfalls on the horizon with which to pay off debt. The financial decisions they make to get through the month may contribute to food insecurity and be detrimental to their long-term well-being.

THE FREQUENCY AND PROCESS OF BUDGET TRADE-OFFS

We calculate how often adults age sixty and older with household incomes below the poverty line were unable to meet basic needs. The Survey of Income and Program Participation asked respondents about their ability to pay for several basic needs in 2020, including their rent or mortgage, utility bills, and food. Our analysis, shown in figure 2.1, finds that among poor older adults, nearly 8 percent reported being unable to pay their rent or mortgage, 12 percent were unable to pay their utility bills, and 19 percent were food insecure. While 73 percent of poor older adults were able to pay for these basic needs, 18 percent were unable to cover one of these essential expenses, 6 percent were unable to cover two of them, and 3 percent were unable to pay for any of the three. For all basic needs, Black adults had higher rates of being unable to pay than did White adults.

During our in-depth interviews, we asked our respondents ten questions about whether in the last twelve months they had been unable to pay their full rent, utilities, medical expenses, and phone bills; whether they had ever been evicted or had utility services terminated; and whether they had ever been called by collection agencies or had ever stolen something. Two-thirds responded yes to at least one question. They report debt or unpaid bills piling up, risk of losing power or housing, or calls from collection agencies. Patty, age sixty-nine with low food security, described how her tight budget leaves nothing extra. "And when you're on a budget and you don't have extra $25, you know, that's like $250 for somebody that doesn't have money."

Carmen, age sixty-five with low food security, barely covers her monthly bills and then has almost nothing to spare. "Exactly what I have, because I pay my mortgage. The mortgage is $400 dollars . . . my phone bill, my water bill. When I come to check the bank, sometimes I have $6 or $7 left. . . . I called the bank yesterday. I've got $14 dollars."

Deb, age sixty-two and food secure, can barely pay her bills, particularly in light of recent inflation. "I barely make it, but I get there. I pay the bills, yeah. . . . I feel with everything going up, we'll have less than what we—we'll be having less than what we need. Everything goes up, except our money."

Difficulty affording food continues to be a significant problem for older adults. In a report from the American Association for Retired People (AARP), one in two adults age fifty and older in December 2022 indicated that rising food prices impacted their ability to access food in the previous two weeks. Further, this survey asked how food insecurity influences nonfood aspects of daily life—specifically, when low-income older people have to choose whether to pay for food, medical care, housing, utilities, transportation, personal and household supplies, or clothing.[22] As shown in figure 2.2, when asked if they had to make trade-offs between paying for food and paying other expenses in the past month, 12 percent reported making trade-offs in transportation, 11 percent in utilities, 10 percent in medical care, 9 percent in housing, and 8 percent in prescription drugs.[23]

Figure 2.2 Trade-Offs Between Food and Other Expenses Within the Last Month (Adults Age Fifty and Older)

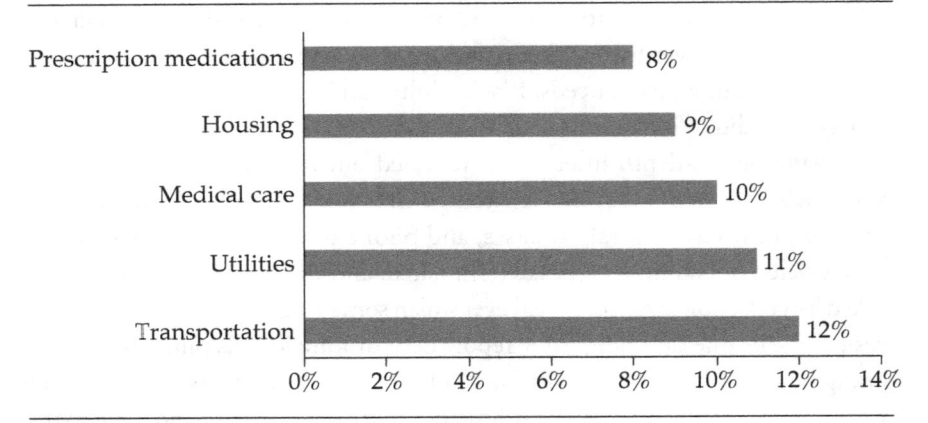

Category	Percent
Prescription medications	8%
Housing	9%
Medical care	10%
Utilities	11%
Transportation	12%

Source: Authors' figure based on data from Keenan and Lampkin 2023.

While survey responses such as these document the frequency with which older adults make difficult choices about monthly essential expenses, they do not explain the results of such choices. For example, when someone indicates that they had to choose between food and transportation, we do not know which choice they made. As a result, despite evidence of these ongoing trade-offs, we do not know how low-income older adults handle meeting their food needs versus covering other essential expenses. Further, we lack understanding of the role that previous experiences over the life course and local access to sources of support play in shaping these choices.

Our qualitative interviews provide insight into these strategies and decisions. We asked eight questions about whether respondents had chosen between paying for food and other household expenses; 67 percent responded yes to at least one question. They made trade-offs between food and medical expenses, housing, utilities, transportation, personal and household cleaning supplies, and phone and internet bills. We focus on each of these major budget categories in the following sections.

Medical Expenses

Budget trade-offs between food and medical expenses, medical supplies, prescriptions, and dental care contribute to food insecurity and poorer health among older adults. Out-of-pocket medical expenses are the greatest financial worry for adults of all ages.[24] Medical expenses tend to rise with age; on average, 12 percent of lifetime health expenditures occur between ages twenty and thirty-nine, 31 percent between forty and sixty-five, and 49 percent at age sixty-five or older.[25] Though nearly all older adults in the United States are covered by Medicare, respondents younger than sixty-five are not yet eligible for the program unless they qualify through disability benefits. Adults who are eligible for Medicare face numerous out-of-pocket expenses, including premiums; co-payments; deductibles; exclusions; and vision, dental, and hearing care. Households with at least one member covered by Medicare spend an average of 13.6 percent of income on medical expenses, twice that of other households.[26]

As adults age, they tend to accumulate medical debt. In 2020, 7 percent of older Americans, or 4 million people, reported unpaid medical debt—a total of $54.8 billion.[27] Low-income older adults paying out-of-pocket medical expenses may divert money away from purchasing food and adversely affect their health, which may lead to an increased need for medical care and even more unpaid medical bills.

People who are poor enough may qualify for Medicaid at any age, though eligibility and benefits vary substantially by state.[28] This variability demonstrates how social ecological factors shape the risk of older adult food insecurity. The share of the total population in each state covered by Medicaid ranges from 11 to 34 percent.[29] Medicaid has relatively few out-of-pocket expenses and hence slows the accumulation of medical debt. Older adults who are dually eligible for Medicare and Medicaid should have very low medical debt because Medicaid covers most of Medicare's out-of-pocket expenses. Yet the Consumer Financial Protection Bureau reports that 10 percent of dually eligible adults have medical debt, in part due to error-prone, complex billing systems and in part due to providers charging beneficiaries for amounts they do not owe.[30]

In our study, respondents sometimes accumulated medical debt before they were old enough to qualify for Medicare or poor enough to qualify for Medicaid. Low-income respondents on fixed incomes may have medical debts, such as unpaid co-payments from doctor visits, surgical procedures, or hospital stays, that interfere with their ability to buy food. The priority of food versus medical needs varies across our respondents and across time. Lionel, age sixty-five with very low food security, pays for food before paying medical bills. "In other words, we didn't have nothing to eat. Better pay for that and have something to eat than paying for the medical. We had to substitute. . . . We just had to go on make that decision."

Violet, age sixty-three with low food security, pays for her medical care first and spends less on food to compensate. When the medical bills are high, she eats beans. "I would try to keep up on the medical piece and eat more beans or whatever, cheaper protein."

For Helen, age seventy with marginal food security, the medical bills are far too large to be offset by lower food purchases. She often has to choose between food and medical bills, and the medical bills are piling up. "Oh, yes, paying them bills . . . I got bills and I can't get them together. I got X-ray and this eye surgery and—if it ain't one thing, it's another. And that gives you a big headache."

Low-income adults may have to choose between paying for food and paying for medical supplies. Medical supplies, including inhalers, glasses, and dentures, often are not covered by Medicare or other health insurance programs. Kate, age sixty-one with marginal food security, prioritizes food over medical supplies by postponing buying glasses so that she can buy food. Deciding whether eating or seeing is more important is a terrible spot to be in.

> Yeah, I guess there have been times that I've had to decide—you know, like I needed glasses and it's been—did I need to not go to buy some extra food items or did I need to save that to—you know save that for when I needed to get my glasses. Take that out of the extra food money and, you know, put it toward my glasses. Yeah, I did need to do that.

Lena, age seventy-three with low food security, tends to buy medical supplies first and food later. She is well aware of how much food she can buy if she does not have to pay for her inhaler. "Quite often since you know, I need certain medicines. But like I say, the inhaler is $7 so if I don't get one from the doctor, I have to buy it. $7 I could have spent on bananas or avocado or something."

Low-income adults may have to choose between filling prescriptions and paying for food, a trade-off known as a "treat or eat" decision.[31] In one study, 19 percent of adults reported food insecurity, 23 percent reported cost-related medication underuse, and 11 percent reported both.[32] In another study of older adults with hypertension diagnoses on SNAP and Medicaid, one in four did not have enough medication to provide daily treatment; among those with diabetes, one in three did not have enough medication throughout the year to control their disease.[33]

Further, among older adults previously diagnosed with hypertension, SNAP participation, particularly when it is consistent and not interrupted by periods of administrative difficulties, is associated with higher levels of medication adherence to antihypertensive medication compared to nonparticipation or intermittent participation in SNAP.[34]

The prioritization of food and prescriptions varies. Some of our respondents described delaying prescription refills so that they have enough money to buy food. Wallace, age sixty-four with very low food security, did not fill his prescription during the month of our interview because he needed money for food. "Tell you the truth I had to, I didn't get my medicine this month, I had to get the food. But . . . I had some medicine left over from the other one. So I had to choose."

Kasha, age sixty-seven with low food security, asks her pharmacy to let her delay payment for the prescriptions she needs until a subsequent month so that she can buy food. "I just bought my groceries, and I told the pharmacy that I would pay next month on my medicine."

Conversely, Scarlett, age sixty-seven with very low food security, saves money for her prescriptions by spending less on food. "It was on the Xarelto. It was like do I pay that $200 or do I eat. . . . And I did save up the money for the medicine. . . . I get my medicine every three months."

Budget trade-offs between food and dental care may also contribute to food insecurity among older adults. Proper dental care, including regular brushing, flossing, and visits to the dentist, is particularly important at older ages because it affects so many aspects of physical and emotional well-being for older adults.[35] Lack of proper dental care leads to adverse physical health consequences, including higher rates of stroke,[36] cardiovascular disease,[37] heart disease,[38] hypertension,[39] and viral and bacterial infections.[40] Poor dental care can also lead to tooth loss. Fifteen percent of adults age sixty-five and older have no natural teeth; those with incomes below the poverty line are five times as likely to not have natural teeth as those with higher incomes.[41] People with poor dental health often need, but lack access to, softer foods.[42] Even when readily available, softer foods may be nutritionally deficient and highly processed.

Lack of dental care can leave older adults in pain, and they may lack the energy to prepare and consume proper meals. Older adults without teeth may find it difficult or unappetizing to eat. Because eating is typically a social activity, those who lack proper dental care are more likely to become socially isolated, depressed, or poorly nourished.[43] Those with poor dental health may limit social interactions for fear others will detect their missing teeth, ill-fitting dentures, or bad gums.

Traditional Medicare specifically excludes dental coverage, except in exceptional circumstances.[44] Medicare Advantage, in which 54 percent of Medicare enrollees now participate, are more likely to cover dental plans, but plans vary widely and many require an extra premium.[45] In 2021, while 94 percent of Medicare Advantage enrollees had at least some dental coverage, and 86 percent had preventive and restorative dental coverage, 78 percent were in plans that capped dental benefits at an average of $1,300 a year.[46]

Dental coverage is optional for state Medicaid programs and varies widely by state.[47] In 2019, Alabama, Delaware, Maryland, and Tennessee did not cover dental services for adults; twenty-eight states covered only emergency or limited dental services; and only nineteen states covered extensive dental services for adults.[48] People who have comprehensive dental coverage through Medicaid find that many dentists will not accept Medicaid because the reimbursement rates are relatively low. They may encounter dentists who provide poor-quality care, dentists who want to pull rather than repair teeth, and general administrative confusion about what services are covered.

Ultimately, approximately one-half of Medicare recipients lack dental insurance because traditional Medicare does not cover routine services. The remaining half of Medicare recipients have dental coverage through a variety of public and private plans: 26 percent through Medicare Advantage, 16 percent through private plans, 8 percent through Medicaid, and 3 percent through dual Medicaid/Medicare Advantage policies.[49] Even those who do have dental insurance often face formidable out-of-pocket expenses. Low-income older adults tend to have poorer dental health and less access to needed dental care throughout their lives, which leads to accumulated disadvantage in old age.[50]

Our respondents reported not having dental insurance or the ability to pay for needed dental care. As a result, they sometimes delay making appointments until they can afford to pay expenses out-of-pocket or until the pain becomes unbearable. Alice, age seventy-seven with low food security, receives only Medicare, which provides no dental coverage. She often chooses between food and other expenses and has trouble paying for dental expenses. "I haven't had dental care in years because I didn't have an insurance that made provision for that. You don't have the money, and you don't have the insurance. You don't have dental care. That's why there's a lot of people that have no teeth."

Marie, age sixty-one with very low food security, has Medicaid but does not have a regular dentist. She visits the local college dental clinics when she can get an appointment and self-medicates when she cannot. "If I'm feeling a tooth pain and some gum issues or something like that, I do a rinse with peroxide."

Lionel, age sixty-five with very low food security, has Medicare coverage that does not cover his dental expenses, so he pays for costs out of pocket. He, too, prioritizes food over dental care. He must work extra hours as a handyman to earn enough money to see a dentist. "I told you I have to get out there and hustle—got to get out doing handywork."

Housing

Budget trade-offs between food and housing may contribute to food insecurity among older adults. Housing stock and affordability varies substantially by location. The uneven availability of affordable and accessible housing is one more example of how unevenly distributed social ecological factors shape the risk of food insecurity for older adults. Housing burden, defined as paying more than 30 percent of income on housing, rises with age. Housing burden is common among both homeowners and renters and more common among older Black adults and older Hispanic adults than other groups.[51] In 2021, 26 percent of all homeowners age sixty-five and older, and 43 percent of older homeowners with mortgages, spent more than 30 percent of their income on housing; 56 percent of all older renters, and 73 percent of older renters with incomes below $25,000, spent more than 30 percent of their income on housing.[52]

Subsidized housing, which limits the cost of rent and utilities to 30 percent of household income, helps alleviate housing burden. But it is not a panacea. Waiting lists for subsidized housing can be long; for example, U.S. Housing and Urban Development data shows that 49 percent of people waiting for housing-choice vouchers wait two or more years for subsidized housing.[53] Among the 43 percent of our respondents living in subsidized housing, paying rent sometimes remained difficult.

Our respondents generally reported paying for rent before food to avoid eviction. Violet, age sixty-three with low food security, describes how she pays the rent first and then adjusts her food intake according to what money remains. "It's housing a priority and then adjust the food."

Ophelia, age sixty-nine with low food security, lives in a household of four that includes two children. She says it is preferable to be hungry over homeless. "Because I'd rather go hungry than not pay rent. I say I'd rather be without a little food and not, you know, being able to pay rent. Because I'm always going to try to keep a roof over my head."

Some respondents, like Faye, age sixty-four with marginal food security, turn to charitable organizations such as Catholic Charities or the Salvation Army, which will sometimes cover one month of rent per year for people in need. The availability of such emergency housing supports varies markedly by place of residence. For Faye, the support has been invaluable as she alternates rent and utility payments to avoid eviction and power cuts. "Like yeah, last month I had to get help with the rent. This month I had to postpone my electric bill. I had to get an extension on my due date."

Eviction is a steady worry for some respondents, though during the pandemic landlords were generally prohibited from evicting renters. Theo, age sixty-six with very low food security, has come very close to being evicted and knows exactly how the process works. He strives to make sure he and his family are not evicted. That often means less money is available for food.

> We have to pay rent. Yes ma'am we pay rent out of the food money. They just can't leave $25 and pay the other next month. They said no, you can't do that. Then, we'll get a $50 bill paper and then the next time we'll get a $70 bill and then it will be an eviction paper.

Budget trade-offs can only go so far. At some point, without enough money, debt accumulates. At the time of the interview, Meredith, age sixty with very low food security, was behind on rent, dental, phone, and utility bills. She had little choice but to forgo food. Given her fixed income, it is hard to imagine she will ever recover.

> I stopped paying rent and that's why I'm going to be homeless, but I still didn't have enough to pay the co-pay to pay the bill, to get this other tooth pulled. And that's a problem when you only have a couple of hundred dollars. You've got to pay the rent. . . . I put food last, but I know I'll fix my phone first so if I need to pay off my utilities and pay for car insurance and gas and car maintenance and breakdowns and tires—you know?

Energy Security

Trade-offs between paying for food and paying for energy bills may contribute to food insecurity, especially if low-income older adults prioritize utilities over food. Older adults have more difficulty than younger adults going from uncomfortable heat or cold to homeostasis; fluctuations in temperature during cold spells and heat waves, therefore, are particularly problematic for older bodies.[54] The Environmental Protection Agency reports that every year since 1999, people age sixty-five and older are much more likely than the general population to die of heat-related cardiovascular disease.[55] In 2022, they were three times more likely. More than 2,000 deaths per year in the United States have been linked to either extreme cold or extreme heat, and the likelihood of each increases significantly with age and lower incomes.[56] Heat-related deaths at any age are increasingly common as a result of global warming, yet older adults remain twice as likely as the rest of the population to die from cold.[57]

Older adults have little choice but to adjust their thermostat to protect their health and well-being. Heating or cooling homes accounts for a substantial portion of utility bills, especially in inner-city areas where large portions of Black and Hispanic people reside and where the urban heat-island effect has a strong impact.[58] Insufficient or excess heat in certain geographic regions is shaped by social ecological factors outside of one's control. Heaters and air conditioners increase energy costs and divert money from food budgets.

Older adults may live in older homes that have poor insulation or outdated heating and cooling systems and as a result spend more money on utility bills.[59] Given that they typically live on fixed incomes, fluctuations in utility bills may be particularly problematic. Planning for bills of unknown amounts is difficult. The cost of utilities, including electricity and heating, during some months may consume significant portions of older adults' incomes, leaving less money available for groceries.[60] High utility bills adversely impact health when they lead to poor nutrition, restricted food intake, reduced medical adherence, and complications with chronic conditions.[61]

In our own analysis of Household PULSE Survey data, we estimate that the prevalence of low-income adults age sixty and older who reported reducing their expenses on "basic household necessities, such as food or medicine, in order to pay an energy bill" increased from about 31 percent in July 2021 to more than 40 percent by November 2022. By November 2022, one in three low-income older adults reported keeping their house at unsafe temperatures to save money. Often, avoiding excess energy costs is not enough to avoid food insecurity. More than one in ten low-income older adults reported both being food insufficient and reducing basic necessities to cover energy costs; nearly one in twenty reported keeping their homes at unsafe temperatures and being food insufficient.

Our respondents who reported keeping the heat low and the lights off tend to prioritize utilities before food. Violet, age sixty-three with low food security, pays the utility bills first and then adjusts by reducing her food budget. "Usually, I'd see where I can make changes with the food budget."

Julie, age sixty-two with low food security, struggles to pay for food and power in a good month. In a bad month, such as when the power bill is more than triple the usual cost, she cannot cover her bills. Her situation is especially tricky because she must keep reminding her granddaughter to be more energy conscious. She lives in fear of yet another thing going wrong.

> Like, you know, for the last two months my power bill has been so horrible. I've never had a power bill so high. So that money to pay a $258 power bill takes a lot away from other things because I'm used to a $70 a month power bill. You know, so that's why some months, you know, there's not enough for food. . . . And my granddaughter has no—I can tell her I don't know how many times you can't turn the air conditioner up. . . . You have to turn off the lights.

Edith, age seventy-one with very low food security, pays utility bills first then tries to make sure she has enough food by going to the food pantry. "Yeah, I usually pay the utility bills and then I figure other stuff out. Then I go to the food bank or whatever."

Carl, age sixty-seven and food secure, was behind on his rent and his air conditioning bill when we interviewed him. Now he juggles both carefully with the hope that he will not face eviction or a power outage.

> That's something—I'm doing that now; they said I owed [$75 for air conditioning], so I'm going to go ahead and pay it and you know, I'm paying it in installments because I'm not—you know, because this month, we have to pay the rent and then for the next three months we have to pay you know, for the air conditioning.

Our respondents described strategies for keeping utility bills as small as possible: They use as little heat, air conditioning, light, and water as their aging bodies will tolerate. But these steps may adversely affect their health and well-being. Russell, age sixty-four and food secure, is so keen to minimize his electric bill that he leaves the lights off as much as possible. "I get my heat covered but I pay electricity. . . . Mainly I stay in the dark. I don't need no light. You know what I mean?"

Wallace, age sixty-four with very low food security, has been behind on his gas bill for some time. Sometimes the utility company cuts his power off and, because he is not good at handling administrative burden by phone, he has to go to the office to get his power restored.

> Yeah. I owe for gas now. I don't pay them, I don't pay this month here, I owe for gas now. . . . They make me sweat but I always manage. . . . I might get cut off for about a day or two. . . . It happened about four or five times. I go down there. See I ain't that good on the tapping on the phone or something like that. I go down there to the place.

During COVID, Turner, age sixty-eight with low food security, was behind on his energy bill, but he knew the utility company could not cut off his service during the pandemic.

> Well behind on my utilities right now. . . . We just applied to a special pandemic thing to get our utility arrears paid, we're waiting to see if that goes through. . . . Need to contact them to see what's going on, they're supposed to pay all your electric and gas arrears up to the present. They're not allowed to right now for most of the pandemic . . . not allowed to cut you off.

Low-income older people often turn to programs such as the Low-Income Home and Energy Assistance Program (LIHEAP) to help pay their energy bills. LIHEAP is a federal program operated at the state and community level that provides financial assistance to pay home energy bills for heating or cooling. It targets low-income households with a high energy burden, especially people who are older or have disabilities, and young children.[62] The program is funded as a block grant that allocates a set amount of money and does not increase if need increases. Funds are usually exhausted each year.

Applying for LIHEAP is not simple.[63] Applicants must provide copies of recent utility bills, as well as proof of identification, Social Security numbers, income, and income tax returns for each person in the household. Moreover, eligibility requirements, the size of benefits, and time on waiting lists vary dramatically by state.[64] LIHEAP and federal weatherization assistance funding have served only a small portion of people eligible for such benefits.[65] The Department of Health and Human Services web page warned applicants in 2024 that only 20 percent of people who are qualified receive benefits.[66] To stretch limited resources during high demand, low-income older people may also turn to local charitable agencies that agree to cover one monthly utility bill a year per applicant. Even so, many cannot afford to cover their utility bills in full each month.

Though LIHEAP is designed to make monthly bills more predictable and manageable, some respondents found that it did not stabilize utility bills, was difficult to enroll in, or did not provide enough relief. Kira, age sixty-eight and food secure, uses LIHEAP to manage her utility budget, but the bills are still too high. She sets the heat low and uses blankets and sweaters to stay warm.

> No, because I have the LIHEAP grant covers most of it and when the HEAP grant runs—I usually keep the heat at sixty. . . . You know, I just put on a blanket and an extra sweater and I cover my head so my heat grant lasts a long time."

Kasha, age sixty-seven with low food security, has been trying unsuccessfully to sign up for LIHEAP. When she ran the air conditioner during a heat spell, she worried about the next month's bill.

> I worried about this winter. . . . They let you pay your light bill, but my funds are low now. The heat bill, that's what it was. I was out of heat and it's run out. So I'm worried about my bill. . . . Yes, I am worried, for next month. I had to run my air conditioning because it's been in the nineties. And then winter is coming up. A very big concern.

Transportation

Budget trade-offs between food and transportation may contribute to food insecurity among older adults. Transportation to grocery stores, food banks, work, and medical and dental appointments is vital for the well-being of low-income older adults. The availability, reliability, and affordability of public transportation varies markedly by region. Where public transportation is abundant, inexpensive, and accessible, obtaining food is easier; where public transportation is scarce, expensive, and difficult, it may be unusable.[67]

Even when buses run on time and older adults can afford the nominal fees, scaling the steps on the way home with arms full of groceries may be an insurmountable task. Some respondents described how they rely on affordable public transportation when it runs in their neighborhood and they are able to climb the steps; others described taking the bus regardless of the difficulties posed by doing so. At age seventy-seven, Alice has low food security and sometimes has to trade off between expenses like transportation and food. Her car is inoperable, so she uses her walker and takes the bus. But sometimes, particularly during COVID, the bus would drive by without picking up riders.

> I rely on my walker, walking with my walker. I thank God that I have the stamina to do that, but other than that, it has to be the bus. No. I did own a car, but it's dead. It's been dead for a while. Primarily it's on foot, and then other than that, it's on the bus; but you have to get to the bus, the bus you need to take; and they have policies. For example, if there's ten people riding the bus, they drive right past you, because they don't have to pick up anybody else if they have ten people on the bus.

Other respondents rely on medical transport for visits to the doctor and paid car rides for trips to the grocery store. The latter are often convenient, but the nominal fees involved may force budget trade-offs and contribute to food insecurity. Tamarah, age sixty-four with marginal food security, used her stimulus money to fix her car, making it easier to obtain food. But her car is still not working properly, so she pays for Metro Mobility, "Because of my difficulties, I'm signed up for Metro Mobility. So I can schedule a ride and then pay them. . . . They'll take you anywhere. It's $3.50 a trip."

Respondents who own cars reported that aging cars tend to become money pits. Personal vehicle expenses, such as the costs of the car, gas, maintenance, inspections, and insurance, are particularly likely to force trade-offs with food expenses. Low-income older adults may be forced to leave car bills unpaid and cars undrivable when budgets are stretched tight. When respondents choose between food and transportation, there is no clear pattern to which expense they prioritize, largely because transportation is required to obtain food.

Gerald, age sixty-seven with very low food security, pointed out how difficult buying food is when his car is not working. He struggles to walk or use public transportation, so he pays for a ride. He wants to spend his small amount of money on food, but then how will he get to the grocery store? "Food is definitely more important than transportation. Sometimes I can't pay but I need the ride to get food."

Lena, age seventy-three with low food security, has multiple chronic conditions and struggles to walk or use public transportation. Six months out of the year, she has to decide whether she can afford food and her car or make do with less of one or the other. She often has to trade-off paying for transportation or food, "Yes, I'd say half the year I have [to] decide between gas and maintenance and food."

A few of our respondents went into debt to either repair or purchase personal vehicles. Debt is worrisome on a fixed income, but they need a way to get groceries. Zachariah, age sixty-three and food secure, had to buy a different car and now has $333 monthly car payments, which adds to his financial stresses.

> I rely on the car for every mode of my transportation, medical appointments, grocery store, everything. Without the car I wouldn't go. . . . My car is a necessity for me. . . . And I have arthritis. I cannot ride buses, I can't stand up that long, on them bumpy buses. . . . So I ended up having to get another car. . . . So it actually threw me back, threw me in debt. . . . I always worry about it, because it's an added expense.

Against her own best judgment, Kate, age sixty-one with marginal food security, and her husband got a credit card in case their car breaks down. Now they worry about accumulating debt that they cannot absorb in their tight fixed monthly budget.

> I just applied for a credit card from my bank, tried to get a lower cost credit card just in case . . . we ever break down while we're traveling. . . . I don't want the temptation of racking up costs. . . . I have a 2009 vehicle that I am still paying on and I just took it to get its inspection. . . . I put $500 down and I still owe $250.

Personal and Cleaning Supplies

Trade-offs between paying for food and affording personal and cleaning supplies may contribute to food insecurity in old age. Older adults on tight incomes can delay paying for personal and cleaning supplies but not indefinitely. When managing household budgets, they must balance the need for food against the need for toilet paper, winter boots, dish soap, and laundry soap.[68] In our study, the prioritization of these expenses varied from respondent to respondent and from month to month.

Everyone needs personal care items such as toothpaste, deodorant, soap, and toilet paper. For people on limited incomes, these items can be cost prohibitive. Respondents described how they stretch their budgets to cover personal items by using such items sparingly or buying them at dollar stores. The best-case scenario is when they receive such supplies for free from food banks; this demonstrates how solutions that are broader than providing food help to relieve food insecurity. Spending money needed for food on shampoo or shaving cream is a source of great frustration. Bobby, age sixty-two with marginal food security, explained that if he does not have enough money, he simply can't buy personal supplies. At the time of the interview, he was prioritizing food, yet needed many personal supplies, "Like I need deodorant, I need toothpaste, I need toilet paper and those things I can't buy if the money's not right."

Maggie, age sixty-three with low food security, shifts the prioritization of food and personal supplies from month to month. She buys toilet paper in bulk so that she does not have to buy it again for a few weeks. This makes it harder to buy food in the weeks she stocks up on personal supplies.

> I try to stock up on some of these items where I don't have to buy them every month, so wow, this month I don't have to buy toilet paper, I don't have to buy paper towel, because I got three big old—you know, I buy the 24, I don't buy the one pack. I buy the double rolls, so I'm always double stacked on stuff, I don't try to let stuff run out because I'm on a tight budget. And my budget is very limited what I can buy each month.

Nate, age seventy-two and food secure, did not state his priorities but did state that his struggles to purchase food and personal supplies were growing more difficult as inflation pushed prices steadily upward, "Toothpaste, bars of soap, alcohol pads which I use a lot of with the recovering and the diabetes. . . . Those things cost. Toilet paper, Scott towels. There's a run on those and they hiked the price at every store you go to."

Trade-offs between food and cleaning supplies were fairly common among our respondents. They described how the cost of cleaning supplies is prohibitive on their fixed incomes. Scarlett, age sixty-seven with very low food security, explained how she diverts some of her food money to pay for cleaning supplies, "Some months I pay less for food to make sure I get the other ones. You can't go without them. I don't use paper towels. I use cloth rags. You can always wash them. Yeah laundry soap, cleaning supplies, and the normal things like that."

Edith, age seventy-one with very low food security, relies on her church food bank for her personal and household cleaning supplies. But they tend to run out, so she still has to choose between food and supplies.

> I'll let that go because I can get toothpaste and shampoo and toothbrushes at church. Our church food bank, they give out toilet paper, ladies' feminine items, razorblade, dish soap, shampoo, spic and span, stuff like that. Every couple months I have to figure it out. . . . I don't use a lot so it'll last me a long time. . . . I have to choose [between food and personal expenses] probably four or five times in a year.

Costs associated with doing laundry may contribute to food insecurity as well. Laundry often involves purchasing detergent, as well as paying for coin-operated washers and dryers. Buying in bulk is often cheaper at the per-unit price but very difficult to manage on a fixed income. Meredith, age sixty with very low food security, noted that when she pays for the large jug of laundry detergent, she has little money left for food. She told us she can only afford to do laundry every other week, "Usually I can't. Well, not super often, I mean, because when you finally get that jug of laundry soap it'll last. But I usually can't do my laundry for the last two weeks in a month. I have to go two weeks without doing it."

At the time of the interview Wallace, age sixty-four with very low food security, needed laundry supplies but had to use his money to buy food instead. He was trying to stretch the little bit of soap he had left, and he had no laundry detergent.

> I had to choose between food because this month here I couldn't even get my cleaning supplies. The last two months. I got some, all I could get this month was some dishwashing detergent. . . . I had just a little bit left over to clean the floors and stuff, and the sink, and stuff like that. But I didn't have something to wash my clothes. I try to stretch it.

Buying clothing can be difficult on a tight budget. Our respondents generally reported that they buy food before clothing. They have not bought new clothing, other than undergarments, in years or even decades. When they buy clothing, they buy used clothes from thrift stores or yard sales. Winter coats and boots are particularly difficult to purchase. Respondents sometimes wait years for a donated coat. Alice, age seventy-seven with low food security, must use her money for food rather than clothing. She makes do with used clothing.

> Yes. My clothes are old, and they're not very good shape. My God. I've had them forever. I don't buy clothes, shoes, or things like that. I buy groceries. Clothes fall into the category, especially shoes and underwear and stuff like that—no. If it's a tossup, you're going to get food.

Gerald, age sixty-seven with very low food security, needs a new coat but has to use the money for food, "I would say we have to have warm clothing. I needed a coat but it was hard. Couldn't buy a coat and have enough food."

Phone and Internet Bills

Prioritizing phone and internet bills over food may contribute to food insecurity. However, many of our respondents described using what they refer to as Obama Phone. They likely have discounted cell and internet service provided by a private company under authorization from the Federal Communications Commission's Lifeline Program to households with incomes below 135 percent of the federal poverty line and those who participate in federal programs such as SNAP, Medicaid, Supplemental Security Income, and housing assistance.[69] The Lifeline Program is another example of how solutions beyond food supply help to relieve food insecurity. Respondents with Obama Phones are generally pleased with the affordability of their service, while others are struggling to cover phone and internet bills. Helen, age seventy with marginal food security, frequently chooses between food and other household expenses. She also frequently faces budget shortfalls. She has lost phone service multiple times after failing to pay her bill, "I don't pay the full phone bill. . . . They [cut it off] before . . . yeah, so it happened before."

Kristi is sixty-one with low food security. Despite her best efforts, she sometimes does not pay her phone bill in full, and occasionally her service is terminated. She frequently chooses between paying for food and paying for other household expenses. She knows well that losing phone and internet service is problematic for anyone and that it makes the administrative burden involved in getting service reinstated particularly difficult.

Stretching a modest fixed income across an entire month and across all necessary household expenses, from medical expenses to phone expenses, is difficult. Budget trade-offs between food and other household expenses contribute to food insecurity in old age.

CONCLUSION

Even with Social Security, many older adults' fixed incomes do not cover all their necessities or provide much leeway to adapt to unexpected price increases for food or other essential expenses. As a result of poor health, limited mobility, and difficulty getting hired, many older adults are unable to augment their incomes with earnings. In the face of chronic economic disadvantage, in which they do not have enough money to meet all their essential needs, food often ranks below housing and energy costs and competes with medical expenses and transportation, personal and cleaning supplies, and phone and internet coverage. About 10 percent of adults over age fifty choose between food and other household expenses;[70] 27 percent report budget shortfalls.[71] For older adults, forgoing medical care, prescription drugs, heating or cooling, safe housing, or transportation may have health consequences that increase health-care costs. If the old age safety net were to better address nonfood expenses, food insecure older adults would be better able to afford healthy food. Instead, tight budgets divert money away from the procurement of sufficient nutritious food, adversely affecting health, increasing health-care costs and utilization, and decreasing quality of life. In chapter 6, we present ideas for how to support food security by strengthening income support for older adults.

CHAPTER 3

Beyond Income: Compounding Problems for Food Insecurity

Although financial factors play a large role in increasing the risk of food insecurity in old age, nonfinancial factors also shape that risk—notably poor physical, cognitive, and mental health; lack of access to healthy food; and transportation challenges.

Theo, age sixty-six, and his wife have very low food security. They are no strangers to hard times. Theo left school in seventh grade and worked as a janitor at a technology firm. Over the years, he and his wife, who has a disability, have developed multiple health issues that compound their food insecurity. Theo has high blood pressure, high cholesterol, difficulty breathing, and poor circulation in his legs. They live on the second floor of an apartment building and increasingly struggle to carry groceries up the stairs. They sometimes skip meals, particularly at the end of the month or when they have been feeding their nonresidential grandchildren.

> I tell my wife sometimes that you can tell when it get the end of the month, because the refrigerator be getting low. . . . I have not eaten all day. Yes ma'am, my wife didn't eat all day. Two or three times a month. . . . Well to tell you the truth ma'am, . . . I'm used to it.

They are increasingly lonely, to the detriment of their mental health. They see their children and grandchildren regularly, which gives them joy, but feeding the grandchildren sometimes means Theo and his wife have to skip meals.

https://doi.org/10.7758/rzos2617.8314

They would love to resume going to church each week but have nothing to give for the offering. "In fact, we wanted to go to church on Sunday. Our daughter said to come back. But see we wanted to have a little bit of money to put in—you know, pay what church. We don't even have that."

The free and subsidized food that they receive is mostly poor quality, which contributes to their poor health. They are only permitted to go to the food pantry once a month; their pantry offers very little fresh produce or other nutritious foods. The food is usually canned, and the meat is often freezer burned. Theo said that they get "green beans and stuff like that. Canned goods. . . . I've gotten meat there that won't be too good. . . . The meat's kind of burnt meat. Freezer burnt meat."

They face numerous transportation challenges that make procuring food more difficult. There is little public transportation nearby. When Theo walks to the closest bus stop, he gets short-winded and feels the poor circulation in his legs. Hence, the journey is formidable. "We got to go two lights—three lights—and the hill to get up before we can get to the [bus on the] main highway." Given Theo's and his wife's limited mobility, it would be much easier for them to drive their car to eat meals at senior nutrition sites and to pick up food at commodity giveaways, but often Theo cannot afford gas money. "We go to do it but we don't have no gas to do that. Because gas has gone up."

In addition, they can only drive during daylight and warmer months. They are struggling to find funds to repair the taillight and heater in their car. The police have warned Theo five times about the taillight.

> Right now, I got a taillight out. And then my heater. . . . Because I just don't have it. I told my wife I said well, we just have to put on thick coats and some blankets. . . . Just don't have the money because they want $105 for the taillight bulb switch and the taillight. . . . We go in the daytime. We don't go at night.

The future looks rather bleak. They are eager to move to subsidized housing so that they can save money, leave their second-floor walk-up apartment, and avoid the gun violence of their current neighborhood. But after five years on the waiting list for subsidized housing, they were just denied.

Theo's food insecurity is linked to a lifetime of hardships, including lack of education, physically demanding work, and multiple chronic conditions. It is also linked to the paucity of available community support in subsided housing, affordable transportation, or healthy food from pantries.

Theo and his wife are not alone. Nonmonetary factors that contribute to food insecurity include poor physical health, mobility, and stamina; mental health issues, such as depression, anxiety, and loneliness; lack of access to healthy food; and transportation challenges. For some older adults, these problems represent the culmination of decades of hard living, whereas for others, they represent the declining economic security that once accompanied middle and old age. For some people, these issues are offset by resource-rich neighborhoods, while for others, they are exacerbated by the paucity of local programs aimed at reducing food insecurity among older adults.

Moreover, these challenges are sometimes interactive or cyclical with food insecurity. That is, food insecurity may lead to the deterioration of physical and mental health, which may further undermine the ability to obtain and prepare healthy food. In this chapter, we examine how nonfinancial factors shape food insecurity for low-income older adults.

A 2022 survey from the AARP asked older adults about the factors that affected their access to food within the previous two weeks. While rising food prices and low wages were the top issues, 24 percent of respondents cited the presence of a physical disability, 15 percent the distance to a store, and 15 percent limited transportation as a factor.[1] See figure 3.1. Importantly, each of these factors, which contribute to what is referred to as logistic food insecurity,[2] was cited more often by adults between the ages of fifty and sixty-four than adults age sixty-five and older, suggesting the higher levels of cumulative disadvantage of the population approaching retirement age compared to those past retirement age.

POOR PHYSICAL HEALTH

Poor physical health, chronic conditions, and disabilities contribute to food insecurity among older adults and increase with age. In 2021, 13.6 percent of adults assessed their health as fair or poor. The percentage increased with age: 6.9 percent of people age eighteen to forty-four, 16.8 percent of those age forty-five to sixty-four, 22.6 percent of those sixty-five to seventy-four, and 27 percent of those seventy-five and older assessed their health as fair or poor.[3]

Chronic conditions also increase with age. In 2018, the Centers for Disease Control and Prevention asked adults if they had ever been told by a health-care provider that they had hypertension, coronary heart disease, stroke, diabetes, cancer, arthritis, hepatitis, weak or failing kidneys, asthma, or chronic obstructive pulmonary disease (COPD). Among adults age eighteen to forty-four,

Figure 3.1   Factors That Negatively Impacted Respondents' Access to Food in the Prior Two Weeks, by Age

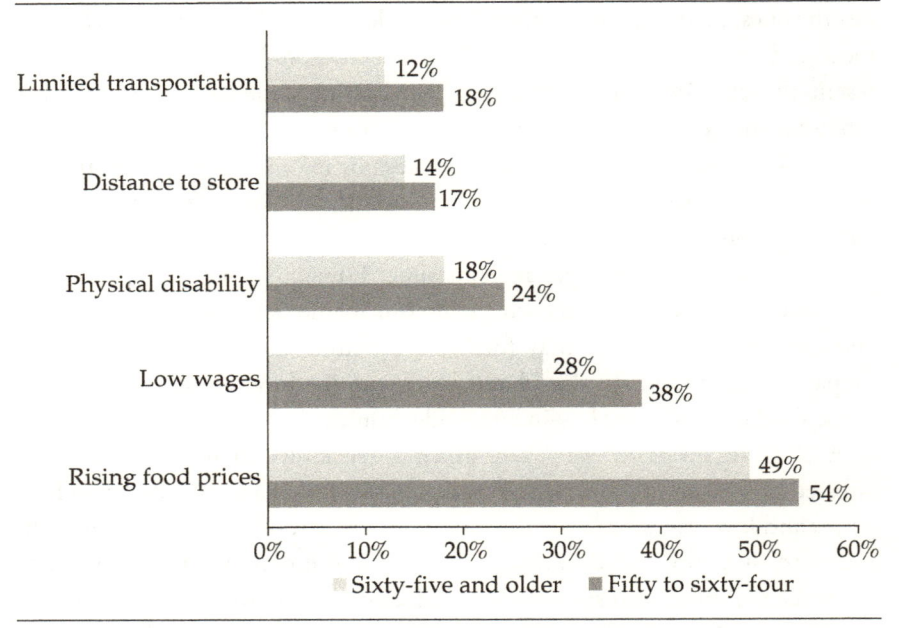

Factor	Sixty-five and older	Fifty to sixty-four
Limited transportation	12%	18%
Distance to store	14%	17%
Physical disability	18%	24%
Low wages	28%	38%
Rising food prices	49%	54%

Source: Authors' figure based on data from Keenan and Lampkin 2023.

20.7 percent had one chronic condition and 6.7 percent had two or more; among those age forty-five to sixty-four, 30.4 percent had one chronic condition and 33.0 percent had two or more; and among those age sixty-five and older, 23.9 percent had one chronic condition and 63.7 percent had two or more.[4]

The prevalence of disabilities also increases with age. In 2022, the Centers for Disease Control and Prevention asked adults whether they had any disabilities in the following six categories: hearing, vision, cognition, mobility, self-care, and independent living. Roughly 24 percent of people age eighteen to forty-four, 29.1 percent of those age forty-five to sixty-four, and 43.9 percent of those age sixty-five and older had at least one disability.[5] The older people get, the more likely they are to have disabilities. In 2020, only 22 percent of people age seventy and older could fully manage self-care and mobility activities, 38 percent could manage with devices, and 40 percent reported that they had difficulty or needed assistance.[6]

The most common disabilities for older adults are mobility limitations.[7] Nearly one in five adults age sixty-five and older reported that a physical disability limited their ability to access food in the past two weeks, as shown in figure 3.1. Mobility limitations may interfere with the ability to obtain, carry, and prepare food. Adults who lack sufficient mobility to go to the food pantry or grocery store, or sufficient stamina to stand and chop vegetables, are more likely to be food insecure. This is one of many reasons why food insecurity is more prevalent in people with disabilities and why households with disabilities constitute a large share of the overall food insecure population.[8] In fact, in 2009 and 2010, 31.8 percent of all food insecure households, or 4.96 million households, contained an adult age eighteen to sixty-four with a disability.[9] Work-limiting disabilities are twice as common among older adults, as are cognitive limitations such as having memory loss or difficulty managing money. One in two adults age sixty and older reports having a limitation to daily activities, one in three reports a mobility limitation, and one in five has difficulty seeing. Previous research has shown that the prevalence of any of these disability measures increases the risk of household food insecurity.[10]

Poor health and disability in old age are not randomly distributed. Older Black and Hispanic adults, older adults in low-income households, and less educated older adults are more likely to have accumulated disadvantages across their life courses and to live in areas with less comprehensive community services and programs. As a result, they are more likely to have worse overall health, higher levels of morbidity, more chronic conditions, higher rates of disability, and more functional limitations than other older adults.[11]

Managing chronic health conditions and functional limitations requires good nutrition, the lack of which can exacerbate such conditions. It is a two-way street. In some cases, physical health conditions lead to food insecurity; in others, food insecurity—which the U.S. Department of Health and Human Services identifies as a social determinant[12]—triggers or acerbates underlying health conditions. For example, diabetes requires careful supervision, but food insecurity may interfere with the ability to follow doctors' orders to take medicine with food or to adhere to a low-sugar and low-carbohydrate diet. Then, lack of access to sufficient healthy food may lead to poorer health, higher health-care bills, and less mobility, all three of which may interfere with the ability to obtain and prepare nutritious meals.

Physical health and food insecurity connect through at least three pathways: by limiting income from employment, by reducing cognitive abilities, and by reducing mobility.[13] First, health issues can limit individuals' ability to work and households' available financial resources even when they impose no constraints on mobility or budgeting abilities. Generally, disabilities are likely to reduce employment opportunities.[14] Work-limiting health limitations can be physical, mental, or emotional in nature; by reducing the financial resources available from earnings to support adequate food consumption, they may increase food insecurity. We describe this relationship between health and food insecurity in chapters 1 and 2.

Second, the presence of cognitive limitations might make it harder to plan financially and juggle the household expenses required to make ends meet or to stretch available food.[15] In addition, reduced cognitive functioning can limit access to formal sources of support, such as SNAP, further limiting household resources that support food consumption.[16] When these issues are extremely severe, an individual may not be in charge of their food procurement or preparation; but in less severe cases, cognitive issues may reduce the ability to successfully manage financial resources in order to avoid food insecurity. While we know that the links between cognitive issues and food insecurity are strong, few of our respondents talked about their own cognitive decline. Alana, age sixty-five and food secure, is a notable exception. She feels her cognitive decline is directly linked to the poor quality of the food she is eating. "Makes me sluggish, sluggish. And I can't sleep well. And then not as productive . . . especially when you're eating the wrong things and not balanced. . . . Not eating the right types of foods can affect your brain, I think."

Finally, physical limitations to mobility and the ability to care for oneself may interfere with the ability to buy food, transport it home, prepare it, and eat it without assistance. These types of limitations are likely to be more common among older adults, particularly those living alone, who cannot rely on another household member for help with these tasks. Obtaining groceries, carrying them up the steps, and preparing meals are all difficult for those with poor physical health, mobility, and stamina. One study finds that during COVID, older adults with three or more physical limitations were more likely to have what scholars referred to as economic and logistic food insecurity.[17]

Respondents told us that getting groceries can be difficult. Shopping for food requires walking, reaching, lifting, and carrying. Groceries are heavy. Getting them in and out of a car trunk, up stairs at home, and into a kitchen requires strength, agility, and stamina. Though it hurts for Pepper, age sixty-eight and food secure, to get in and out of the car, she can drive her own car to the store. But filling the grocery cart and carrying the groceries to her home are becoming more difficult. She is now too weak to go to the grocery store alone.

> Like you're going to the grocery store, you take it off the shelf, you put it in the cart, take it out the cart, you put in on the belt, and you're bagging, comes off the belt into the bag, you take those bags out to the trunk, you get them upstairs in your home, and take them out the bag again. That's crazy.

Faye, age sixty-four with marginal food security, uses a cane; at the grocery store she leans on the shopping cart for stability. "At times I use the cane. . . . When I go to the grocery store I hold the cart, right next to the cart, so I just hold the cart. I don't take cane or anything. . . . Just to walk outside It's hard."

Anna, age seventy-six with low food security, is not strong enough to carry groceries home from the store. "I simply can't carry it, and I get too tired to go to the grocery store, too tired to drive there. I have no grocery store close enough that you could walk to. And besides I couldn't carry it anyway."

Our respondents described various adaptive strategies to overcome serious mobility limitations. They move to first-floor apartments, use canes and walkers, or most often, depend on the kindness of others. Helen, age seventy with marginal food security, cannot climb steps and uses a cane, a walker, and a scooter to get around. Fortunately, the grocery store is next door, so she can walk there with her cane when the weather is good.

> I don't climb steps. I use a scooter and a walker and I have a quad cane. I use my walker and scooter when I go out. . . . I was going to walk over to the store. The store is just next door. And I'll get my walker and walk over there if it ain't raining. You know?

Lena, age seventy-three with low food security, has serious back issues, fluid on her knee, and a numb foot, which make it difficult to walk. She uses a cane and often asks strangers to lift or carry items for her.

> I go to the grocery store still, but it would be nice if I could send somebody and not be walking around getting stuff. I drive there and you know, sometimes like even a watermelon is too heavy for me to pick up. . . . If I see anybody walking in the parking lot, I'll say can you put this in the basket for me? And they do.

Pepper, age sixty-eight and food secure, is one of few respondents who has a home health aide, though several others are on waiting lists to obtain one. Pepper often relies on her home health aide to help select and carry groceries.

> I really like doing a little bit when my home health aide is here because getting up and down from the electric cart, that in itself, can be painful at the end of the evening. So I give the list to my health aide and I follow her around and stalk her. And she gets it all up here.

Housing, particularly housing without steps, for people with poor mobility or disabilities is in short supply, which may contribute to food insecurity. A 2009 survey finds that 12 percent of adults age fifty to sixty-four, 20 percent of those age sixty-five to seventy-nine, and 41 percent of those age eighty and older have difficulty leaving their homes because of medical conditions.[18] Only 4 percent of residential units are suitable for people with moderate mobility disabilities, and only about 1 percent are wheelchair accessible.[19] Many older adults need to make their homes more age friendly but find that such accommodations are costly, and they often have more immediate priorities to meet before they can do so.[20] Shortages of housing with few steps, secure railings, ample lighting, in-kitchen seating, and other age- or disability-friendly accommodations may make it even more difficult to get groceries, carry them up the steps, and prepare meals.

Steps pose one of the greatest hurdles to getting groceries home for older adults. It is easy to imagine Vera, age seventy-six with low food security, getting upstairs with the help of a railing, but it is harder to imagine she can do that while carrying bags of groceries. "I get around, but with difficulty. I very much need knee replacements from arthritis. I see the surgeon next month. . . . Yeah, I kind of haul my butt up by grabbing the railing."

Beth, age sixty with low food security, has trouble bringing her groceries up the stairs to her second-floor apartment. Despite steroid injections, her knee gets sore.

> Right now I am having a little trouble climbing steps because I have a knee that's bothering me. . . . I have a little bit of arthritis plus the cartilage is wearing out so the bones are rubbing each other so they hurt and I live on the second floor . . . especially [hard] when I have to bring up groceries.

After breaking her foot, Tamarah, age sixty-four with marginal food security, had screws put in her bones, which she later had removed because she could not tolerate them. As we conducted the interview, she was elevating and icing her foot. She avoids steps whenever possible. Climbing steps while carrying bags of groceries is out of the question. "Well, yeah, climbing steps because of my foot surgery, I don't really climb steps that often."

People with poor stamina and mobility may have difficulty preparing meals, which may contribute to food insecurity. Once they have brought groceries home, they still need to chop, stir, and fry food, as well as wash dishes and clean kitchens. Cooking requires a lot of standing and bending, and respondents reported difficultly being on their feet long enough to prepare a meal. Pepper's struggles continue after she manages to get the groceries home. She is sixty-eight and food secure but is not able to stand up long enough to prepare meals due to a serious spine injury. "Just like if I decided to cook a meal. I'm preparing and I'm sitting down. I'm preparing and I'm sitting down. The hot spot is my lower back. . . . If I'm cooking something over the weekend, my health aide will stand up and do all the chopping for me."

Marie, age sixty-one with very low food security, has two years of college and makes $10,000 a year working at the food pantry. She can eat meals at the pantry and take food and toiletries home. Marie has access to enough food but lacks the energy to prepare it. She wishes she had somebody who would cook for her.

> It was like it was just too much damn work. . . . And even though I have the resources and have the food here, I'm hungry most of the time. . . . The pain makes me get up, but it doesn't help me cook a balanced meal. . . . I mean I think what I do is make sure I get enough to survive. But I know that sometimes I know I can eat enough to where I get full, and then sometimes I don't eat enough to . . . cause I don't want to go back in there and fix no more.

Lena, age seventy-three with low food security, has a bad back and knee and finds it difficult to stand. She obtained a little cart she can sit on while preparing meals.

> I have one of those push things that you can turn around and sit on. So when I'm in the kitchen cooking, I do that because my back is weaker. You know? But my knees . . . my ankles are swollen. . . . That's why I got that thing I can turn around and sit on. You've got to stand up to get it and sit back down and whatnot. . . . I'm having more trouble now.

It might be tempting to ask why people with poor health, mobility, and stamina don't just order home delivery of their food. Home-delivered food can be an important source of support for people with health and mobility issues, but only if certain barriers can be overcome. Ordering delivery from restaurants or grocery stores is increasingly common but has some serious limitations. The four most common platforms, Amazon, Instacart, Uber Eats, and Walmart, now cover 93 percent of the U.S. population, and 90 percent of people in lower-income, lower-access tracts have at least one of these platforms available in their neighborhood.[21] About 4.5 million Americans, however, live in rural areas without services that provide home delivery, and 17 million households do not have broadband internet connection to facilitate ordering.[22]

In addition, even though the use of internet, smart phones, and various online platforms has risen steadily among the older population, older adults lag behind younger age groups. For example, in 2024, while nearly all adults younger than sixty-five reported using the internet, only 90 percent of those age sixty-five and older did.[23] Our interviews reveal some older adults may not be technologically savvy or confident enough to use electronic devices. Some older adults may be reluctant to use credit cards to make online purchases for fear of making errors, building up credit card debt, or risking credit card fraud. Also, providers often charge more for food that is being delivered, and delivery prices have been growing steadily.[24] Respondents on fixed incomes with tight budgets often cannot afford to pay online prices. Finally, given the extra costs of having food delivered, older adults often attempt to order as much food as possible per delivery. But the extra food may turn bad before they are able to consume it, particularly if they live alone.

Because of mobility problems, Harriet, age sixty-five with marginal food security, has food delivered. Often, however, the produce goes bad before she can use it, so she eats frozen dinners instead.

> Yeah, sometimes when I buy—when I'm picking out my food online and stuff, yeah, I can buy fresh produce and stuff. But like lettuce. I make a salad. That might be once or twice a week. Well almost that whole head goes to waste. . . . Tomatoes to put in the salad. They mold before I can eat them all. It's not so much a matter of buying them as it is storing them and throwing them away. I hate to throw away food. So prepared meals, you know, frozen dinners and stuff that's mostly what I eat, macaroni and cheese.

POOR MENTAL HEALTH

Poor mental health may contribute to food insecurity for older adults. A lifetime of accumulating disadvantages such as low education, low income, poor physical health, or little social control leaves many older adults with mental health challenges such as depression, anxiety, or loneliness. All three of these conditions are linked to higher food insecurity.

As with the relationship between physical health and food insecurity, the relationship between mental well-being and food insecurity is bidirectional. Higher levels of food insecurity are associated with higher rates of depression, anxiety, and sleep disorders.[25] Higher levels of mental health issues are associated with higher levels of food insecurity,[26] in part because people with poor mental health may be less able, or less motivated, to work, manage their finances, prepare meals, or buy groceries.[27] It can be difficult to disentangle the causal direction when a trigger event leads to a cascade of negative outcomes.

Food insecurity may harm emotional well-being through common pathways associated with changes in health. First, stressful life conditions, such as experiencing a period of food insecurity, are known to increase stress hormones in the body, which can impair biological processes that support emotional well-being. Second, food insecurity may limit nutritional adequacy in one's diet and decrease access to needed micronutrients that are supportive of emotional well-being.[28] A meta-analysis of nineteen studies from ten different countries that explored the link between food insecurity, depression, stress, and anxiety showed that food insecurity has a significant effect on depression and stress, particularly in North America.[29] In 2020, at the height of the pandemic, one in four older Americans reported depression or anxiety. That rate jumped to more than one in three among those with incomes below $25,000 and nearly one in two among those with poor or fair health.[30]

Though many of our respondents reported excellent mental health, others struggled with depression or anxiety, which often affected their ability to eat and sleep. Sometimes the high cost of food fuels anxiety and depression. Lena, age seventy-three with low food security, told us much of her anxiety is due to the increasingly high cost of food.

> Yeah, the food issues bother my mental health. . . . Yeah, when you know you should be eating certain stuff and you go in the store and it's so high, you know, you put it back or you put some of it back. . . . I try to eat a banana every day

but you go in there and they're 49 cents a pound or, you know, whatever a pound. . . . So you get four.

Kasha, age sixty-seven with low food security, has anxiety linked to her fear that she will soon no longer be able to live independently. Her chronic illness makes it difficult for her to prepare her own food. "I have concerns about my living arrangement . . . that I won't be able to take care of myself when the Parkinson's progresses badly. . . . Worried that I won't be able to prepare my food because I'll be shaking so much. It's worse in my hand. It shakes in my hand."

Diane, age sixty-five and food secure, lives in a great deal of pain. She struggles to take care of her granddaughter and finds it almost impossible to make meals for herself. She told us she contemplates suicide.

Some days I don't want to get up. I force myself to get up. I think it's because I have obligations to my granddaughter and I want to make sure she gets on this bus and gets off this bus safe. . . . Every time my legs is on fire. . . . If had a choice I would take a pill and end it all. . . . I don't have that choice.

Social isolation and loneliness may further exacerbate food insecurity. Social isolation refers to the objective state of having few social relationships or infrequent social contact with others, and loneliness is a subjective feeling of being isolated.[31] Social isolation is associated with a significantly higher risk of premature death from any cause and a 50 percent increased risk of developing dementia; loneliness is linked to a higher likelihood of premature death and hospitalization; and poor social relationships as a result of social isolation or loneliness are linked to a 29 percent increased risk of heart disease and a 32 percent increased risk of stroke.[32]

Isolation and loneliness generally increase with age because older adults are more likely to experience living alone, the loss of family or friends, chronic illness, and sensory impairments.[33] For example, 43 percent of adults age sixty and older, compared with 35 percent of adults age forty-five and older, report feeling lonely.[34] The rates for isolation and loneliness are substantially higher for older adults in poor to fair physical health and those with lower incomes.[35]

The relationship between isolation or loneliness and food insecurity is often bidirectional. Loneliness directly affects the physical health of older adults.

It also exacerbates the negative health consequences of food insecurity. Food insecurity may also affect social well-being, including how often family members visit, care for each other, or share meals. Socially isolated older people may have limited access to social support networks, including family, friends, or community organizations. This lack of social connections can make it difficult for them to seek assistance with everyday tasks, including obtaining food.

According to a study by the Pew Research Center, older people in the United States spend around seven hours a day alone, and those who live by themselves average ten hours.[36] Women tend to spend the most time alone, especially at older ages, because they tend to outlive their male partners.[37] Furthermore, the COVID lockdown proved to be especially traumatic for many adults who lost paid jobs and access to volunteer and social activities.[38] The Urban Institute finds that 55 percent of older adults who identify as lonely also report poor health.[39]

When older adults live with other people, they eat better and maintain healthy nutrition levels.[40] One study of older adults living in subsidized housing communities finds that, despite having access to SNAP, many older adults with limited mobility or who lived alone were food insecure because they shopped for groceries less often than other older adults who shopped with family and friends.[41] A study of older adults in rural areas finds that although participants feared being food insecure and lonely, participation in informal networks kept many of them engaged in cooking, eating, and grocery shopping together.[42]

Our respondents demonstrated how people who are food insecure may become more socially isolated and how those who are more socially isolated may become more food insecure.[43] Some respondents have rifts with families, live too far away, or fear that contact with neighbors or old friends may be bad for their health. Sharing meals with extended family is difficult for people who do not see their family for months or years. Alice, age seventy-seven with low food security, has only been able to see her family once a year. Loneliness is dampening her appetite and her mental health.

> It's very bad for a person my age and in my circumstances to be so far removed from my family. It's terrible. It takes a psychological toll. . . . I don't have the means. . . . I know what it is to have a social life. Unfortunately, I'm not in a position to have one at this time. Where? With who?

For people of all ages, strong social ties with family and friends tend to positively affect a wide range of health behaviors, including eating.[44] Living and eating alone tends to undermine good eating habits. People who have to cook for one—whether they are widowed, divorced, or never married—often find doing so is not worth the trouble, whereas eating with a spouse or other family members promotes healthy, consistent meals. Respondents noted that making the effort to cook properly for one is challenging. Faye, age sixty-four with marginal food security, explained how living with other people enhances her food security.

> So if I lived alone I probably would not eat, but when someone else is counting on you for food, I don't want to say you're forced to do it, but I kind of am, you know.... Maybe even once a week because I'm just not hungry or don't have an appetite that particular day, but I'm saying when someone else is counting on you, you're kind of forced to have something.

Beth, age sixty with low food security, finds it difficult to summon the motivation to cook for one.

> I'm not eating the right stuff. I'm eating junk food and I'm not really eating how I'm supposed to eat because I live by myself. I rarely cook so I just eat junk food.... Now trying to eat more vegetables and fruits but being on a diet is all so expensive.

Respondents reported becoming more socially isolated during the pandemic, giving up potlucks with friends and neighbors, book clubs, church socials, and family dinners. While national studies suggest that younger age groups struggled more than older age groups with loneliness and anxiety during COVID, several of our respondents reported feeling more loneliness, anxiety, and depression linked to fewer social opportunities to enjoy food.[45] Nick, age sixty-six with marginal food security, struggled with depression prior to COVID. It grew worse during the pandemic because he was not able to see his family members. "I have some issues with depression and stuff. This whole epidemic thing has really played up to this.... Being quarantined kept people away."

Depression, anxiety, and loneliness cause some people to eat too much, and others to eat too little. Beth, age sixty with low food security, was too inactive and ate too much during the quarantine period. Now she is depressed about her weight gain.

> I think that's why I've gained so much during this pandemic, because watching TV and eating junk food and candy. At the beginning you could barely go out. It was scary to go out thinking you would get infected. . . . Right now I'm depressed because of that weight gain. I don't like the way I look. I don't feel happy. I have low self-esteem.

Kristi, age sixty-one with low food security, often felt too worn out from depression and physical disabilities during COVID to bother eating a proper meal.

> Some days I have been without food. . . . During depression. Because during the pandemic it was kind of lonely, you know. I think I told you, if I—sometimes if I pick up a pan my arm gives out, and I don't want to have hot grease in my hand and let it drop, so I don't take that chance. . . . I just eat a cup of soup.

Respondents sometimes decline social invitations because they cannot afford to pay for the food associated with most social interactions. Julie, age sixty-two with low food security, must sometimes decline social invitations because she cannot afford to bring a dish or pay for a meal.

> Well like you know, say someone invites us to a barbeque and we have to take something with us, you know, we may not go because we don't have anything to take with us. So stay home. And if somebody's going out to eat, you know, we can't afford it so we'll say no, we can't go. We're going to stay home.

Kasha, age sixty-seven with low food security, often declines social invitations but is too embarrassed to tell her friends she lacks funds.

> Yes, I'm invited for pizza but I don't have the money. . . . Like my girlfriend wanted me to go with her last Saturday. They were going and I didn't want to tell her I didn't have any money. I just told her I didn't want to go. Well, she wanted to go the beach last summer, I didn't have money to eat at the beach, so I didn't go.

LACK OF ACCESS TO HEALTHY FOOD

Lack of access to healthy food may contribute to food insecurity among older adults. Social ecological theory suggests that where one lives matters a great deal when attempting to obtain nutritious fresh food. An AARP study reported that one in seven adults age sixty-five and older reported that distance to the store limited their ability to access food within the last two weeks, as shown in figure 3.1. Some respondents told us that they live near wonderful grocery stores with affordable fresh produce and easy transportation. Others complained about the lack of nearby grocery stores with healthy and affordable food options. An abundance of nearby nutrient-rich food options may offset a dearth of individual resources for procuring healthy food, whereas a lack of nearby nutrient-rich food options may exacerbate difficulties accessing food.

Some low-income older adults live in food deserts, areas in which residents have little access to supermarkets. The U.S. Department of Agriculture defines a food desert as "a tract in which at least 100 households are located more than one-half mile from the nearest supermarket and have no vehicle access; or at least 500 people, or 33 percent of the population, live more than 20 miles from the nearest supermarket, regardless of vehicle availability" and estimates that about 6 percent of the U.S. population lives in a food desert.[46] A study of food deserts finds that older adults without private vehicles are 12 percent more likely to be food insecure than are those who have private transportation. In fact, lack of transportation may have a larger effect on food insecurity among older adults than living in a food desert itself.[47]

Low-income households often face higher food prices because they are less likely to live near suburban supermarkets that tend to charge lower food prices and more likely to live near supermarkets in low-income neighborhoods that tend to charge higher prices.[48] A recent Brookings study finds that premium grocery stores are significantly less likely to invest in poor and predominately Black neighborhoods, leaving residents of those areas with fewer options to purchase high-quality food.[49] By contrast, Dollar Stores are significantly more likely to be located in poor and predominately Black neighborhoods.[50] If low-priced high-quality grocery stores are further away, and transportation and mobility are challenging, low-income older adults may be more likely to purchase less healthy foods from higher-priced convenience stores, such as corner bodegas and Dollar Stores, rather than supermarkets.[51]

Some low-income older adults we interviewed live miles away from a good grocery store with fresh food at affordable prices. Others report that produce at nearby grocery stores either is too expensive or goes bad before they can eat it. Much of the fresh, unprocessed food they can afford to purchase is damaged or about to expire. When they run out of healthy, affordable options, they are more likely to eat highly processed food, which contributes to poorer health.

Respondents told us of their frustration over the lack of good grocery stores near their residences. The neighborhood where Bobby, age sixty-two with marginal food security, lives has no good grocery stores selling high-quality produce at reasonable prices, and he has difficultly finding transportation to the stores that are further away. Out of necessity, he frequents the store in his building where he pays far too much for food with far too little nutritional value. The combination of overpriced corner groceries with few healthy options and lack of transportation to larger stores with better prices and produce has him irritated.

> To go [to] a grocery store with decent prices . . . I would have to catch a bus or maybe give somebody a few dollars and get a ride. But see they got a store downstairs which is my main concern. . . . These corner stores is ridiculous. There's no reason why they should be jacking up their prices like that. . . . I wish I could buy a car. . . . They used to have a bus that would go out to grocery store. I think it was every Saturday to the grocery store and they don't do that no more. . . . Why there ain't no grocery store in our area?

Our respondents asked why no grocery stores with healthy food were located in their own neighborhoods. Their frustration at not having a good way to obtain good food was palpable. Living far from the good grocery stores, coupled with lack of transportation, causes Wren, age seventy with marginal food security, to overpay for food. She wishes it was easier to get transportation to the better stores, which have better deals, particularly on days they break apart family packs and slash prices.

> Being able to go in and actually see the things that are on sale or things—see the meats that have been reduced, because usually on Monday or Tuesday they'll mark them down and hey, they'll actually put—break packages down to make it a little bit easier, too. So that has been I think my biggest problem over the past year and a half.

Other respondents asked why they do not have access to better transportation to the better grocery stores. Nancy, age seventy-one with very low food security, faces serious limitations to her mobility, and mostly uses a wheelchair. Her wheelchair is broken, however, and she has been waiting months to get it fixed. She has no grocery stores near her home, and transportation options are limited. Sometimes she is unable to get to the grocery store.

> I'm in a wheelchair and I have a disability. I can't walk far. I have a bad back. I have a fractured shoulder. I have a herniated disc. I got an umbilical hernia. . . . My wheelchair has been not keeping a charge. So they're coming tomorrow to fix my wheelchair. . . . I can't go to the grocery store. Sometimes I can get others to go for me. . . . There's not a grocery store close by to where we live.

When respondents have no choice but to shop at what they consider inferior but nearby grocery stores, the fresh food is often no longer fresh. Much of the food Bobby, age sixty-two with marginal food security, buys at the grocery store in his building is about to expire.

> Well, when I go grocery shopping downstairs I just lose my whole appetite. . . . I was like, "You got some sausage in there and the sausage is still in there and the expiration date is expired." OK. He said, "There's nothing wrong with the sausage." I said, "It is, after you defrost it. It's expired." I said, "It's frozen now because it's frozen." Nobody want no expired food. . . . Sometimes you gotta check your labels and check the dates on them.

Our respondents echoed the main point raised by scholars and policymakers alike: access to nutritious food is a critical social determinant of health. Researchers explore the links between health conditions and food insecurity from both directions. In one direction, among adults age sixty and older, work-limiting health conditions increase the risk of food insecurity by 2.1 percentage points. Each individual functional limitation increases the risk by 0.6 percentage points, and having difficulty managing money due to cognitive limitations increases the risk by 1.9 percentage points.[52]

In the other direction, studies show that experiences of food insecurity disrupt biological processes. The stress associated with food insecurity may lead to an increase in cortisol, which is associated with a host of negative biological outcomes. Food shortages may lead to reductions in medication adherence.

And poor-quality food may result in obesity or macronutrient deficiencies. In both directions, the results are clear: food insecurity and poor health are integrally connected.[53]

Our respondents described how relying on poor-quality food makes them ill. They know that they need healthy food for healthy bodies, but nutritious food is often too costly. Carl, age sixty-seven and food secure, put it very simply. "When I run out of the foods that are more beneficial for my body, then [I eat] a lot of the junk food."

Health professionals tell Susan, age sixty-five and food secure, that she needs to eat more fresh and less processed food so that her cancer treatments will be more effective. Unfortunately, she cannot afford more fresh produce.

> And I've got to get over it because they tell me since they got this cancer out of me, they tell me I've got to stop eating foods with—I need to go vegetarian like because of the inflammation it causes on your body when you have radiation And that's the part I think that really affects you.

Though we often think of people who are food insecure as being underweight, in fact in the United States, food insecure people tend to be overweight or obese, because they generally have access to food that is high in calories and low in nutritional value.[54] Nick, age sixty-six with marginal food security, is one of several respondents who said eating unhealthy food is making him gain weight and this is contributing to his anxiety. "I'm gaining weight when I shouldn't be and part of that is eating too much and not watching what I eat the way I should. And at my age gaining weight it not a good thing."

TRANSPORTATION CHALLENGES

Transportation challenges may contribute to food insecurity among older adults. Social ecological theory points out that where one lives impacts transportation options in substantial ways. An AARP study reported that one in eight adults age sixty-five and older said that transportation problems limit their access to food, as shown in figure 3.1. Transportation problems tend to be more pronounced in low-income, minority, southern, and rural areas. In one study of individuals who had requested food assistance, 43 percent reported that they did not have transportation to get groceries.[55] Another study finds that 2.1 million households located twenty miles from a grocery store do not have private vehicles.[56] Low-income households, and particularly low-income minority households, are the least likely to own automobiles.[57] In one study of 2,000 municipalities, 34 percent had no access to public transportation. These areas were more likely to be in the South and have populations of fewer than 2,500 people.[58] Even when public transportation is available, it often involves changing buses multiple times, paying fees, or struggling to carry groceries up and down bus steps. People who own cars are unable to drive them if they cannot afford registration, repairs, gas, or other expenses. Such transportation obstacles make it more attractive to shop at nearby convenience stores and buy poor-quality, less-nutritious food.[59] Some of our respondents face no transportation problems. Either their cars work well and they are readily able to drive, public transportation is affordable and convenient, or they can easily call for a ride. Others, however, are not so lucky.

Some of our respondents said that public transportation was too inconvenient or unreliable. Catching the bus is difficult for Carmen, age sixty-five with low food security, especially when it is cold outside. Sometimes she rides with a friend and offers payment.

> Yeah, sometimes in the wintertime it's hard for me to catch the bus because I've got to walk all the way down the street and stand in the bus stop and wait for the bus and sometimes it be really cold. But sometimes if I have like, you know, a few dollars to give my friend for gas, I guess she just takes me.

Valerie, age sixty-eight and food secure, finds public transportation unreliable, particularly when bus drivers drive right past her. "I get a bus pass, free bus pass. . . . There is a bus stop just a block down the road, but you can't depend on that bus. So I walk a mile to the bus stop, where they change buses and get on the bus there."

Ginny, age sixty-two with very low food security, has an unreliable car, so she takes the bus.

> Oh, Lord. It needs an oil change, and there are some mechanical issues going on with it, but I'm going to drive it till it falls apart. . . . My concern is that it's not going to hold up much longer. . . . Sometimes they'll have where the bus is behind and they reroute the bus and you don't get your bus until, like, the following time to go around.

Respondents described how the buses in their areas were not accessible for people with disabilities who are unable to climb the bus's steps, sit for long spells, or transport walkers or scooters on the bus. Because they cannot drive a car of their own, they rely on others for rides or pay for rides, both options that divert money away from food. Tilly, age sixty-eight and food secure, cannot manage the steps on the bus so she relies on rides from her son and husband and her scooter.

> I can't ride a bus or anything, because I can't lift my foot up to get on step. Now my son's back at school, my husband has to—he goes with me. I have a scooter that comes apart in five pieces, goes in trunk of my car, and you just put it back together. . . . I can't go by myself. Someone has to be able to take care of the scooter.

Nancy, age seventy-one with very low food security, has trouble with transportation in part because she uses a wheelchair. She can only go to the food pantry if she has an accessible ride. She delays food purchases and medical care due to lack of transportation.

> When I can get to the pantry I'll go, but without transportation I can't go . . . because my doctor is only three blocks away from me. I got an appointment Monday and my chair will be fixed tomorrow, so I'll be back on track. Yeah. And it's been delaying my surgery.

Respondents often rely on special buses routed to grocery stores, senior nutrition sites, food pantries, or low-cost shopping outlets. During the COVID pandemic, many of these special routes were discontinued. At the time of the interviews, respondents were hoping special routes would soon be reestablished. Martha, age sixty-four and food secure, hopes her residential building will resume rides to the grocery store and Walmart because the alternatives are too expensive.[60]

> One thing this building did have a bus on Wednesday going to grocery and then on the weekend every other week sometimes they go to stores. . . . On alternative weeks they go to Walmart. But we haven't had that all year and that's been very depressing. . . . I do qualify for Call-a-bus. But it's expensive. It's like $5.00 a day. . . . So I can't use it all the time.

Respondents also face challenges with personal vehicles. The vehicles they own are often unreliable and in need of registration, inspections, repairs, insurance, or gas. These expenses prove formidable for some older adults. Deb, age sixty-two and food secure, cannot afford to fix her car, or pay for car insurance.

"You get one thing fixed. And one thing breaks and then another thing breaks. You got to sit it there until that gets fixed, you know? . . . It's hard to pay the car insurance. It's very expensive."

Lena, age seventy-three with low food security, is unable to drive her car because it needs a headlight, an expense that sounds small unless you are on a very tight budget.

> Right now, I got a headlight out on the passenger side that I just noticed. I went to AutoZone or whatever you call this other place—Advance Auto—and the car only needs one bulb. It comes in a pack of two—$34. So I just won't be driving at night until the third of next month.

Our respondents described relying on family members and friends for rides. Such rides are not free when they are asked to help pay for gas or other expenses. Valerie, age sixty-eight and food secure, has not had a car in eighteen years. She walks most places, though she relies on the bus or a ride from a friend when she can arrange one. "I can't do steps, the curb's too high for me. I can do them, but it's painful because the arthritis is in my knees. Yeah, I have it in my back too, so when I'm done walking, I'm hurting."

Gerald, age sixty-seven with very low food security, does not have a car and cannot take the bus due to his bad back. He said he pays friends for rides to the store. "It's hard to take public transportation. I have a bad disc in my back. I need to have surgery but I'm putting that off. I don't have a car. I kind of get a ride to the store. Yeah, a got a couple of friends—for a fee."

In the absence of affordable, reliable, and accessible transportation, some low-income older adults get around in ways that may be unsafe. Faye, age sixty-four with marginal food security, and her son own a car, but she rarely drives because she feels she is no longer a safe driver.

> I was forced to get my license, my driver's license. I hadn't driven since 2015, when I had the stroke. The boys said you shouldn't drive anymore. You too slow on reflexes. . . . But now that [my son is] gone I'm forced to drive, but I don't unless my son who lives with me comes with me because I'm very nervous. I'm not good at it. It's not for me anymore.

Tamarah, age sixty-four with marginal food security, is afraid to shop in her neighborhood for fear of violence. "Yeah, going to the store. I have worries about that. . . . It's not safe, you know . . . and then it's so dangerous. People here they grab old lady's purses, and one lady hung onto it and they drove away in a car and were dragging her."

Diane, age sixty-five and food secure, has no transportation to the food shelves and does not feel alert enough to push her cart, especially during poor weather.

> My capacity isn't that good and I don't think I would do it anyway. My focus not really that good for me to be going—you know, you got to push a cart, you know, it be cold, it rains. It's different things or the weather is too hot, so when you get to a certain age you don't want to do a lot of things.

CONCLUSION

While affordability is the central barrier to food access for older adults, nonfinancial factors also contribute to food insecurity. An AARP survey documented that among adults age sixty-five and older, 18 percent cited a physical disability, 14 percent cited the distance to a store, and 12 percent cited limited transportation as an issue that reduced their access to food within the last two weeks.[61] Our interviews show that food insecurity in old age is also linked to nonfinancial factors, including poor physical health, mobility and stamina; mental health issues, including depression, anxiety, and loneliness; lack of access to healthy food; and transportation challenges. Our respondents reported being unable to obtain nutritious food or prepare balanced meals because they lacked either the physical or emotional strength and stamina or adequate transportation. When they do not have the stamina to obtain or prepare healthy food, they skip meals, reduce their food intake, or eat packaged and frozen meals. When they do not have transportation to sources of healthy food, they make do with unhealthy food. It is a vicious circle: older adults who lack the health, well-being, and resources to obtain and prepare healthy food have little choice but to rely on less healthy prepared and packaged food, and that reliance on poorer quality food in turn leads to poorer health. In chapter 6, we discuss how measures of older adult food insecurity should incorporate these financial barriers to food access. We also propose that people working with older populations should regularly screen for food insecurity to evaluate how food insecurity may be impacting their health and how their health may be impacting their food insecurity.

CHAPTER 4

Understanding the Limits of SNAP

SNAP, the focus of this chapter, is one of the most successful and largest U.S. food and nutrition assistance programs. It is designed to address the economic roots of food insecurity. In fiscal year 2024, on average 12.2 percent of the U.S. population participated in SNAP each month, and the average monthly household benefit was $352.[1] Research finds that SNAP participation increases food consumption and reduces health-care utilization and costs.[2] Recent estimates show that if everyone ages sixty and above received SNAP, the thirty-day food insecurity rate would be reduced by 76 percent relative to a world in which no one received SNAP.[3] SNAP is good for older people and it is also good for the economy: $1 billion in SNAP benefits generated $1.5 billion in gross domestic products in 2016.[4]

However, Edith's experience with SNAP reveals some of the program's limitations. Edith, age seventy-one, has very low food security. She has no children living in her home, but because she frequently feeds her pregnant daughter and her young nieces and nephews, we asked her all eighteen Food Security Scale questions, and her score was 11/18. She has worked hard throughout her life to maintain financial stability. As a young woman, her life course trajectory was hopeful; she completed a degree in teaching, married, and had two children. Her trajectory changed following her divorce. As a single mom raising her children, she relied on SNAP occasionally when she was without work. Now an older woman with multiple health problems and irregular gig work for employment, she has again applied for SNAP but finds the administrative burdens difficulty to navigate. During recertification, she worked with

https://doi.org/10.7758/rzos2617.7667

a novice caseworker who made multiple errors and cut her from the program, requiring her to appeal the decision. She typically receives $28 a month from the program, though during COVID she received an extra $225 a month. "Well, I've had food stamps off and on through the last few years so it depended. . . . They cut me off for September and I appealed it. There were four mistakes in my report from—so I appealed it, and then I got them back."

Her frustration with the red tape at SNAP is palpable. She spent inordinate amounts of time on the phone and going to the SNAP office to straighten out the caseworker's errors.

> I had a new caseworker and she couldn't—we did an interview over the phone and she couldn't figure things out, so she had to call me back the next day because . . . she was importing things wrong. . . . Plus, uh, they said that I was cut off because I didn't turn these papers in either, three different papers, and I said, "I have them right here, in front of me, and they're date-stamped from the office. I did turn them in." The case worker made three mistakes on there, and then they said I didn't turn the paperwork in. And I took every single piece of paper down there and talked to them, and the lady called me a week later and said, "We're going to drop your appeal and reinstate you because obviously there were mistakes made."

She eventually received back benefits for the benefits she missed during her appeal. But during the appeal she had to find ways to obtain food without SNAP. "It took a couple weeks before I could get it all straightened out, getting on the phone with people and taking my paperwork back down there and . . . I was hurting because I wasn't really working that much."

Throughout middle age, she accumulated health problems and medical debt, which she still struggles to pay off. She has an autoimmune disease, diabetes, asthma, arthritis, and degenerative disc disease. She worries about how much longer she will be able to work and struggles to pay off her home before she must retire.

She was able to manage her diabetes when she received increases to her SNAP benefits during COVID, but doing so is more difficult without the additional benefits. She works part-time as a bartender at special events, so her hours and paychecks fluctuate from month to month. SNAP eligibility is based on monthly income; hence her benefits also change from month to month. During COVID, when most special events were canceled, her hours and paychecks nearly disappeared altogether. Life was easier when she had the COVID SNAP supplement.

> It works when I have [the extra] $225 food stamps. When I don't have food stamps I have a hard time. That's when I'm going to the food banks and get canned food. . . . When I don't have food stamps and I'm sort of stuck, you know, like I can't reapply right away or I don't know. Because if I have a big check like from December, it's going to make me not get any of the food stamps.

Instability in her SNAP benefits also made it more difficult for Edith to fix her car. For several months, she had no car and had to take the bus or walk everywhere. It proved difficult to get to work, fill prescriptions, and obtain food.

> I was without a car for five months. I rode everywhere on the bus, it was horrible. It was like two-hour bus ride just to go to the grocery store. . . . It would take me all day in the winter. It was ridiculous. And I'd have to bundle up and layer clothes and then get to the grocery store and take everything back off.

Edith's health is deteriorating. Lately, she often feels too sick to eat, which is particularly problematic given her diabetes. "Probably two to three days a month I don't feel like eating. I have protein drinks in the refrigerator. And if I'm nauseated or depressed or I just don't feel like eating, I'll just drink one of those. Because of my diabetes I have to have something."

The disadvantages Edith has amassed since she became a single mother and accumulated chronic health conditions may outweigh the advantages she accrued earlier in life. Her food insecurity is alleviated somewhat by food from the pantry and the farmers market, but could be alleviated more if local and federal policies provided transportation assistance or more generous and stable SNAP benefits.

Low-income older adults with accumulated health disadvantages, such as Edith, face both economic barriers to food security, and noneconomic barriers, including poor physical health, mental health issues, transportation problems, and access to nutritious food. In this chapter, we highlight SNAP's strengths and limitations in addressing such barriers.

The share of SNAP participants age sixty and older has risen since 2000, but participation rates lag. In fiscal year 2022, 55 percent of eligible older people received SNAP benefits, compared with 88 percent of overall adults.[5] SNAP is particularly difficult for older adults in three respects: the high levels of administrative burden associated with eligibility, certification, and benefit-determination processes; the low value of SNAP benefits compared with the high costs associated with redeeming them; and the high levels of state variation in SNAP policies that produce substantially different local conditions for SNAP.[6]

AN INTRODUCTION TO THE SNAP PROGRAM

Policymakers enacted the food stamp program, the predecessor to SNAP, in 1939 during the Great Depression. In its early years, people received 50 cents of blue stamps, which they could redeem for surplus food items when they purchased $1 of orange stamps, redeemable for normal food items. It operated in half of all U.S. counties, reaching approximately 20 million people before ending in spring 1943. Based on studies and reports of the initial success of the food stamp program, President John F. Kennedy's first executive order in 1961 was to create a pilot food stamp program in eight areas, which over the next four years expanded to forty-three areas in twenty-two states. In 1964, the program became permanent, although it did not become available nationwide until 1974.[7]

Policy changes introduced in the 1980s and 1990s changed participation criteria and benefit levels, allowed for the electronic benefit transfer (EBT) to replace physical stamps, and created SNAP education and training programs. Legislation in the late 1990s created time limits for able-bodied adults without dependent children, further changed the eligibility formula, and reduced eligibility for legal immigrants, although eligibility was restored for some groups in 2002.[8] That same year, federal legislation allowed states to adopt waivers to federal certification requirements, and states began experimenting with administrative processes that created variation in the program at the state and county level. At the national level, policymakers renamed the program to the Supplemental Nutritional Assistance Program in 2008, although states now use a variety of names to describe the program.

When conditions warrant it, policymakers have increased SNAP benefits to help low-income households weather significant economic downturns. During the Great Recession of 2007 to 2009, policymakers temporarily increased SNAP benefits by 13.6 percent. This temporary benefit increase resulted in a 2.2 percent reduction in food insecurity and a 5.4 percent increase in food expenditures among low-income households.[9] Similarly, during the COVID pandemic, the federal government temporarily increased SNAP benefits by 15 percent and allowed states to provide emergency allotments, or the maximum SNAP benefit for the household size.

Since the start of the program, SNAP benefits have been narrowly targeted as vouchers redeemable only for food purchases and not as cash for general consumption that can be spent on any household necessities. SNAP is different from an income benefit: participants cannot use SNAP benefits to cover housing, energy costs, medical expenses, clothing, or personal and cleaning supplies. On the one hand, this program design means that benefits only support food consumption, which makes SNAP more effective at addressing food insecurity than it would be if the program provided the same amount of benefits as cash income. On the other hand, for most families, an extra dollar of SNAP benefits results in less than an extra dollar of food consumption, because households use some of the cash that they would have spent on food to cover other essential expenses.[10]

SNAP is a countercyclical program, which means that as unemployment increases, SNAP participation should increase and act as an economic buffer at both the household and the macroeconomic level. At the household level, SNAP benefits are designed so that low-income households spend no more than 30 percent of their disposable income on the food needed to ensure access to the Thrifty Food Plan, the most conservative of four food plans created by the U.S. Department of Agriculture. At a more macroeconomic level, SNAP benefits the local economy, because participants spend SNAP benefits at local food retailers, supporting local employers and creating jobs. In fact, according to one estimate, each $1 billion of expenditures in SNAP benefits generates $1.5 billion in benefits throughout the economy.[11]

Figure 4.1 shows the size of the national SNAP caseload. After the food stamp program became available nationwide in 1974, the size of the caseload was relatively stable for the next twenty years, before increasing during the recession of the early 1990s. It then fell throughout the late 1990s and early 2000s, before rising dramatically during the Great Recession starting in 2008. The size of the SNAP caseload then dropped until the start of the COVID pandemic. While SNAP participation expanded during the pandemic, caseloads remained below the historic high of 2013.

In general, the size of the SNAP caseload is a function of economic, policy, and demographic factors. The need for SNAP varies with economic conditions including changes in the labor market, the unemployment rate, and structural

Figure 4.1 Total SNAP Caseload, Fiscal Years 1969–2024

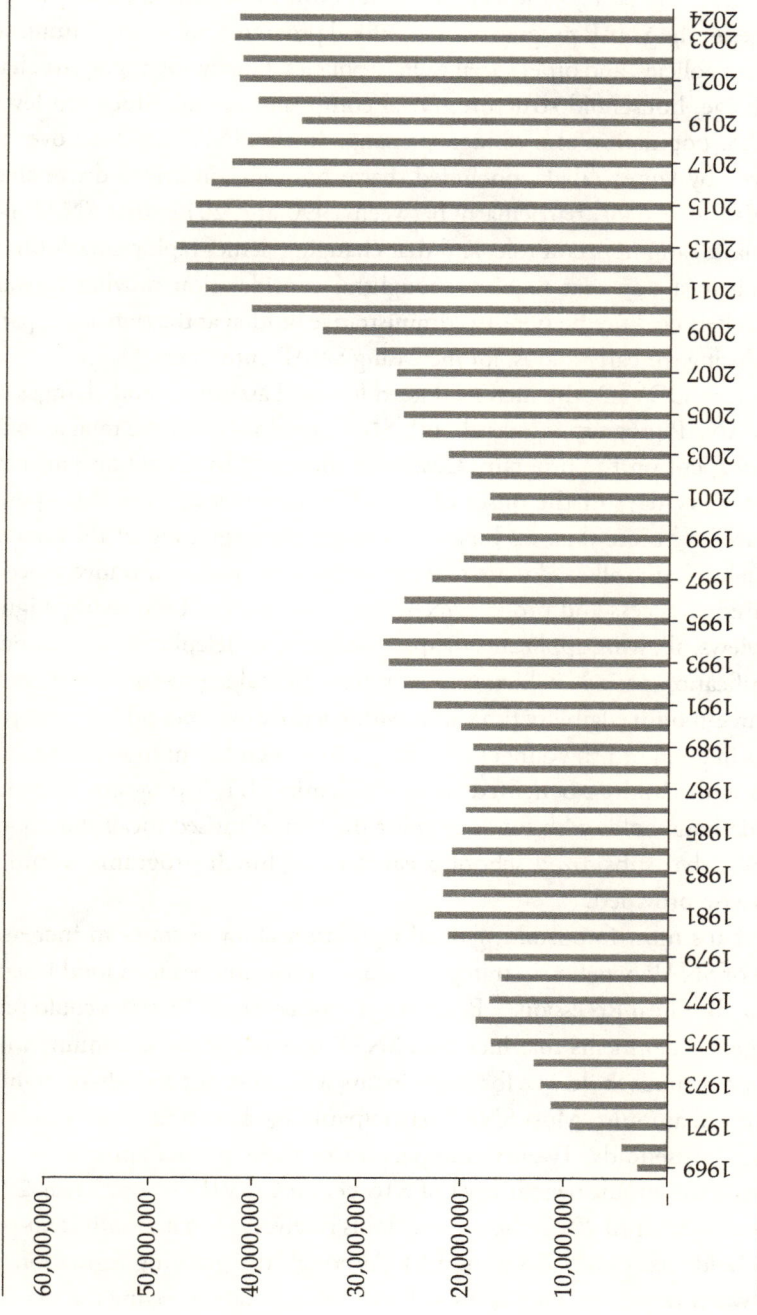

Source: Authors' calculations based on U.S. Department of Agriculture (2025d) SNAP data at the individual level.

inequality. The policy landscape includes both food-related policies, such as changes in the SNAP program, and nonfood programs, such as minimum wage laws, tax policies, and other social welfare policies. Finally, demographic changes in the age, household structure, racial composition, and education levels of the U.S. population also influence change in the SNAP caseload over time. Analysis by James Ziliak concluded that economic conditions drove changes in SNAP caseloads, particularly between 1990 and 2011, that SNAP policy also played an important role, and that changing demographic conditions were shifting in a way that requires thoughtful consideration moving forward.[12] Researchers credit reductions in administrative burden at the state level, particularly during the early 2000s, for increasing SNAP enrollment.[13]

During COVID, the increased need for food assistance and changes made to the SNAP program increased both SNAP caseloads and the total amount of money spent on the program. Caseloads increased by 4 million participants within sixty days of the onset of COVID, and average monthly spending increased by more than $2 billion.[14] During the beginning of the pandemic, federal legislation allowed states to temporarily modify administrative procedures required to access and process SNAP benefits, such as by waiving eligibility interviews, allowing applicants to apply online or by telephone, and extending recertification periods (which vary by state). Federal legislation also eliminated the three-month eligibility time limit within a three-year period for unemployed adults in good health younger than fifty without children. In addition, households with children benefited from Pandemic-EBT, a program designed to provide households with funds to cover the cost of missed meals due to school closures that subsidized school breakfast and lunch programs would have otherwise provided.

Perhaps most important, federal legislation allowed states to increase the value of SNAP benefits, a strategy that had previously reduced food insecurity during the Great Recession.[15] Beginning in fiscal year 2020, states could provide emergency allotments that increased SNAP benefits to the maximum amount allowed by household size for participants who were not already receiving the maximum amount. Most SNAP participants age sixty and above live in one-person households. Twenty-one percent of these participants received the monthly minimum benefit level of $16 before COVID in fiscal year 2019.[16] Beginning in April 2020, these households received $194 a month (two-person households received $355 a month). Although the granting legislation originally was interpreted to not apply to households already receiving the maximum

SNAP benefits for their household size, this was reinterpreted in April 2021 to provide a minimum monthly benefit increase of $95 to all SNAP households. States differed in how long they offered these higher benefits, with eight states ending emergency allotments by October 2021 and nine more states no longer providing higher benefits by September 2022. From January through September 2021, federal-level SNAP benefits temporarily increased by 15 percent for all participants (estimated at about $28 per person per month). Another permanent increase, unrelated to COVID, followed in October 2021 after a congressionally mandated reconsideration of the Thrifty Food Plan. In March 2023, the emergency allotment provision ended for SNAP participants in the thirty-five states that had not already discontinued this option, resulting in an increase in food insufficiency of 8.4 percentage points.[17]

During our interviews, respondents were aware that the emergency allotment provision would soon end and that their SNAP benefits would decrease, and they were concerned about how they would make ends meet. Willow, age seventy-four with low food security, receives the minimum SNAP benefit, which had increased to $23 a month after COVID. She is concerned about how she will pay for food, because she often must pay her other bills before she can buy food. "I'm going to struggle. Because I'll pay my bills before I'll buy food. . . . Food is not even on the list. It's not on the list. I figured it out. It's going to be [about] $20 a month. I can buy my milk and cereal with that every month."

ACCESSING SNAP BENEFITS

To receive SNAP benefits, participants age sixty and older must first show that their net household income, after relevant deductions, is below the poverty line for their household size. Potential deductions from household income include 20 percent of earned income; the standard deduction, which is $204 for one-to-three-person households in fiscal year 2025; the excess shelter deduction, which caps shelter expenses at 50 percent of household income; and adjusted medical costs, which allow households with adults who are older or have disabilities to subtract medical expenses greater than $35. A small set of states also apply asset tests, which disqualify households with adults who are age sixty and older or who have disabilities with assets greater than $4,500 in fiscal year 2025.[18] Documentation required for eligibility determination includes birth certificates for everyone in the household, proof of residence, bank statements, utility bills, rental lease or property tax payments, and medical receipts.

Most states have switched to computerized application processes that allow applicants to submit materials without physically going to an agency. For many SNAP households, particularly working family members who no longer need to take time off work to go to the local social service agency to apply for SNAP, these process changes have resulted in better access. However, current processes require applicants to be able to access the internet, be comfortable using computerized systems, and understand the questions being asked on the application. As states have modernized their application systems, they have closed many brick and mortar offices and replaced them with phone centers for both efficiency and labor-cost reduction.[19] However, for older adults who may have to apply on their phones rather than on laptops, who may not understand how to complete what might appear as obvious computer functions to people who use technology every day (such as using a drop-down menu), who have difficulty remembering passwords and pins, or who do not feel safe disclosing personal financial information online, these systems may be difficult to navigate. While some agency locations offer paper applications and help filling out the forms, the application process is no longer designed to support face-to-face contact consistently for all residents.

The final step for eligibility determination is an interview. If an applicant walks into a SNAP office and completes the form with all the right documentation and has no income, the interview can often be completed immediately. In most other cases, the interview can be completed later by phone. Some places provide applicants with a phone number to call and complete the interview when it is convenient for them. However, in other locations, they give applicants a day and time window (Tuesday from 1 to 3 p.m., for example) when they need to be available for an eligibility worker to call them to complete the interview. In practice, the interview is often not completed during the assigned window, because either the eligibility worker does not call or the applicant is not available. During the interview, the eligibility worker confirms income and household size, clarifies any aspects of the application that are unclear or missing, and then approves the application.[20] In the best situations, the eligibility worker connects applicants to other programs for which they qualify and provides information about where to find emergency food assistance.

Recipients periodically must repeat this process of proving eligibility, with the frequency varying by state. During the recertification process, many participants who are eligible fail to complete the process and experience a lapse in their benefits before finishing the paperwork and reenrolling a month or two later.[21] Researchers refer to this as administrative churn. In all states, however, older adults and those with disabilities do not have to recertify as frequently as other adults do. The less-frequent recertification requirements recognize that the income that these households receive—Social Security, SSDI, and SSI payments—is more stable than households whose members are more likely to be working, and that complying with recertification procedures might be more difficult. In some states, while the recertification period is as short as six months for most households, those with older adults have between twelve and thirty-six months before they need to prove eligibility again.[22] In fiscal year 2022, 34.6 percent of adults sixty and older had a twelve-month recertification period, 24.2 percent had a twenty-four-month period, and 29.9 percent had a thirty-six-month period.[23]

Once applicants certify their eligibility, federal benefit formulas determine the level of benefits awarded at the household level, which is tied to the cost of the Thrifty Food Plan. Each year, the U.S. Department of Agriculture updates SNAP benefit levels to account for increases in the cost of food. Each household's monthly benefit increases with household size and is set to ensure that the household can eat according to this food plan without spending more than 30 percent of its disposable income on food.

In fiscal year 2022, four in five households receiving SNAP included children, people with disabilities, or those age sixty and older. These households face no limits on the length of time that they can receive SNAP, nor any work requirements. The remaining one in five SNAP households is only eligible for three months of SNAP benefits within a three-year period without fulfilling work requirements. The minimum SNAP benefit for one- and two-person households with adults age sixty and older is $23 per month in fiscal year 2025, and the average monthly SNAP benefit for all households in November 2024 was $361.70 per household, or $192.82 per person.[24] In 2023, 51.9 percent of households that received SNAP reported being food insecure.[25]

SNAP PARTICIPATION AMONG OLDER ADULTS

In fiscal year 2022, the latest year for which characteristics of the SNAP population are available, 7.2 million adults age sixty and older received SNAP benefits. Households with an adult age sixty and older made up 31.4 percent of all SNAP households. SNAP households with older adults tended to be

Figure 4.2 Sources of Income for Adults Age Sixty and Older on SNAP, Fiscal Year 2022

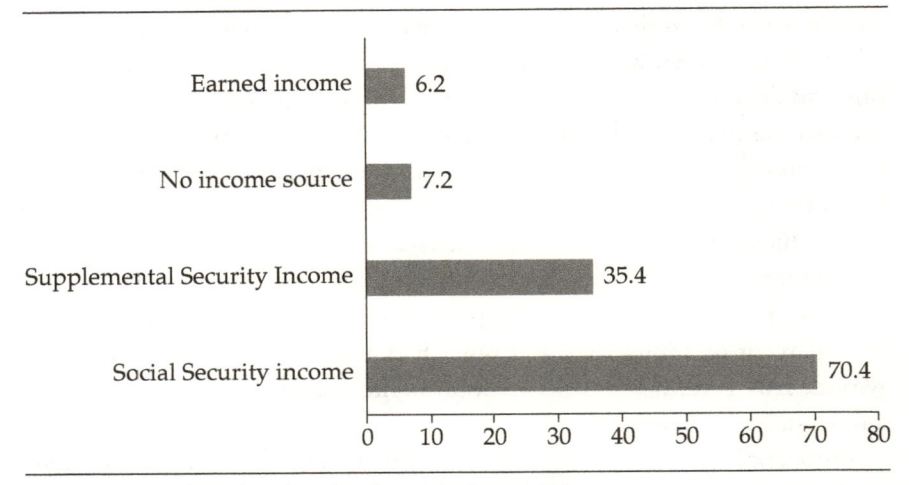

Source	Percent
Earned income	6.2
No income source	7.2
Supplemental Security Income	35.4
Social Security income	70.4

Source: Authors' figure based on data from Monkovic 2024.

smaller on average than the average SNAP household (1.2 versus 1.9 individuals). In fact, 82 percent of older adult SNAP households were single-person households. The average monthly SNAP benefit for older adults in fiscal year 2022 was $137 for recipients living alone and $208 for multiperson households. Because SNAP benefits are a function of both income and household size, average SNAP benefits were higher in households without older adults ($360), because older adult households tend to have higher incomes and fewer household members. To put these benefit amounts in context, the U.S. Department of Agriculture estimates that the cost of a month of food using the Thrifty Food Plan for women age seventy-one and older in January 2024 was $248.[26] In terms of sources of income, as shown in figure 4.2, 35 percent of older adult SNAP households received SSI and 70 percent received Social Security income in 2022. Although 6 percent had earned income, fully 7 percent of SNAP households with older adults had no source of income.[27]

In figure 4.3, we present the demographic characteristics of the SNAP caseload for adults aged sixty and above in fiscal year 2022. Similarly to people in poverty, most SNAP recipients age sixty and older are female—64.1 percent. In terms of the racial composition, 41.2 percent of heads of SNAP households containing older adults were White non-Hispanic, 20.9 percent Black non-Hispanic, 15.2 percent Hispanic of any race, 7.4 percent Asian, 0.9 percent

Figure 4.3   Demographic Characteristics of Adults Age Sixty and Older in SNAP Households, Fiscal Year 2022

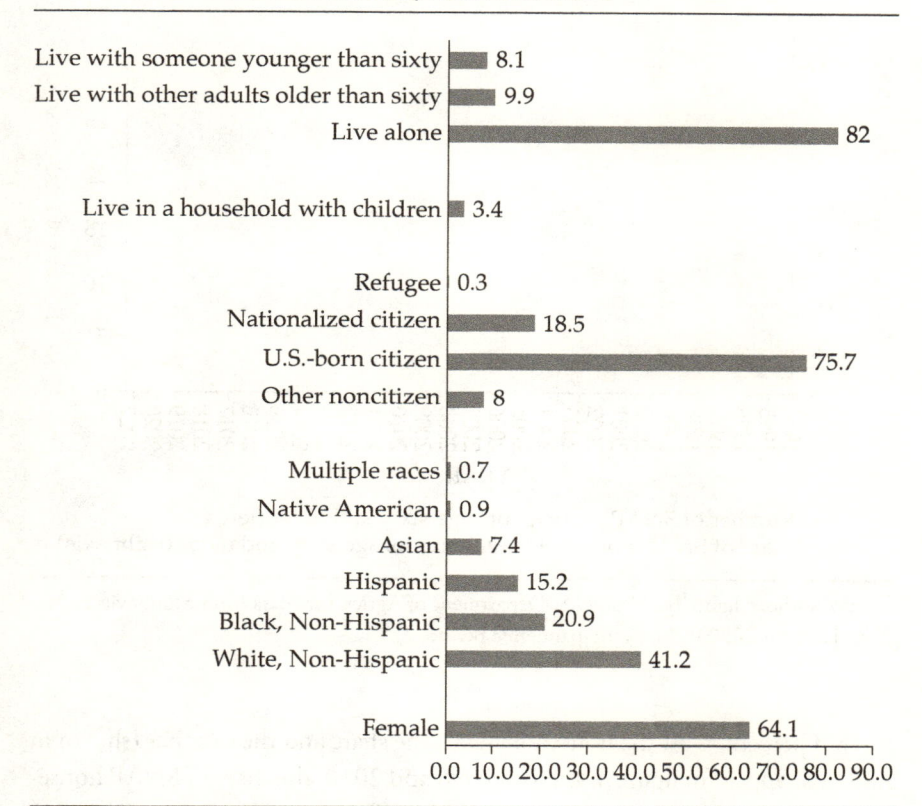

Category	Value
Live with someone younger than sixty	8.1
Live with other adults older than sixty	9.9
Live alone	82
Live in a household with children	3.4
Refugee	0.3
Nationalized citizen	18.5
U.S.-born citizen	75.7
Other noncitizen	8
Multiple races	0.7
Native American	0.9
Asian	7.4
Hispanic	15.2
Black, Non-Hispanic	20.9
White, Non-Hispanic	41.2
Female	64.1

Source: Authors' figure based on Monkovic 2024.

Native American and 13.7 percent were of unknown race and ethnicity. In terms of citizenship, 75.7 percent of older adults in SNAP households were U.S.-born citizens, 18.5 percent were naturalized citizens, 0.3 percent were refugees, and 8 percent were other noncitizens. Four out of five adults age sixty and older on SNAP lived alone, one in ten lived with another older adult, and one in ten lived with someone younger. About 3 percent of households with children, the majority of whom were school-aged children, also contained an older adult.[28]

The composition of the SNAP caseload that consists of older adults is changing at a rapid pace. At the individual level, the share of SNAP recipients who are older adults grew 50 percent between 2013 and 2022, from 9 percent

100 FOOD FOR THOUGHT

Figure 4.4 SNAP Recipients Age Sixty and Older, 1994–2022

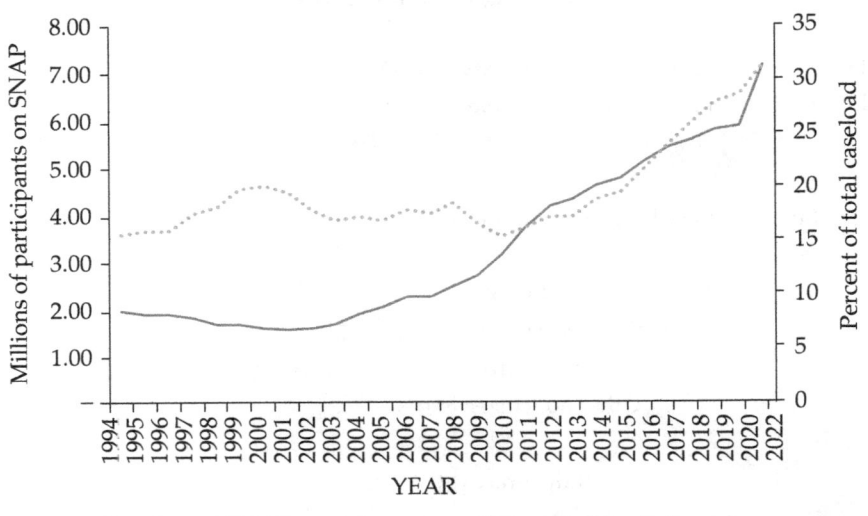

——— Number of SNAP participants age sixty and older (left axis)
······· Share of SNAP households with adults age sixty and older (right axis)

Source: Authors' figure based on U.S. Department of Agriculture data from Monkovic 2024.
Note: Data for 2020 includes pre-pandemic period.

to 18.3 percent.[29] At the household level, the share and the number (shown in millions) appear in figure 4.4. From 1998 and 2010, the share of SNAP households containing adults age sixty and older fluctuated between 16 percent and 21 percent, but since 2010, the share has steadily increased, reaching 31.4 percent by 2022. The raw number of older adult SNAP participants grew slowly from 1.9 million in 1994 to 2.7 million in 2009 before growing more rapidly to the 2022 level of 7.2 million participants.[30]

Figure 4.4 demonstrates that older adults on SNAP compose an increasingly greater share of the SNAP caseload, and that their raw numbers are growing. How do we think of this caseload growth in light of the low participation rates for adults age sixty and older? We begin by estimating time trends in who is eligible for SNAP in the first place and then look at the share of those eligible who participate in the program.

Using restricted-access data from the Health and Retirement Study, a unique source that contains detailed household income, expense, and asset data and

Figure 4.5 Trends in Estimated SNAP Eligibility Rate by Age, 2002–2018

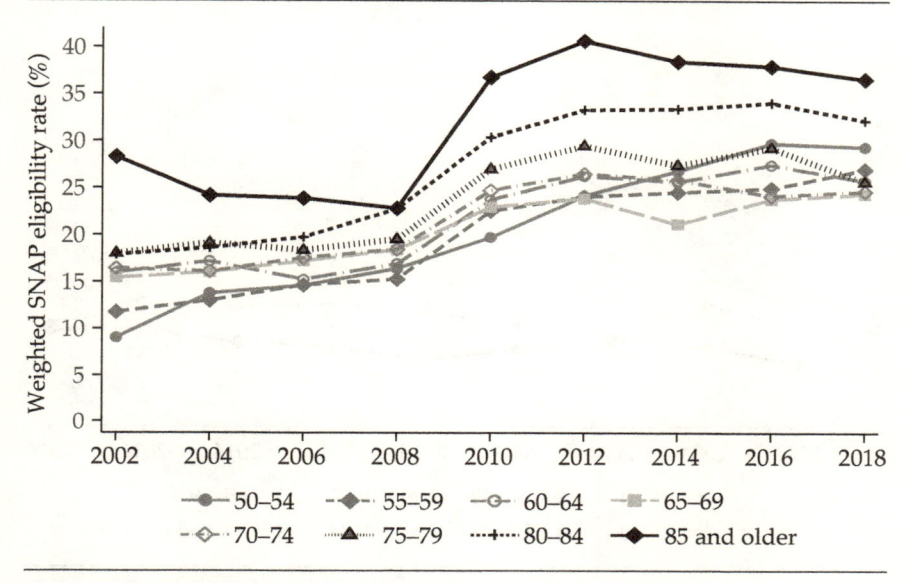

[Line chart showing weighted SNAP eligibility rate (%) from 2002 to 2018 for age groups: 50–54, 55–59, 60–64, 65–69, 70–74, 75–79, 80–84, and 85 and older.]

Source: Authors' calculations using Health and Retirement Study data.

that allows researchers to consider the variation in state policies over time, Colleen Heflin and colleagues estimated SNAP eligibility following a process pioneered by Steven Haider and colleagues and refined by Jordan Jones and colleagues for 2002 to 2016.[31] Using the same method, we present estimated SNAP eligibility from 2002 to 2018 by age in five-year bins in figure 4.5, beginning with age fifty to fifty-four. Estimated eligibility increases as adults age: among adults age fifty and older, the oldest older adults are more likely to be eligible for SNAP than are younger older adults, with adults most likely to be eligible for SNAP at age eighty and older. State policy changes, such as the adoption of broad-based categorical eligibility, which increases household income limits and removes asset tests, as well as other provisions, such as allowing adults age sixty and older to subtract the cost of out-of-pocket medical expenses from net household income calculations, are designed to increase SNAP coverage.[32] As figure 4.5 shows, estimated eligibility increased for all adults age fifty and older from 2008 through 2012. By 2018, estimated SNAP eligibility was higher for all ages by about 8 percentage points relative to 2002, with even higher increases in estimated eligibility for adults age seventy-five and

102   FOOD FOR THOUGHT

Figure 4.6   Trends in SNAP Uptake Rate by Age, 2002–2018

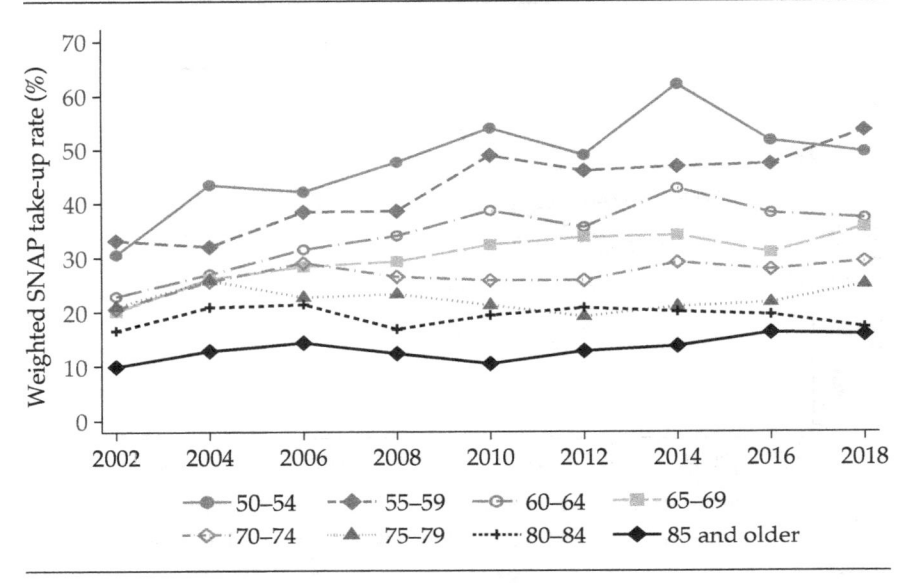

Source: Authors' calculations using Health and Retirement Study data.

older. Thus, state and federal policy changes, as well as the changing demographic profile of older adults, increased the pool of older adults eligible for SNAP over this period.

Using the sample of older adults predicted to be eligible in figure 4.5, we show the trend in SNAP uptake among people predicted to be eligible by age in figure 4.6. Here, the patterns are the opposite of those for eligibility, with the oldest age groups the least likely to uptake SNAP and the youngest groups the most likely. SNAP uptake declined from around 50 percent between the ages of fifty and fifty-four to 15 percent at age eighty-five and older in 2018. Stated differently, 50 to 85 percent of older adults who are estimated to be eligible for SNAP do not participate in the program. Additionally, most of the changes in SNAP uptake over time occurred between 2002 and 2010, and this is concentrated among the younger age groups; from 2010 to 2018, SNAP uptake was relatively constant for all age groups.[33]

Together, these two figures tell us that estimated SNAP eligibility consistently rose with age, a trend that also increased over time (figure 4.5); that means that more adults age sixty and older are eligible for SNAP. However, at the same time, SNAP uptake consistently declined as age increased (figure 4.6).

As a result of these two trends moving in opposite directions, the age gap in older adult SNAP participation has grown rapidly over time. This is a troubling trend that essentially is moving in the wrong direction.

We must acknowledge, however, that not everyone who is eligible for SNAP would necessarily see their access to healthy food improved by participating in the program. A study by Haider and colleagues, which used the 1998 and 2000 waves of the Health and Retirement Study to estimate both SNAP eligibility and uptake, concludes that the eligible seniors who did not uptake SNAP appeared to not be very needy according to measures such as skipped meals and median housing values.[34] Indeed, some older adults may not participate in SNAP even though they qualify, because they are able to meet their food needs without SNAP. In addition, as health declines, many older adults move to residential care settings that provide meals. Residents of assisted living facilities who receive more than half of their three daily meals as part of their normal services are ineligible for SNAP unless they live in federally subsidized housing for older adults. For the rest of the older adult population that is eligible but not receiving SNAP, we believe that most of the reasons for this pattern lie within the program itself.

EXPLAINING LOW SNAP UPTAKE AMONG OLDER ADULTS

The level of SNAP participation among the population eligible, referred to as the uptake rate, varies at the state level. According to data from fiscal year 2018, the latest year for which state estimates are available, uptake rates for older adults at the state level vary from 22 to 78 percent, reflecting differences in social ecological conditions across states.[35] According to recent U.S. Department of Agriculture estimates for fiscal year 2022, 55 percent of adults age sixty and older who qualify for SNAP receive benefits, compared with 88 percent of overall eligible adults who do so.[36] For comparison, the Social Security program has an uptake rate of 97 percent.[37] Further, analyses of formal state policies report that efforts to increase eligibility among older adults have only been modestly effective at increasing uptake, and state efforts to reduce the stigma or transactions costs of SNAP, such as eliminating fingerprinting, as well as outreach efforts, such as TV or radio advertising campaigns to raise awareness of the program, are not effective.[38]

What are the potential explanations for the consistent pattern of declining uptake during the aging process? We focus on the nonparticipation in SNAP among older adults that is attributed to the high administrative burden associated with eligibility, certification, and benefit-determination processes; the relatively low benefit amounts received and the difficulties associated with redeeming those benefits; and the significant state variation that exists in the policies determining both the costs and benefits of participation.[39]

Administrative Burdens Embedded in SNAP Processes

Policymakers designed SNAP, a means-tested program that is limited to low-income households, with a set of administrative processes to ensure that the program awards benefits to cover the food needs of households without other means of support such as savings, assets, or work opportunities.[40] Application and recertification processes should identify and prevent fraud. The term *administrative burden* often refers to the process individuals go through to access benefits. Researchers frequently identify three types of administrative burdens that pertain to social programs: learning costs, compliance costs, and psychological costs. Individuals encounter learning costs when trying to figure out specific program rules and procedures. Compliance costs involve providing necessary documentation and meeting eligibility requirements. Personal psychological costs may result from the stigma or mental burden associated with interacting with the government.[41] Recent research has begun to consider how some forms of administrative processes may benefit, rather than burden, clients, as well as explore how some processes, such as the interview requirement, may decrease learning costs while increasing compliance costs.[42]

Not everyone we spoke to had trouble accessing SNAP. Some of our respondents live in areas where agencies streamlined enrollment and recertification processes and strived to enroll applicants in as many programs as possible. Those that are lucky enough to live in areas with processes that embraced principles of human-centered design were happy to describe how helpful that process can be. Nate, age seventy-two and food secure, described how SNAP case managers helped him enroll in Medicare and Medicaid as well. "There were good people to sign me up. . . . Then I got into everything—Medicare, Medicaid, the SNAP program. . . . It's automated or whatever. You can do most of it by phone."

Turner, age sixty-eight with low food security, also described an efficient and effective administrative process, saying "Because we had no money in the household, they considered it emergency benefits and we got [them] in less than seven days."

Victor, age sixty-six and food secure, explained that during his application for SNAP, he received a free Lifeline phone with unlimited calls and texts, "In the state of Florida if you have SNAP, the government provides you a free phone. . . . It's called Lifeline. And I've had that since I first started getting food stamps, so I haven't had a phone bill in six years."

However, in our interviews, the negative aspects of accessing SNAP were more apparent than the occasional positive examples. Kira, age sixty-eight, has high food security in part because she receives $135 a month from SNAP. That said, she is overwhelmed by the amount of paperwork.

> Well, I hate doing all that damn paperwork once a year. I mean, God, I haven't changed anything, stop putting me through this. I recently recertified for food stamps and I'm just—goodness gracious, I'm poor, leave me alone. . . . When you do the annual recertification, then you've got to take it over to social services and drop it off and document that you get a receipt that you turn into paperwork.

Martha, age sixty-four and food secure, received $200 a month from SNAP during COVID. She described the compliance and psychological costs associated with waiting by the phone for calls from SNAP officials that never came.

> It's just every so often I have to recertify and they say they're going to call and I have to stay home and they never do call. . . . And before it [SNAP benefits] has stopped because they were supposed to call me. They didn't and they didn't get something and it [my benefits] ended.

Even though she has very low food security, Scarlett, age sixty-seven, does not currently receive SNAP. She summed up her frustration with the compliance costs.

> Not worth the hassle. Oh, having to go in, fill out all this—I hate filling forms out and my income can vary with $100 each month. . . . And I don't have computer, so I can't go to the computer and change anything. To me it's just not worth the hassle. I probably would bring in $50 anyway. . . . I just think that sometimes they ask too much of you.

Annual changes in the size of SNAP benefits, which are linked to the cost-of-living changes in Social Security in January, and adjustments for inflation in food prices in October may feel arbitrary. For older adults trying to manage a tight budget, and perhaps facing cognitive decline, these changes may seem frequent and random, making SNAP support feel unstable and imposing a psychological cost to reapplying. Maggie, age sixty-three with low food security, described the seemingly ever-changing amount of her SNAP benefit.

> We get the little $20 [increase] of the Social Security check or the food stamps go up $2, it's a lot. So I was getting $16, I was getting $12, I was getting $200, I was getting $97, was getting $76, so it just all depends on whatever the government decides to give us.

Francis, age sixty-three with low food security, said her benefits frequently change unexpectedly as well. "What I don't understand on SNAP is, you know, I get—like I say, right now I get $81, but it'll knock it back down to $45. They change it every time you turn around."

As a group, older adults and those with disabilities are more likely than younger adults to find the administrative processes associated with SNAP to be a barrier to participation. Recent research using the Health and Retirement Study finds that SNAP uptake among eligible older adults was lower among those who had dementia than those with normal cognitive functioning. Reductions in the probability of SNAP uptake were especially salient for female older adults and those living alone who may have lower levels of social support to help them navigate the SNAP eligibility process.[43] Additionally, an examination of administrative data from Oregon finds that the initial application challenges may be a larger barrier to participation than recertification in some states.[44] All three types of administrative burden vary markedly by county, state, and region of the country. As social ecological theory points out, where one lives matters.

The compliance costs associated with SNAP administrative processes sometimes lead to administrative churn, which occurs when households stop receiving SNAP benefits for one to three months, often when they need to recertify their program eligibility, before returning to the program.[45] Overall, churn is more likely among Black older adults and older adults who live in households with more people or in urban areas. Both the agency processing the SNAP case, which bears the cost of closing and then reopening a SNAP case, and the SNAP household members, who often do not find out that their benefits were not renewed until they are at the grocery store and are unable to purchase groceries with their SNAP EBT card, must suffer the costs of administrative churn.[46] Rates of administrative churn vary at the state level from 17 to 28 percent.[47] A study that focused on households with children in South Carolina finds that half of all SNAP exits were associated with a failure to recertify.[48] Another study reports that households that fail to recertify lose, on average, $550 in benefits in the following year.[49]

Administrative churn in SNAP benefits is less likely among older adults than it is among younger adults.[50] However, for cases due specifically for recertification, administrative churn appears more likely among older adults than it does among other SNAP recipients.[51] For example, in Missouri, at the halfway point of the recertification period—the default period is twenty-four months for households that contain an older adult and twelve months for most other SNAP households[52]—households must confirm eligibility by completing a mail-in form indicating that their financial situation has not changed.[53] Those who do not return the form on time may find their SNAP benefits interrupted even though they remain eligible. Perhaps because many states have longer recertification periods for older adults than for the rest of the SNAP population, overall administrative churn and exits among older adults remain lower despite possibly higher rates of churn specific to recertification.[54] Zachariah, age sixty-three and food secure, struggled with SNAP initially because he did not attend his recertification meeting at the beginning of COVID.

> In the beginning of the pandemic I actually had a . . . redetermination appointment. And on the news, hey, state of emergency and all the places were closing down. So I did not go, and . . . about a week later, I got a letter . . . telling me they were going to cut me off because I didn't do redetermination.

Patty, age sixty-nine with low food security, struggles with the compliance costs of having to produce evidence of her medical costs to gain eligibility. "I did have a gap with SNAP because I didn't fill the paperwork out, you know. I had to go get copies from where I had medical procedures or what I had spent on that. . . . They don't just go by your word. You have to prove it."

Ruth, age sixty with very low food security, described suddenly finding out that her EBT card had no benefits when she called to check the balance. She still does not understand why.

[I am] supposed to get $250 a month. Well, I could call on my [EBT card] and there was nothing on it. . . . And then I called—I kept calling. I hadn't heard anything but then I think—I looked on my postal service website today and I think there's a notice in the mail.

Most of what we know about administrative churn among adults age sixty and above comes from a study using administrative data from Missouri.[55] Between 2006 and 2014, one in four older adults in Missouri experienced a spell of churn, about half the rate of the adults younger than sixty in the state. Roughly 60 percent of churn episodes occurred at the twenty-four-month recertification point. The median length of a churn spell (the number of days that an individual is without SNAP benefits) was thirty-one days; 25 percent of churn spells lasted ten or fewer days but another 25 percent lasted at least fifty-three days. Older adults who experienced churn suffered an average loss of $111; most did not retrospectively receive their lost benefits, so this was a permanent loss.[56]

Ophelia, who lives in the Northeast, experienced a similar loss in SNAP benefits due to churn. Age sixty-nine with low food security, Ophelia used to receive $234 a month in SNAP benefits. Her benefits were disrupted, however, when she missed her recertification because SNAP mailed the papers to her old address. The benefits lost during the period when she was out of compliance were never replaced.

My food stamps had stopped for a month. You know we have to recertify every year and because of the COVID, you know, I hadn't been doing it every year. So they sent it to my old address. . . . I didn't get the papers. I didn't realize it until I didn't get the money.

Valerie, age sixty-eight and food secure, received $194 a month from SNAP during COVID. When she had to reapply, she told us that she had to walk a mile each way to the SNAP office.

I've had [SNAP] for three and a half years. I've hit a glitch here and there when I've had to reapply. . . . I don't know if my papers got lost or if they didn't do them, if they threw them away, what they did. I don't know, but then I had to reapply again. And—yeah. [I recertify] every six months, the SNAP office is a mile away. I walk.

Unstable SNAP benefits lead to gaps in the financial means to purchase food and may exacerbate health conditions that are sensitive to diet quality, such as diabetes or hypertension. Chronic disease among older adults is common: three out of four adults age sixty or older live with hypertension, and one in four adults age sixty-five and older has diabetes.[57] Additionally, hypertension and diabetes are among the leading causes of morbidity and mortality in the United States.[58] Among food insecure older adults, diabetes and hypertension are a special cause for concern, because both disease conditions are prevalent in this population.[59] In addition, low-income food insecure households are less likely to have proper disease control, either as a direct result of a poor-quality diet or an inability to afford daily medications.[60]

The connection between older adult food insecurity, administrative churn associated with SNAP participation, and health-care costs associated with diabetes and hypertension related to medication underuse is a significant problem in the United States. Among adults who reported a chronic illness in the National Health Interview Survey, 23.4 percent also reported cost-related medication underuse, 18.8 percent reported food insecurity, and 11 percent reported both.[61] Among the older adult SNAP population in Missouri in 2006–2014, 69 percent had hypertension, and roughly 25 percent of these individuals did not have enough medication on hand to manage their hypertension for more than 20 percent of the year. For the 40 percent of the older adult SNAP population with diabetes, 35 percent did not have enough medication on hand to manage their disease condition for more than 20 percent of the year.[62]

Medicaid-insured older adults living with hypertension are more likely to have consistent access to hypertension medications when they have consistent access to SNAP benefits; those who stably receive SNAP benefits in all twelve calendar months have the highest level of medication adherence.[63] Heflin and colleagues also find a relationship between health-care utilization patterns and the stability of SNAP benefits: SNAP recipients who experienced gaps in their benefits were less likely to have prescription drug claims, see a doctor in an outpatient setting, or go to the emergency room than were those with stable benefits.[64] In fact, the only type of health care that was more likely to be accessed by those experiencing unstable SNAP was hospitalizations, suggesting that adults may forgo health-care needs during times when SNAP is not available to support food consumption at the expense of their health.

Social Security provides a good model for how policymakers might redesign SNAP administrative processes to reduce administrative burden for older adults.[65] The Social Security program is simple to access and efficiently administrated, with an uptake rate of 97 percent at a cost to administer of just 0.4 percent of the total program cost.[66] Workers age twenty-five and older have access to an annually updated statement of benefits that provides an estimate of the amount of Social Security benefits they will receive conditional on different retirement ages.[67] This reduces learning and psychological costs. The process to start receiving benefits is straightforward and uniform throughout the country, which reduces compliance costs. Finally, local Social Security Administration offices, in which one can update an address, replace a lost card, or have questions answered, are located throughout the country. Once retirees begin receiving Social Security benefits, they will continue to receive those benefits until death unless they take some action. In essence, the process for accessing Social Security is well designed for older adults, while SNAP is not.

SNAP Benefit Redemption and Adequacy

Once older adults start receiving SNAP benefits, additional hurdles lie between them and food security. For some recipients, SNAP benefits may be difficult to redeem, due to difficulty getting to a food retailer that accepts benefits. Or, as some respondents we interviewed reported, the size of the benefits was too small to cover food costs (a conclusion backed up by a National Institute of Medicine recommended study conducted by the US Department of Agriculture) and changed too frequently to allow for planning.[68] Finally, the type of food covered by SNAP, staple items designed to be cooked and eaten at home, may be heavy to carry, time consuming to cook, and difficult to adjust to portions suitable for a person living alone. Most older adults on SNAP live in single-person households. We describe these issues using a combination of U.S. Department of Agriculture studies and the experience of our respondents.

Recipients often exhaust SNAP benefits early in the calendar month, resulting in a reduced caloric intake at the end of the month.[69] SNAP redemption data indicates that recipients spend nearly 17 percent of SNAP benefits on the day that they are received and 57 percent by the end of the first week; they spend 78 percent within the first two weeks and almost 90 percent by the third week. By the end of the month, 96 percent of SNAP households have exhausted their benefits. Households consisting entirely of adults age sixty and older or who have disabilities were more likely both to exhaust their benefits within the first week and to have unspent funds at the end of the month than were other households. Black and Native American households were also less likely to have unspent funds than were other households, controlling for other household characteristics.[70] The average amount of SNAP benefits carried over into the next month was $10.72, and only 6 percent of households went a month without spending their SNAP benefits.[71]

Although food costs vary geographically, the value of SNAP benefits is fixed across the United States (except for Hawaii and Alaska) and food insecurity is higher in areas with higher food prices.[72] For more than one-quarter of SNAP households, benefits are too low to cover the cost of the Thrifty Food Plan at the stores where they shop.[73] Recent estimates that include the 2024 cost-of-living adjustment indicate that the cost of a modestly priced meal was not covered by SNAP in 98 percent of counties in the United States. Nationally, the average meal cost was $0.53 more than the average maximum SNAP benefit of $2.84 per meal, which means that SNAP benefits fell short by $49.29 per thirty-one-day month.[74]

Respondents told us about running out of SNAP benefits well before the end of the month. When we talked to Carmen, age sixty-five with low food security, she described how her benefits and food supplies lasted "at least the first two weeks of the month before the food ran out" and she had "no money to restock."

In contrast, Faye, age sixty-four with marginal food security, received $431 a month from SNAP during COVID for her and her grandson and had a clear strategy to make the benefits stretch across the month. She spends most of her benefits on canned and boxed food on sale because these food items will not go bad.

> When I first get the food stamps . . . I try to buy stuff that will stay fresh like canned soup. [My grandson] likes that, like, the Progresso, or those TV dinners, when they go on sale. Like in Publix, they put them four for $10. Because he'll eat them like that late at night. He likes cereal, but, again, cereal is very expensive, so I try to buy it when it's buy one get one free.

Ginny, age sixty-two with very low food security, worries about running out of SNAP benefits, which is negatively affecting her health. She was receiving $27 a month when we interviewed her.

I get my food stamps on the first of the month. You know, there's been times by the 21st, 22nd, I'm starting to run out of food. . . . I believe that if I wasn't worried about the amount of food stamps I get, or the amount of food that I have in the house, that my general health would be better. I think the stress weighs on my general health. . . . I think my mental health would be better if I didn't have to worry so much about food.

Redemption costs are one final form of administrative burden associated with SNAP benefits for this age group. Redemption costs involve the challenges beneficiaries encounter in learning how to use their benefits.[75] To use SNAP benefits, recipients must find a food retailer that accepts the EBT card as a form of payment. To qualify as a SNAP retailer, food retailers must sell staple foods, which are defined as basic food items that make up a significant portion of an individual's diet and are usually prepared at home and consumed as a major component of a meal. Food retailers also must meet specific requirements for the diversity of foods sold or the volume within a single staple area. Staple foods do not include heated foods, prepared foods, or accessory foods including snacks, desserts, beverages, or spices. While virtually all large food retailers qualify, new participants may not be aware which neighborhood stores accept SNAP. A U.S. Department of Agriculture tool located on their website allows recipients to enter their address or zip code to locate SNAP retailers within a particular radius.[76]

Overall, fiscal year 2023 recipients redeemed 75 percent of SNAP benefits at supermarkets or superstores and used only 3.5 percent to buy food at large or medium grocery stores and less than 1 percent to buy food at small grocery stores. Despite rhetoric otherwise, redemption data indicate that SNAP participants used less than 6 percent of benefits to buy food at convenience stores.[77] Critics of SNAP sometimes point to out-of-state sales as evidence of fraud. However, nationally, less than 3 percent of SNAP households used their benefits to purchase food out of their state at least twice within one year, and they made 71 percent of those purchases at supermarkets or superstores in fiscal year 2017, the last year that this information is available. Adults age sixty and older were less likely to make out-of-state purchases, perhaps due to reduced access to transportation. Overall, households with adults age sixty and older have fewer SNAP transactions, shop at fewer stores, and spend less per month than other household types.[78]

According to a 2018 U.S. Department of Agriculture survey, SNAP participants of all ages reported difficulty getting to a grocery store to buy food with their benefits, but the issues were particularly salient for older adults. One in five SNAP recipients indicated lack of transportation to a grocery store was a problem. Another one in five indicated that the distance to a grocery store was a problem. In terms of travel time, 80 percent of SNAP households reported traveling twenty minutes or fewer to their primary grocery store. However, households with older adults were more likely to report longer time travel times, less likely to report using a car to go grocery shopping, and, most surprisingly, more likely to report walking, biking, or using public transportation. Overall, older adults were more likely to report that distance was a barrier to a healthy diet.[79]

Anna, age seventy-six with low food security, received $234 a month in SNAP benefits during COVID. She explained how high gas prices make the long drive to the grocery store prohibitive.

> Car repairs and gas has gone up so high now that it costs me nearly $50. So I wasn't buying gas, and I wouldn't go when I needed to go to the store to buy food. I would wait and try and get it all into one big shopping, so I didn't have to run up and down and use gas. $50 for me to put gas in the car is a real hardship. . . . And that's a mistake because you may have food stamps, but you may not have enough gas in your car to go get the food. And I have no grocery store in walking distance. I have to travel several miles to get to a grocery store.

In 2012, the Institute of Medicine and the National Research Council recommended that the U.S. Department of Agriculture examine the barriers to SNAP adequacy at the individual, household, and environmental level.[80] A 2018 survey of SNAP recipients revealed that households with older adults were more likely to be food secure than were those without older adults. However, overall, 88 percent of SNAP recipients identified a barrier to maintaining a healthy diet throughout the month.[81] The most common environmental barrier reported by three of five SNAP recipients was the affordability of healthy food.[82] Our respondents frequently discussed affordability as a serious issue as well. Ingrid, age sixty-four with low food security, described how she tries to stretch her SNAP benefits by forgoing produce. "Instead of doing three—like a meat, potato, and a veggie . . . if I'm making Rice-A-Roni, let's say, I will just have that for my meal instead of making other things."

Russell, age sixty-four and food secure, lives alone. He explained how his $194 monthly SNAP benefits cover mostly TV dinners.

> I only buy . . . what I eat. You know, I like them little TV dinners, I like them, you know, because I can pop one in the oven, you know, they have like mashed potatoes, peas, they might have a piece of meatloaf or something like that. So yeah, and they don't cost but like $.89 cents. . . . I get the paper and see what's on sale, and as soon as I see it and it's not far, I'm going to get it. . . . Like my [SNAP benefits] went on today. And then I've got groceries still from last month, and I have, like, $37 dollars left on my card.

Victor, age sixty-six, is food secure, yet he worries daily about having enough food for the next day. He stopped working at age sixty when a work-related injury left him legally blind. During the pandemic, he received $125 a month from SNAP. "It's like I said, I'm living day by day, month by month. . . . I prepare enough to where I know I can have my share that night. And then I know I have enough for the next night also. . . . So I try to do the best I can."

According to the 2018 survey of SNAP recipients, households with older adults were more likely than households without older adults to report finding it difficult or very difficult to afford fruits, vegetables, and whole grains.[83] As Carmen, age sixty-five with low food security, explained, purchasing healthy food is particularly important for people with chronic conditions such as diabetes.

> Because it's hard, being diabetic is hard. . . . Like I told my doctor, it's, you know, it's expensive to buy diet food. . . . The doctor says you've got to have your breakfast, lunch, and dinner and in between breakfast and lunch you've got to have a snack, and between lunch and dinner you've got to have a snack. And you've got to have a snack before I go to bed. . . . So I try to . . . eat more—depends how much they had, the fruits, the fruits I eat bananas, apples, peaches. So I can have one before I go to bed if I've got the money. . . . Yeah, once or twice a month, or three times a month [I eat] the vegetables.

Willow, age seventy-four with low food security, is eager to enjoy some peaches but cannot afford to purchase them. "Right now peaches are on sale and I love peaches. But I don't have the money to go buy any. . . . My bills get paid before I buy any food or detergent or anything else."

Our respondents repeatedly told us the size of the SNAP benefit was insufficient to cover their food needs. Francis, age sixty-three with low food security, receives $81 a month from SNAP. Her entire monthly allotment can disappear during a walk down a single grocery store aisle. "I got food stamps. I had the food grant. . . . I mean you can take $45 and go to the grocery store and walk down the meat aisle and it's gone before you get there."

Wallace, age sixty-four with very low food security, never has enough SNAP benefits for three meals a day. He received $214 a month from SNAP during COVID. Nearly every month, when his SNAP benefits run out, he stops eating altogether. This happens so often that he has lost weight. "When my food stamp run out, no ma'am. Sometimes I don't eat. . . . That's why I lost the weight because sometimes I run out. I just don't eat. When I ain't got no money I just skip [meals]. Sometimes it just about happen every month."

Respondents described strategies for stretching their SNAP benefits that could be dangerous for their health, such as buying food that was dented, damaged, or near the expiration date, all of which pose food safety issues. Francis, age sixty-three with low food security, described how she searches out damaged goods to save money.

> I go to Town and County and they got this buggy and they have bad groceries and when they slice to take them out of that plastic, they'll slice the front of the bread, the package. Well, you know, they may mark the corn meal, or corn flour down, it may be a $5 pack but they might got it, knock it down to $1.50. I got a deal of baking soda, or baking powder the other day for 25 cents because the can had got crushed.

Kate, age sixty-one with marginal food security, received $234 a month from SNAP during COVID. She buys food that is close to the expiration date.

> There's another store called Sharp Shopper. . . . It's a store that gets products that are close to the dates and products that are overstocked or whatever. We take a cooler and they have like big bags of frozen vegetables. . . . They have some meats and stuff that are maybe getting to the date, but you can freeze them. . . . You have a considerable amount of savings and if we go by there, we always stop in there and get really good savings on things, so those are stores that we use to help stretch the budget.

In 2018, the Agriculture Improvement Act mandated that the Institute of Medicine review the adequacy of SNAP benefits. As a result, SNAP benefits increased in October 2021 because of changes in the cost associated with the redesigned Thrifty Food Plan. The U.S. Department of Agriculture designed the Thrifty Food Plan to represent the minimal cost nutritious diet by household size and is the basis of the SNAP benefit size. It had not updated the Thrifty Food Plan, beyond the cost of inflation, since 1975 and, as such, the plan no longer reflected the current dietary and food preparation patterns of low-income households. As a result of this review, the U.S. Department of Agriculture permanently increased the maximum SNAP benefits by 21 percent, raising average SNAP benefits by 27 percent, or $1.20 per day or $36 per month in October 2021. Researchers at the U.S. Department of Agriculture estimated that this increase would result in households spending more money on food overall ($5.30 per week in food eaten at home and $0.65 in food eaten away from home), an increase in the nutritional adequacy of the food eaten, including whole fruit, and a 6 to 7 percent increase in the amount of key nutrients. Additionally, they predicted that since most SNAP households spend some of their own income covering food expenses, the increased benefits would also likely shift income that would have covered food to pay for other expenses.[84]

The October 2021 adjustment to the Thrifty Food Plan reduced the number of counties for which the maximum SNAP benefit did not cover the cost of a modestly priced meal to 21 percent (down from 96 percent in 2020). However, rising food prices in 2022 increased the share of counties where SNAP benefits fell short back to 99 percent. The U.S. Department of Agriculture increases SNAP benefits in October each year based on the rising cost of food prices, and the 2022 cost-of-living adjustment then narrowed the gap to 78 percent.[85]

A variety of policy changes during COVID resulted in higher SNAP benefit levels. Most respondents we interviewed do not know which policy changes led to their specific benefit level change. However, they often cited the increase in SNAP benefits during COVID as allowing them to eat healthier food, stock up on pantry supplies, pay off other household bills, and reduce reliance on food pantries and other high-risk sources of food during COVID. Patty, age sixty-nine with low food security, enjoyed being able to purchase more nutritious food such as fruits, vegetables, and meats.

I've been getting the extra money for like a year, more than a year. And you know, I'm able to get fruits and vegetables—fresh things. It's been better. . . . I have salads all the time. You know, things—like I used to do peanut butter and jelly sandwich and that would be a meal . . . just to save money. And [now] tuna and chicken.

Martha, age sixty-four and food secure, described how she has also been eating healthier and stocking up.

So I'm trying to eat more nutritiously, and food stamps increased temporarily. So, I've had a full refrigerator which I've never had in my life. . . . I usually stock up and keep things in my freezer and stuff for when it ends. . . . Oh, yeah, yeah. I have stuff I never could have before and I never had that much food in my fridge, you know.

Low-income households often make trade-offs between essential expenses when resources are tight, and because food is often the easiest place to cut corners, the dedicated subsidy that can only be spent on food may free up cash for other expenses.[86] During COVID, Diane, age sixty-five and food secure, told us that she got ahead on paying some of her other bills because the extra SNAP benefits covered her entire food bill and freed up household funds for other expenses. "I get $52 a month in food stamps. But when it was COVID they gave you extra money. . . . COVID helped me a lot with the checks and stuff."

Valerie, age sixty-eight and food secure, told us that she stopped going to the food pantry when SNAP was expanded during COVID but now has to return again, no matter how arduous the journey. "I was going to the food pantry weekly until we got the extra SNAP benefits during the pandemic. I haven't really had to go, but I might have to start going back now. . . . It's a mile from here and I walk."

Helen, age seventy with marginal food security, was dreading the end of higher emergency SNAP benefits.

Since the pandemic—when that runs out and they quit doing that, it's going to be back down and I'm going to have to figure out well what can I get for $16 or whatever they're going to give me. Like $16 or $50 you go to the store and buy—the food is high. You know? So I'm worried about when that time comes.

As you might expect, older adults on SNAP eat and shop differently than do younger beneficiaries. Among SNAP participants, 82 percent of those age sixty and older report that "on most days I eat a healthy diet." SNAP households with older adults are more likely to report that they cook their meals eaten at home from scratch (66 percent for older adults versus 60 percent overall) and the least likely to report that they assemble meals using ready-made ingredients (21 percent for older adults versus 27 percent overall). Like all SNAP households, most older adult households indicate that the person cooking the meals knows how to cook healthy meals (94 percent) and prepares healthy meals (90 percent).[87] Anna, age seventy-six with low food security, explained the importance of well-honed cooking skills.

> I do get the food stamps and I do know how to cook. And that helps, so I can cook food from scratch. So I've had a wide variety and I am grateful for the food stamps. I will tell you that much. If I didn't have that I'd be in big trouble.

Vera, age seventy-six with low food security, stretches her food budget by preserving as much food as she can. But canning peaches is a physically demanding job. She worries she will not have the stamina for it much longer. "I'm concerned about how long I'll be able to maintain caring for myself on the level I am, which is one of the reasons for downsizing. It's physically hard work if you're canning. It's exhausting."

Like other SNAP households, only about 10 percent of households containing an older adult cited lack of cooking skills as a primary reason or barrier to eating healthy meals in 2018. Meanwhile, 8.7 percent cited lack of equipment to prepare healthy meals, 13 percent cited lack of storage, and nearly 10 percent cited lack of time to go shopping, levels that are slightly below those of all SNAP households. Unsurprisingly for a population that is less likely to be working, only about 20 percent of older adults cited lack of time to prepare meals as a barrier, compared with more than 33 percent of all SNAP households. In contrast, 21 percent of older adults, compared with 15 percent of all SNAP households, cited physical disability as a barrier to eating healthy meals.[88]

Harriet, age sixty-five with marginal food security, points out that older people sometimes do not have enough energy or good health to prepare meals but still need to eat. Though she received $259 a month from SNAP during

COVID, she found it difficult to prepare proper meals due to multiple health problems and considerable pain.

> We don't feel like getting up and cooking a meal and stuff, [but] we still have to eat. . . . Almost every day I debate whether I really want to get up and go fix something to eat because just going across the room, even with my oxygen on, I get out of breath and with the fibromyalgia and arthritis and stuff, it just—it hurts to move. . . . Do I put in a pan of lasagna? No, I'll grab a sandwich.

Martha, age sixty-four and food secure, receives $200 a month from SNAP. Because she cannot stand long enough to prepare a meal, she must keep sitting down.

> Well I have stenosis of the spine so I only can stand for so long. So I have to keep taking breaks. It's not severe. And my legs are weak because of the spinal stenosis. So I'll do something for a little while and then I go and sit down. You know, I can't keep watch. I can't stand in front of the stove and watch things.

SNAP covers fruits and vegetables, meat, poultry, fish, dairy products, breads and cereals, snack food, nonalcoholic beverages, and seeds or plants that produce food for the household to eat.[89] SNAP does not cover beer, wine, liquor, cigarettes, tobacco, vitamins, medicines, supplements, most live animals, and any nonfood items such as pet food, cleaning supplies, paper products, household supplies, hygiene items, or cosmetics. Our respondents expressed frustration that SNAP does not cover personal and household cleaning supplies, given that these items too are necessities. Faye, age sixty-four with marginal food security, said she has to buy food before cleaning supplies no matter how desperately she needs the latter. "I'd eat before I'd go spend money on that if it came down to making a choice. . . . That always comes first to me because if you're hungry you're no good to anybody."

When we interviewed Gerald, age sixty-seven with very low food security, his additional COVID SNAP benefits had already been repealed. He receives just $16 a month. Gerald often runs out of cleaning supplies, but he needs his money for food. When we asked him if he runs out of money, he told us: "Definitely. Sometimes I'm short on soaps because I need the money for food. Oh, yes, definitely, yes run out of money for paper towels and stuff."

Figure 4.7   Older Adult Uptake in SNAP by State, Fiscal Year 2018

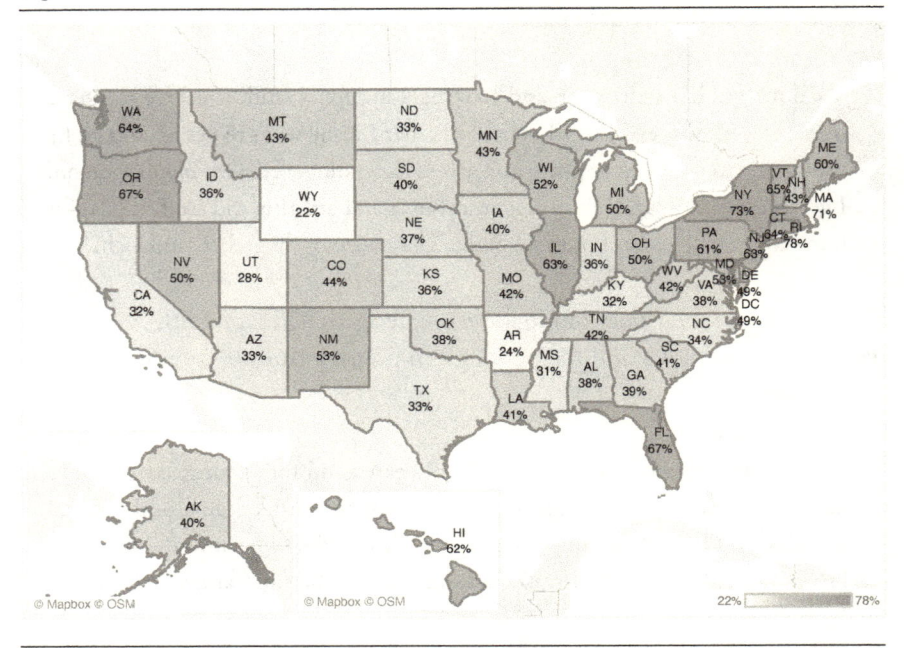

[US map showing older adult SNAP uptake percentages by state: WA 64%, OR 67%, CA 32%, NV 50%, ID 36%, MT 43%, WY 22%, UT 28%, AZ 33%, CO 44%, NM 53%, ND 33%, SD 40%, NE 37%, KS 36%, OK 38%, TX 33%, MN 43%, IA 40%, MO 42%, AR 24%, LA 41%, WI 52%, IL 63%, MS 31%, AL 38%, TN 42%, KY 32%, IN 36%, MI 50%, OH 50%, WV 42%, VA 38%, NC 34%, SC 41%, GA 39%, FL 67%, PA 61%, NY 73%, VT 60%, NH 65%, ME 60%, MA 43%, CT 71%, RI 78%, NJ 64%, DE 49%, MD 63%, DC 49%, AK 40%, HI 62%. Scale: 22% to 78%.]

Source: Authors' figure using U.S. Department of Agriculture (2021a) data.

Local Variation in SNAP Experience and Uptake

Although SNAP is a federal program, state officials administer it. The program varies significantly across states as a consequence. Further, in ten states, county officials administer SNAP to their local population, and local administrative practices can differ across the state.[90] Although the federal government fully funds SNAP benefits and covers 50 percent of the cost of administering SNAP, since the early 2000s, states can make decisions regarding the household income and asset levels that determine eligibility; the shelter, utility, and out-of-pocket medical expenses that can determine benefit size; the complexity of application processes; the frequency of recertification processes; and the restrictions on redemption of benefits.[91] The U.S. Department of Agriculture has a state waiver process through which states can choose to make benefits more or less generous for participants, to increase or decrease eligibility criteria governing who qualifies for benefits, and to make the process of application and recertification more or less onerous. As a result, in fiscal year 2018, SNAP uptake varied from 22 percent among eligible older adults in Wyoming to 78 percent in Rhode Island, as shown in figure 4.7.[92]

States apply some of the waivers and options that they can adopt to the entire state SNAP population, such as the treatment of utility expenses in the SNAP benefit calculation process. Julie, age sixty-two with low food security, argues that her benefits would be higher if the state took into account all of her housing and utility expenses.

> We only get $66 a month in food stamps. So that doesn't go very far. And they only count—you know, they count what I pay in rent and then they count one utility and that's it. You know, nothing else is counted toward—you know, so you know, there should be more things counted. But there's not. That's the way it is.

States provide some waivers to specific populations that may include older adults, such as a waiver or modification to the federal drug felony ban permanently prohibiting SNAP benefits to anyone convicted of a felony involving a controlled substance. Some states target other waivers to increase uptake in SNAP for the subgroup of adults age sixty and older.

Three waivers available to states are particularly noteworthy for older adults. First, in fiscal year 2024, seventeen states participated in the Combined Application Project (CAP), which policymakers designed to make it easier for adults receiving SSI to participate in SNAP by linking the application process. Second, twenty-three states participated in the Elderly Simplified Application Project, which reduces verification processes, provides a thirty-six-month certification window, and eliminates the recertification interview for adults age sixty and older without earnings. Third, twenty-five states participated in the Standard Medical Deduction (SMD), which allows states to establish a higher deduction amount for adults age sixty and older who can demonstrate $35 a month of out-of-pocket medical expenses.[93]

During COVID, federal policymakers gave states, and where relevant counties, the option of adopting changes to their eligibility protocols, but they were not required to do so. States that decided to adopt provisions also could decide when to sunset the changes. As a result, local variation in SNAP was even greater during COVID than previously experienced, with changes occurring month to month and even county to county within some states. Heflin and colleagues report that in spring 2021, among the ten county-administered states, only 27 percent of counties chose to implement the interview and physical presence waivers designed to keep both clients and workers safe, as well as reduce administrative burden. The adoption of the interview waiver by local agency officials was not associated with local public health conditions, economic conditions, food security levels, or partisan leaning, but it was a meaningful decision—counties that implemented the waiver had SNAP caseloads that were 5 percent higher than those that did not.[94]

COVID also prompted states to adopt policies that they long had the flexibility to consider, such as allowing SNAP benefits to be used for online purchases. The federal 2014 Farm Bill originally allowed this provision, but New York state was the first state to pilot the program in 2019. As of March 2020, Alabama, Iowa, Oregon, and Washington had pilot programs in place at the beginning of COVID. Now, all fifty states have programs, and 8 percent of all SNAP benefits in fiscal year 2023 were redeemed at online retailers.[95] While the list of participating retailers varies by state, in most states, it includes major grocery stores such as Amazon, Walmart, and Sam's Club. Harriet, age sixty-five with marginal food security, received $259 a month from SNAP during COVID and appreciates ordering food online.

> Yes. I order online. Walmart lets you pay with food stamps online. And then [my daughter] goes by and picks it up for me. . . . And Walmart lets me pay with food stamps and then if I go over or buy something that needs to be paid with cash, I can also use my debit card at the same time.

Historically, SNAP has not covered food that is hot at the point of sale, but during COVID, states had the option to change that rule. Though many respondents mentioned that SNAP coverage of prepared hot meals expanded during COVID, Turner, age sixty-eight with low food security, reported rotisserie chickens were still not covered where he lived. He pointed out the irony when hot prepared food is excluded.

> Well they've got certain rules about not being allowed to buy hot food or prepared food, but I noticed some local places like stores or takeout food/fast food places are starting to accept SNAP benefits now. . . . They're trying to make it easier for someone to get a hot meal or a prepared meal who don't have the facility to prepare one. . . . Anything hot, for example, let's say you want to buy a fried chicken that's cut up, like in eight pieces, you can't buy that hot, but they have it packaged in the refrigerated section where it's cold and you can buy it that way. That's kind of silly to me. . . . You go home and you heat it up and you have the same thing that you're not allowed to buy.

Perhaps one of the most significant examples of state variation in SNAP policies is how childless adults between the ages of eighteen and forty-nine are treated.[96] The program traditionally limits such households to three months of receipt within a three-year period unless they meet certain work requirements. However, in 2023, federal SNAP rules governing the population subject to work requirements for SNAP raised the age limit from forty-nine to fifty-four, with the age change rolled out over time. States have the option to request a waiver from this restriction for areas in which the unemployment rate is greater than 10 percent or in which there are insufficient jobs.[97] In fiscal year 2025 (second quarter), seven states had a full state waiver and twenty-four states had a partial waiver in place; but twenty-two states provided no waivers, and the three-month limit applied to all SNAP participants in this category.[98] Adults in their early fifties who live in areas that limit SNAP eligibility to three months within a three-year period without participation in work requirements may be more likely to enter older age with the markers of having consumed a less healthy diet, showing once again how life course theories and social ecological theories underline the mechanisms leading to an increased risk of food insecurity at old age.

Some states and counties put out the welcome mat for older adults, encouraging applications, recertifications, and expenditures by linking SNAP to other income-based benefits, such as SSI. Meanwhile, other states and counties gatekeep by placing administrative hurdles that discourage participation in SNAP. These hurdles may prove especially difficult for older adults with health or cognitive limitations.

Previous research examining the relationship between state policy decisions and the size of the SNAP caseload finds that these decisions are quite important.[99] However, research focused more narrowly on older adult participation is more mixed, finding only modest impacts (while still finding much larger changes in participation among other populations).[100] While common sense and respondent interviews tell us that local policy choices shape the experience of older adult SNAP participants, empirical evidence suggests that older adult SNAP participation decisions are not as sensitive to policy choices that are not targeted at their specific barriers to participation, compared with policies that are targeted to them.

A related question is what interests are driving state and county choices around SNAP access. Are localities dialing up (or down) access to SNAP intentionally? Results are mixed here as well. While plenty of studies find that

Democratic party control results in more generous social policies in general,[101] research specific to SNAP is often mixed.[102] Additionally, recent research that has tried to explain county adoption of SNAP waivers finds that local public health risk, demographic vulnerability and economic need, and political orientation in the county were not statistically significant predictors of waiver use.[103] Overall, there is clearly a great deal of variation in local conditions that shape SNAP use, but whether this variation is intentional is less clear in the case of older adults. As a result of the mixed evidence base, we do not subscribe intentionality to the current situation and, instead, believe that policymakers most likely are not designing SNAP policies with older adults in mind.

CONCLUSION

While SNAP is a vital source of support for many adults age sixty and older, only 55 percent of those eligible participate, despite the importance of access to healthy and nutritious food to support healthy aging. Why? Policymakers designed SNAP to provide supplemental resources to support food consumption for the entire low-income population, but they did not design it with older adults in mind. As a consequence, administrative processes associated with applying and recertifying for benefits are more difficult to manage for older adults with limited computer literacy and access, physical limitations, transportation problems, cognitive decline, stigma, and distrust of providing personal information. Additionally, the minimum SNAP benefit level is quite low, $23 a month in fiscal year 2025, and the costs of redeeming SNAP benefits may be high: one in five SNAP recipients older than sixty reported in 2018 that transportation problems limited their ability to redeem their benefits, and one in five reported that the physical distance to the store posed a problem.[104] Finally, the U.S. Department of Agriculture allows states and some counties to determine how to implement SNAP. As a result, some states and counties encourage applications, simplify recertification, increase benefits for older adults, and link SNAP to other poverty-based benefits, while others enforce administrative processes that reduce participation in SNAP. Consequently, in fiscal year 2018, SNAP uptake among older adults who are eligible ranges from just 22 percent in Wyoming to 78 percent in Rhode Island.[105] In chapter 6, we discuss how bundling social programs would increase participation among eligible nonparticipants and propose specific initiatives to improve SNAP for adults age sixty and older.

CHAPTER 5

Understanding the Limits of Community-Based Free and Subsidized Food Programs

Policymakers designed SNAP to address the economic roots of food insecurity, but community-based programs must address the remaining gap in resources and problems food insecure older adults face related to physical health, mental health, access to nutritious food, and transportation. Free and subsidized food programs provide much needed food, but the robustness of the programs varies remarkably, the services often limit choice and provide food that may be of lower nutritional value, and low-income older people, particularly those with mobility limitations, may find them difficult to access.

Ophelia, age sixty-nine with low food security, relies on community-based food programs to augment her food supply. She lives in a household of four with her daughter, her pregnant granddaughter, and her grandson. Her family has been waiting to enter subsidized housing, which would loosen their budget and open up funds for food. In the meantime, she told us she often skips meals because their monthly SNAP benefits have not yet arrived, the grandchildren need food, and she no longer has enough food to feed everyone. "Sometimes I just have enough food for maybe breakfast and dinner. . . . I'm going to make sure the kids eat even if I don't."

Her life course was once on a positive trajectory: she earned a college degree and worked for twenty-five years at a day care center. But she was a single mother, and paying the bills was never easy. Her family does not have a car, and she must pay $2.50 to ride the public bus. Sometimes she does not have

https://doi.org/10.7758/rzos2617.7779

transportation to the grocery store, the food pantry, or the senior center to obtain food.

> Well if I go to grocery store I use the MTA. Yeah, where they come to your house and pick you up and take you where you got to go. I have to pay $2.50 each way. . . . Sometimes I would go to the market, and I just had enough money to call a cab which was the $3 . . . but there was a couple times I didn't even have money to get to the market.

She had been volunteering at a center where she was eating two free meals a day but had to stop because of COVID. She also had augmented her food supply by eating at the senior center three times a week, but with the pandemic, the free bus to the nutrition site was eliminated. "Before the COVID when I went up to the senior center, they offered free transportation and now they don't have it anymore. So, if I go I have to get up there by my own means."

Now Ophelia goes to the senior center to eat meals only one day a week, and it must be the same day that the nearby food pantry is open.

> I would go up there three days a week and, you know, we get a meal, but we had to pay for it. It's called Eating Together. It was only $1.25. Before the COVID, yeah it was more than once a week. Yeah, now once a week. . . . I only go up to the senior center on Tuesdays and the church [food pantry] is located next door to the senior center. And I only allotted money in my budget to go to the senior center once a week. . . . Yeah see my friends when I go to the senior center. . . . We run our mouth. We play cards.

During the pandemic, many group meal sites gave out free food boxes that participants could take home. Ophelia relied heavily on these boxes but explained that once COVID waned, so did the practice of offering food boxes to go. COVID revealed that we can adapt policies quickly in the face of structural hardships, such as a recession or pandemic.

> At the senior center sometimes they would give out meals and stuff . . . meals to take home. Meals on Wheels used to come and, you know, bring leftover meals. And they would give it to us at the senior center, you know to bring home and eat. . . . Sometimes it was like maybe six meals.

Most of the food from the food pantry and the senior center is highly processed. Ophelia rarely obtains enough fresh fruits and vegetables. The scarcity of fresh produce affects how she feels.

> I don't think I eat a lot of fruit and vegetables. . . . I feel terrible . . . because sometimes if I want it, I don't care how much it [costs]. Well yes I do. But if I want it bad enough, I'll try to figure out a way to get it.

Nationwide, the quality of food from pantries varies markedly, and the pantry in Ophelia's neighborhood provides lower-quality food. Weary of the meager food pantry options available in her neighborhood, Ophelia is frustrated that she has to travel far to get better-quality food at a pantry in a distant neighborhood.

> OK put it this way. They should have a place in maybe every neighborhood where you could go like if they give out food. I most likely would have to take a long walk to get there or use transportation. . . . See because the area of the city I live in, they don't give out much. . . . It's certain sections of the city they more readily give out stuff than where I live at.

For a while, Ophelia augmented her household food supply through home-delivered meals. She received home-delivered meals for free during the pandemic, but when the program returned to its usual sliding-scale fees, which she found prohibitive, she halted the service.

> Meals on Wheels was bringing people meals for like three months, but they stopped that. Right. They would deliver maybe a week's worth of meals. They were frozen but they were only like dinner meals, yeah. . . . It was during COVID. But then they stopped because they say now you had to pay for them.

Ophelia now buttresses her household food supply by going to food giveaways. But she has to walk and wait in long lines during the summer to access this food. "Yeah, so like once a month in the summer I would go stand in a line that was giving out food."

Ophelia also makes use of the farmers market coupon program. However, sometimes she does not have a way to get to the farmers market. "Yeah, but other than that that's it. And then I got the food coupons where I could go to the farmers market. . . . I use them. I have to use transportation to get there."

Many of the difficulties Ophelia faces are the result of a lifetime of hardships; she and her progeny have accumulated more disadvantages than advantages over the years. But her difficulties are also the result of living in a resource-poor area. Because she lives in an area with a lower-quality food pantry, inconvenient and expensive public transportation, long lines at food giveaways, and a long wait for subsidized housing, her food security is low. The social ecological model makes clear that if the paucity of her individual resources were offset by a resource-rich neighborhood, Ophelia and her family would be less likely to struggle with food insecurity.

In this chapter, we focus on community-based free and subsidized food programs, which we categorize into three groups—group meal programs, home-delivered meals, and food provided to be eaten off-site. We conducted our interviews during COVID, which gives us insight not only into the impact of an international pandemic but also into other shocks to the system, such as economic recessions, inflation, supply-chain disruptions, and labor shortages. As the comments from our respondents demonstrate, free and subsidized food programs expanded and responded mightily in some areas and restricted and closed in others.

Three consistent themes that are particularly important for older adults emerged from our interviews. First, consistent with social ecological theory, where one lives determines the quantity and quality of available community-based free and subsidized food programs.[1] The extent to which all three of the types of community-based programs are available varies throughout the United States. Additionally, programs may limit their service to residents of particular neighborhoods or zip codes. Some people live in neighborhoods with multiple food program options, a wide selection of days and hours, ample fresh fruits and vegetables, and convenient transportation, while others live in neighborhoods with none of these conveniences. The differences in their experiences are evident in the comments from our respondents.

Second, the programs that older people use to cope with food insecurity typically limit recipients' ability to choose what they eat. Sometimes the food is of poor nutritional quality. Older adults who are women, Black, Hispanic, or low-income or who live alone or have disabilities, because they are more likely to be food insecure, are also more likely to be affected by the complexities and inefficiencies of community-based free and subsidized food programs.[2]

Third, being older, having mobility limitations, or having disabilities often makes it difficult to participate in the complicated web of community-based free and subsidized food and nutrition assistance programs. Most community-based food programs require participants to complete an application process and periodically recertify eligibility, which often involves a combination of paperwork, computer sessions, phone calls, and office visits that may be particularly difficult for older adults to complete. While community-based food programs may be helpful in shoring up food security, they typically limit participation to specific times, dates, and locations. Some also require recipients to have transportation and fairly high levels of individual mobility and stamina.

TRENDS IN COMMUNITY-BASED FREE AND SUBSIDIZED FOOD PROGRAMS

The United State has a complicated set of community-based programs, paid for by federal, state, and local governments in partnership with private charities that provide free and subsidized food to low-income people. The Older Americans Act designed group meal and home-delivered-meal programs to provide food to older recipients to relieve the economic burden of securing a healthy diet in a format of ready-to-eat meals, to address many of the physical health barriers to food insecurity, and to provide social connections to support mental health.[3] In 2023, 2.6 percent of older adults received a free meal in the previous twelve months (7.7 percent of older adults in households with income below 185 percent of the federal poverty line).[4] The remaining programs, food pantries and farmers market coupons, provide food to be prepared at home, offer more food choices for recipients than the other programs, and are generally open to low-income people of any age. In 2023, 6.6 percent of older adults received free groceries in the previous twelve months (18 percent of older adults in households with income below 185 percent of the federal poverty line).[5]

The community-based food landscape changes over time, with access to some programs growing and access to others contracting. Using data from the IRS reports filed by nonprofit organizations, available from the National Center for Charitable Statistics, we plot the trend in the number of nonprofit organizations that report offering one of the following four programs, as defined by the National Center for Charitable Statistics:[6]

- Congregate meals: Organizations, typically known as nutrition sites or senior nutrition programs, provide hot meals on a regular basis, usually for individuals who are older or have disabilities or other target populations.
- Senior centers: Organizations provide or coordinate a wide variety of programs and services that meet the needs and interests of the senior population. This includes organizations that administer funding for senior services under Title III of the Older Americans Act. By far, the most common type of congregate meals are offered at senior centers.
- Home-delivered meals: Organizations prepare and deliver regular hot meals to elderly individuals, people with disabilities, or people with AIDS or other targeted conditions who are unable to shop, prepare food for themselves, or travel to a site that serves a meal. This is also known as Meals on Wheels.
- Food banks and pantries: Organizations gather, store, and distribute food, and sometimes personal or cleaning supplies, to low-income people at no charge or at a low cost.

Figure 5.1 shows the trend in the availability of community-based nutrition assistance programs between 2000 and 2021. It is important to note that these figures do not include services that are operated directly by the local government and therefore represent an undercount of the total availability of these services nationwide. Congregate meal sites, which are much less commonly operated by nonprofit organizations nationally than food banks, grew from 132 in 2000 to 202 in 2013, a 53 percent increase, then remained consistently around this level until 2021. Senior centers remained relatively stable over the time period, with about 2,600 nonprofit administered senior centers nationally. Home-delivered-meal programs fluctuated slightly over the time period, going from 366 in 2000 to 428 in 2009, then back down to 382 in 2021. The number of food banks grew from 515 in 2000 to 1,501 in 2020, nearly tripling in size, before falling to 1,441 in 2021.

Overall, among the 35 percent of SNAP households with adults age 60 and older surveyed in 2018, only 17 percent reported eating a group meal at a community program or senior center, and slightly more than 5 percent reported eating a home-delivered meal.[7] Low usage rates are worrisome, because some research finds a link between Older Americans Act services and reduced food insecurity.[8] However, not all studies agree on this point.[9]

Figure 5.1 Nonprofit Programs That Mainly Provide Nutritional Assistance to Older Adults, 2000–2021

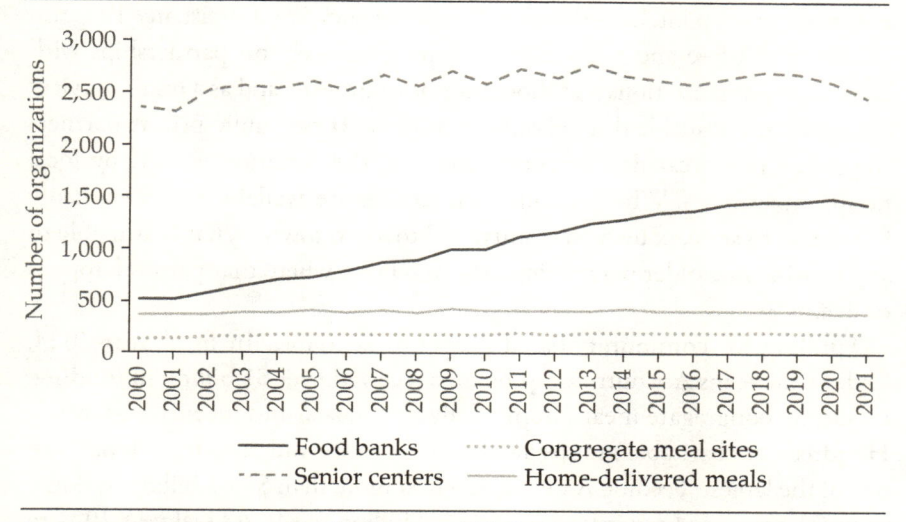

Source: Authors' calculations based on data available from the National Center for Charitable Statistics core files (Lecy 2024).

During COVID, food assistance programs expanded quickly but unevenly. In December 2019, 13.9 percent of older adults reported receiving charitable food assistance in the last 30 days; by April 2020, the number receiving assistance in the last seven days fell to 7.3 percent, then rebounded to 11.1 percent in July 2020.[10]

FUNDING FOR COMMUNITY-BASED FREE AND SUBSIDIZED FOOD PROGRAMS

Group meal and home-delivered-meal programs receive funding from Title III(C) Nutrition Services Programs under the Older Americans Act of 1964, and the Administration on Aging in the Department of Health and Human Services administers them. In addition to supporting nutrition, these programs offer social interaction and connection to other needed services, such as transportation and referrals to medical care. States receive funds from the federal government to support community planning, social service delivery, and infrastructure assistance such as personnel training in the field of aging.

Emergency food programs that offer recipients the ability to choose their food often serve all ages and receive funding primarily through the U.S. Department of Agriculture and private donations. The U.S. Department of Agriculture provides federal funding for a network of food banks that stock local food pantries and soup kitchens through The Emergency Food Assistance Program (TEFAP). All free and subsidized food programs rely on partnerships with community organizations and thousands of volunteers, and as a result, services are not evenly available throughout the country. These public-private partnerships require a great deal of coordination at the community level by local nonprofit agencies. Whether and when services are available varies markedly from state to state, county to county, and town to town. What is available to any low-income older person depends largely on where that person happens to live.

Funding for community-based programs is sizable. In fiscal year 2024, Older Americans Act nutrition programs received over $1 billion in funding, including congregate meals, home-delivered meals, and incentive grants.[11] Hundreds of charitable groups also rely on private and corporate donations: one of the largest, Feeding America, received more than $5.01 billion in donations for goods and services to provide 5.9 billion meals in fiscal year 2024 to those in need.[12] Each type of community-based food program may blend funding targeted toward adults age sixty and older with funding for all ages programs from federal funding sources such as the U.S. Department of Agriculture and the U.S. Department of Health and Human Services, state and local governments, and private funding. Generally, older adults may eat group meals at congregate meal sites and soup kitchens, receive home-delivered meals through Meals on Wheels, and receive food to be prepared at home through food pantries and farmers market coupons. Nonprofit organizations, governmental agencies, or public-private partnerships may deliver these programs.

GROUP MEALS: CONGREGATE MEALS AND SOUP KITCHENS

Group meal sites provide prepared meals and an opportunity to socialize for adults age sixty and older. In addition, many group meal sites provide connections to other services, such as nutritional education, health screenings, and transportation assistance. Group meals are also known as congregate dining and can be accessed across a variety of community-based agencies, including senior centers, Salvation Army buildings, church halls, senior-housing facilities, and other nonprofit facilities. Nearly all sites provide lunch, and many also provide breakfast. Among their most popular offerings, according to our respondents, is bingo. In fiscal year 2024, the federal government allocated $565 million to congregate dining, and congregate meal sites provided an estimated 50.3 million meals.[13] As of 2016, 87 percent of local providers recommended that participants contribute to the cost of the meal.[14] The cost of the contribution does not cover the full cost of the meal and varies by location. In Cayuga County, New York, in February 2025, the suggested contribution is $3.50 per meal, but the county website indicates that no one will be denied services because of an inability to pay.[15]

During COVID, most group meal programs closed their doors for on-site dining. But many were quick to adapt their services, diminishing the health risk to staff and clients by providing drive-through meals, telephone assessments, take-home boxes including several weeks of frozen meals, grab-and-go meals, and grocery drop-offs.[16] To foster the social connections common at group meal sites, many sites invited participants to online meals through Zoom or other platforms, coordinated buddy systems to foster paired virtual dining, and arranged for telephone check-ins or outside events when safe and weather appropriate. Once vaccines became available, group meal sites became an important source for vaccine information and access.[17]

Who participates in group meals? In 2023, the average group meal participant funded through the congregate dining program was seventy-seven years old, and 57 percent of participants lived alone.[18] While financial tests are not allowed as a requirement of participation, a majority of participants are low income; 31 percent have income below the poverty line and most of the remainder have incomes between 100 and 200 percent of the poverty line.[19]

Despite the increasing share of older adults in the U.S. population and increasing rates of food insecurity among older adults, the rate of older adults who report eating meals at a community program or senior center on the Current Population Survey has remained remarkably stable from 2002 to 2019, at about 6 percent of older adults in households with income below 185 percent of the federal poverty line, as shown in figure 5.2, or less than 2 percent of all older adults. During COVID, most group meal sites closed in 2020, and participation fell to 2.9 percent before rebounding to 4.3 percent in 2021. According to our calculations, in 2021 older adults who reported eating group meals were more likely to be Black, older, or unmarried or to live in a nonmetropolitan area.

Figure 5.2   Adults Age Sixty and Older with Household Income Below 185 Percent of the Federal Poverty Line Reporting Having Eaten Prepared Meals at a Community Program or Senior Center in the Previous Thirty Days, 2001–2021

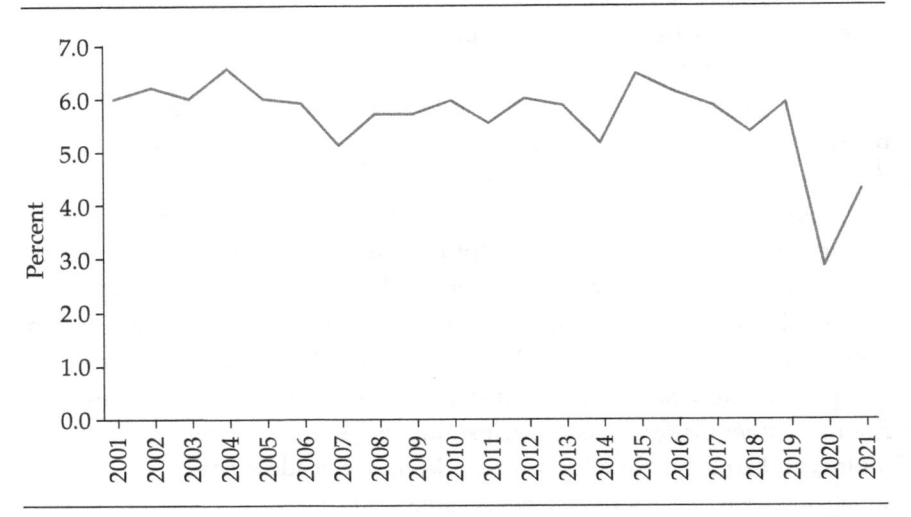

Source: Authors' calculations based on data from the 2001–2021 Current Population Survey (Flood et al. 2024).
Note: The item wording changed after 2021 and comparable data from more recent years are not available.

Prior to COVID, most older adults who ate at group meal sites receiving congregate dining funding did so frequently—82 percent received three or more meals per week and 43 percent received five or more meals per week. Further, most participants develop a lasting relationship with a specific site and set of people, with most receiving meals from the same site and attending for longer than one year.[20]

Our respondents described going frequently to group meals to see friends, eat tasty and nutritious breakfasts and lunches, play bingo, and access other services. Carmen, age sixty-five with low food security, summarized the social advantages of congregate dining succinctly.

> I go to the community place. I go Monday, Wednesday, sometimes Thursday. . . . They just opened because they were closed because of the pandemic. We go to the center, we play bingo. And we talk. . . . We get there like around 9, 9:30, and

10 o'clock bingo starts. Then we take a break. We talk, you know, "Did you watch the news, did you see what happened?" Yeah, every day. Every other person in there have a different conversation. But we get along really well. Really well. I like them.

Respondents also described how one of the most important aspects of group dining is the opportunity to connect to other services that are available. Deb, age sixty-two and food secure, emphasized the importance of connecting with people to learn what other services are available.

You just have to get up and move and know where to go and connect with people that they'll know, "Oh, man, go over there. They have this on sale. Or go over here, they have this. Guess what? The pantry has this this week. Do you need potatoes?" . . . You connect with people in the community that'll tell you things, and word of mouth.

For Nate, age seventy-two and food secure, participating in group dining means, in addition to good meals, that he is able to learn from other people about the services that are available to him. To his delight, the center dropped off meals for him after a surgery.

It was a good place because they served meals—lunch meals five days a week. It was good food but man, they was the hooking up with people and finding out about ride share and rides. So I got all that hooked up and when I had the surgery . . . they brought me a meal five days a week. . . . And they brought me two on weekends. On weekends. So it was great because I didn't have to worry about going to get food at the pantry.

Congregate Meals and Geographic Variation in Availability

Despite recent growth in the program, the number of nonprofit organizations that provide congregate meals as a primary activity remains low. As figure 5.3 demonstrates, California, with eleven registered nonprofit organizations, stands out as the state with the most nonprofit organizations claiming this as a main activity in 2000. Between 2000 and 2021, Florida, New York, and Texas reported large increases in the numbers of nonprofit organizations indicating that they

Figure 5.3 Number of Nonprofit Organizations That Mainly Provide Congregate Meals to Older Adults by State, 2000 and 2021

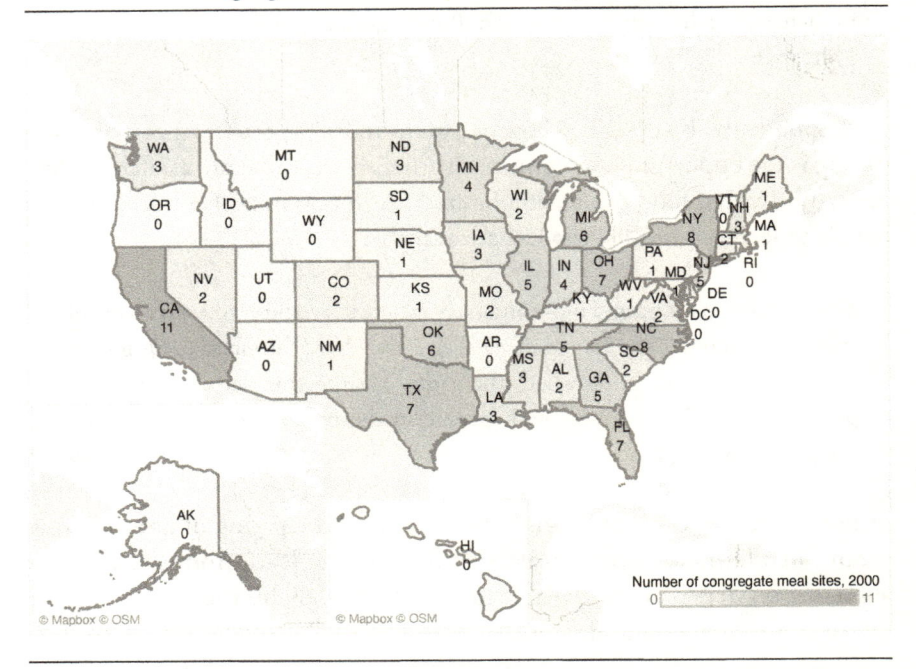

Source: Authors' calculations based on data available from the National Center for Charitable Statistics core files (Lecy 2024).

provided congregate meals as a prime activity—seven, six, and five, respectively—while Illinois experienced a decrease of two. Thirteen states did not have any such organizations in 2000, but by 2021 all but Hawaii and Montana had nonprofit organizations that offered congregate meals as a primary activity. In Hawaii and Montana, congregate dining may have been available, but no nonprofit organizations in these states listed providing group meals as a main activity.

The availability and quality of congregate meals vary dramatically from one location to another. Respondents told us they did not eat at group sites, or limited their visits, if they found the food unhealthy or inedible. Diane, age sixty-five and food secure, tried the food at one site and stopped going. "No. No. I don't like that. The food is not good. I don't care what nobody say it's not good."

Figure 5.3   (continued)

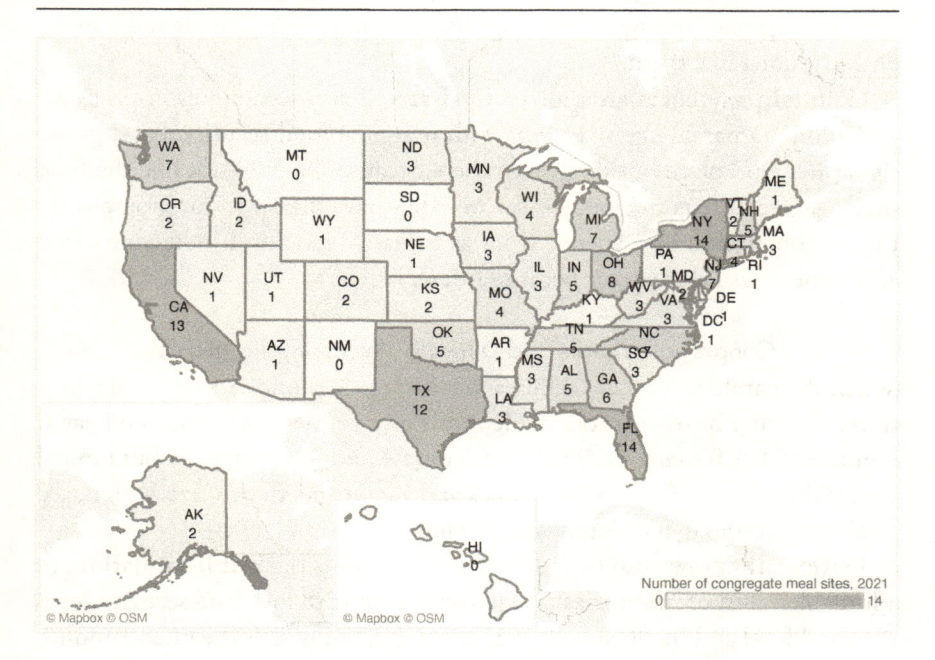

[Map of United States showing number of congregate meal sites by state, 2021. Values: WA 7, OR 2, CA 13, AK 2, ID 2, NV 1, UT 1, AZ 1, MT 0, WY 1, CO 2, NM 0, ND 3, SD 0, NE 1, KS 2, OK 5, TX 12, MN 3, IA 3, MO 4, AR 1, LA 3, WI 4, IL 3, MS 3, AL 5, MI 7, IN 5, KY 3, TN 1, GA 6, FL 14, OH 8, WV 1, VA 2, NC 1, SC 3, PA 1, MD 3, DE —, DC 1, NY 14, NJ 4, CT 5, RI 1, MA 3, VT 2, NH 1, ME 1, HI 0. Legend: Number of congregate meal sites, 2021, scale 0 to 14.]

Congregate Meals and Access to Nutritious Food

Group meals provide half or more of total daily food for the day for 46 percent of participants.[21] However, an important issue that we return to in chapter 6 is that the food provided at congregate meals sites is unhealthy in some respects. A 2017 evaluation reported that group meals met 2010 Dietary Guideline recommendations for total fruit, whole fruit, total vegetables, greens and beans, dairy, and total protein foods, but not for whole grains. Further, 94 percent of congregate meal participants had usual intakes that exceeded the Dietary Guidelines in place at that time for sodium, and 89 percent had usual intakes that exceeded the recommendations for saturated fat.[22]

Our respondents made it clear that the quality of the food ranges widely. Maggie, age sixty-three with low food security, said congregate meals are tasty and healthy. "Me and my sister . . . we can go with seniors and eat free with healthy lunch and stuff. And we go there sometimes and eat. It's good healthy food."

However, Valerie, age sixty-eight and food secure, said she cannot eat the food at congregate dining, explaining, "Remind me of TV dinners and I just—oh I just don't like them."

Cultural preferences around the food served also sometimes impact participation. Tamarah, age sixty-four with marginal food security, has a group site at her workplace but rarely eats there because she does not like the food that is served. "It's at my job, you know? They have that, a senior program. So I get it sometimes, but where I work at is Native food and Indigenous food and sometimes I don't get it because I don't like it."

Congregate Meals and Difficulty Accessing Programs

When the pandemic forced facilities to close, our respondents reported sometimes receiving boxes of ready-made meals or groceries that they could eat at home. As COVID rates declined, sites in some locations reopened but limited on-site dining to one or two days a week and augmented those meals with boxed meals or groceries that clients could take home.

Participation may also be reduced by food limits, lack of information, or affordable transportation. Kasha, age sixty-seven with low food security, loves the good food and bingo at her group meal site, but wishes the once-a-month take-home food box was a once-a-week supply.

> I go to the senior center. . . . We congregate together, socialize. . . . Twice a week. I do enjoy it. We play bingo. Food its very good. And they give us a pantry once a month. Yes. Like tomorrow, I get some food to bring home. Yes. We can pick out our vegetables. We seldom get fruit, unless it's in a can. Food pantry once a week? That would be wonderful.

Lena, age seventy-three with low food security, is limited to a few days a week of on-site dining, but grab-and-go meals augment her food supply.

> Yeah. I'm going to one today because it's Friday and they give you a hot meal. But Monday they give you a hot meal and they give you something for Tuesday. . . . It might be a can of ravioli. It might be a can of chicken noodle soup along with a fruit and a drink.

Lack of information about the availability of congregate meals programs impedes participation as well. Martha, age sixty-four and food secure, had only just found out about congregate dining when we interviewed her and was hoping to try it soon.

> But I just heard about a senior program, and they pick you up and they have lunch there. . . . They had programs where you exercise and stuff like that. . . . I don't know how often I would go. Maybe one day a week. . . . Something different to be around regular people.

Finally, a lack of affordable transportation also interferes with access to congregate meals. Programs for low-income recipients often are not located in the neighborhoods where low-income recipients live.[23] Gerald, age sixty-seven with very low food security, can only afford to taxi to his group meal site twice a week. He misses the food and he misses his friends.

> I go to the senior nutrition site twice a week when I can. I bring home food once a month. But I can't go because I have to pay for a taxi to get over there. . . . And two or three times a week I go to the center—to the senior citizens. . . . I talk to a few of them quite a lot over the phone.

Despite the evidence about the nutritional quality of the food provided, participants in congregate meals are generally satisfied with their program. Data from a 2023 survey of the Older Americans Act nutrition program participants indicate that 90 percent of congregate meal participants rated their program as good, very good, or excellent; 76 percent reported that the program helped them eat healthier, and importantly, 75 percent reported that the program helped them live independently.[24] However, recent research does not find that the participation rate among eligible seniors was associated with a reduction in food insecurity.[25]

Soup Kitchens

Soup kitchens also provide prepared group meals to be eaten on-site, usually within short time spans around mealtimes. Each of the main issues found with other forms of group meals is also present in soup kitchens. Soup kitchens are not organized formally under a national membership organization, such as Feeding America, that could provide support to or collect data from the network. The result of this highly decentralized organizational structure is that we do not know how many soup kitchens exist across the country, where they are located, how they are funded, how many days per week they are open for meals, or the nutritional quality of the food that they serve. We also know very little about how they responded during COVID. According to our analysis of Current Population Survey data, about 1 percent of adults age sixty and older reported eating at a soup kitchen in 2021, although this rises to 11 percent when we focus on low-income older adults.

Unlike the group meals served at senior nutrition sites, soup kitchen meals obtain funding almost entirely from charitable donations, do not face oversight in terms of nutritional content, and are usually run by teams of volunteers through local nonprofit agencies, churches, and Salvation Army centers. The quality of one's local soup kitchen depends on where one lives. Food may be donated from local restaurants, grocery stores, churches, farmers, or individual households. Because donations often rely on local networks, the quality and quantity of food available varies considerably over time, by geography, and by the demographic composition of the neighborhood. We know from personal experience volunteering and from respondent reports that the quality of food available at each soup kitchen can vary substantially. Wallace, age sixty-four with very low food security, has eaten at soup kitchens for several years. He can no longer stomach one of them, but he has a hard time getting a ride to the two he likes because they are farther away.

> Like I said I been to three different . . . soup kitchen[s]. The one downtown . . . I don't eat there. I go in there and eat, it smell, everything. I remember it's been a while, but I don't eat in there anymore. I will not eat in there. It's terrible. The other two are all right. I'll go in there and eat.

Respondents said that some soup kitchens serve the same food every single time and that the lack of variety has become difficult over the years. Alice, age seventy-seven with low food security, has grown weary of repetition in the menus. "The Salvation Army, there's a menu. The problem with that is, I've been here four years. The menu hasn't changed in four years. There's things that you like, but then you get sick to death of the same thing over and over and over and over again."

Access to food varies widely. Some soup kitchens serve two meals a day, seven days a week; others serve just one meal a week. One of the nation's largest soup kitchens, Project Open Hand, works with 125 volunteers to provide 2,500 meals and 200 bags of groceries a day in the San Francisco area.[26] Like the respondents who access congregate dining opportunities at senior centers, our respondents who eat at soup kitchens appreciate a warm meal that they do not have to cook themselves, as well as the socialization that soup kitchens offer. Alice relies heavily on her soup kitchen and wishes it was open on weekends. "Yes. There's a Salvation Army site only about four blocks. In spite of a little bit of a walk, but I can go there and get a meal, which I rely on very much, only I can't get it on the weekends."

Marie, age sixty-one and food secure, frequently eats at the soup kitchen and, in addition to eating a meal there, she brings home leftovers for additional meals. "I eat there most of the time, and they got leftovers. So I can bring the leftovers home, so it's all good. It's really good."

Kira, age sixty-eight and food secure, said her soup kitchen accommodates her food preferences. She missed the food while they were closed during the pandemic. She is so grateful for her soup kitchen that she donated a small part of her stimulus check to help keep them going during the pandemic.

> Yeah. Well, there are soup kitchens that I used to go to before the pandemic, and they knew I was a vegetarian. . . . They would make a special veggie burger for me. But then when the pandemic hit I stopped going. . . . [A] month ago I dropped in to say hello and I had breakfast, but you had to take the breakfast to go. . . . You know that money, extra money for the pandemic? Yeah, well, I gave one of the soup kitchens $50. . . . I said to them, "You've always been very nice to me."

Some of our respondents volunteered at soup kitchens regularly in exchange for meals or other necessities. Scarlett, age sixty-seven with very low food security, volunteers twice a week at her soup kitchen. Then she eats a meal and takes home a box of food or household supplies. "I also volunteer twice a week at a food kitchen. . . . They're very generous. . . . Once in a while toilet paper or shampoo . . . a food giveaway. . . . I've been going since about—I'd say at least eleven years. . . . I'll get me a sandwich."

Soup kitchens are geographically distributed unevenly across the United States. Some low-income older people may have several soup kitchens nearby, while others have none. There are no soup kitchens near where Deb, age sixty-two and food secure, lives. Gerald, age sixty-seven with very low food security, must travel quite far to get to his soup kitchen. "Every now and then I get to a rescue mission to eat a meal. . . . It's a little out of my area."

Sometimes soup kitchens do not feel safe. Soup kitchens meet the needs of the most vulnerable and needy populations in society. As a result, they serve a mix of adults, including some who are mentally ill or dealing with behavioral health issues, such as substance abuse. Long-standing ideas about who constitutes the deserving poor—namely those who are older or have disabilities, but less so those with mental illness or addiction issues[27]—shape how accepting and comfortable volunteers and clients are around other clients. Kira, age sixty-eight and food secure, is strategic about who she waits in line with and who she sits with, because some of the clients are struggling with mental health issues.

> Well, we have a little clique of people we would—you had to decide who you could tolerate most, of all the crazy people at the soup kitchen you know? . . . But we had a little clique of people. We would all wait in line and we'd just— you know, you go down, you pick your table, you get your cup of coffee. . . . Because I don't have to cook, I don't have to do the dishes and I get to hang out with some people.

HOME-DELIVERED MEALS

Home-delivered meals are designed to address food and nutrition security for homebound older adults. They are often known as Meals on Wheels, which is by far the nation's biggest supplier of home-delivered meals, and provide fully cooked meals. Meals on Wheels served an estimated 251 million meals in fiscal year 2024 to more than two million seniors through a network of five thousand community-based organizations.[28] Home-delivered meals also offer an opportunity for socialization through contact with the people delivering the meals, who may provide nutritional education, screening, and counseling. Like congregate meals, income is not a formal factor in determining eligibility, although services are targeted toward those with the greatest need and waiting lists may be long. Home-delivered-meal programs may offer their services for free, request a donation, or charge a fee. In 2016, the average recommended contribution was $2.95 per meal, with 22 percent of programs suggesting $1.50 or less and 28 percent suggesting $3.50 or more.[29] In Onondaga County, where we live, the February 2025 voluntary contribution level is $4.00 for two meals ($4.50 for two kosher meals), but the local website also indicates that any level of contribution is accepted and payment is not required.[30]

A study of Meals on Wheels shows that it is effective at counteracting loneliness, social isolation, and in some cases food insecurity. In 2015, two-fifths of the people who receive Meals on Wheels said that it was the only form of human interaction that they were getting and they felt less isolated.[31] A study conducted at a Meals on Wheels program in Central Florida, using a validated food security scale, finds that 40.3 percent of the participants were food insecure at the beginning of the program, and within this group, 30.6 percent had very low food security.[32] After two months on the home-delivered-meal program, none of the participants had very low food security, and only 21.6 percent reported having low food security.[33] However, more recent research using nationwide data does not find a relationship between access to home-delivered meals and food security.[34] According to Meals on Wheels, in addition to providing meals, 66 percent of providers also connect seniors to other services in the community, 50 percent offer home repair and modification services, and 44 percent provide pet assistance.[35]

Budgets for home-delivered meals are relatively small, in part because the programs receive funding through public-private partnerships with the Older Americans Act, the U.S. Department of Agriculture, state and local governments, and local foundations and individuals. As a result, such programs are unevenly distributed and rely on legions of volunteers to prepare and deliver the meals. In fiscal year 2020, the federal government spent $263 million on providing 199 million meals to 1.4 million homebound older adults through such programs.[36] During COVID, the federal government allocated an additional $160 million to fund home-delivered meals in 2020 through the Families First Coronavirus Response Act. The CARES Act allotted another $480 million to states for both congregate and home-delivered meals with another $750 million flowing to these two programs from the American Rescue Plan in 2021.[37] More recently, Medicaid and Medicare funding is becoming available in some states for a specialized version of home-delivered meals called Medically Tailored Meals, an intervention that is part of the movement of piloted interventions that recognize that food is medicine. In fiscal year 2024, $381 million from the Older Americans Act was spent on home-delivered nutrition.[38]

Who receives home-delivered meals? In 2023, participants were, on average, seventy-eight years old, and 59 percent of participants lived alone. Home-delivered meals provided half or more of their total food for 60 percent of participants, and 48 percent reported difficulty going outside the home.[39]

Participation tends to be very stable: 71 percent of participants received five or more meals per week, and 85 percent received three or more meals per week.[40]

Susan, age sixty-five and food secure, briefly received home-delivered meals following a surgery and appreciated the service. "I had a hip replacement and . . . after I got out of the hospital, they delivered meals for me for a week or so. . . . Oh yeah, they were good. Better than what they cooked me there."

Zachariah, age sixty-three and food secure, received home-delivered meals, which were provided through contact-free delivery at the beginning of COVID because he was afraid to leave his home. He stopped receiving home-delivered meals because the food was aggravating his chronic health conditions.

> Yeah, and that lasted for about, I want to say, six weeks. And they came once a week, and they gave you enough meals for breakfast, lunch, and dinner . . . and I knew I have underlying conditions that put me at a greater risk . . . the obesity, the COPD [chronic obstructive pulmonary disease] . . . and it stopped.

We estimate that nationally from 2001 to 2019, between 4 and 5 percent of older adults in households with income below 185 percent of the federal poverty line received food from home-delivered meals in the previous thirty days (or less than 2 percent of all older adults), as shown in figure 5.4. Then the percentage increased to 6.7 percent in 2020 due to COVID, a nearly 50 percent increase in one year before returning to 6.0 percent in 2021. Among our low-income respondents, 22 percent used home-delivered meals in 2021.

Home-Delivered Meals and Geographic Variation in Availability

Only a small number of nonprofit organizations list the provision of home-delivered meals as their main activity in annual tax reports to the IRS. In fact, the average county does not have a single organization that is devoted to primarily providing home-delivered meals. And though demand has increased, the supply has decreased between 2014 and 2021.

Figure 5.5 demonstrates the state variation in the availability of home-delivered meals. In 2000, most states had at least one nonprofit organization that reported to the IRS that home-delivered meals were its primary activity. Notably, Nevada and Utah had no such organizations in 2000 and in 2021.

Figure 5.4 Adults Age Sixty and Older with Household Income Below 185 Percent of the Federal Poverty Line Reporting That They Have Received Home-Delivered Meals in the Previous Thirty Days, 2001–2021

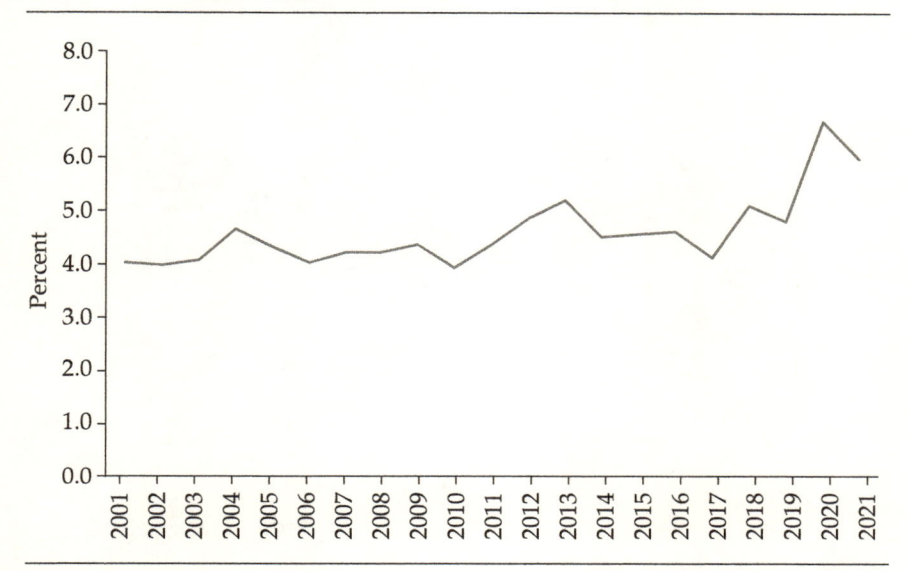

Source: Authors' calculations based on data from the 2001–2021 Current Population Survey (Flood et al. 2024).
Note: The item wording changed after 2021 and comparable data from more recent years are not available.

California and Pennsylvania, two of the three states with more than thirty sites in 2000, also experienced the largest increase between 2000 and 2021, reaching forty-three and forty-eight sites respectively. However, New York, the third state, saw a decline from thirty-six sites in 2000 to thirty-three in 2021. Missouri experienced the sharpest decline, dropping from twenty-two sites in 2000, to nine in 2021.

Home-Delivered Meals and Access to Nutritious Food

According to interviews conducted in 2015–2016, while most home-delivered-meal participants reported eating three times a day, 29 percent described their appetite as poor or fair, and 34 percent were on special health-related diets to control nutritionally sensitive conditions such as diabetes or hypertension.

Figure 5.5   Number of Nonprofit Organizations That Mainly Provided Home-Delivered Meals by State, 2000 and 2021

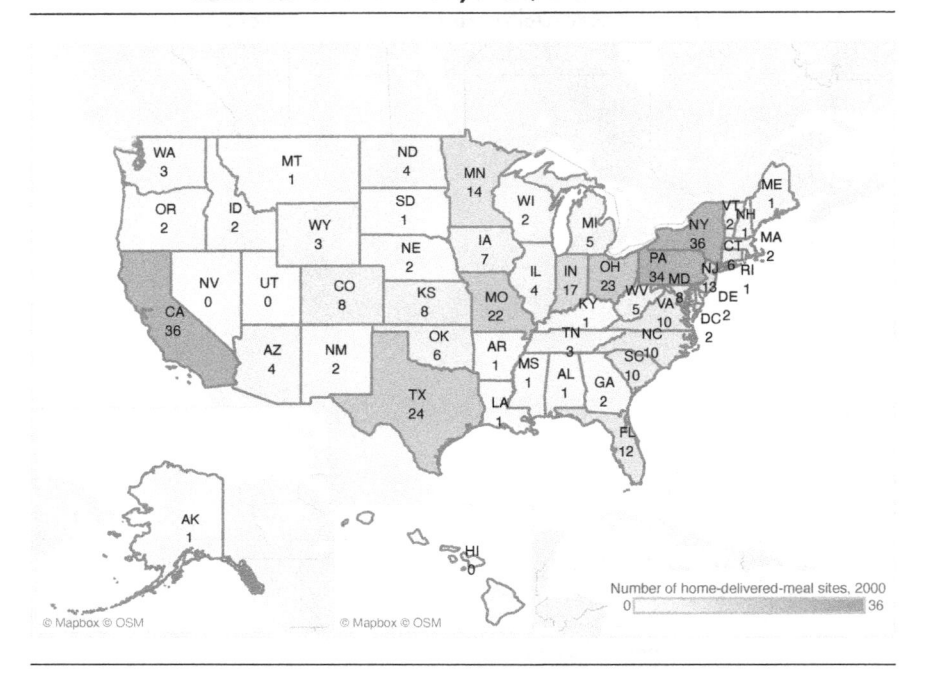

Source: Authors' calculations based on data available from the National Center for Charitable Statistics core files (Lecy 2024).

About 33 percent reported being unable to prepare a hot meal if necessary. Consequently, 41 percent of participants' daily calories came from the delivered meals.[41] In terms of diet quality, a 2017 evaluation of the nutritional quality of the meals provided indicated that the meals, like congregate meals, scored highly in terms of meeting the 2010 Dietary Guidelines for total fruit, whole fruit, total vegetables, greens and beans, dairy, and total protein but that 72 percent of home-delivered-meal participants exceeded the recommended intake of saturated fats, 69 percent exceeded the recommended intake of sodium, and only 28 percent met the guidelines for whole grains.[42] Nonetheless, a 2023 survey of participants found that 81 percent reported that they ate healthier because of the meal program, 88 percent rated their meal as good to excellent, and 91 percent reported that the program helped them to live independently.[43]

Figure 5.5   (continued)

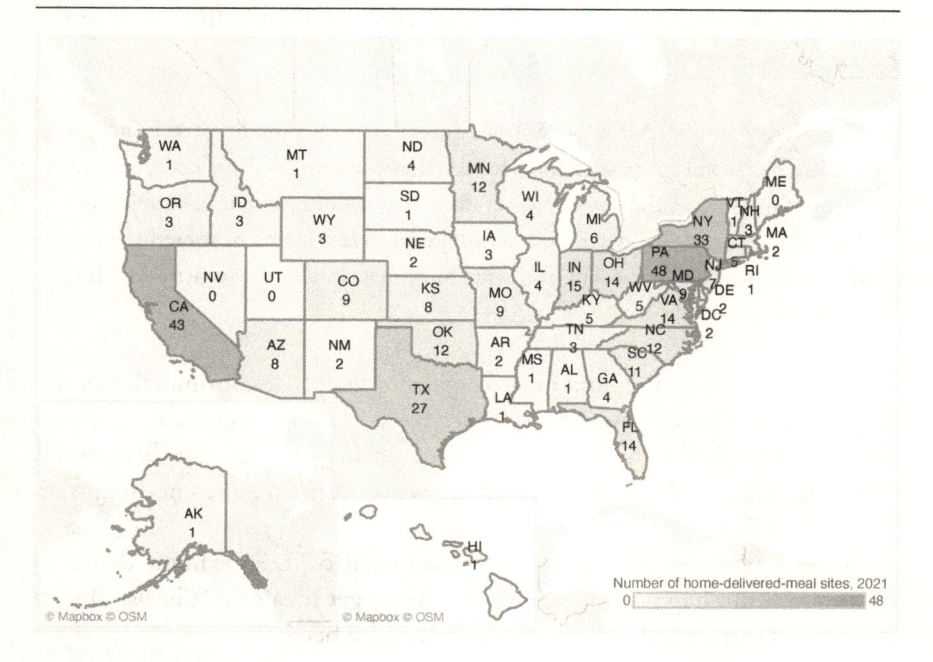

[US map showing number of home-delivered-meal sites, 2021: WA 1, MT 1, ND 4, MN 12, ME 0, OR 3, ID 3, WY 3, SD 1, WI 4, MI 6, NY 33, VT 1, NH 3, MA 2, NE 2, IA 3, PA 48, NJ 5, CT 2, RI, NV 0, UT 0, CO 9, KS 8, MO 9, IL 4, IN 15, OH 14, WV 9, MD 7, DE 1, CA 43, AZ 8, NM 2, OK 12, AR 2, KY 5, VA 14, DC 2, NC 2, TN 3, SC 12, TX 27, MS 1, AL 1, GA 4, LA 1, FL 14, AK 1, HI. Scale: 0 to 48.]

Perhaps unsurprisingly, people who participate in home-delivered-meal programs are in worse health than those who participate in other nutritional assistance programs. About 50 percent of participants in home-delivered-meal programs describe their health as fair or poor, and 6 percent report being underweight. Roughly 25 percent report difficulties with their teeth or gums; 82 percent report taking three or more prescription medications daily. In terms of chronic health conditions, more than 50 percent of participants report having high cholesterol, arthritis, eye conditions, or hypertension, and 41 percent report a history of heart disease. Finally, functional limitations are common—64 percent have difficulty climbing stairs and 12 percent cannot walk.[44]

Respondents who try the service sometimes find that they cannot eat the food because it interferes with their ability to manage chronic conditions. Doctors tell them to replace processed food with fresh food, but home-delivered-meal providers are not necessarily able to heed that advice. Respondents noted that very little from home-delivered meals was fresh. Barbara, age sixty-eight with very low food security, had to discontinue the delivered meals because they were making her sick, but now she has little food in her house and sometimes goes hungry.

> They were giving me Meals on Wheels, but they couldn't modify it so I can't eat that anymore, and then I got Mom's Meals. They couldn't modify it again, because some of the stuff in there was making me sick and so I have not been able to— I couldn't eat it so I'm stretching a pot of greens to last a week or something like that, and then I've got beans and stretching that to where—sometimes I just don't eat.

Martha, age sixty-four and food secure, also had to discontinue the service because it conflicted with her health needs. "My doctor had me on a special diet. . . . And they were having a problem getting me the right diet. And it was actually like once a week. Everything was frozen. So there's nothing fresh or anything."

Ginny, age sixty-two with very low food security, receives home-delivered meals but is not happy with the quality. "Yes, I get Meals on Wheels. Once a week. . . . I just wish the Meals on Wheels tasted better."

Home-Delivered Meals and Difficulty Accessing Programs

As with other forms of nutrition assistance programs, receiving home-delivered meals requires an application process that involves providing information about one's living situation, household income, and health conditions (to tailor the food provided). Respondents are sometimes frustrated by long waits to enroll in services and invasive application questions. In 2025, one in three local providers report a waitlist that is, on average, four months long.[45] Harriet, age sixty-five with marginal food security, applied but has not yet been able to begin services due to a waiting list. "I called to see about getting on the home delivery, which they have here in New Mexico. But they're full. They don't have any spaces and that was two years ago."

Ruth, age sixty with very low food security, said the questions asked during the intake process were too invasive so she halted her application.

> They just seemed too nosy to me. . . . People want to make everything their business. You know, I'm not that kind of person. I thank you and bless you and

I thank you for helping me. But don't try to get into my business because it's not going to work. . . . Yeah, they want you to tell the condition of this and tell the condition of that.

FOOD TO BE PREPARED AT HOME: FOOD PANTRIES AND FARMERS MARKET COUPONS

Food pantries, which provide food to be prepared off-site, form the backbone of the emergency food assistance system and emerged as a community-based solution around 1979.[46] The Ronald Reagan administration's cuts to the food stamp program (now SNAP) in the early 1980s induced community organizations to provide private emergency food assistance. Additionally, the reemergence of the government-commodities program in the early 1980s—which used charitable organizations to distribute food that the government purchases to support farm prices, such as canned fruits and vegetables, peanut butter, beans and canned meat, to low-income populations—helped shift the network from an ad hoc to a more permanent status. Now, most of the food distributed through food pantries is donated by private sources, such as grocery stores, restaurants, and other corporate, charitable, and individual donations. Private organizations such as churches and schools host food drives for local food banks and pantries; farmers and growers donate excess foods; grocery stores donate food that is nearing expiration; and food banks purchase food at reduced rates from grocery stores.[47]

The network relies heavily on thousands of volunteers, including some who are themselves food insecure. Currently, the U.S. Department of Agriculture's TEFAP employs the food pantry system to distribute significant amounts of government commodities that the government purchases from farmers and growers to control pricing, reduce food waste, and provide food to those in need.[48] In fiscal year 2021, food pantries distributed 1.3 billion pounds of commodity food, four times the 422 million pounds of commodity food distributed in 2000.[49]

Food pantries vary considerably, from informal closets in churches that are open only once a month to multimillion dollar operations with regular daily hours that distribute millions of pounds of food a month. Protocols for receiving food also vary in terms of how one qualifies, the amount of food available, and the frequency with which one can access food from that site. Perhaps most

Figure 5.6 Adults Age Sixty and Older with Household Income Below 185 Percent of the Federal Poverty Line Reporting That They Received Food from a Food Pantry in the Last Twelve Months, 2001–2021

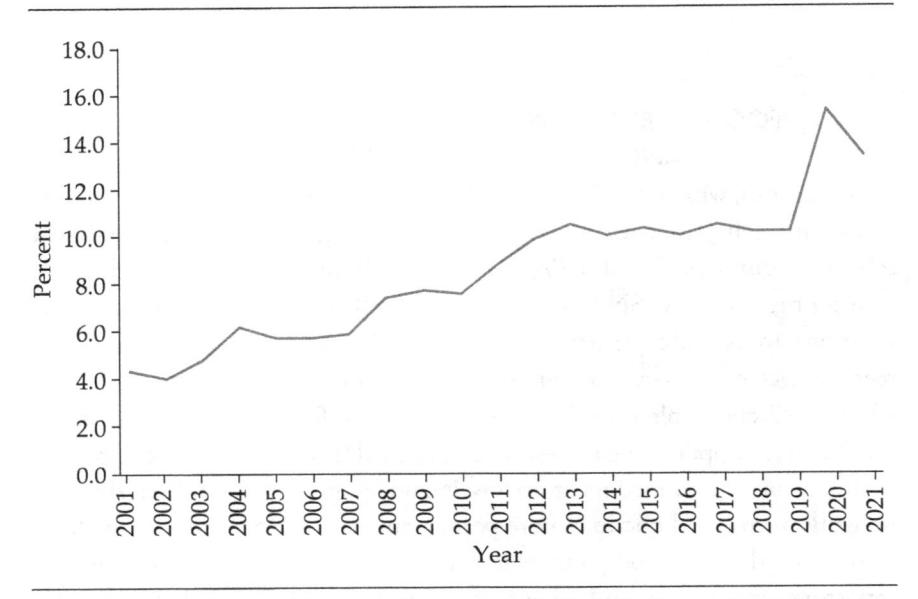

Source: Authors' calculations based on data from the 2001–2021 Current Population Survey (Flood et al. 2024).
Note: The item wording changed after 2021 and comparable data from more recent years are not available.

important, the quality of the food varies remarkably in terms of content, freshness, and healthiness.

Older people make up a growing share of food pantry users. Heflin and Ashley Price use data from the Current Population Survey for 2002 to 2014 to examine changes in reported use of food pantries and document how the age composition of food pantry users has shifted over time.[50] Between 2002 and 2014, the share of food pantry users with household heads who were age fifty to sixty-four increased from 18 to 34 percent, and the share with household heads who were age sixty-five and older increased from 11 to 18 percent. By the end of the Great Recession in 2010, the food pantry population was much older than it had been at the beginning of the decade.

Food pantry users have continued to age since the Great Recession. According to our analysis, shown in figure 5.6, the percentage of older adults with household incomes below 185 percent of the federal poverty line who reported receiving food from food pantries in the previous twelve months increased by 40 percent, from 4.4 percent in 2001 to 6.3 percent in 2008. It increased by 65 percent again to 10.5 percent in 2013, after which it remained between 10 and 11 percent until 2020 when it jumped by 50 percent again to 15.4 percent before returning to 13.3 percent in 2021. Among our low-income respondents, 78 percent reported using food pantries.

Demand on food pantries increased dramatically during COVID and has remained high.[51] Vera, age seventy-six with marginal food security, said that pantries have been extremely efficient, in part because they have legions of volunteers.

> I think the food pantry is doing an excellent, excellent job.... I think was last week there was like three hundred cars in line.... They're totally efficient. It starts at 5 o'clock exactly. And everybody's lined up then you start through. You have your trunk open. They check off your name because you have to register ahead of time. And then they just—it's like a little army of them and they put the boxes in and click and next and next and next. And I think even if I show up late, which I did last time, so I was right at the end of the line, it took maybe an hour and a half.... And the firemen and the church people do it.

According to our analysis of self-reports of food pantry usage in the Current Population Survey, non-Hispanic Black and Hispanic older adults are more likely to report receiving food from food pantries than are non-Hispanic White older adults. Similarly, one in four older adults with less than a high school degree reported receiving food from a food pantry in 2020, compared with one in ten older adults with a college degree or higher education. Finally, married older adults are much less likely to receive food from a food pantry than are nonmarried older adults.

The majority of food pantries are small and staffed entirely with volunteers. Food pantries with some paid administrative staff historically have paid relatively low wages for long hours of often physically and emotionally demanding work. In both scenarios, staff turnover tends to be quite high. Volunteers may be food insecure themselves and volunteer by unloading food trucks, organizing food, preparing food boxes for delivery, or helping clients at pickup in exchange for taking home food for themselves. In recent years, paid staff have received pay increases as food pantries strive to make sure they do not impoverish their own workers.[52]

Figure 5.7 Number of Nonprofit Organizations That Mainly Provide Food Pantries by State, 2000 and 2021

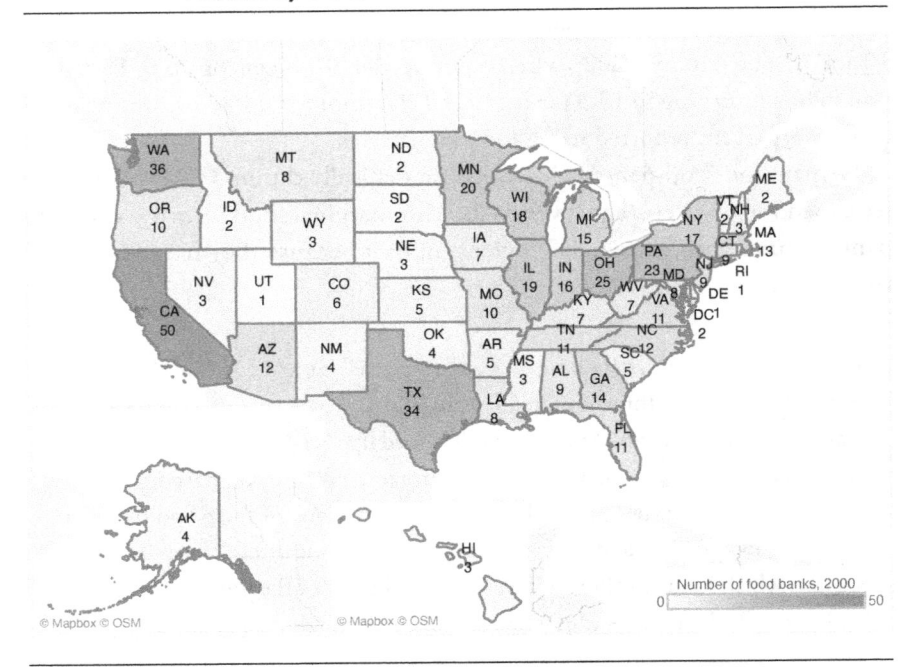

Source: Authors' calculations based on data available from the National Center for Charitable Statistics core files (Lecy 2024).

Respondents sometimes volunteer at food pantries in part so that they can give back and in part because it gives them access to more, and often better, food and household supplies. Nick, age sixty-six with marginal food security, finds that volunteering gives him early access to the best food. "When I volunteer for the food pantries . . . I kind of get the first choice."

Marie, age sixty-one and food secure, volunteers in exchange for donated food or household supplies that she can take home with her. "We get fringe benefits though. We can get some donated, you know. And we get a lot of donations whether it's household supplies, toilet paper, food, clothing. I actually furnished my whole apartment from there."

Food Pantries and Geographic Variation in Availability

As figure 5.7 shows, the number of food pantries has grown steeply since 2000, yet they remain geographically unevenly distributed. According to our analysis

Figure 5.7 (continued)

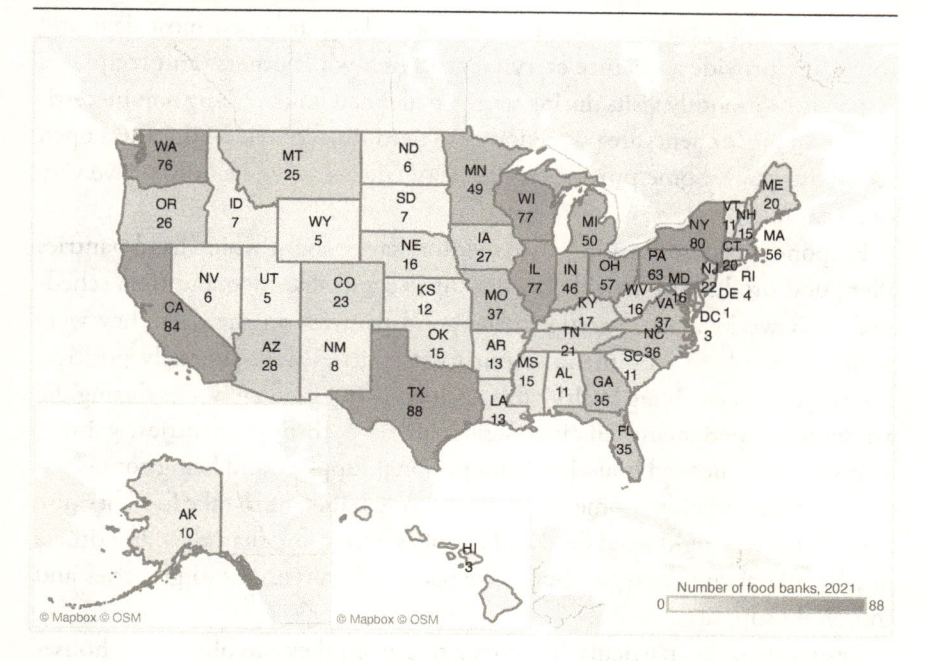

Number of food banks, 2021

of IRS data, we find that every state had at least one food bank and pantry in 2000, and the number of organizations distributing food increased dramatically after the Great Recession in 2008. In 2000, the states with the most organizations focused on food distribution to low-income families were California with fifty, Texas with thirty-four, and Washington with thirty-six. Between 2000 and 2021, four states—Illinois, New York, Texas, and Wisconsin—experienced an increase of more than fifty food pantries. Similarly, many states in the South and along the East Coast doubled the number of organizations that distributed low-cost or free food. Reflecting the lower level of need, less populated states in the Midwest and West did not experience the level of organizational increases seen in the rest of the country.

As is the case with other community-based programs, food pantries vary dramatically in terms of quality, convenience, and access. Some provide their clients with an abundance of fresh produce, pantry items, and nonfood household items such as toilet paper or detergents, while others provide limited canned and boxed goods, produce that is near its expiration, or few if any household items. Some are conveniently located near public transportation, related social services, and churches, while others are difficult, even dangerous, to get to without a car. Finally, some allow clients to come daily, are open most days and hours, and provide assistance carrying groceries, while others limit recipients to weekly or monthly visits during narrowly defined hours. Many require certification to prove clients are poor enough to need the services, while others open doors to anyone. Some provide services very efficiently, while others have very long wait lines.

Respondents described how they became savvy about which food pantries offer good produce or provide free toothpaste and shampoo and then scheduled their weeks around going to the good pantries on the days they were open. Respondents' comments about food pantries were generally positive. They described receiving healthy food, appreciating food deliveries during the pandemic, experiencing efficient service at drive-through pantries, gaining access to much needed household and personal supplies, and being connected to other social services. Some respondents were reluctant to take food because they felt others might need food and supplies even more than they did; others volunteered at the pantry to both give back and gain access to groceries and household supplies.

Respondents are particularly appreciative when they can obtain free household and personal supplies at pantries. Nonfood items such as household cleaning and personal hygiene products can be expensive and often compete with food in tight budgets. Receiving these items for free opens up more of household budgets for food. As these next quotes demonstrate, some pantries offer higher quantities and a wider array of household and personal supplies than others do. Willow, age seventy-four with low food security, takes food and as much soap and toilet paper as her pantry will allow.

> They ask you if you want detergent and it's usually just a small sandwich bag size of detergent. So I turn that down. But they do give you a bar of soap, which I take. They give you two rolls of toilet paper. And so they include a lot of the essentials that you need besides all that canned goods that they give out.

Kira, age sixty-eight and food secure, goes to a food pantry that offers a wide variety of personal and household cleaning supplies. "They have dishwashing soap and shampoos and deodorants and paper towels and things that I can't get with food stamps, you know? So yeah, I hit up that one for some of the stuff I can't afford."

Zachariah, age sixty-three and food secure, may select from an even broader array of household and personal items at his food pantry.

> You can go every two weeks. . . . I like this place because they give you things you can use. Toilet paper . . . hand sanitizer, bottled water . . . a case or two . . . also they have stuff like antihistamines, Advil, stuff like to dust your furniture, clean your furniture, light bulbs. . . . You can pick soap and you can take paper towels, or you can pick Kleenex or whatever.

Respondents are especially grateful when food pantries connect them with other social services. They helped connect Alex, age sixty-five with low food security, with counselors. "Then there's another one where you really get some good food over there, is the . . . it's called the Community Resources. And they do other things too, like they help . . . they've got counseling there, and if you need, school supplies and help with utilities."

The food pantry connected Alana, age sixty-five and food secure, to free legal services.

> I've gone to the food pantry. . . . Usually once every two weeks, Yes. Like yesterday I went in the Hispanic area and they had . . . I went to a free legal service, I qualified. And I wanted to do my will and I'm just trying to get everything in order, you know. And when I left, soon as I went around the corner, they were giving food away and so it's such a blessing.

The food pantry connected Ezra, age seventy-two and food secure, to subsidized housing.

> I go up there once a week to pick up some veggies and stuff. This is one of the services they offer. They've helped me with low-income housing, too, but. . . . Actually, they lay out the vegetables and stuff on the table and you come over and take what you want. . . . There's vegetables, fruits, canned good[s] . . . that sort of thing.

Wallace, age sixty-four with very low food security, visits a church-run pantry that connected him to a service that will pay his utility bill once a year if he falls short. While getting to the pantry is not safe, he feels it is worth the risk.

> They got a food pantry but it's a dangerous highway, you know, but I be very careful. It's going over a hill and it's very dangerous, and I don't like it. They'll pay a bill for me. Like I say I know how to survive. They'll pay a bill for me maybe up to $170. They got churches that will do that.

Food Pantries and Access to Nutritious Food

Food processors or distributors donate much, though certainly not all, of the food to pantries for tax write-offs; the donated food might otherwise be considered food waste because it cannot be sold due to some defect in manufacturing or because it is expired or dented.[53] Where one lives determines the type of food that local farms, groceries, and food processors donate and therefore, the type of food one receives. For example, central New York pantries give out surplus apples, central Missouri pantries give out chicken, and Idaho pantries offer potatoes.

Respondents were delighted by access to fresh food at some pantries. Whether they select their allotments in person or receive boxes of food slipped into their trunks or delivered to their door, these respondents described receiving healthy food. Food pantries help them stretch tight budgets and assure that they do not go hungry. Vera, age seventy-six and marginally food secure, described the healthy food that she receives every other week when she drives through the church parking lot. It makes all the difference. Without the food pantry, she would not have enough food.

> I do get food from the food bank every two weeks, which is wonderful and generous and really good quality.... Let's see, I get taco shells, which I love because I eat my scrambled eggs in a taco shell in the morning. And I get cheese.... Last couple of weeks it's been five chicken legs and a couple pounds of ham. And there's eggs, there's milk ... cucumbers, couple onions, avocados. There's always a bag of potatoes. There's sometimes fresh lettuce.... They put [the food] in your car for you. You drive ... through the church.... It's a couple of small boxes, usually three.... And there's both canned goods, bagged goods, and fresh goods.... I don't think I could make it without the food boxes now.

Carl, age sixty-seven and food secure, is pleased with the quality of the vegetables he receives from the food pantry. On the day of our interview, he was making soup.

> And most of the time, the broccoli that I just got, it was excellent broccoli that they had at the food shelf, and I got three heads, and I'm going to be chopping that up today. . . . When I made that dish last night, I had three bags of spinach that I didn't want . . . to go to waste. So, I cooked it . . . because all I had to do was make it thinner, more soupy, then I could just add some more water and a little more this sort of like bouillon but it has hydrogenated vegetables.

In stark contrast, other respondents reported that much of the food from their local pantry is processed, canned, or boxed and that the pantry lacks fresh produce and meat. Barbara, age sixty-eight with very low food security, is not able to eat canned food, and she no longer accepts it. However, her pantry does not offer enough fresh produce or meat to offset the loss.

> Where I am at they have food boxes. . . . The bad part about that is, the majority of the stuff you get in there is canned goods so I'm able to keep the juice. . . . So you might get a bag of potatoes, a bag of apples, a bag of oranges, cabbage, or onions that you can use in there, and every now and then they might put some meat in there. That's the extra box and you have to qualify for that. . . . There are other food banks but, like I say, [they] mostly give canned goods and it doesn't make sense to waste food so I don't do the canned goods.

Carl, age sixty-seven, wishes the food boxes being delivered contained meat.

> It comes in a box, and there's perishables and nonperishable. . . . You got more stuff, you know, if you go out to the facility and a lot of times, you'll get meats and stuff but when they deliver to our building, they don't. Because it's perishable. . . . And they deliver, you know, food every other week. . . . Every year, we have to recertify.

When we spoke with Willow, age seventy-four with low food security, she was incredulous that, after waiting in a long line at the food giveaway, she received a case of plastic bags of chocolate syrup.

We do have some things around here that's called food pop-ups . . . and they hand out food. But the majority of the food that you get from them is . . . well, for instance, I've gone and got a case of huge plastic bags of chocolate [syrup] for, like ice cream, you know. What are you going to do with—to me, that's useless.

Respondents described some food from the pantry as old and about to expire or turn bad. Anna, age seventy-six with low food security, stopped going to the food pantry because the food was too old, and she is too tired to travel all the way to the pantry to get poor-quality food.

Sometimes the food I was getting from the food banks was moldy and I would have to throw it out. Yes, I do. I do sometimes have to do that. Yeah, well they brought the food was already old on the day they brought it. And it was like I had pears, and I just looked at them and they were just way past the point of being safe to eat. So it was hard for me to get food from food banks. I get a lot of spoiled food.

Ruth, age sixty with very low food security, finds that the produce is often about to go bad, and if she does not use it right away, she must throw it out.

Yeah but I been going to the food bank. . . . But a lot of that stuff if you don't take it and do something with it right then, in two days it's going to be turned and you're going to have to throw it out anyway. . . . But I got beef yesterday. . . . I mean it was frozen and it was kind of dark brown instead of red. But you don't know what happens to it. If I open it and it don't smell right, it's out of here.

Perhaps most important, respondents noted that processed food from the pantries adversely affects their health. Martha, age sixty-four and food secure, has chronic conditions and the processed food makes her feel worse. "I shouldn't be eating anything processed at all, but I still do once in a while. . . . I have osteoarthritis. If I do eat processed stuff, I'm in a lot more pain and I think I have more mental fog."

Alice, age seventy-seven with low food security, once received a two-pound bag of processed cheese. She has now stopped receiving the food boxes altogether.

I stopped getting the food box because, after about two years . . . it was repulsive to me. I didn't need another two pounds of processed cheese. I couldn't eat more beans. I had enough rice. It's very cheap food. . . . They would often give us a lot of sweet cereal, real sugary cereal.

Meredith, age sixty with very low food security, reported that the poor-quality food from the pantries is causing her to gain weight. "It's hard to live off of food banks. . . . Like, you don't necessarily lose weight from not having food. Sometimes you gain it. . . . I mean, you have enough to keep going, but you're eating crap and that makes you gain weight."

Food Pantries and Difficulty Accessing Programs

Our respondents indicated that participation at food pantries is sometimes limited by burdensome administrative processes, long lines to receive food, lack of convenient transportation, or a less than welcoming attitude by some staff members.

Respondents described burdensome administrative processes to sign up for food pantries. They put a great deal of effort into figuring out where the best food pantries are located, which days and hours they are open, and how often they are able to visit. This comment from Wallace, age sixty-four with very low food security, provides a sense of how complicated the systems can be for individual users.

I go every weekend, it's part of my life. I go—I meant to go yesterday but a friend of mine wanted me to help him put some mulch down. . . . He gave me $60. There's a food pantry, I didn't go yesterday, there was one every Thursday, and there's another one every Wednesday. But you can go every fourteen days. But there's one you can go every Thursday, three times a month.

Visitors to food pantries typically have to qualify on an annual basis. In some places, clients qualify for specific levels that dictate how many days a week they can attend as well as how many boxes of food they can take. Julie, age sixty-two with low food security, lives in a household of four that includes children. She wishes she could go to the pantry every day because she does not have enough food.

We have a food bank. I mean we could go there every day if they have it. . . . They have rules. It would be nice if they could apply—like it doesn't matter if my power bill is $50 or if it's $250. It counts the same, you know, as far as what they can help me with. . . . Like if my car breaks, I've still got to pay everything else, you know. And I still only have so much for food.

Pantries' insufficient capacity to provide services may limit participation. Patty, age sixty-nine with low food security, applied for a food box delivery to her home, but it has never been delivered. "I contacted somebody about having some food delivered and they never came. It was a nonprofit that somebody was doing, and I saw it on Facebook and I contacted her and gave her my information and then they didn't come."

In some areas, food pantries always have long waits. Lines grew longer during COVID and continue to be long after the pandemic, largely because of reduced SNAP benefit amounts and ongoing food inflation.[54] On Harrington Meyer's drives through Harlem and Brooklyn, for example, she often sees people who are older or have mobility limitations standing in lines that stretch around the block. Clients might stand in hot sun or light rain, waiting for their turn at the food pantry and hoping to get inside before the food runs out for the day. Many pantries have switched to car lines, popping prepared boxes of food into car trunks to minimize the spread of pathogens. This allows recipients to wait in their cars rather than on foot, but also sharply reduces their ability to choose food, and it nearly eliminated participation among those who do not have cars or sufficient gas.

Francis, age sixty-three with low food security, said the line of cars is always very long at her monthly distribution, but the extra box of food she qualifies for is worth the wait. "When I went to the Food Room last month . . . I mean there was cars lined up like crazy. . . . We have one food pantry and it's once a month and this time they give us, say, if you were sixty or older, they had an extra box."

Long waits in cars for drive-through pickups can mean using up precious gas. Lena, age seventy-three with low food security, endures very long wait times, during which she worries about whether she has enough gas in the tank.

No, it's just the line of people. You have to change your time and stuff because being older, you know, you've got to either wait in the car. . . . So the struggle is just sitting, waiting. But if you want it you've got to wait. And then the gas and your car. You turn the motor off. This guy kept asking me why I was cutting my motor off every time I move up. I said because I'm riding on fumes. And he gave me $10 for gas.

Waiting in a car can be frustrating, expensive, and uncomfortable, but waiting on foot can be downright painful, especially for people with mobility issues. Sometimes people wait a long time, only to find out that the pantry has run out of food and that they will have to return another day. Gerald, age sixty-seven with very low food security, learned firsthand that this was particularly likely to occur during COVID.

> At the senior center, they used to have . . . abundant food but being so many people was in the pandemic, we would get the food from the food bank and it was hurting. Oh, my God, it was hurting. During COVID they did not have enough food at the food bank.

Sometimes, transportation to and from food pantries is a formidable problem. Some food banks are conveniently located near public transportation or other public services, but others require a car or a long walk to get there. It can be difficult for anyone to walk home from the food bank with a load of groceries, more so for people who are older and have chronic health conditions. Alice, age seventy-seven with low food security, says some food pantries have more fresh produce, but she's not able to get to the good pantries because she relies on public transportation and has poor health.

> The food bank . . . you get more vegetables and stuff. There are food banks if I can get to them, but since I have to rely on public transportation, and I'm having trouble with both my kidneys at this time, it's difficult for me to take the public transportation and do the walking that is necessary to get to the food bank.

Martha, age sixty-four and food secure, used to go regularly to a food pantry that had particularly high-quality produce and meats, but now she does not have transportation to get there. She can only go if a friend or coworker offers to take her.

> Well my work used to take me to the fresh food pantries and that was wonderful. There's a long wait but there was a lot of fresh food you can get. And sometimes

they gave out a rotisserie chicken or yogurt. That was really good. So I used to go there once a week with her but now I have no transportation there. . . . But today a worker took me to . . . two of them. It's mostly canned stuff. You know? And boxed. And I can't eat a lot of canned stuff because I can't have sodium.

Tilly, age sixty-eight and food secure, uses a wheelchair and is only able to go to the food pantry if someone drives her and can help carry all the items home. She relies on the grandson she lives with, her husband, and a friend. She tries to visit food pantries that load the produce into the car for clients.

Once a week. We have three different ones, I usually try to pick up at two. Because I am in a wheelchair, I can't always go. . . . Right now, only one, where someone has kind of a vehicle. And I have a friend that does that with me. And then the other two, you just drive around and they load it in your car.

Respondents appreciated it when food was delivered to their buildings during COVID, eliminating the need for transportation to the food pantry. However, many of these delivery services ended as the pandemic receded. Anna, age seventy-six with low food security, said that at the beginning of COVID, the deliveries made all the difference.

I would say last year, maybe the first six months of last year, were very bad because I didn't have enough of a lot of basic needs items. . . . First you had to go to the food bank. Now they're delivering the food, so in the last six months it's gotten better. But before that I did have days where I was totally kind of out of certain kinds of food but not everything. Maybe I didn't have say fresh fruit, but I had other pantry items.

Respondent perceptions of attitudes among the staff may also discourage some older adults from going to food pantries. Kate, age sixty-one with marginal food security, described the psychological costs of receiving food from her local food pantry because she is uncomfortable with the way the staff express their "Christian attitudes" toward her. As a result, she avoids the food pantries when she can. "In my town, like my food pantry, I wish was a little bit different. You know like my food pantry comes with a little bit of attitude. This is our town. They're heavy on the Christian literature and, you know? There's just some things I don't like about it."

Lena, age seventy-three with low food security, said some of the staff treated clients as if they were going to take the goods to sell them for drug money. But Lena has worked hard to qualify for three food pantries that provide the fresh food and household goods she needs.

> Yep, I go to the three places that I like. You know, because some of the places they treat you like you know, you're just coming to get the stuff to sell it like you're on dope or something. But the places I like to go, they give out really what you need like toilet paper, nutritious food that don't be outdated. Because some of these places give you stuff that'll kill you. . . . No. You just have to go in and, like I say, give your history and sign up and get a card and it's usually good for a year. And then you have to re-sign up again. But this one senior program I got like a nickel over and I can't go there anymore.

Obtaining welfare benefits for the poor at any stage of life can be stigmatizing and lead to feelings of shame.[55] Respondents reported feeling embarrassed to use the food pantries or being put off by the attitudes of the staff. Tamarah, age sixty-four with marginal food security, avoids the food pantries because it feels stigmatizing to go there, but when they bring the truck to her building it feels much less stigmatizing. She's more comfortable participating when they come to her.

> I hate going to a food shelf. . . . It feels degrading to me. I try not to go. . . . But when the truck comes [to my building], you can see what they have on the list outside. It's got a big chalkboard. If it's something that I wanted, like fish or something like that, then I will do it. And I don't feel that shame because they're coming here and a lot of people in this building use that service.

Farmers Market Coupons

Another community-based program that allows recipients to select their own food items to cook at home is the Senior Farmers Market Nutrition Program (SFMNP), which provides coupons to low-income older adults that can be exchanged for fresh food at roadside stands, farmers markets, and community-supported agricultural programs. In many communities across the country, farmers markets also accept SNAP benefits. SFMNP served over

750,000 participants in FY2022. Only 16 percent of our respondents use farmers market coupons.

Geographic variation in the availability of farmers market coupons is a significant issue. The U.S. Department of Agriculture offers grants to states to operate the SFMNP. Funding and participation levels alike vary substantially across states, counties, and farmers markets. For example, in 2022, Colorado did not participate in the program, while California received $983,000 in funding and Alabama received $1.7 million.[56] As a consequence, access to SFMNP is very limited by geography.

Our respondents uniformly described how SFMNP coupons, unlike the other sources of food discussed in this chapter, routinely provide affordable access to fresh fruits and vegetables. In fact, respondents wish the benefits were more generous. Studies examining the dietary outcomes of SFMNP participants generally find that participation is correlated with an increase in fresh fruit and vegetable consumption.[57] However, they largely do not find a strong link between participation in the program and reductions in food insecurity.[58]

Maggie, age sixty-three with low food security, uses her coupons at different farmers markets and enjoys not only the fresh produce but the food samples and the educational advice available from the vendors.

> I go to farmers markets. And I buy fresh vegetables, like green tomatoes and green onions and stuff like that. . . . You can go to the one close by you. . . . People make guacamole and different people have samples of food they want to get you into, healthy foods and stuff . . . how to keep it fresh for three days. . . . I mean those Farmer's Market checks . . . the $25. Everything there is just really cheap, like a $1.50, $2. And you get a lot so if you buy freezer bags and you come home and freeze stuff and you've just got to know how to save.

Barbara, age sixty-eight with very low food security, goes to her farmers market as often as she is able to do so.

> I do go to the farmers market where I can buy produce and most of it is $3 a bundle or like that there, but at least I can get some potatoes or better yet some greens or fresh vegetables to make a salad or I can cook a pot of greens, you know?

The difficulties in accessing food through the SFMNP that respondents described fall into two categories: transportation problems and administrative processes. Getting to a farmers market can be difficult, and getting home with the fresh produce and vegetables can be even more so. Martha, age sixty-four and food secure, would like to go to the farmers market more often, but the cost of transportation and her difficulties walking in the heat cause her to limit her visits.

> Once in a while they will—they had something posted where they were giving away farmer's market coupons. . . . And they gave away twenty of them and I went down for the appointment and I got them. But I can't go while it's hot out so I have to wait until September. . . . Well to walk to a cab, I can go out. But to go to the farmers market and walk down there—I have COPD and asthma and it's too humid. I can't breathe.

Scarlett, age sixty-seven with very low food security, loves the farmers market, but it is twenty miles from her house and very difficult for her to get there. Some markets are closer to her but only open during the hours while she is at work. For her, the annual administrative process to recertify her eligibility for the program is straightforward. She simply calls for an application form that she completes and mails in; in return, she receives a booklet of coupons. "During the summer I get vouchers for fresh vegetables or fruits at farmers market . . . $40 worth of coupons. . . . I went last Saturday. I got food. . . . I just wouldn't be able to get out there again to use them . . . about twenty miles."

However, other respondents described the eligibility and redemption process as more burdensome. Wren, age seventy with marginal food security, said that registering farmers market coupons in her town takes a significant amount of time and that many of the vendors do not accept the coupons.

> To get them you have to go down and sit and register and it takes hours, that's been my experience with it. . . . We have lots of farmers markets in the area, but most of them don't take these senior vouchers; if you go there, there's usually maybe about ten different vendors that are set up and only two of them take these vouchers.

Kate, age sixty-one with marginal food security, likes the farmers market coupons but her program gives each recipient only six coupons, so she goes to the market only six times per year.

I get the farmers market vouchers for the farmers market. You know for fresh fruit and vegetables. I don't know how many tickets there are; there's probably like six stubs I think, so you could go to the farmers market like six times I think. . . . If you wanted to go to six farmers markets or whatever, you have like six stubs.

CONCLUSION

Every year, the U.S. federal government disperses billions of dollars, which are joined by private donations and state and local government funds, to distribute food at the community level to people in need. In 2023, among older adults with household incomes below 185 percent of the federal poverty line, 7.7 percent received free meals and 18 percent received free groceries in the last twelve months. Participants must learn about, qualify for, and then figure out how to access benefits from a wide array of charitable and government community-based organizations that provide group meals, home-delivered meals, and food to be prepared at home. By describing their experiences with community-based food programs during COVID, our respondents shed light on food programs' ability to respond to a major social and economic upheaval. The programs are unevenly dispersed geographically. The strength of the local emergency food assistance system, as well as its ability to respond to major shocks in the system, varies dramatically depending on where one lives. The quality of the food and access to that food vary considerably. Although policymakers designed many of these programs to meet the food needs of older adults and to address the noneconomic barriers to food security that older adults face, many are still difficult to access for people with physical limitations, cognitive issues, or transportation problems. To be poor and at the mercy of local food programs when living in a resource-poor area is a difficult spot to be in. In chapter 6, we discuss ways to strengthen the emergency food assistance system.

CHAPTER 6

Policy Recommendations to Address Old Age Food Insecurity

As the number of older people at risk of food insecurity continues to rise, we must reexamine policy responses to food insecurity in the United States from the vantage point of low-income older people. Food insecurity is often part of a complex web of insecurities. In the face of chronic economic disadvantage, when older adults do not have enough money to cover all of their basic needs, our respondents revealed that they use the money that they would otherwise spend on food to pay for medical care, prescription drugs, housing, energy bills, transportation expenses, personal and cleaning supplies, and their phone and internet. Food insecurity in old age is often linked to nonfinancial factors as well, including physical health, stamina, and mobility, and mental and cognitive health issues, lack of access to healthy food, and transportation problems. By focusing exclusively on whether respondents have enough money for food, the current measure of food insecurity provides an incomplete description of the challenges older adults face in securing access to healthy and nutritious food.

The current policy response to old age food insecurity is complex, costly, and ultimately ineffective. SNAP and the entire web of community-based free and subsidized food programs are not designed well for older adults. Programs are difficult to access, and the benefits and food available are often insufficient in size and nutrition and not supportive of the health of older adults. Moreover, where one lives plays a significant role in shaping one's experience with SNAP, as well as the quantity and quality of community-based free and subsidized food programs available.

https://doi.org/10.7758/rzos2617.7130

In this chapter, we suggest specific policy solutions to the issues we identified. Our policy recommendations reflect the theoretical approaches that we presented in chapter 1 and embedded throughout the book. First, life course theory stresses how cumulative disadvantages throughout the life span leave older adults increasingly vulnerable to food insecurity as they age. To fully address older adult food insecurity, we propose a comprehensive approach to income support that begins before age sixty, so that people arrive at old age healthier and with more economic resources to meet their basic needs. In addition, social ecological theory stresses the importance of the local context—from the built environment, public transportation, and location of grocery stores to the quantity and quality of support available from community, local, and state agencies. While local variation may allow communities to take advantage of local resources and more fully address local needs, it also creates great gaps in the safety net, in which older adults with similar needs do not have access to similar levels of support. We recommend that the federal government take a greater role in providing older adults consistent access to support.

We have five main suggestions for measuring and responding to old age food insecurity: Policymakers should measure food security in multidimensional ways, treat food security as a health issue, combine SNAP benefits with other programs benefits, encourage state adoption of SNAP policies for older adults, and increase income supports for older adults. Our solutions are multifaceted because the problem of old age food insecurity is multifaceted.

RECOMMENDATION 1: MEASURE FOOD SECURITY IN MULTIDIMENSIONAL WAYS

Older adults face several barriers to accessing healthy and nutritious foods that support a healthy and active lifestyle. Measures of food security should do a better job of capturing the full range of these barriers. In the United States, the U.S. Department of Agriculture's Food Security Supplement formally defines food security by focusing on affordability as the main constraint to accessing healthy and nutritious food. While affordability poses the largest constraint to food insecurity in the United States, our research suggests that three additional dimensions, which are not included in the formal measure of food insecurity, limit older adults from being food secure—physical, nutritional, and transportation barriers to food security. By not measuring these barriers, policymakers and researchers undercount the number of older adults who struggle with food security. We believe that a holistic approach to understanding the problem of food security is essential to defining and evaluating future policy solutions.

In chapter 3, we described how common physical limitations among older adults, such as limitations in walking, standing, and cognitive issues, can interfere with the ability to access, prepare, and consume healthy and nutritious food. AnnieBelle Sassine and colleagues, including several U.S. Department of Agriculture researchers, created a six-item scale of physical food insecurity to capture older adults' inability to access food and prepare meals.[1] These items include having difficulty with indicators such as lifting or carrying something as heavy as ten pounds; doing chores around the house; preparing meals; eating, such as holding a fork, cutting food, or drinking from a glass; standing or being on feet for about two hours; and going out to do things like shopping. Whereas the standard U.S. Department of Agriculture measure focuses exclusively on whether respondents have enough money for food, this six-item scale emphasizes whether health and mobility interfere with food access. Researchers have also proposed a mixed measure that incorporates limitations in functional ability, social support, and economics resources.[2] We encourage the incorporation of issues related to cognitive decline into measures of physical food insecurity and the widespread screening for this issue among older adults.

Additionally, in chapter 3, we demonstrated how the food that older adults access is not always healthy and nutritious. This finding leads us to support the growing interest in nutrition security. According to U.S. Department of Agriculture, "Nutrition security means consistent access, availability, and affordability of food and beverages that promote well-being, prevent disease, and, if needed, treat disease, particularly among racial/ethnic minority, low-income, and rural and remote populations including Tribal communities and Insular areas."[3] Food insecurity connects to nutrition security in that while food security focuses on securing an adequate quantity of calories, nutrition security emphasizes the nutritional quality of those calories and the implications for disease reduction. Researchers are currently developing numerous measurement tools for assessing nutritional security, and we believe that their inclusion in measures of food security will highlight the importance of the quality of food that older adults consume.[4] We hope that the focus on nutritional security will lead to a stronger emphasis on the quality of food that is available throughout the community-based food system.

In chapter 3, we described the special challenges that lack of transportation and distance to food retailers can pose for older adults, particularly those with mobility limitations. Finally, in chapters 4 and 5 we documented the large geographic variation in access to food and nutrition assistance programs. Our findings are consistent with the growing recognition that a spatial dimension to food access constrains the ability to secure healthy and nutritious food. We provide the U.S. Department of Agriculture definition of a food desert in chapter 3, but policymakers and researchers increasingly recognize that access to food has multiple components. The U.S. Department of Agriculture has created an interactive tool, the Food Access Research Atlas, that allows users to examine three specific aspects of food access: accessibility to healthy food sources, using a measure of distance to food retailers or the number of food retailers within a spatial designation; individual-level resources, such as household income or vehicle availability; and neighborhood-level resources, such as average household income and the availability of public transportation.[5] Additional research efforts have focused on refining transportation measures by incorporating the ability to bike or walk to food retailers, incorporating different time and distance measures of food accessibility, and refining socioeconomic measures. Because the link between household-level food insecurity and food deserts remains low,[6] food insecurity and food deserts are not substitute terms. Researchers should view them as measuring different dimensions of the problem. Our research also suggests that the two issues are interactive and that policymakers therefore must consider physical food insecurity in the context of the food environment. Increased funding for home-delivered meals, increased access to food-delivery services, and medically tailored meals should be part of the solution to increase food access for older adults.

To be clear, the U.S. Department of Agriculture's food security measure, which focuses on the financial means to buy food, is an important and critical benchmark that policymakers and researchers should not abandon.[7] However, the singular focus on affordability as the only constraint to food security ignores many important dimensions of the social problem that are particularly problematic for older adults. We believe that improving the consistency of measurement of these other dimensions will aid in the development of policies that are focused on solving all dimensions of food insecurity and will ultimately lead to conditions that support access to healthy and nutritious food for older adults.

RECOMMENDATION 2: TREAT FOOD SECURITY AS A HEALTH ISSUE

Old age is often a time of growing health-care needs, including chronic conditions such as diabetes, hypertension, and obesity that are sensitive to nutritional intake. Given the growing recognition of the negative health consequences of food insecurity and the growing strength of interventions that recognize that food is medicine, clinicians should screen older adults regularly for food security. The Hunger Vital Sign, a two-item screening tool (see appendix table A.2), has been validated for clinical use among older adults.[8] The Veteran's Administration currently uses it, and the Center for Medicare and Medicaid Services includes it in its Accountable Health Communities Screening Tool.[9] In addition, private primary-care organizations are beginning to follow the practice and incorporating the Hunger Vital Sign into their screening of social determinants of health. Given our first recommendation that policymakers and researchers should assess food insecurity with multidimensional measures, screening protocols should also consider other factors beyond affordability barriers to food security. This approach is consistent with calls for greater consideration of the social determinants of health within the medical field.[10]

Disease management of many chronic conditions that are prevalent among older adults, such as diabetes, hypertension, and depression, requires consistent access to healthy food. Yet, clinicians can easily overlook the presence of food insecurity when they are not specifically screening for the condition. The main barrier to screening is that clinicians are often unclear about what they would do with the information.[11] Clinically, such information may be important to identifying appropriate disease-maintenance protocols, such as diabetes medication levels, as well as the ability of patients to take medicines with food and adhere to dietary treatment protocols.[12]

Additionally, too often the emergency food system addresses issues of industrial and commercial food waste and overproduction rather than proper nutrition. While redistributing edible food for consumption is better than throwing it in landfills, policymakers need to treat diet and nutrition as the critical pillar of health that it is and not rely on donated foods that are high in sodium and saturated fat to nourish economically vulnerable populations. We support the 2019 recommendations by the Government Accountability Office for increased research and guidelines on the nutritional needs of older adults. Given that health-care providers increasingly give referrals to home-delivered-meal programs and senior nutrition sites, and that evidence suggests that these meals do not meet all the dietary guidelines, we support these recommendations for increased oversight by the U.S. Department of Health and Human Services, the Administration of Community Living, and the U.S. Department of Agriculture to ensure that meals provided for older adults are consistent with the nutritional guidelines.[13]

More innovative health-care settings are going a step further and experimenting with nutritional interventions targeting specific patient populations. One such program is Prescription Produce, which provides vouchers that can be redeemed at local grocery stores for fresh fruits and vegetables to targeted groups such as those with diabetes or hypertension. Other health-care settings are experimenting with Medically Tailored Meals, which delivers fully cooked meals to targeted groups, such as those with congestive heart failure, dental problems, renal failure, or diabetes. In addition, food delivery services such as Instacart have developed the ability to partner with local or state health agencies that want to provide delivered food benefits that can be specifically tailored or prescribed in a Medically Tailored Grocery approach (such as protein supplements, fresh fruits and vegetables, or infant formula) without being tied to a specific food retailer. Even food pantries, such as the Northern Illinois Food Bank, are allowing participants to order food for pickup or delivery to address access barriers in the food pantry system.[14] Policymakers should combine innovation in this field with rigorous evaluation to ensure that programs meet the food security and health needs of demographically and geographically diverse patient populations. In addition, nutritionally targeted interventions, such as Prescription Produce, Medically Tailored Groceries and Medically Tailored Meals, must complement and not replace the food choice that SNAP provides.

Finally, health-care policy, including dental care, should more fully focus on supporting food security.[15] Dental problems that cause pain when eating are more common among older adults and among people on SNAP.[16] Medicare, the federal health insurance program offered to older adults, does not include dental coverage. Medicaid, the public health insurance program that is administered at the state level, offers dental coverage in forty-nine states, but only eight of those states provide a level of coverage that dental professionals categorize as extensive across all eight categories of dental services assessed.[17] When food security is treated as a health issue, dental health rises in importance.

RECOMMENDATION 3: ENCOURAGE STATE ADOPTION OF SNAP POLICIES TARGETED TO INCREASE BENEFITS AND PARTICIPATION AMONG OLDER ADULTS

Older adults in the United States participate in SNAP at levels that are 63 percent of those of the general population.[18] Recent work by Jordan Jones and colleagues suggests that existing SNAP policies aimed to reduce the administrative burden associated with applying for SNAP do not effectively increase SNAP participation among older adults.[19] This may be due to the reliance of modernized digital application systems on web-based interfaces for assistance instead of in-person aid, which older adults may prefer. However, Jones and colleagues did find that efforts to broaden eligibility are associated with a small increase in SNAP participation among older adults. More recent policy changes and research suggests new directions that policymakers should consider. Specifically, we suggest increasing the minimum SNAP benefit amount and indexing benefits to the local food costs, expanding the U.S. Department of Agriculture Restaurant Meals Program, improving access to home delivery, removing the requirement for states to offset costs when adopting a standard medication deduction, and expanding state participation in the Elderly Simplified Reporting Program.

Increase Minimum SNAP Benefit and Index to Local Food Costs

Many older people report that the minimum SNAP benefit amount of $23 per month is not worth the hassle of applying for benefits. Additionally, as we demonstrate, the hurdles to participation may be higher for older adults, given their declining physical and cognitive health as well as transportation and mobility problems. We also demonstrate how the benefits of SNAP participation may extend to higher levels of medication adherence and reduced health-care costs. Given the extent to which this individual and societal cost-benefit calculation differs for older adults, the SNAP benefit formula should differ too. In households that contain adults age sixty and older or those with disabilities, we support an increase in the minimum SNAP benefit from $23 per month (set to 8 percent of the maximum benefit size for a one-person household) to $146 per month, or 50 percent of the maximum benefit size for one-person households.

Additionally, research consistently indicates that SNAP benefits are too low to cover the cost of the Thrifty Food Plan. However, if policymakers indexed SNAP benefits to local food prices, they could redistribute the total benefits from low-cost areas to high-cost areas without an increase in total expenditures.[20] We recommend that the U.S. Department of Agriculture index SNAP benefits to local food prices to allow for purchasing parity across geographic areas.

Expand SNAP's Restaurant Meals Program

To address the needs of people who lack the physical and cognitive ability to cook meals for themselves or who lack access to a kitchen to store and prepare food, the U.S. Department of Agriculture provides states the option to participate in the Restaurant Meal Program (RMP). The RMP allows SNAP participants who are older, have disabilities, or are homeless to purchase prepared meals at restaurants using their EBT cards.

As of 2024, nine states had implemented RMP (Arizona, California, Illinois, Maryland, Massachusetts, Michigan, New York, Rhode Island, and Virginia). In each of the states, the program is being piloted in some counties, or only a few restaurants are authorized to participate, limiting the reach. In fiscal year 2023, 4,653 authorized firms provided private restaurant or meal-delivery services through the program, and spending on these services was 0.24 percent of overall SNAP redemption spending.[21] Given the barriers to cooking that older adults with significant health conditions often experience, the RMP addresses both the affordability and the access issues of food consumption, while supporting food choice. We support both evaluation efforts of the effectiveness of this program, and assuming it is found to be effective at supporting food security for older adults, the expansion of RMP to other states and retailers.

Expand SNAP's Online Purchasing Program

Before the COVID crisis, the U.S. Department of Agriculture rolled out the SNAP online purchasing pilot, which allows SNAP customers to use their EBT cards to purchase eligible groceries online for home delivery or store pickup. The original focus was to improve access to food among people who lived in food deserts and people unable to access a grocery store due to physical and mobility limitations or lack of transportation. During COVID, the program expanded to allow all SNAP participants to obtain groceries while maintaining social distancing requirements.

Today, the program is widely available in all fifty states (except for Alaska and Montana) and Washington, DC. Retailer participation varies by state and is often limited to primarily large retailers. By fiscal year 2023, nearly 12.5 million households had participated in the program.[22] All states should expand the program and include retailers such as Instacart that work with a large variety of food merchants in a single area, proving additional food shopping choice. In addition, the federal government should work to limit and subsidize any fees associated with home delivery from private services. Given the widespread use of online purchasing, older adult SNAP participants should have the ability to purchase food in the same manner as other shoppers. Early pilot programs suggest that home delivery can be an effective approach for saving money on transportation costs associated with accessing food, as well as for expanding receipt of charitable food.[23]

Eliminate the SNAP Offset Requirement for the Standard Medical Deduction (SMD)

To increase SNAP participation among older adults and those with disabilities, twenty-five states have adopted the SMD, which allows applicants to receive a state-specific deduction for medical expenses if they show that they spent a minimal amount ($35).[24] This reduces the cognitive and administrative burden of demonstrating income eligibility and can increase both participation and benefit size.

However, the U.S. Department of Agriculture requires states that decide to adopt the SMD to offset its costs elsewhere, essentially requiring them to reduce SNAP benefits for other populations. Using national data from 2004 to 2019, Jun Li and colleagues find that adoption of the SMD was associated with increased SNAP participation among SMD-eligible households, both in terms of aggregate household counts (20 percent) and as a share of households receiving SNAP (5 percentage points).[25] However, while estimated annual SNAP benefits per state increased for SMD-eligible households, they decreased (although reductions were not statistically significant) for non–SMD eligible households. This suggests that the requirement to offset SNAP costs may have benefited households with older adults and households with people with disabilities at the expense of others. To encourage state adoption of the SMD, the U.S. Department of Agriculture should eliminate the requirements for cost offsets.

Expand SNAP's Elderly Simplified Reporting Program

The U.S. Department of Agriculture allowed states to pilot a series of SNAP policies specifically aimed to improve uptake in households with members who are older or have disabilities, such as lengthening the recertification period to thirty-six months, eliminating the initial and recertification interviews, adopting the SMD, and providing a simplified application that is only two pages in length. Early evaluation results of the Elderly Simplified Reporting Program do not find strong evidence that these efforts increased SNAP uptake. However, results also suggest that the initial certification interview is an important opportunity to educate older adults about the application process, eligibility regarding potential deductions, and expectations for recertification periods. States also found that even though they waived recertification interviews, many older adults still contacted the agency with questions, underscoring that administrative processes that may be burdensome for some populations may be helpful to others.[26]

The U.S. Department of Agriculture now provides guidance for states regarding how to apply for the Elderly Simplified Reporting Program waivers, as well as a variety of other practices that can be put into place to make signing up for SNAP easier for older adults. We encourage all states to apply for the Elderly Simplified Reporting Program waiver.

Finally, we encourage the federal government to approve new state waivers aimed to increase older adult SNAP uptake with appropriate evaluation. Given the barriers that we identified in chapter 4, we believe that further innovation is necessary to make SNAP more easily accessible, more valuable, and easier to use for older adults.

RECOMMENDATION 4: CONNECT FOOD ASSISTANCE PROGRAMS WITH OTHER SOCIAL WELFARE PROGRAMS

Dealing with the administrative burden associated with participating in multiple social welfare programs is more difficult for older adults to manage because of physical limitations, transportation problems, cognitive decline, and low computer literacy and access. However, recent estimates by researchers at the Urban Institute predict that if all eligible adults age sixty-five and older received SNAP and SSI, then the supplemental poverty rate would fall from 15.7 to 13.9 percent.[27] The government knows how to make programs more user friendly. Recall that the Social Security program has an uptake rate of

97 percent.[28] But many social welfare programs are not designed for maximum uptake. The uptake rate for Medicaid is only 50 percent;[29] the uptake rate for SNAP is 55 percent for older adults;[30] the success rate for SSDI applications is 21 percent initially and 31 percent after appeals;[31] the success rate for SSI disability applications is 33 percent after appeals;[32] the wait for housing-choice vouchers averages two and a half years;[33] and only 20 percent of people eligible for the Low-Income Heating and Energy Assistance Program receive benefits.[34]

To increase program uptake, policymakers should bundle application processes for food assistance with other social welfare programs. In partnership with the Social Security Administration, the U.S. Department of Agriculture offers CAP, which allows SSI recipients to simultaneously enroll in SNAP in participating states. CAP was designed to reduce barriers to SNAP because SSI benefits are so modest that SSI recipients who do not receive SNAP are often at risk of food insecurity.[35] Current program guidelines are already aligned so that SSI recipients are categorically eligible for SNAP. Since 1997, federal law has required that applicants for SSI be given the opportunity to file a SNAP application at the Social Security Administration office when applying for SSI. However, in the U.S. Department of Agriculture's own words, this "has not always worked as seamlessly as originally intended."[36]

As of 2022, the latest year for which national data is available, seventeen states have implemented one of the two versions of CAP.[37] The Urban Institute case study of the program finds that from 2000 to 2008, CAP states experienced a 48 percent increase in SNAP participation levels among one-person SSI households, while other states saw little change.[38] While significant issues still exist with the implementation of CAP, including limited eligibility and low benefit levels, recent research supports the finding that CAP increases uptake among eligible older adults.[39] Importantly, recent policy changes address the issue from the other side by making it easier for SNAP recipients to qualify for SSI.[40]

Our qualitative data suggests that lack of transportation is a significant barrier to accessing SNAP, senior center services, farmers markets, food pantries, and soup kitchens, as well as getting to the grocery store. Future research needs to provide evidence about the scope and nature of the problem in different communities and populations, as well as to pilot different approaches to addressing the problem. We encourage innovation in this area to address transportation issues around food access for older adults at the individual, neighborhood, and community levels.

Furthermore, policymakers should extend the models of combining applications with SNAP and other programs. For example, have SNAP send out simplified applications to households that are known to be eligible for other programs that low-income older people are likely to rely on such as housing subsidies, home-delivered meals, congregate meals, Medicaid, LIHEAP, transportation assistance, and low-income phone and internet service. Simplifying and aligning eligibility and documentation requirements and sharing across programs would make participation in multiple programs much easier for older adults who are more likely to experience cognitive decline and mobility and transportation difficulty getting to agencies, as well as who lack comfort with and access to modernized online application systems. Connecting these programs more readily to each other and to eligible beneficiaries could reduce food insecurity across the life course. Change is very possible in this area: program bundling is one of the policy innovations identified in the Biden-Harris Administration's National Strategy on Hunger, Nutrition and Health so that individuals who participate in one program receive the benefits from all programs for which they are eligible.

RECOMMENDATION 5: INCREASE INCOME SUPPORT FOR OLDER ADULTS

As we saw in chapter 2, retirement insecurity is related to food insecurity among older adults. Older adults would not require the complicated web of current social welfare programs if they had enough money to live comfortably. Our respondents told us that given insufficient economic resources to cover their essential needs, particularly housing and utilities, they may view food as the lowest priority. They can live without a meal but not without a roof over their heads. A long line of research debates the utility of providing food assistance in the current form, that is, as food vouchers that recipients can use only to purchase food, versus providing cash that they can use to cover competing needs. Pilot studies conducted in the late 1980s and early 1990s indicated that converting food stamp benefits to cash reduced food spending by 5 to 20 percent, as recipients used the money to cover other essential needs.[41] In fiscal year 2022, however, the average benefit level for older adult SNAP households was $158 per month, and 18.7 percent received the minimum SNAP benefit level of $20.[42] As a result, they need other economic resources to secure access to healthy and nutritious food. Until SNAP and community-based sources of emergency food are generous enough to meet the nutritional needs of older adults, providing cash payments to older people would be an effective approach to addressing food insecurity. While it would be easiest to do so through a single program, the social safety net is a complex patchwork of programs. We therefore offer suggestions for the array of programs that touch low-income older adults.

Work-based strategies to address low levels of household income are not politically feasible or, in many cases, physically possible at older ages. For a short time during the COVID pandemic, the federal government provided cash payments directly to most adults, regardless of age, to stimulate the economy, as well as expanded the Child Tax Credit. Additionally, states had the option to award SNAP recipients the maximum benefit for their household size from March 2020 to February 2023. Researchers credit these policy changes with keeping the national food insufficiency rate consistent from 2019 to 2021.[43] Affirming these national statistics, many of our respondents described being more food secure during COVID than they had been before the pandemic.

Increase Social Security Benefits for Low-Income Recipients

Sources of income support, such as Social Security receipt and increases in benefits, are linked to reduced food insecurity among older adults.[44] Changing the benefit formula to increase benefits for low-income households and reducing the penalty for early retirement due to disability would help address food insecurity and reduce the size of the problem in the future. Given that the Social Security trust fund reserve is expected to be depleted by 2033, most policymakers aim to cut benefits and delay benefit eligibility.[45] However, some scholars propose a targeted minimum benefit that would increase Social Security benefits among low-income beneficiaries and reduce poverty, and as a result food insecurity, in old age.[46]

Increase the Maximum SSI Benefit and Index Asset Limits to Inflation

SSI, the means-tested program that provides cash payments to low-income older adults, should be increased from the current maximum value of $943 per month for a single eligible person and $1,415 for a couple. Additionally, asset limits for SSI have remained the same since 1989 and not adjusted for inflation—currently, individuals with assets over $2,000, and couples with assets over $3000, do not qualify for the program.[47] Asset limits for SSI should be reset at $9,000 for individuals and $13,500 for couples, indexed to inflation, and allowed to grow with the standard of living.[48]

Simplify Access to SSDI Benefits

Given the evidence that cumulative disadvantage leads to food insecurity among older adults, the application process for SSDI should be easier and faster, and it should provide more income support to adults with disabilities so that they have more resources as they enter old age. Low-income older adults with physical or mental disabilities who are unable to obtain SSDI benefits need a source of support to tide them over until they are eligible for Social Security benefits. The program does not approve nearly 80 percent of initial claims, and on average, it does not approve 67 percent of appealed claims.[49]

Consider Additional Program Expansions

Other important programs include federal housing subsidies and LIHEAP. Even though older adults are included in their target group, these programs lack sufficient funding to meet the needs of all who qualify, and as a result, waiting lists may be long. U.S. Housing and Urban Development data shows that 49 percent of people waiting for housing-choice vouchers wait two or more years.[50] The Department of Health and Human Services warns applicants that qualifying for LIHEAP does not mean they will receive benefits.[51] Only 20 percent of those who qualify receive benefits, and once money allocated for the year runs out, so do benefits. Our interviews clearly demonstrate that many food insecure older adults struggle to cover the cost of housing and energy bills. More generous policies in these areas would free up resources that could be spent on food. Finally, new evidence suggests that mortgage borrowing, an underutilized option that is only available to people who own their own homes, is also associated with lower food insecurity, and deserves greater inclusion in future discussions.[52]

In 2021, food insecurity increased for older adults while it decreased for households with children and remained the same for most other demographic groups.[53] That year, most households with children temporarily received the Child Tax Credit, a one-year program that subsidized their incomes. Analysis suggests that food insecurity decreased among these households as a result.[54] We have every reason to believe that increasing income support for older adults would also reduce food insecurity for this age group.

CONCLUSIONS

Making sure low-income older adults have access to healthy and nutritious food will yield many rewards, including improved physical, mental, and cognitive well-being; improved social integration and declines in loneliness and isolation; decreased health-care costs linked to better diet and medical compliance; and better options for living longer in the community and delaying the transition to residential care. Unfortunately, no single program is likely to address all the barriers that older adults face across the country. As a result, the United States needs a multipronged, comprehensive set of policies.

How likely is it that public policy will adapt and change to support older people in the United States? We need only look at the federal response to COVID to recognize that our governmental institutions have the ability to move quickly and effectively to face national challenges. The federal government dispersed cash payments to most U.S. households, suspended the need for administrative procedures that slowed down processing of social programs, and increased the size of SNAP benefits when faced with a national public health crisis. The Biden-Harris administration released a National Strategy on Hunger, Nutrition and Health in September 2022, with a call to end hunger (or very low food security) in the country by 2030.[55] As we go to press, it is also too soon to know the extent of the actions the Trump administration will take and their consequences for older-adult food insecurity. However, we continue to believe that change is possible.

The United States sits on the edge of a precipice with regard to older adult food insecurity. Without substantial change in the way that policymakers and researchers conceptualize food insecurity, an increase in the surveillance of food insecurity within the health-care sector, and substantial policy changes to address the needs of older adults, stories like Alex from the introduction to this book are going to become increasingly familiar. Publicly funded health-care costs will continue to skyrocket as the health consequences of a lack of access to affordable and nutritious food exacerbates the cost of treatment of chronic health conditions such as diabetes, heart disease, and cognitive decline. The ability for older adults to live independently within the community will be diminished if we, as a society, do not figure out how to make it easier for older adults to access nutritious foods in their homes. While the challenges that we have outlined are daunting, we believe that change is not only possible but the only way forward.

APPENDIX

APPENDIX A: FOOD PROGRAMS AND FOOD INSECURITY MEASURES

Figure A.1   State Food Insecurity for Adults Sixty and Older, 2023

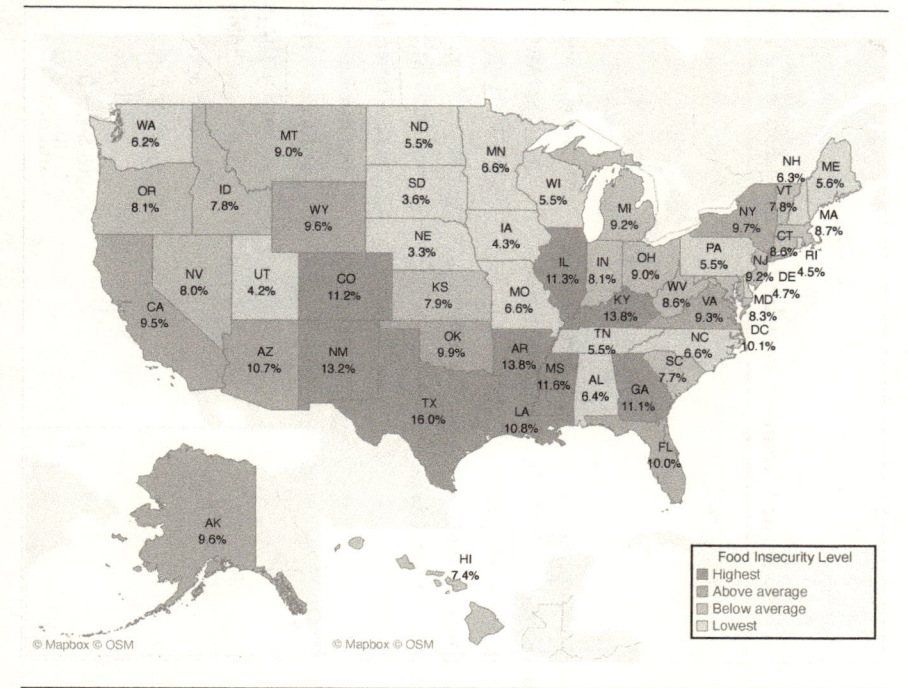

Source: Authors' calculations based on 2023 Current Population Survey (U.S. Census Bureau 2024).

https://doi.org/10.7758/rzos2617.8680

Table A.1   Major Food Programs Available to Older Adults in the United States

What Is the Program?	Who Pays for It?	Who Is Eligible?	Where Is It Available?	How Big Is the Program? (Fiscal year 2024 unless otherwise specified)
Supplemental Nutrition Assistance Program (SNAP): EBT card that works as a monthly voucher for food purchased to be cooked and eaten at home.	U.S. Department of Agriculture, Food and Nutrition Service.	People of all ages can access SNAP.[a] Special eligibility requirements for people age sixty and older whose net income (after shelter and medical deductions) is less than or equal to the poverty line. Households with an adult age sixty or older or a person with a disability can have up to $4,500 in assets and still qualify.[b]	Universally available throughout the country. State agencies administer the program, varying policies and application assistance exist.	41.7 million participants.[c]

Group Meal Programs

Congregate Meals (Congregate Nutrition Program): Meals available to be eaten on-site at senior centers, churches, schools, and other nonprofit organizations, with the intent of fostering community engagement.	U.S. Department of Health and Human Services, Administration on Aging; private donations and fees.	Available to people age sixty or older who are in social and economic need; specific eligibility requirements vary by state and local entities.[d]	Available in all U.S. states, American Samoa, the District of Columbia, Guam, the Northern Mariana Islands, Puerto Rico, and the U.S. Virgin Islands.	50.3 million meals served (expected for FY2024).[e]
Soup Kitchens: Prepared food available to be eaten on-site at little to no cost.	Public and private donations.	People of all ages may participate. Eligibility criteria varies (low barrier, typically no income or means test).[f]	Availability varies.	An estimated 864,000 people utilized soup kitchens in 2021.[g]

(Table continues on p. 186.)

Table A.1 (continued)

What Is the Program?	Who Pays for It?	Who Is Eligible?	Where Is It Available?	How Big Is the Program? (Fiscal year 2024 unless otherwise specified)
Child and Adult Care Food Program: Reimbursements for nutritious food items for eligible children and adults enrolled at participating care centers such as day cares and adult day care centers to promote healthy child and adult development.	U.S. Department of Agriculture, Food and Nutrition Service.	Children who are enrolled in an eligible care center or home, or adults older than sixty with a disability enrolled in a care center. Income-based test used to determine eligibility for free or reduced meals.[h]	Available in all U.S. states, the District of Columbia, Guam, the Northern Mariana Islands, Puerto Rico, and the U.S. Virgin Islands.	1.7 billion meals served.[i]
Delivered Meal Programs				
Home-Delivered Meals: Prepared meals delivered to individual homes of adults age sixty and older who are physically compromised, live alone, or cannot leave home. Fosters social interaction and promotes a healthy diet.[j]	U.S. Department of Health and Human Services, Administration on Aging; private donations and fees.	Available to low-income people age sixty and older; no income limit or means test.[k]	Available in all U.S. states, American Samoa, the District of Columbia, Guam, the Northern Mariana Islands, Puerto Rico, and the U.S. Virgin Islands.	211.9 million meals served (expected for FY2024).[l]

Food for Home Preparation and Consumption

Food Pantries: Food items available to be prepared at home.	Public and private donations, USDA funding.[m]	All ages may participate. Eligibility criteria varies (typically low-barrier).[n]	Availability varies.	An estimated 19.3 million people utilized food pantries in 2021.[o]
Senior's Farmers Market Nutrition Food Program: Coupons are exchanged for eligible foods at participating farmers markets, fruit stands, and community-supported agriculture programs.	U.S. Department of Agriculture, Food and Nutrition Service.	Program is available to people age sixty and older with incomes no higher than 185 percent of the federal poverty line.[p]	Available in 46 states, the District of Columbia, Puerto Rico, the U.S. Virgin Islands, and Indian Tribal Organizations.[q]	757,751 participants (FY2022).[r]
Commodity Supplemental Food Program: Monthly package of shelf stable foods, such as juice, peanut butter, oats, rice, pasta, dry beans, canned meat, fish, fruit, and vegetables.	U.S. Department of Agriculture, Food and Nutrition Service.	Limited to people age sixty and older with incomes at or below 150 percent of the federal poverty line; state eligibility requirements may vary by, for example, local residency or determination of nutritional risk.[s]	Available in all states, the District of Columbia, Puerto Rico, and Indian Tribal Organizations.	716,027 participants.[t]

(Table continues on p. 188.)

Table A.1 (continued)

What Is the Program?	Who Pays for It?	Who Is Eligible?	Where Is It Available?	How Big Is the Program? (Fiscal year 2024 unless otherwise specified)
Special Supplemental Nutrition Program for Women, Infants and Children (WIC): EBT card that works as a monthly voucher for targeted food purchased to be cooked and eaten at home; healthy eating education and healthcare referrals.	U.S. Department of Agriculture, Food and Nutrition Service.	Women who are pregnant, breastfeeding, or postpartum (up to six months), infants (up to age one) and children (up to age five) who are determined to be at nutritional risk. Limited to those who meet the income eligibility standards determined by state agencies and the residential requirement.[u]	Universally available across the country. State agencies administer the program.[v]	6.7 million participants.[w]

Source: Authors' compilation.

[a] To receive SNAP without a waiting period, eligible participants must be a U.S. citizen, or a noncitizen who meets the specific USDA criteria for eligibility (U.S. Department of Agriculture 2013a).

[b] U.S. Department of Agriculture 2024f.
[c] U.S. Department of Agriculture 2025c.
[d] There are no citizenship requirements for eligibility (Administration for Community Living 2023b).
[e] Administration for Community Living 2024.
[f] Immigrant eligibility varies.
[g] Congressional Research Service 2023.
[h] There are no citizenship requirements for eligibility (U.S. Department of Agriculture 2025c).
[i] U.S. Department of Agriculture 2023a, 2025c.
[j] Administration for Community Living 2023b.
[k] There are no citizenship requirements for eligibility (Administration for Community Living 2023b).
[l] Administration for Community Living 2024.
[m] U.S. Department of Agriculture 2024g.
[n] Immigrant eligibility varies.
[o] Congressional Research Service 2023.
[p] There are no citizenship requirements for eligibility (U.S. Department of Agriculture 2023e).
[q] U.S. Department of Agriculture 2023e.
[r] U.S. Department of Agriculture 2023f.
[s] There are no citizenship requirements for eligibility (U.S. Department of Agriculture 2019).
[t] U.S. Department of Agriculture 2025c.
[u] Immigrant eligibility can vary by states. (U.S. Department of Agriculture 2023h, 2024i).
[v] U.S. Department of Agriculture 2022a.
[w] U.S. Department of Agriculture 2025c.

Table A.2   Various Measures of Food Hardship

Survey	Measure of Food Hardship Used
Current Population Survey	Eighteen-item U.S. Department of Agriculture Food Security Measure
Household PULSE Survey	Single-item food insufficiency measure indicating if households sometimes or often did not have enough to eat
Health and Retirement Study	Single-item report if respondent household has not always had enough money to buy the food it needed over the past two years
2018 Survey of Income and Program Participation	Six-item scale adapted from eighteen-item U.S. Department of Agriculture Food Security Measure
Hunger Vital Sign	Two-item scale: (1) Within the past twelve months, we worried whether our food would run out before we got money to buy more. (2) Within the past twelve months, the food we bought just didn't last and we didn't have money to get more.

Source: U.S. Department of Agriculture 2024b.

Eighteen-Item U.S. Department of Agriculture Food Security Measure

The following questionnaire is used by the U.S. Department of Agriculture to measure respondents' levels of food insecurity.[1]

1. "We worried whether our food would run out before we got money to buy more." Was that often, sometimes, or never true for you in the last 12 months?
2. "The food that we bought just didn't last and we didn't have money to get more." Was that often, sometimes, or never true for you in the last 12 months?
3. "We couldn't afford to eat balanced meals." Was that often, sometimes, or never true for you in the last 12 months?

4. In the last 12 months, did you or other adults in the household ever cut the size of your meals or skip meals because there wasn't enough money for food? (Yes/No)
5. (If yes to question 4) How often did this happen—almost every month, some months but not every month, or in only 1 or 2 months?
6. In the last 12 months, did you ever eat less than you felt you should because there wasn't enough money for food? (Yes/No)
7. In the last 12 months, were you ever hungry, but didn't eat, because there wasn't enough money for food? (Yes/No)
8. In the last 12 months, did you lose weight because there wasn't enough money for food? (Yes/No)
9. In the last 12 months did you or other adults in your household ever not eat for a whole day because there wasn't enough money for food? (Yes/No)
10. (If yes to question 9) How often did this happen—almost every month, some months but not every month, or in only 1 or 2 months?

Questions 11 through 18 were asked only to households with children age 0 through 17.

11. "We relied on only a few kinds of low-cost food to feed our children because we were running out of money to buy food." Was that often, sometimes, or never true for you in the last 12 months?
12. "We couldn't feed our children a balanced meal, because we couldn't afford that." Was that often, sometimes, or never true for you in the last 12 months?
13. "The children were not eating enough because we just couldn't afford enough food." Was that often, sometimes, or never true for you in the last 12 months?
14. In the last 12 months, did you ever cut the size of any of the children's meals because there wasn't enough money for food? (Yes/No)
15. In the last 12 months, were the children ever hungry but you just couldn't afford more food? (Yes/No)
16. In the last 12 months, did any of the children ever skip a meal because there wasn't enough money for food? (Yes/No)
17. (If yes to question 16) How often did this happen—almost every month, some months but not every month, or in only 1 or 2 months?
18. In the last 12 months did any of the children ever not eat for a whole day because there wasn't enough money for food? (Yes/No)

APPENDIX B: QUALITATIVE SAMPLE

Table B.1 Qualitative Sample Characteristics

	N = 63	%
Gender		
Male	15	24
Female	48	76
Race		
White	28	44
Black	32	51
Hispanic	2	3
Native American	1	2
Other/Mixed	5	8
Education Level		
Less than high school	10	15
High school	13	21
Some college	25	40
Bachelor's degree	12	18
More than bachelor's degree	3	5
Marital Status		
Single	17	27
Married	8	12
Divorced	26	41
Separated	3	5
Widowed	9	14
Rent or Own		
Rent	50	79
Own	13	21
Living Area		
Rural	16	25
Suburban	15	24
Urban	32	51
Residential Grandchildren		
Yes	3	5
No	60	9

Table B.1 (continued)

	$N = 63$	%
Person in Household with Disability		
Yes	44	70
No	19	30
Military Service		
Yes	2	3
No	61	97
Receiving Social Security		
Yes	50	79
No	13	21
Receiving SSI		
Yes	17	27
No	46	73
Receiving SSDI		
Yes	18	29
No	45	71
Receiving Medicare		
Yes	54	86
No	9	14
Receiving Medicaid		
Yes	38	60
No	24	38
DK	1	2
Receiving Veteran's Benefits		
Yes	1	2
No	62	98
Food Security Scale		
0	20	32
1–2	12	19
3–5	17	27
6+	14	22

(Table continues on p. 194.)

Table B.1   (continued)

	$N = 63$	%
Budget Tradeoff Scale		
0	21	33
1–2	16	25
3–5	23	37
6+	3	5
Budget Shortfall Scale		
0	20	32
1–2	23	37
3–5	16	25
6+	4	6
Receiving SNAP		
Yes	49	78
No	14	22
Dines at Congregate Dining Sites		
Yes	21	33
No	42	67
Receives Home-Delivered Meals		
Yes	14	22
No	49	78
Visits Food Pantry		
Yes	50	79
No	13	21
Visits Soup Kitchen		
Yes	8	13
No	55	87
Receives Farmers Market Voucher		
Yes	10	16
No	53	87
Owns a Car		
Yes	42	67
No	21	33

Table B.1   (continued)

	N = 63	%
Self-Rated Physical Health		
Excellent	5	8
Good	25	40
Fair	25	40
Poor	8	12
Self-Rated Mental Health		
Excellent	6	9
Good	38	59
Fair	16	27
Poor	3	5
Subsidized Housing		
Yes	27	43
No	36	57
Household Size		
1	50	79
2	8	13
3	1	1
4	4	6
Location (State/Region) (Census 2021 Regions)		
Northeast	16	25
South	16	25
Midwest	20	32
West	11	17

Source: Authors' tabulation from phone survey of food insecurity conducted between March 2021 and November 2021; sample selection limited to adults age sixty and older with household incomes less than 130 percent of the federal poverty line.

Note: **Northeast:** Connecticut, Maine, Massachusetts, New Hampshire, Rhode Island, Vermont, New Jersey, New York, Pennsylvania. **South:** Delaware, District of Columbia, Florida, Georgia, Maryland, North Carolina, South Carolina, Virginia, West Virginia, Alabama, Kentucky, Mississippi, Tennessee, Arizona, Louisiana, Oklahoma, Texas. **Midwest:** Illinois, Indiana, Michigan, Ohio, Wisconsin, Iowa, Kansas, Minnesota, Missouri, Nebraska, North Dakota, South Dakota. **West:** Arizona, Colorado, Idaho, Montana, Nevada, New Mexico, Utah, Wyoming, Arkansas, California, Hawaii, Oregon, Washington.

Figure B.1   Qualitative Sample Characteristics Compared with Nationally Representative Poor and Food Insecure Adults Age Sixty and Older

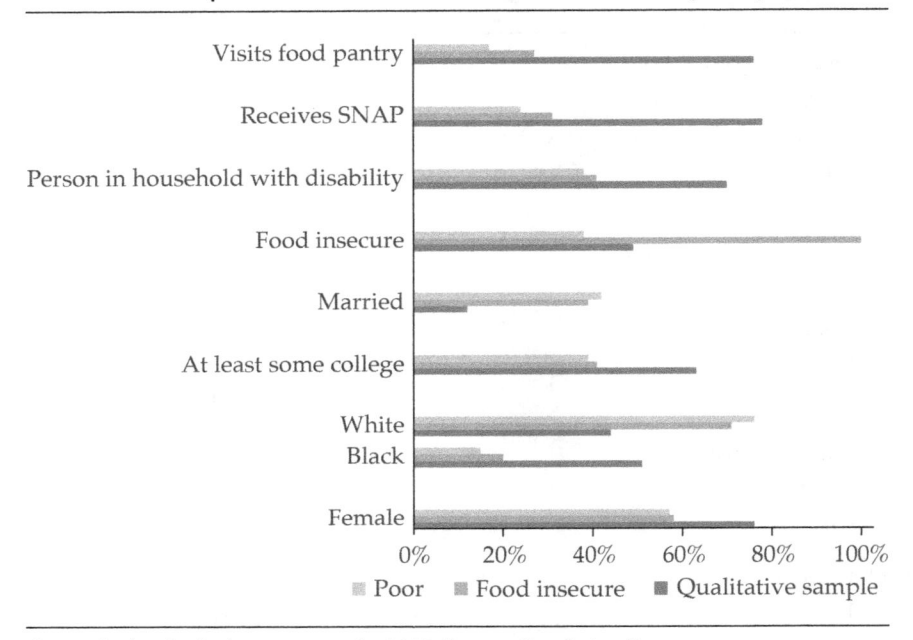

Visits food pantry
Receives SNAP
Person in household with disability
Food insecure
Married
At least some college
White
Black
Female

■ Poor ■ Food insecure ■ Qualitative sample

Source: Authors' calculations using the 2022 Current Population Survey.

Table B.2 Individual Characteristics

Alias	Gender	Race/Ethnicity	Education	Marital Status	FSS Scale	Budget Scale	Bills Scale	SNAP	Home-Delivered Meals	Food Pantry	Soup Kitchen	Farmers Market Vouchers	Congregate Meals
Alice	F	Mixed	MA	NM	4	2	0	19	No	Yes	No	No	Yes
Barbara	F	Black	BA	NM	10	6	6	30	Yes	Yes	No	Yes	Yes
Carl	M	Black	<BA	NM	0	0	2	DK	No	Yes	No	No	Yes
Deb	F	Mixed	BA	NM	0	0	0	DK	Yes	Yes	No	Yes	Yes
Alex	M	White	HS	M	3	3	4	NA	No	Yes	No	No	No
Beth	F	Hispanic	HS	NM	3	0	0	232	No	No	No	No	No
Carmen	F	Other	<HS	NM	4	3	1	234	No	No	No	No	Yes
Diane	F	Black	HS	NM	0	0	2	152	No	No	No	No	No
Alana	F	Black	<BA	NM	0	0	1	NA	No	Yes	No	No	No
Betty	F	Black	HS	NM	2	2	1	16	Yes	Yes	No	No	Yes
Bobby	M	Mixed	<BA	NM	1	1	4	190	No	Yes	No	No	Yes
Anna	F	White	BA	NM	3	3	2	234	Yes	No	No	No	Yes
Clara	F	Black	<HS	NM	2	0	0	114	No	Yes	No	No	Yes
Francis	F	Black	BA	NM	5	2	3	81	No	Yes	No	No	No
Ginny	F	White	<BA	NM	7	4	4	27	Yes	Yes	No	No	No
Harriet	F	White	<BA	NM	2	3	1	259	No	No	No	No	No

(Table continues on p. 198.)

Table B.2 (continued)

Alias	Gender	Race/Ethnicity	Education	Marital Status	FSS Scale	Budget Scale	Bills Scale	SNAP	Home-Delivered Meals	Food Pantry	Soup Kitchen	Farmers Market Vouchers	Congregate Meals
Ingrid	F	White	HS	NM	4	3	3	NA	No	Yes	No	No	No
Julie	F	White	HS	NM	7/18	3	0	66	No	Yes	No	No	No
Jeane	F	Black	HS	NM	0	0	0	235	No	No	No	No	No
Meredith	F	White	<BA	NM	6	5	6	NA	No	Yes	No	No	No
Helen	F	Black	<BA	NM	1	5	4	16	Yes	Yes	Yes	No	Yes
Kristi	F	Black	<HS	NM	4	4	6	DK	No	Yes	No	No	No
Liza	F	Black	<HS	NM	3	1	2	180	No	Yes	No	No	No
Lucy	F	Black	<BA	M	1	0	1	193	Yes	Yes	No	No	No
Kira	F	White	>BA	NM	0	1	0	135	No	Yes	Yes	Yes	Yes
Martha	F	White	BA	NM	0	1	1	200	Yes	Yes	No	Yes	No
Maggie	F	Black	HS	M	3	0	0	19	No	Yes	No	No	Yes
Nate	M	Black	<BA	NM	0	1	1	NA	Yes	Yes	No	No	Yes
Nancy	F	Black	<HS	NM	8	1	1	186	Yes	Yes	No	No	No
Pepper	F	Black	BA	NM	0	0	0	55	No	Yes	No	No	No
Valerie	F	White	<BA	NM	0	0	0	194	No	Yes	No	No	No
Willow	F	White	HS	NM	5	3	1	200	No	Yes	No	No	No
Patty	F	White	MA	NM	4	4	2	200	No	Yes	No	No	Yes

Rose	F	Black	<HS	NM	0	0	1	200	No	No	No	No	No
Queenie	F	Black	<BA	NM	3	4	1	234	No	Yes	No	No	No
Yolanda	F	Black	<BA	NM	0	1	4	DK	No	No	No	No	No
Russell	M	Black	<HS	NM	0	0	0	194	No	Yes	No	No	No
Zachariah	M	Black	<BA	NM	0	0	0	234	Yes	Yes	No	No	Yes
Violet	F	White	BA	M	5	5	0	NA	No	Yes	No	No	Yes
Scarlett	F	White	<BA	NM	9	3	4	NA	No	Yes	Yes	Yes	Yes
Tamarah	F	Other	BA	NM	1	2	1	125	Yes	Yes	No	No	No
Wren	F	White	BA	NM	1	1	2	NA	No	No	No	Yes	No
Theo	M	Black	<HS	M	10/1013/18	3	2	16	No	Yes	Yes	No	No
Wallace	M	Black	<HS	NM	8	5	8	214	No	Yes	No	No	No
Ruth	F	White	<BA	NM	10	6	2	NA	No	No	Yes	No	No
Victor	M	White	<BA	NM	0	0	0	125	No	Yes	No	No	No
Tilly	F	White	<BA	M	0/18	0	0	NA	No	Yes	No	No	No
Susan	F	White	<BA	NM	0	1	0	16	Yes	Yes	No	No	No
Turner	M	White	BA	M	5	0	3	250	No	Yes	Yes	No	No
Kenneth	M	Mixed	<BA	NM	6	5	5	210	No	Yes	No	No	No
Lionel	M	Mixed	<BA	NM	8	3	5	NA	Yes	Yes	Yes	No	Yes
Kate	F	Mixed	<BA	NM	1	1	0	234	No	Yes	No	Yes	No
Lena	F	Black	<BA	NM	4	6	4	NA	No	Yes	Yes	No	No

(Table continues on p. 200.)

Table B.2 (continued)

Alias	Gender	Race/Ethnicity	Education	Marital Status	FSS Scale	Budget Scale	Bills Scale	SNAP	Home-Delivered Meals	Food Pantry	Soup Kitchen	Farmers Market Vouchers	Congregate Meals
Nick	M	White	BA	NM	1	1	0	NA	No	Yes	No	No	No
Marie	F	Black	<BA	NM	0	0	3	200	No	Yes	Yes	No	No
Kasha	F	Black	<HS	NM	3	3	2	184	No	Yes	No	No	Yes
Gerald	M	Black	GED	NM	6	4	3	16	No	Yes	Yes	No	Yes
Vera	F	White	<BA	NM	2	1	2	NA	No	Yes	No	No	No
Ophelia	F	Black	BA	NM	7/18	3	2	234	No	Yes	No	Yes	Yes
Ezra	M	White	<BA	NM	0	0	0	NA	No	Yes	No	No	No
Edith	F	White	<BA	NM	10/10 11/18	5	3	253	No	Yes	No	Yes	No
Faye	F	White	HS	M	2	0	4	431	No	Yes	No	No	No
Holly	F	Black	<BA	NM	0	0	0	NA	No	No	No	No	No

Source: Authors' tabulation.

Note: M = married; NM = not married.

Qualitative Methods

Much of the analysis in this book is based on secondary analysis of quantitative data. The remainder is based on qualitative data from in-depth interviews. We collected data about our national, nonrepresentative sample of sixty-three adults age sixty and older who were below 130 percent of the federal poverty line by phone between July 2021 and November 2021. Our mixed-methods approach uses transcripts from our in-depth interviews to supplement the quantitative data.[2] We use qualitative data to address questions that previous research has only partially answered, such as why food insecurity rates drop with age even as many of the predictors of food insecurity rise; and why uptake of SNAP is so low among eligible older adults. Chapter 1 describes several ways research might undercount food insecurity in old age, and chapter 4 explains several reasons for low SNAP use among older adults.

As Mario Luis Small and Jessica McCrory Calarco note, we can assess good qualitative work based on the five principles of cognitive empathy, heterogeneity, palpability, follow-up, and self-awareness.[3] We worked hard to adhere to these principles as we developed the interview guide, conducted the interviews, analyzed the transcripts, and wrote the manuscript. We emphasized cognitive empathy by beginning the interviews asking about where and with whom our respondents live to develop an easy rapport. We emphasized heterogeneity by following up on, and writing about, comments that were positive and negative, grateful and critical, humorous and heart-wrenching. We emphasized palpability by describing in our writing what the respondent was doing on the day of the interview, including elevating and icing a sore leg, making soup before the produce spoils, or waiting for mechanics to fix a wheelchair. We followed up extensively during the interviews, probing and confirming questions and responses, but we did not follow up with subsequent interviews. We emphasized reflexivity by hiring and training diverse sociodemographic interviewers and working to create a sample that was diverse on a wide array of measures.

Our shortcomings in such diversity efforts are noted in the following sections. At their best, good qualitative interviews provide, what Stefanie DeLuca refers to as intimate revelations of everyday experiences.[4] Our goal was to weave the everyday experiences of lower income older adults into the fabric of policy discussions about food insecurity.

Development of Interview Guide

We designed our interview guide to first gather context about the respondent, and then to focus on issues more closely related to food insecurity. The initial components of the guide ask about household, employment, and income. These broad questions help to develop rapport with respondents, giving them the opportunity to tell us about their life course and any difficulties they have faced, and providing the interviewer with context that assists comprehension as the interview unfolds. Then we ask about participation in welfare programs, transportation, health, social life, and meals in general. Finally, we ask three sets of questions from well-respected scales drawn from the literature to measure food insecurity, budget trade-offs, and how respondents pay the bills. For these three sets of questions, interviewers read the questions as written and then return to all yes responses to ask for clarification, examples, and additional information. We reserve these final questions for the end of the interview because they tend to reduce the amount that respondents say during their responses.

Recruitment

Our recruitment of respondents shifted throughout the pandemic. First, we had planned to visit, call, email, and post flyers at a wide variety of social institutions in all regions of the U.S., including through colleague referrals and at churches, libraries, Area Agencies on Aging, congregate nutrition sites, food pantries and kitchens, Salvation Armies, veterans' organizations, SNAP offices, home-delivered-meal sites, and other locations where people age sixty and older tend to congregate. We had planned to speak to people as they arrived or departed and to use the recruitment script to ask them whether they might be interested in doing an interview. However, because of concerns about COVID with an older population, state regulations, and Syracuse University policies, we were not able to do any face-to face recruitment. We instead mailed flyers to administrators at these agencies, called them, and emailed them. We mailed 250 packets of recruitment flyers around the country to administrators. However, most offices were closed or not seeing clients. These early efforts yielded no interviews. Over time some offices reopened, but we still struggled to recruit participants: workers were overworked as demand outstripped supplies; many places opened only for contactless service provision, and many older people were still fearful of exposure to COVID.

Following International Review Board (IRB) approval, we then contacted the Cornell University Social Sciences Research team and asked for a sampling frame of phone numbers. The team referred us to Marketing Systems Group, which provided roughly 4,000 phone numbers for households with at least one person age sixty or older who were near or below the 130 percent poverty threshold. The group pulled numbers equally from all four regions of the country, and the numbers included 40 percent landlines and 60 percent cell phones. This approach eliminated potential exposure to COVID for the researchers and the respondents. Our plan was that we would call the numbers, use the already approved recruitment script, and arrange appointments for phone interviews. However, we called a few hundred of these numbers per week, and this cold-call technique yielded no interviews.

Then with IRB approval, we implemented a token of $50 on a prepaid cash card to respondents. We paid for and placed Facebook ads in all fifty states. Finally, we posted a flyer on Craigslist. These efforts yielded interviews.

We also resumed mailing and emailing techniques. As COVID declined and vaccines became available, we began live recruiting, passing out flyers at food pantries and kitchens in New York City, Minneapolis–St. Paul, and Washington, DC. People began to respond and we conducted interviews.

Each interview began with a three-question screen to be sure the respondent met our selection criteria, asking if they were older than sixty, if their household income was less than 130 percent of the federal poverty line, and if they had been hungry in the past year due to lack of money for food.

Our response rate was good: while many people never answered their phones or did not return our calls, only eight people who actually scheduled an interview subsequently did not conduct the interview.

We conducted sixty-three one-to-two hour phone interviews from March 2021 to November 2021. Everyone who completed an interview received a cash card with a $50 honorarium.

Sample Description

Our qualitative data is from a national, nonrepresentative sample of sixty-three people age 60 and older with household incomes below 130 percent of the federal poverty line, whom we interviewed over the phone between July 2021 and November 2021. This is a convenience sample that is national in scope but not nationally representative. In general, 76 percent of our respondents were female, 51 percent were Black, 44 percent were White, 63 percent had at least some college education, 12 percent were married, 68 percent answered affirmatively to at least one question about food insecurity, 49 percent were food insecure, 5 percent had residential grandchildren, 70 percent included a person in the household with a disability, 78 percent were receiving SNAP, 43 percent lived in subsidized housing, and 79 percent used food pantries. The sample is diverse in terms of the causes and consequences of poverty and food insecurity. Some members of our sample had almost always been poor and were very familiar with food insecurity. They started out life with few resources and throughout their life course, accumulated more disadvantages than advantages. Others had only recently become poor and were new to the challenges of food insecurity. The sample is described in detail in appendix table B.2. While we had a great deal of ethnic diversity among our sample, no respondents identified as Asian alone; 13 percent identified as mixed or other races. Our goal was to provide a thick description of how older people currently experience food insecurity in the United States in order to help us design public policy for the next twenty years.

Analysis of Data

We recorded all interviews and paid Transcript DIVA to transcribe them. The interviewer then checked each transcript for accuracy, listening to the recording if the transcriber had not been able to understand the speaker. The primary investigator (PI) and research assistants (RA) then read each transcript and addressed questions about accuracy. The interviewer then used the transcript to write a synopsis of the interview. We then read each synopsis and addressed any questions about accuracy.

The interviewer then coded the interview along an Excel spreadsheet, and we double-checked these codes for accuracy. Much of the information in the spreadsheet, such as age, race, marital status, is factual, but the spreadsheet also includes more complex factors about respondents, such as whether their housing was at risk, they had transportation challenges, they were concerned about the poor quality of food they were obtaining, COVID was making it hard to get food, or they were getting food from church or family members.

The PI then read and reread each transcript and created lists of themes that emerged from the interviews. This was an iterative process that required several reads through the transcripts. We then highlighted quotes, color coding by themes such as budget trade-offs, budget shortfalls, difficulties with administrative burden, transportation challenges, difficulty obtaining healthy nutritious foods, physical health problems including mobility and stamina issues, or mental health challenges such as depression, anxiety, and isolation. While we expected to come across many of these themes, given our literature review, other themes that emerged from the transcripts were surprising. These less-expected themes that emerged from the interviews included having extra difficulty using public transportation during COVID, not seeing family members due to substance use, becoming disabled due to injury on the job, using stimulus checks to stock up the food pantry, food from grocery stores or from free and subsidized food programs turning bad before they had a chance to use it, sharing or leaving food with others who might have greater need, paying rent or utilities before buying food, the difficulties of getting groceries up the stairs, stretching food to the end of the month, being too tired to stand and chop or stir to prepare meals, facing administrative burden for free and subsidized food programs, making soup to stretch food until more money would arrive, and describing how inflation was undermining the purchasing power of the extra SNAP benefits.

We then collected and assembled quotes organized around each one of these themes. For example, we copied all quotes about feeding grandchildren together into a document, then checked for accuracy and completeness, making sure that all quotes about feeding grandchildren but no other material were assembled there. We organized these quotes about feeding grandchildren from most positive to most negative, or along another emerging dimensions such as whether they were custodial grandparents. In another example, many respondents had positive comments about food pantries but almost no positive comments about home-delivered meals. As another example, many had difficulties with public transportation, and the PI organized these comments separately based on whether the difficulties were linked to COVID or were related to public transportation. During this process of analysis, we fine-tuned the themes, dividing some into subtopics, separating some that were multidimensional, and collapsing some that were more closely related than they initially seemed.

The PI then pulled quotes from these themes to write each section of the chapters. In the process of writing, the PI returned to each transcript numerous times to write relevant descriptions of, or introductions to, each speaker. Rereading the transcripts provided an excellent opportunity to double-check for accuracy, review the development of themes, and elucidate our main points.

Sample Recruitment Flyer

Syracuse University

Research Opportunity: Older Adults, Household Expenses, and Food Insecurity We invite you to participate in a research study of how older people manage household expenses and food insecurity. To be eligible you must be: **(1)** age 60 or older and **(2)** live in a household with income below these amounts.

$16,744 for a **single** person
$22,646 for **two** persons
$28,548 for **three** persons
$34,450 for **four** persons
$40,352 for **five** persons
$46,254 for **six** persons
$52,156 for **seven** persons

Participation is voluntary. You can take as much time as you wish to decide and ask questions at any time. It takes 1-2 hours and responses are confidential.

For a completed interview, I will give you one **$50** Visa gift card. We will interview you by phone. Please call and leave a message with your name and phone number.

Principal Investigator: Madonna Harrington Meyer, University Professor, Department of Sociology, Center for Policy Research, Syracuse University,

Interview Guide
Screening Script (In person, by phone, or via computer)
1. Are you 60 or older? ___ What year were you born? _____
2. Was your total household income for 2019 less than this?
   Household size 1 income less than $16,237   Yes   No
   Household size 2 income less than $21,983   Yes   No

Household size 3 income less than $27,729   Yes   No
Household size 4 income less than $33,475   Yes   No
Household size 5 income less than $39,221   Yes   No
Household size 6 income less than $44,967   Yes   No
Household size 7 income less than $50,713   Yes   No

3. In the last 12 months, was there any day that you or anyone in your household went hungry because you did not have enough money for food? Yes ____ No ____

Completed Consent Form Yes ___ No ____   Recording Yes___ No___

Demographics: Tell me a little bit about you
1. Date _____ Interviewer _____ Case #_____
   Alias _____ Location of interview_____
   Phone   Face-to-Face   Computer
2. Respondent name _____ phone number_____
3. Age ____ Race _____ Ethnicity _____
4. Education: highest earned degree? _____
5. Current marital status _____ marital history? _____

Household and Family: Tell me a little bit about your household and family
1. Place of residence: state ____ own or rent? rural, urban, suburban?
2. Household members:
   Name   Age   Relationship   Race   Marital Status
3. Family members:
   Name Age Relationship Race Proximity FQ Contact Mar Stat
4. Number of grandchildren_____ ages, how many minutes away do they live, frequency of contact?
5. Providing or receiving custodial or co-residential care with grandchildren, older parents, or other relatives?
6. Does anyone in the household have a disability _____ need care? Who? Does anyone in the family have a disability, need care?
7. Looking ahead do you have any concerns about your living arrangements?
8. Have you moved, or are you considering moving for the sake of the HH budget or for the needs of others?

Employment: Tell me a little bit about your work
1. Current employment status, work history, type of work, hours of work, if retired?
2. Salary or wages, benefits, health insurance, private pension, paid vacation, paid sick leave, other?
3. Gaps in employment—due to illness, care work, loss of job, disability?
4. Military service, history?
5. Reasons for leaving work, interrupting employment?

Sources and Amounts of Household Income—Anyone in HH
1. Names of household members with earned income, and amounts of income each?
2. Money received from Social Security? Other pensions? Annuities?
3. Money received from Supplemental Security Income?
4. Money received from Disability Insurance?
5. Money received from VA? Pension or disability compensation?
6. Money received from other family members?
7. Other sources of money for the household?
8. Total respondent annual income?
9. Total household annual income?
10. Currently, compared to your HH needs, would you say you have more money than you need, exactly what you need, or less than you need?
11. Looking to the future, do you feel you will have more money than you need, exactly what you need, or less than you will need?

Participation in Benefit Programs: Do you or others in HH receive
1. Social Security old age pension: current status, history, ever applied, ever received, reasons for gaps in benefits, struggles to get benefits? Others in the HH?
2. Social Security disability insurance: current status, history, ever applied, ever received, reasons for gaps in benefits, struggles to get benefits? Others in the HH?
3. SSI: low income or disability: current status, history, ever applied, ever received, reasons for gaps in benefits, struggles to get benefits? Others in the HH?
4. Medicare: current status, history, ever applied, ever received, reasons for gaps in benefits, struggles to get benefits? Others in the HH?

5. Medicaid: current status, history, ever applied, ever received, reasons for gaps in benefits, struggles to get benefits? Others in the HH?
6. Veteran's Benefits or Compensation: current status, history, ever applied, ever received, reasons for gaps in benefits, struggles to get benefits? Others in the HH?
7. TANF, WIC: current status, history, ever applied, ever received, reasons for gaps in benefits, struggles to get benefits? Others in the HH?
8. SNAP: current status, history, ever applied, ever received, reasons for gaps in benefits, struggles to get benefits? Others in the HH?
9. Senior nutrition site meals: current status, history, ever pursued, ever received, reasons for gaps in benefits, struggles to get benefits? Others in the HH?
10. Home-delivered meals (Meals on Wheels): current status, history, ever applied, ever received, reasons for gaps in benefits, struggles to get benefits? Others in the HH?
11. Commodity supplemental food program: current status, history, ever applied, ever received, reasons for gaps in benefits, struggles to get benefits? Others in the HH?
12. Food pantry or kitchen: current status, history, ever pursued, ever received, reasons for gaps in benefits, struggles to get benefits? Others in the HH? Did you eat at the pantry or kitchen or take food to eat at home?

Transportation: Tell me a little bit about how you get around
1. Do you own a car, car working well, use public transportation, get rides from others, offer rides to others, any transportation difficulties? Others in the HH?
2. How do you get to the grocery store, to doctor, to work, to social program offices, to food programs or nutrition sites, any difficulties? Others in the HH?
3. Looking ahead, do you have any concerns about transportation?

Health and Health Care: Tell me a little about your health and health care
1. How do you rate your physical health, and why? Excellent, good, fair, poor
2. How do you rate your mental health, and why? Excellent, good, fair, poor

3. Do you have any diagnosed health conditions, disabilities, problems getting around, or climbing steps? Does anyone else in the HH?
4. Do you have any difficulties with depression, anxiety, sleeping, suicidal thoughts, alcohol use, or drug use. Does anyone else in the HH?
5. Do you have a regular doctor, health insurance, any difficulties making appts, getting to appts, paying for care, taking your medications properly? Have you or others in the HH ever delayed getting care, and why?
6. Do you have a regular dentist, dental insurance, any difficulties making appts, getting to appts, paying for care? Have you or others in the HH ever delayed getting care and why?
7. Do you have a regular counselor or therapist, any difficulties making appts, getting to appts, paying for care? Have you or others in the HH ever delayed getting care and why?
8. Do you get much exercise, how often, what types, why or why not, how do you feel about it? Do others in the HH?
9. Do you feel you get enough rest and relaxation, how often, what types, why or why not, how do you feel about it? Do others in the HH?
10. Are you concerned about the health or health care of another person in the HH or family?
11. Do you ever help pay for health care of others in the HH or family? Does anyone help pay yours?
12. Looking ahead do you have any concerns about health or health care for anyone in your HH or family?

Family and Friends: Tell me a little about your family and friends

1. How satisfied are you with your family relationships and why? Very, somewhat, not very, not at all
2. How often do you see members of the family, how do you get along, are there any conflicts?
3. Do you have any hobbies or pastimes, how often, why or why not, how do you feel about it?
4. Do you spend time with friends, people your own age, how do you get along, what do you usually do?
5. Do you attend church, volunteer, belong to any clubs or groups, how often, why or why not, how do you feel about it?
6. Looking ahead do you have any concerns about participating in any social activities?

Meals: Tell me a little bit about your meals

1. How would you rate your diet and why? Excellent, Good, Fair or Poor
2. With whom do you usually eat breakfast, lunch, supper, where are these meals?
3. Who prepares the meals, who plans the meals, buys the groceries, cleans up afterward?
4. Do you prepare to take food elsewhere, feed others, who and where, do you lend food to others, or do others ask to borrow from you?
5. How often do you eat out at restaurants, or carry out, take out, with whom?
6. Do you feel you eat enough fruits and vegetables, proteins, balanced meals?
7. Do you ever waste food, have to throw food out?

Food Insecurity Questions
Circle Responses[5]

1. "We worried whether our food would run out before we got money to buy more." Was that **often, sometimes,** or **never true** for you in the last 12 months?
2. "The food we bought just didn't last and we didn't have money to get more." Was that **often, sometimes,** or never true for you in the last 12 months?
3. "We couldn't afford to eat balanced meals." Was that **often, sometimes,** or **never true** for you in the last 12 months?
4. "We relied on only a few kinds of low-cost food to feed our children because we were running out of money to buy food." Was that **often, sometimes,** or never true for you in the last 12 months?
5. In the last 12 months did you or other adults in the household ever cut the size of your meals or skip meals because there was not enough money to buy food? **Yes No**
6. "We couldn't feed our children a balanced meal because we couldn't afford that." Was that **often, sometimes,** or **never true** for you in the last 12 months?
7. In the last 12 months did you eat less than you felt you should because there wasn't enough money for food? **Yes No**
8. If yes to Q5, how often did this happen? Was this **almost every month, some months but not every month,** or in **only 1 or 2 months**?

9. "The children were not eating enough because we just couldn't afford enough food." Was that **often, sometimes,** or **never true** for you in the last 12 months?
10. In the last 12 months were you ever hungry, but didn't eat, because you couldn't afford enough food? **Yes No**
11. In the last 12 months did you lose weight because you did not have enough money for food? **Yes No**
12. In the last 12 months, did you ever cut the size of any of the children's meals because these wasn't enough money for food? **Yes No**
13. In the last 12 months did you or other adults in your household ever not eat for a whole day because there wasn't enough money for food? **Yes No**
14. In the last 12 months, were the children ever hungry but you just couldn't afford more food? **Yes No**
15. If yes to Q13, how often did this happen? Was this **almost every month, some months but not every month,** or in only 1 or 2 months?
16. In the last 12 months did any of the children ever skip a meal because there wasn't enough money for food? **Yes No**
17. If yes to Q16, how often did this happen? Was this **almost every month, some months but not every month,** or in **only 1 or 2 months**?
18. In the last 12 months, did any of the children ever not eat for a whole day because there wasn't enough money for food? **Yes No**

For Q1–18, return to all YES responses, repeat their response, and ask: tell me about it, give me an example.

19. What things make it easy for you to have enough of the right kinds of food?
20. What things make it hard for you to have enough of the right kinds of food?
21. If you could change one thing what would it be?
22. Do food issues affect your physical health? How so?
23. Do food issues affect your mental health? How so?
24. Do food issues affect your social life? How so?

Budget Trade-off Questions
Circle Responses[6]
In the last 12 months,

1. Did you or someone in your household have to choose between paying for food and paying for medicine or medical care? **Yes No** If yes, how often? Tell me about it.

2. Did you are someone in your household have to choose between paying for food and paying for utilities? **Yes No** If yes, how often? Tell me about it.
3. Did you or someone in your household have to choose between paying for food and paying for housing, rent? **Yes No** If yes, how often? Tell me about it.
4. Did you or someone in your household have to choose between paying for food and paying for transportation including gas, oil changes, car repairs, subway passes, bus tickets? **Yes No** If yes, how often? Tell me about it.
5. Did you or someone in your household have to choose between paying for food and paying for education, including tuition, books, school supplies? **Yes No** If yes, how often? Tell me about it.
6. Did you or someone in your household have to choose between paying for food and paying for clothing including coats, underwear, or shoes? **Yes No** If yes, how often? Tell me about it.
7. Did you or someone in your household have to choose between paying for food and personal supplies such as diapers, baby wipes, shampoo, toothpaste? **Yes No** If yes, how often? Tell me about it.
8. Did you or someone in your household have to choose between paying for food and paying for household items such as lightbulbs, laundry soap, paper towels, cleaning supplies? **Yes No** If yes, how often? Tell me about it.
9. Did you ever feel that it was just too much trouble to prepare a meal? **Yes No** If yes, how often? Tell me about it.
10. Did you just lose interest in eating? **Yes No** If yes, how often? Tell me about it.
11. Did you ever feel that the others did not appreciate your efforts to provide meals? **Yes No** If yes, how often? Tell me about it.
12. Did you ever feel that it was not important that you eat? **Yes No** If yes, how often? Tell me about it.

Paying the Bills
Circle Responses[7]
In the last 12 months,

1. Did you ever not meet all of your essential expenses? **Yes No** If yes, how often? Tell me about it.

2. Did you ever not pay for the full amount of the rent or mortgage? **Yes No** If yes, how often? Tell me about it.
3. Were you evicted for not paying rent or mortgage? **Yes No** If yes, how often? Tell me about it.
4. Did you not pay the full amount of the gas, oil, or electric bills? **Yes No** If yes, how often? Tell me about it.
5. Did the gas or electric company turn off the service, or the oil company not deliver the oil? **Yes No** If yes, how often? Tell me about it.
6. Did you not pay the full phone bill? **Yes No** If yes, how often? Tell me about it.
7. Did the phone company disconnect service? **Yes No** If yes, how often? Tell me about it.
8. Did you need to see a doctor or go to the hospital but did not go? **Yes No** If yes, how often? Tell me about it.
9. Did you receive calls from collection agencies? **Yes No** If yes, how often? Tell me about it.
10. Did you or anyone in the family ever steal something because money was tight? **Yes No** If yes, how often? Tell me about it.

Final Questions
1. Looking ahead do you have any concerns about buying or preparing meals in your HH or family?
2. Do you have suggestions for how we could improve SNAP, home-delivered meals, senior nutrition sites, commodity food programs, food pantries or kitchens?
3. Do you have any questions for us? Anything you think I should have asked?

Recruitment Script
(In person, or by phone, flyer, or email)
We would like to invite you to participate in a research study of how older people manage household expenses. To be eligible you must be age 60 or older and live in a household with income below 130% of the federal poverty line. We want to get a sense of what strategies you use and how it affects your wellbeing. Participation is voluntary. You can take as much time as you wish to decide and ask questions at any time. If you participate in the interview, I will give you up to a $50 Visa gift card.

If you think you would like to participate, we will interview you. The interviews take 1-2 hours, all interviews will be conducted by telephone, and your responses will be confidential. When would it be best to do the interview? Day, time?

Thank you. I look forward to talking with you at the interview.

NOTES

INTRODUCTION: THE NEED TO ADDRESS OLDER ADULT FOOD INSECURITY

1. Authors' calculations based on 2023 Current Population Survey and official food security measure.
2. Coleman-Jensen et al. 2021, 2.
3. Authors' calculations based on 2023 Current Population Survey and official food security measure.
4. Levy 2022 using data from the Health and Retirement Study, a long-running study that follows a cohort of older adults every two years and measures food insecurity using a single item measure indicating if the household has not always had enough money to buy the food they needed over the previous two years.
5. Gregory et al. 2019; Leung et al. 2014; Leung and Tester 2019; Zizza et al. 2008.
6. Desilva and Anderson-Villaluz 2021.
7. Baugreet et al. 2017.
8. Administration for Community Living 2022a; National Council on Aging 2024a.
9. When writing about disabilities, scholars are urged to use person-first language, which favors "adults with disabilities." We see a recent shift in the literature from person-first to identity-first language, which favors "disabled adults" (Wooldridge 2023; Andrews et al. 2022). After careful consideration, we decided to use person-first language for two key reasons: the shift to identify-first language is generally advocated by adults with specific disabilities such as autism, whereas we refer to adults with a wide variety of disabilities; and the shift may or may not be temporary. We hope our language use will be acceptable indefinitely. Our intent is to be respectful of people with disabilities.
10. Tavares et al. 2022.

11. Afulani et al. 2015; Gundersen and Ziliak 2021.
12. Vesnayer and Keller 2011.
13. Hughes et al. 2004; Tani et al. 2015; Ohara et al. 2020; Wang et al. 2016.
14. Gundersen and Ziliak 2015, 2021; Leung et al. 2020; Afulani et al. 2015; Herman et al. 2015; Na et al. 2023.
15. Afulani et al. 2015; Gundersen and Ziliak 2015; Siefert et al. 2004; Melchior et al. 2009; Burris et al. 2019; Howe-Burris et al. 2022; Gonyea et al. 2022; Brostow et al. 2017; Wolfe et al. 2003.
16. Berkowitz et al. 2014; Gundersen and Ziliak 2015.
17. Seligman et al. 2010; Bergmans et al. 2019; Knight et al. 2016; Carlson and Keith-Jennings 2018; Tarasuk et al. 2015; Berkowitz, Basu, et al. 2017; Palakshappa et al. 2023.
18. Berkowitz, Basu, et al. 2017; Bhargava and Lee 2017; Tarasuk et al. 2015; Lee and Frongillo 2001b.
19. Vespa 2018; National Institute on Aging et al. 2007; Administration of Community Living 2023a.
20. Vespa 2018; National Institute of Aging et al. 2007.
21. Coleman-Jensen et al. 2020; Ziliak and Gundersen 2016, 2023; Rabbitt et al. 2023a.
22. Wilmoth et al. 2015.
23. Coleman-Jensen et al. 2020; Ziliak and Gundersen 2020; Mathers et al. 2015.
24. Rabbitt et al. 2024.
25. Fry and Braga 2023.
26. Fry and Braga 2023.
27. Burtless 2015.
28. Board of Governors of the Federal Reserve System 2023.
29. Carr 2023.
30. Neumark 2018.
31. Senior Living 2023.
32. Iceland 2013; Creamer et al. 2022; Meyer and Wu 2018.
33. Van de water and Romig 2023.
34. Munnell 2013.
35. Dushi et al. 2017.
36. Coleman-Jensen et al. 2022; Shrider and Creamer 2023.
37. Shrider 2024.
38. Toossi and Jones 2023.
39. Wilde 2018.
40. Vigil and Rahimi 2024.

41. Coleman-Jensen et al. 2021.
42. White House 2022.
43. Mozaffarian et al. 2022.

CHAPTER 1
MEASURING OLD AGE FOOD INSECURITY IN THE UNITED STATES

1. U.S. Department of Agriculture 2024b; Anderson 1990.
2. Authors' calculations based on 2023 Current Population Survey and official food security measure.
3. "Food security exists when all people, at all times, have physical and economic access to sufficient safe and nutritious food that meets dietary needs and food preferences for an active and healthy life." According to this definition of food security developed at the 1996 World Food Summit by the United Nations Food and Agriculture Organization (2008), food security has four components: the physical availability of food; economic and physical access to food; food utilization; and stability of the other three dimensions over time. In the international context of famine and war, where the consistent availability of nutritious food cannot be assumed, all four components are critical.
4. U.S. Department of Agriculture 2024b; Anderson 1990.
5. Gualtieri and Donley 2016.
6. U.S. Department of Agriculture 2012.
7. U.S. Department of Agriculture 2012; Bickel et al. 2000.
8. Ziliak and Gundersen 2023 for 2001 data and authors' calculation for 2023 data. Note that the population cited with marginal food insecurity only includes the population that meets the definition for marginal food insecurity and not low or very low food security.
9. Not all households answer all the questions. A set of screening questions are used to limit the respondent burden for those who are highly food secure. People from households with incomes above 185 percent of the federal poverty line and those who respond to questions in a specific way are not asked all the questions. See U.S. Department of Agriculture 2012 for additional information.
10. Gundersen et al. 2017.
11. For more information on the difference between food insufficiency and food insecurity, see U.S. Department of Agriculture 2024b.
12. Ziliak 2021.
13. Heflin et al. 2009.
14. Sen 2000.

15. Rabbitt et al. 2024.
16. Rabbitt et al. 2024.
17. Mayer and Jencks 1989; Rector 1999; Rector and Sheffield 2011.
18. Elder 1998; Jones et al. 2019; Shanahan 2000; Bengtson and Allen 1993; Braveman and Barclay 2009; Bengtson. et al. 2012.
19. Kuh et al. 2014; Kuh 2019; Cao et al. 2022.
20. Vilar-Compte et al. 2017; Goldberg and Mawn 2015; Strickhouser et al. 2015; U.S. Senate 2013; Keller et al. 2007; Wolfe et al. 2003.
21. Vilar-Compte et al. 2017; Goldberg and Mawn 2015; Strickhouser et al. 2015.
22. Loo and Brown 2024; Brown and Manning 2021.
23. Heflin and Patnaik 2022; Butcher et al. 2023; Generations United 2023.
24. Adams et al. 2015; Balistreri 2019; Brown et al. 2018; Brucker 2016; Brucker and Coleman-Jensen 2017; Brucker and Nord 2016; Heflin, Altman, et al. 2019; Coleman-Jensen and Nord 2013.
25. Reed-Jones 2024; U.S. Department of Agriculture 2023c.
26. She and Livermore 2007.
27. Social Security Administration 2024c.
28. Social Security Administration 2020.
29. Center on Budget and Policy Priorities 2024a.
30. Meyer and Mok 2019; Stephens 2001.
31. Based on authors' calculation using 2023 data from the Current Population Survey. See also Rabbitt et al. 2023b.
32. Attanasio and Hoynes 2000; Heflin et al. 2019.
33. U.S. Bureau of Labor Statistics 2024a.
34. Harrington Meyer 2014.
35. Harrington Meyer 2014.
36. Gavin 2024.
37. Pooler et al. 2019; Office of Disease Prevention and Health Promotion 2023.
38. Marcos 2021.
39. U.S. Department of Agriculture 2025e.
40. U.S. Department of Agriculture 2024e.
41. U.S. Department of Agriculture 2025d.
42. Keenan and Lampkin 2023.
43. Keenan and Lampkin 2023.
44. Bernard et al. 2016; Glaser and Strauss 2017; DeLuca 2022.
45. Jones 2024; Rabbitt et al. 2024; Richterman et al. 2023.
46. U.S. Bureau of Labor Statistics 2024b.

47. Cunnyngham 2023b; Vigil and Rahimi 2024.
48. Lauffer and Vigil 2021; U.S. Department of Agriculture 2021.

CHAPTER 2
THE ECONOMIC ROOTS OF OLD AGE FOOD INSECURITY

1. At the time of the interview, the minimum SNAP benefit was $23 monthly in states without emergency allotments, but she reported receiving $16.
2. Holben and Marshall 2017; Harrington Meyer 2014; Wolfe et al. 2003.
3. Hill and Stephens 1997; Shipler 2005; Edin and Lein 1997.
4. Shrider 2024.
5. Board of Governors of the Federal Reserve System 2019; Hake and Dawes 2024; Brown et al. 2016; Morrissey 2019.
6. Shrider 2024.
7. Dushi et al. 2017.
8. Ghilarducci et al. 2015.
9. Shrider 2024.
10. U.S. Bureau of Labor Statistics 2024b.
11. Senior Living 2023.
12. Organisation for Economic Co-operation and Development 2023.
13. Sullivan and Ghosh 2024.
14. Government Accountability Office 2022.
15. U.S. Department of the Treasury 2023; Kochhar and Moslimani 2023.
16. Li 2021.
17. Dunifon et al. 2014; Ellis and Simmons 2014; Taylor et al. 2010; Wiemers 2014.
18. Ziliak and Gundersen 2016; Hake and Dawes 2024.
19. Heflin and Patnaik 2022.
20. Stone 2024.
21. Heflin and Patnaik 2022.
22. Keenan and Lampkin 2023.
23. Keenan and Lampkin 2023. Each of the reported trade-offs between food and other expenses was more common among those age fifty to sixty-four than those age sixty-five or older.
24. Lopes et al. 2024.
25. Alemayehu and Warner 2004.
26. Ochieng et al. 2024.

27. Carter 2023; Consumer Financial Protection Bureau, Office for Older Americans 2023.
28. Kaiser Family Foundation 2024.
29. Rudowitz et al. 2023.
30. Consumer Financial Protection Bureau, Office for Older Americans 2023.
31. Berkowitz, Seligman, et al. 2014; Gundersen and Ziliak 2015.
32. Berkowitz, Seligman, et al. 2014.
33. Heflin et al. 2022.
34. Ojinnaka et al. 2023.
35. Shuman et al. 2017; Harrington Meyer et al. 2021.
36. Sen et al. 2018.
37. Van Wormer et al. 2012.
38. Shuman et al. 2017.
39. Pietropaoli et al. 2018.
40. Shuman et al. 2017; American Heart Association 2021.
41. Freed, Neuman, et al. 2019.
42. DiMaria-Ghalili et al. 2020.
43. DiMaria-Ghalili et al. 2020; Shuman et al. 2017.
44. Freed, Ochieng, et al. 2021.
45. Freed et al. 2024.
46. Freed, Ochieng, et al. 2021.
47. Shuman et al. 2017.
48. Center for Health Care Strategies 2019.
49. Freed, Ochieng, et al. 2021.
50. DiMaria-Ghalili et al. 2020.
51. Joint Center for Housing Studies of Harvard University 2023.
52. Joint Center for Housing Studies of Harvard University 2023.
53. Acosta and Gartland 2021.
54. Centers for Disease Control and Prevention 2023a; National Institute on Aging 2024.
55. Environmental Protection Agency 2024.
56. Environmental Protection Agency 2021, 2024.
57. Masselot et al. 2023; Berko et al. 2014.
58. Cooper 2022.
59. Oberdorfer and Wiley 2014.
60. Hernández 2016.
61. Jackson et al. 2019; Jih et al. 2018; Leung et al. 2020.

62. U.S. Department of Health and Human Services 2023.
63. Graff and Pirog 2019.
64. Castillo and Daniel 2022.
65. Bohr and McCreery 2020.
66. National Council on Aging 2024b.
67. Abdul and Mohd 2023.
68. During COVID some of our respondents found that they were better off. Stimulus checks, coupled with higher SNAP benefit amounts, made it easier to buy food and other household necessities. Liza, age seventy-three with low food security, used her stimulus checks to purchase household supplies:

    > It happened before we were getting that $1,200 and $600 and all of that. It was during that time things were kind of tight. But after, you know, I got that it was better. I could stock up and, you know, save on a few things. The things was the toilet paper and the paper towels and the detergent and just all of that stuff, you know. Because if you buy once a month thing, you wouldn't be able to buy as much at one time as you did when the COVID came up.

    However, Beth, age sixty with low food security, found that covering extra COVID expenses left less money for much needed food. She told us, "Because of the extra expenses, there was times that I couldn't buy stuff like we had to get all these hand sanitizers, gloves and masks and they were expenses that were not on the budget so I didn't have enough money to buy food."
69. Federal Communications Commission 2023, 2024; Obama Phone 2023.
70. Keenan and Lampkin 2023.
71. Authors' calculations using the 2021 Survey of Income and Program Participation.

CHAPTER 3
BEYOND INCOME: COMPOUNDING PROBLEMS FOR FOOD INSECURITY

1. Keenan and Lampkin 2023.
2. Choi et al. 2021.
3. Centers for Disease Control and Prevention 2023b; Administration for Community Living 2022a.
4. Boersma et al. 2020.
5. Centers for Disease Control and Prevention 2024a, 2024b.
6. Freedman et al. 2021; Freedman and Cornman 2023.

7. Administration for Community Living 2022a.
8. Coleman-Jensen and Nord 2013; Brucker and Coleman-Jensen 2017; Heflin, Altman, et al. 2019; Coleman-Jensen 2020.
9. Coleman-Jensen and Nord 2013.
10. Heflin, Altman, et al. 2019.
11. Zhang et al. 2019; Centers for Disease Control and Prevention 2024a.
12. U.S. Department of Health and Human Services 2025.
13. Heflin, Altman, et al. 2019.
14. Heflin, Altman, et al. 2019.
15. Royer et al. 2021.
16. Zuo and Heflin 2023.
17. Choi et al. 2021.
18. Joint Center for Housing Studies of Harvard University 2016.
19. Chan and Ellen 2017.
20. Housing and Urban Development Office 2017.
21. George and Tomer 2022.
22. George and Tomer 2022.
23. Pew Research Center 2024.
24. Miranda 2023.
25. On depression, see Allen et al. 2018; Burke et al. 2018; Leung et al. 2015; Laraia et al. 2009; Ziliak et al. 2015. On anxiety, see Wolfson et al. 2021. On sleep disorders, see Arenas et al. 2019; Meng et al. 2015; Lee et al. 2021.
26. Brostow, Gunzburger, et al. 2017.
27. Nagata et al. 2019, 2020; Lent et al. 2009; Whittle et al. 2019.
28. Ziliak et al. 2015; Lee and Frongillo 2001a, 2001b.
29. Pourmotabbed et al. 2020.
30. Koma et al. 2020.
31. National Academy of Sciences, Engineering, and Medicine et al. 2020.
32. National Academy of Sciences, Engineering, and Medicine et al. 2020.
33. National Academy of Sciences, Engineering, and Medicine et al. 2020.
34. National Academy of Sciences, Engineering, and Medicine et al. 2020.
35. National Academy of Sciences, Engineering, and Medicine et al. 2020.
36. Livingston 2019.
37. Livingston 2019.
38. Akobundu 2022.
39. Lipman and Waxman 2017.
40. Burris et al. 2019, 31.

41. Gonyea et al. 2022, e5965.
42. Valliant et al. 2022, 606.
43. Burris et al. 2019.
44. Umberson et al. 2010.
45. McDonald et al. 2022.
46. U.S. Department of Agriculture 2022a; Ver Ploeg et al. 2009.
47. Fitzpatrick et al. 2015; Dutko et al. 2012.
48. Kaufman et al. 1997.
49. Rowlands et al. 2023.
50. Rowlands et al. 2023.
51. Kiszko et al. 2015; Kaufman et al. 1997.
52. Heflin, Altman, et al. 2019.
53. Generally, teasing out these different explanations is difficult, although recent research is making good headway in this area. For example, recent clinical studies suggest that household food insecurity is associated with diabetes partially through inflammation and stress hormones (Bermúdez-Millán et al. 2019). Heflin and colleagues have demonstrated that short-term changes in available resources for food related to the monthly timing of SNAP benefits are associated with increased levels of Medicaid-related claims in the emergency room for childhood injuries, pregnancy-related health conditions, and asthma (Heflin, Arteaga, et al. 2020; Heflin, Arteaga, et al. 2019; Arteaga et al. 2018). In addition, short-term changes in SNAP benefits related to administrative processes are associated with a decrease in outpatient care visits and prescription drug claims but an increase in hospitalizations and emergency care visits (Heflin, Hodges, et al. 2020). It is likely that some individuals with disabilities who suffer from limited access to procure, prepare, or cook food but are financially able to afford it are not fully identified with this measure of food insecurity. This measurement error creates a downward bias that attenuates the finding and suggests that the relationship might be even stronger than previous studies have identified.
54. Carvajal-Aldaz et al. 2022.
55. U.S. Hunger 2022.
56. Trust for America's Health 2021.
57. Deokrye 2016.
58. Dumas et al. 2021.
59. Arena and Salerno 2020.
60. During the pandemic, some respondents were frustrated when public buses limited the number of grocery bags riders could bring with them. Martha explains,

"Now they say you can't carry that much on the bus. I'm not going to be able to get what I need on the bus." Others were frustrated when public buses implemented social distancing procedures that caused the buses to drive past them. Helen was left standing at the bus stop waiting for a subsequent bus that might be less full. "Like yesterday I had to walk to Walgreen's to get my medicine and three buses went past me. So it's just . . . about three blocks. I had to do what I had to do. If I had had somebody that would go for me, I didn't have nobody."

61. Keenan and Lampkin 2023.

CHAPTER 4
UNDERSTANDING THE LIMITS OF SNAP

1. U.S. Department of Agriculture 2025d; 12.2 percent calculation based on SNAP average caseload of 47.1 million and U.S. population of 341 million individuals.
2. Bitler 2015; Hoynes et al. 2015; Gregory and Smith 2019; Gregory et al. 2015; Todd 2015; Berkowitz et al. 2017.
3. Heflin and Ziliak 2024.
4. Canning and Stacey 2019.
5. Vigil and Rahimi 2024.
6. Finkelstein and Notowidgdo 2018; Harrington Meyer and Abdul-Malak 2020; Herd and Moynihan 2019; Gundersen and Ziliak 2015.
7. SNAP is still not available in Puerto Rico.
8. For a full timeline, see U.S. Department of Agriculture 2024a; Bartfeld et al. 2015.
9. Nord and Prell 2011.
10. Hastings and Shapiro 2018.
11. Canning and Stacey 2019.
12. Ziliak 2015.
13. Ganong and Liebman 2018.
14. Toossi et al. 2021.
15. Nord and Prell 2011; Guthro 2021.
16. Cronquist 2021.
17. Wells et al. 2024.
18. Center on Budget and Policy Priorities 2024a.
19. Heflin et al. 2012.
20. Giannella et al. 2023.
21. Mills et al. 2014.

22. Benvie et al. 2023.
23. Monkovic 2024.
24. Monkovic 2024; U.S. Department of Agriculture 2024e; U.S. Department of Agriculture 2025d.
25. Rabbitt et al. 2024.
26. Monkovic 2024; U.S. Department of Agriculture 2024b.
27. Monkovic 2024.
28. Monkovic 2024.
29. Monkovic 2024.
30. Monkovic 2024.
31. Heflin et al. 2022; Haider et al. 2003; Jones et al. 2022. The Heflin et al. 2022 methodology is distinct from the microsimulation model used for official estimates of SNAP eligibility detailed in appendix D of Vigil 2019.
32. McConnell et al. 2024.
33. In results not shown, we also examine SNAP participation (using the full population) by age group again using the Health and Retirement Study. When we examine SNAP participation by age group, two patterns are clear. First, SNAP participation increased over time for all age groups, with the sharpest increases after 2008. Second, levels of SNAP participation varied by age to a much larger extent for older adults in 2018 than they did in 2002, with participation declining as age increased. While SNAP participation ranged from 3 to 5 percent in 2002, by 2018 SNAP participation ranged from 15 percent between the ages of fifty and fifty-four to 6 to 8 percent from age sixty-five and older. These patterns are consistent with those reported by Ziliak and Gundersen (2019) using the Current Population Survey.
34. Haider et al. 2003.
35. Cunnyngham 2023a.
36. Vigil and Rahimi 2024; Gundersen and Ziliak 2015.
37. Social Security Administration 2024b.
38. Jones et al. 2022.
39. Finkelstein and Notowidigdo 2018; Harrington Meyer and Abdul-Malak 2020; Herd and Moynihan 2019; Gundersen and Ziliak 2015.
40. Herd and Moynihan 2019.
41. Herd and Moynihan 2019.
42. Barnes et al. 2023; Linos et al. 2020; Fannin et al. 2024.
43. Zuo and Heflin 2023.
44. Giodorno et al. 2022.

45. Mills et al. 2014.
46. Mills et al. 2014.
47. Cody et al. 2007; Mabli et al. 2011; Mills et al. 2014; Rangarajan and Gleason 2001.
48. Ribar and Edelhoch 2008.
49. Homonoff and Somerville 2020.
50. Mills et al. 2014; Heflin, Hodges, et al. 2023; Heflin, Hodges, et al. 2020.
51. Mills et al. 2014.
52. While the median recertification length for SNAP households with adults age sixty and older in Missouri was consistently twenty-four months throughout the observation period, the annual share of cases with adults age sixty and older with recertification periods of twenty-four months varied between 86 to 96 percent of the elderly caseload over our observation period. In addition, online document submission began in 2013.
53. Cronquist et al. 2021; Heflin et al. 2022.
54. Ribar and Edelhoch 2008.
55. Levels of administrative churn for older adults are not known for other states or time periods at this point.
56. Heflin, Hodges, et al. 2023.
57. Ostchega et al. 2020; Fryar et al. 2017; Centers for Disease Control and Prevention 2024.
58. Xu et al. 2016.
59. Bhargava and Lee 2017; Fryar et al. 2017; Jih et al. 2018.
60. Berkowitz et al. 2014; Gundersen and Ziliak 2015.
61. Berkowitz et al. 2014.
62. Heflin, Hodges, et al. 2023; Ojinnaka et al. 2023.
63. Ojinnaka et al. 2023.
64. Heflin, Hodges, et al. 2020.
65. Herd and Moynihan 2019.
66. Social Security Administration 2023b; Social Security Administration 2024b.
67. Social Security Administration 2008.
68. Gearing, Lewis, et al. 2021; National Council on Aging 2023.
69. Todd 2015; Castner et al. 2020.
70. Gearing, Lewis, et al. 2021; Castner et al. 2020.
71. Castner et al. 2020.
72. Christensen and Bronchetti 2020; Gregory and Coleman-Jensen 2013; Li and Çakir 2024.

73. Christensen and Bronchetti 2020.
74. Urban Institute 2023.
75. Barnes 2021; Barnes and Riel 2022.
76. U.S. Department of Agriculture 2024h.
77. U.S. Department of Agriculture 2025b.
78. Castner et al. 2020.
79. Gearing, Lewis, et al. 2021.
80. Castwell and Yaktine 2013.
81. Gearing, Dixit-Joshi, et al. 2021.
82. Gearing, Dixit-Joshi, et al. 2021.
83. Gearing, Dixit-Joshi, et al. 2021.
84. Ver Ploeg and Zhen 2022.
85. Waxman and Gupta 2023; U.S. Department of Agriculture 2024c, 2023d.
86. This is known as the marginal propensity to consume. See Song 2022 and Hastings and Shapiro 2018 for empirical estimates of the marginal propensity to consume food out of SNAP benefits.
87. Gearing, Lewis, et al. 2021.
88. Gearing, Lewis, et al. 2021.
89. U.S. Department of Agriculture 2023k.
90. McConnell et al. 2024.
91. Geller et al. 2019.
92. Lauffer and Vigil 2021; U.S. Department of Agriculture 2021a.
93. McConnell et al. 2024.
94. Heflin, Fannin, et al. 2023.
95. Jones et al. 2022.
96. Referred to as able-bodied adults without dependents, or ABAWDs.
97. U.S. Department of Agriculture 2025a.
98. U.S. Department of Agriculture 2025f.
99. Stacy et al. 2018; Klerman and Danielson 2011; Dickert-Conlin et al. 2016; Ziliak 2015; Ratcliffe et al. 2008.
100. Jones et al. 2022; Heflin and Ziliak 2024.
101. Smith 1997; Barrilleaux et al. 2002; Berry et al. 1998; Fellowes and Rowe 2004.
102. Heflin, Lopoo, et al. 2020; Fannin et al. 2024.
103. Heflin, Fannin, et al. 2023.
104. U.S. Department of Agriculture 2024e; Gearing, Lewis, et al. 2021.
105. Lauffer and Vigil 2021; U.S. Department of Agriculture 2021.

CHAPTER 5
UNDERSTANDING THE LIMITS OF COMMUNITY-BASED FREE AND SUBSIDIZED FOOD PROGRAMS

1. Allard 2017; Dickinson 2020.
2. See figure 1.3 and Hake and Dawes 2024.
3. Although the U.S. Department of Agriculture–funded Child and Adult Care Food Program also provides funding for group meals to day care sites for adults age sixty and older.
4. Authors' calculations based on 2023 Current Population Survey responses to the question: "In the last 12 months, have (you/you or anyone in your household) received a free meal from a church, shelter, home-delivered meal service like Meals on Wheels, or other place that helps with free meals?" Note that question wording changed after 2021, and data are not comparable to those of earlier years.
5. Authors' calculations based on 2023 Current Population Survey responses to the question: "In the last 12 months, did (you/you or anyone in your household) ever get free groceries from a food pantry, food bank, church, or other place that helps with free food?" Note that question wording changed after 2021, and data after this year are not comparable to those of earlier years.
6. Lecy 2024.
7. Gearing, Dixit-Joshi, et al. 2021.
8. Lee et al. 2022.
9. Balistreri 2022.
10. Ziliak 2021.
11. Meals on Wheels America 2025a.
12. Feeding America 2022, 2024; U.S. Department of Agriculture 2024g.
13. Administration for Community Living 2022b, 2022c.; Meals on Wheels America, 2025a.
14. Shenk and Mabli 2020.
15. Cayuga County 2025.
16. Government Accountability Office 2021.
17. Government Accountability Office 2021.
18. Administration for Community Living 2023b.
19. Mabli et al. 2017.
20. Mabli et al. 2017.
21. Administration for Community Living 2023b.

22. Mabli et al. 2017; Niland et al. 2017.
23. Allard 2017; Dickinson 2020.
24. Administration for Community Living 2023b.
25. Balistreri 2022. Congregate meals may be served at either senior centers or adult care centers. Senior centers provide a wide array of services. According to our analysis of data from the National Center for Charitable Statistics, a consistent spatial distribution is apparent: California and New York lead the country with the most organizations that name senior center as a primary service they offer, with Texas, Ohio and Pennsylvania close behind. The changes from 2000 to 2021 are much smaller for senior centers than they are for the other types of organizations, although most states did see small changes in the number of organizations hosting senior centers over the time period.

Adult care centers provide recreation and care, including nutrition services, and may receive funding for nutritional services from U.S. Department of Agriculture's Child and Adult Care Food Program. The number of adult care centers has declined from 2000 to 2021, according to our analysis of National Center for Charitable Statistics data. Because availability is declining and none of our respondents participated in adult day care, we do not discuss it in this book.
26. Project Open Hand 2023.
27. Moffitt 2015; Katz 1989.
28. Meals on Wheels America 2025b.
29. Shenk and Mabli 2020.
30. Onondaga County Aging Services 2025.
31. Lipman and Waxman 2017.
32. Wright et al. 2015, 224.
33. Wright et al. 2015, 225.
34. Balistreri 2022.
35. Meals on Wheels America 2025b.
36. Administration for Community Living 2022b, 2022c.
37. Government Accountability Office 2021; Colello 2020.
38. Meals on Wheels America 2025a.
39. Administration for Community Living 2023b.
40. Mabli et al. 2017.
41. Mabli et al. 2017.
42. Mabli et al. 2017; Niland et al. 2017.
43. Administration for Community Living 2023b.
44. Mabli et al. 2017.

45. Meal on Wheels America 2025b.
46. Daponte and Bade 2006.
47. Morello 2021.
48. National Agricultural Law Center 2024.
49. Ohls et al. 2002; Coleman-Jensen et al. 2022.
50. Heflin and Price 2019.
51. Feeding America 2023.
52. Costanzo 2022.
53. Feeding America 2023.
54. Feeding America 2023.
55. Lapham and Martinson 2022; National Council on Aging 2016.
56. U.S. Department of Agriculture 2023f.
57. For example, in Washington, see Johnson, et al. 2003; in Southern Illinois, see Middleton and Smith 2011; in South Carolina, see Kunkel et al. 2003.
58. Balistreri 2022.

CHAPTER 6
POLICY RECOMMENDATIONS TO ADDRESS OLD AGE FOOD INSECURITY

1. Sassine et al. 2023.
2. Tucher et al. 2021.
3. U.S. Department of Agriculture 2022e.
4. Tufts University, Food is Medicine Institute 2025; Center for Nutrition and Health Impact 2025.
5. U.S. Department of Agriculture 2022c.
6. Mabli 2014; Fitzpatrick et al. 2015.
7. As mentioned in chapter 1, we encourage the department to consider expanding the sampling frame of the Food Security Supplement to include institutionalized older adults or to acknowledge that the measure does not include their experience with food security. In addition, we encourage it to think about how to include the child food security questions in the scale for adults that regularly feed children who are not in their households.
8. Gundersen et al. 2017.
9. Billioux et al. 2017.
10. U.S. Department of Health and Human Services 2025.
11. Pooler et al. 2018; Steiner et al. 2018.
12. McDougall et al. 2022.

13. Government Accountability Office 2019.
14. Fiol et al. 2023.
15. Katch and Van De Water 2020.
16. Bahanan et al. 2021.
17. Carequest Institute for Dental Health 2024; Singhal et al. 2017.
18. Vigil 2024.
19. Jones et al. 2022.
20. Christensen and Bronchetti 2020.
21. U.S. Department of Agriculture 2025b.
22. U.S. Department of Agriculture 2025b.
23. Waxman et al. 2023.
24. McConnell et al. 2024.
25. Li et al. 2023.
26. Levin et al. 2020.
27. Giannarelli et al. 2023.
28. Social Security Administration 2024a.
29. Decker et al. 2022.
30. U.S. Department of Agriculture 2023b.
31. Social Security Administration 2020.
32. Rabbitt et al. 2024.
33. Acosta and Gartland 2021.
34. National Council on Aging 2024b.
35. Food Research and Action Center 2017.
36. Ambegaokar et al. 2017; U.S. Department of Agriculture 2004.
37. McConnell et al. 2024.
38. Dorn et al. 2014.
39. Jones et al. 2022.
40. Social Security Administration 2024b.
41. Fraker et al. 1995.
42. Monkovic 2024.
43. Berkowitz and Palakshappa 2024; Bovell-Ammon et al. 2022; Wells et al. 2024; Shafer et al. 2022.
44. Singleton 2023; Brucker et al. 2022.
45. Social Security Administration 2023a.
46. Herd et al. 2018.
47. Center on Budget and Policy Priorities 2024b.
48. Center on Budget and Policy Priorities 2024b.

49. Social Security Administration 2020.
50. Acosta and Gartland 2021.
51. National Council on Aging 2024b.
52. Loibl et al. 2022.
53. Coleman-Jensen et al. 2022.
54. Karpman et al. 2022; Pilkauskas et al. 2022.
55. White House 2022.

APPENDIX

1. U.S. Department of Agriculture 2024b.
2. Small 2011.
3. Small and McCrory Calarco 2022.
4. DeLuca 2022.
5. These questions come from Ziliak and Gundersen 2019.
6. Adapted from Weinfield et al. 2014.
7. Adapted from the 2008 U.S. Census Bureau Survey of Income and Program Participation Panel Wave 9.

REFERENCES

Abdul Latiff, Abdul Rais, and Saidatulakmal Mohd. 2023. "Transport, Mobility and the Wellbeing of Older Adults: An Exploration of Private Chauffeuring and Companionship Services in Malaysia." *International Journal of Environmental Research and Public Health* 20(3): 2720. https://doi.org/10.3390/ijerph20032720.

Acosta, Sonya, and Erik Gartland. 2021. *Families Wait Years for Housing Vouchers Due to Inadequate Funding*. Center on Budget and Policy Priorities. Last modified July 22, 2021. https://www.cbpp.org/sites/default/files/7-22-21hous.pdf.

Adams, Elizabeth J., Laurel M. Hoffman, Kenneth D. Rosenberg, Dawn Peters, and Melissa Pennise. 2015. "Increased Food Insecurity Among Mothers of 2-Year-Olds with Special Health Care Needs." *Maternal and Child Health Journal* 19: 2206–14. https://doi.org/10.1007/s10995-015-1735-9.

Administration for Community Living. 2022a. *2021 Profile of Older Americans*. U.S. Department of Health and Human Services. https://acl.gov/sites/default/files/Profile%20of%20OA/2021%20Profile%20of%20OA/2021ProfileOlderAmericans_508.pdf.

Administration for Community Living. 2022b. *Older Americans Act: Title III Programs 2020 Program Results*. U.S. Department of Health and Human Services. https://acl.gov/sites/default/files/news%202022-09/OAA%20Report_Module%201_Title%20III_8-26-22%20FINAL_508.pdf.

Administration for Community Living. 2022c. *Title III - Grants for State and Community Programs on Aging FY 2020 Final Allocation (Without Any B/C1/C2 Transfers and Allotments)*. U.S. Department of Health and Human Services. https://acl.gov/sites/default/files/about-acl/2020-09/TitleIII-2020.pdf.

Administration for Community Living. 2023a. "Aging, Independence, and Disability Program Data Portal." U.S. Department of Health and Human Services. Last modified August 22, 2023. https://agid.acl.gov/#NationalTabl.

Administration for Community Living. 2023b. "Nutrition Services." U.S. Department of Health and Human Services. Last modified September 21, 2023. https://acl.gov/programs/health-wellness/nutrition-services.

Administration for Community Living. 2024. "FY2025 Justification of Estimates for Appropriations Commitees." U.S. Department of Health and Human Services. April 1, 2024. https://acl.gov/about-acl/budget.

Afulani, Patience, Dena Herman, Alisha Coleman-Jensen, and Gail G. Harrison. 2015. "Food Insecurity and Health Outcomes Among Older Adults: The Role of Cost-Related Medication Underuse." *Journal of Nutrition in Gerontology and Geriatrics* 34(3): 319–42. https://doi.org/10.1080/21551197.2015.1054575.

Akobundu, Ucheoma. 2022. "Perspectives on Food Security in Older Adults in the Covid-19 Era: What We Know, Where We Go?" Generations Today: American Institute on Aging, May 18. https://generations.asaging.org/food-security-older-adults-covid-19-era.

Alemayehu, Berhanu, and Kenneth E. Warner. 2004. "The Lifetime Distribution of Healthcare Costs." *Health Services Research* 39(3): 627–42. https://doi.org/10.1111/j.1475-6773.2004.00248.x.

Allard, Scott W. 2017. *Places in Need*. Russell Sage Foundation.

Allen, Nickolas L., Benjamin J. Becerra, and Monideepa B. Becerra. 2018. "Associations Between Food Insecurity and the Severity of Psychological Distress Among African Americans." *Ethnicity & Health* 23(5): 511–20. https://doi.org/10.1080/13557858.2017.1280139.

Ambegaokar, Sonal, Zoe Neuberger, and Dorothy Rosenbaum. 2017. *Opportunities to Streamline Enrollment Across Public Benefit Programs*. Center on Budget and Policy Priorities, November 2. https://www.cbpp.org/research/poverty-and-inequality/opportunities-to-streamline-enrollment-across-public-benefit.

American Heart Association. 2021. "Heart Health Recommendations for Those with CHD." Last modified September 20, 2023. https://www.heart.org/en/health-topics/congenital-heart-defects/care-and-treatment-for-congenital-heart-defects/heart-health-recommendations-for-those-with-chd.

Anderson, Sue A. 1990. "Core Indicators of Nutritional State for Difficult-to-Sample Populations.'" *Journal of Nutrition* 120(11): 1555–98. https://doi.org/10.1093/jn/120.suppl_11.1555.

Andrews, Erin, Robyn M. Powell, and Kara Ayers. 2022. "The Evolution of Disability Language: Choosing Terms to Describe Disability." *Disability and Health Journal* 15(3): 101328. https://doi.org/10.1016/j.dhjo.2022.101328.

Arena, Olivia, and Clare Salerno. 2020. "Four Ways to Address Food Insecurity Through Transportation Improvements." Urban Wire, January 28. https://www.urban.org/urban-wire/four-ways-address-food-insecurity-through-transportation-improvements.

Arenas, Daniel J., Arthur Thomas, JiCi Wang, and Horace M. Delisser. 2019. "A Systematic Review and Meta-analysis of Depression, Anxiety, and Sleep Disorders in US Adults with Food Insecurity." *Journal of General Internal Medicine* 34: 2874–82. https://doi.org/10.1007/s11606-019-05202-4.

Arteaga, Irma, Colleen Heflin, and Leslie Hodges. 2018. "SNAP Benefits and Pregnancy-Related Emergency Room Visits." *Population Research and Policy Review* 37(6): 1031–1052. https://doi.org/10.1007/s11113-018-9481-5.

Attanasio, Orazio, and Hilary W. Hoynes. 2000. "Differential Mortality and Wealth Accumulation." *Journal of Human Resources* 35(1): 1–29. https://www.jstor.org/stable/146354.

Bahahan, Lina, Astha Singhal, Yihong Zhao, Thayer Scott, and Elizabeth Kaye. 2021. "The Association Between the Supplemental Nutrition Assistance Program Participation and Dental Caries Among U.S. Adults." *International Journal of Dental Hygiene*, 22(1): 251–57. https://doi.org/10.1111/idh.12562.

Balistreri, Kelly Stamper. 2019. "Food Insufficiency and Children with Special Healthcare Needs." *Public Health* 167: 55–61. https://www.ncbi.nlm.nih.gov/pmc/articles/PMC6419505.

Balistreri, Kelly Stamper. 2022. "Older Adults and the Food Security Infrastructure." *Applied Economic Perspectives and Policy* 44(2): 653–70. https://doi.org/10.1002/aepp.13238.

Barnes, Carolyn Y. 2021. "'It Takes a While to Get Used to': The Costs of Redeeming Public Benefits." *Journal of Public Administration Research and Theory* 31(2): 295–310. https://doi.org/10.1093/jopart/muaa042.

Barnes, Carolyn, Sarah Halpern-Meekin, and Jill Hoiting. 2023. "'I Used to Get WIC . . . But Then I Stopped': How WIC Participants Perceive the Value and Burdens of Maintaining Benefits." *RSF: The Russell Sage Foundation Journal of the Social Sciences* 9(5): 32–55. https://doi.org/10.7758/RSF.2023.9.5.02.

Barnes, Carolyn Y., and Virginia Riel. 2022. "'I Don't Know Nothing About That': How 'Learning Costs' Undermine COVID-Related Efforts to Make SNAP and WIC More Accessible." *Administration & Society* 54(10): 1902–30. https://doi.org/10.1177/00953997211073948.

Barrilleaux, Charles, Thomas Holbrook, and Laura Langer. 2002. "Electoral Competition, Legislative Balance, and American State Welfare Policy." *American Journal of Political Science* 46(2): 415–27. https://www.jstor.org/stable/3088385.

Bartfeld, Judith, Craig Gundersen, Timothy Smeeding, and James P. Ziliak, eds. 2015. *SNAP Matters: How Food Stamps Affect Health and Well Being*. Stanford University Press.

Baugreet, Sephora, Ruth M. Hamill, Joseph P. Kerry, and Sinéad McCarthy. 2017. "Mitigating Nutrition and Health Deficiencies in Older Adults: A Role for Food Innovation?" *Journal of Food Science* 82: 848–55. https://doi.org/10.1111/1750-3841.13674.

Bengtson, Vern L., and Katherine R. Allen. 1993. "The Life Course Perspective Applied to Families Over Time." In *Sourcebook of Family Theories and Methods: A Contextual Approach*, edited by Pauline Boss, William J. Doherty, Ralph LaRossa, Walter R. Schumm, and Suzanne K. Steinmetz. Springer. https://doi.org/10.1007/978-0-387-85764-0_19.

Bengtson, Vern L., Glen H. Elder, and Norella M. Putney. 2012. "The Life Course Perspective on Ageing: Linked Lives, Timing, and History." In *Adult Lives: A Life Course Perspective*, edited by Jeanne Katz, Sheila Peace, and Sue Spurr. Bristol University Press.

Benvie, Catherine, Michael Ribar, John Knaus, et al. 2023. *Supplemental Nutrition Assistance Program: State Options Report*. USDA, Food and Nutrition Service. https://fns-prod.azureedge.us/sites/default/files/resource-files/snap-15th-state-options-report-october23.pdf.

Bergmans, Rachel S., Briana Mezuk, and Kara Zivin. 2019. "Food Insecurity and Geriatric Hospitalization." *International Journal of Environmental Research and Public Health* 16(13): 2294. https://doi.org/10.3390/ijerph16132294.

Berko, Jeffrey, Deborah D. Ingram, Shubhayu Saha, and Jennifer D. Parker. 2014. "Deaths Attributed to Heat, Cold, and Other Weather Events in the United States, 2006–2010." *National Health Statistics Report* 30(76): 1–15.

Berkowitz, Seth A., Sanjay Basu, James B. Meigs, and Hilary K. Seligman. 2017. "Food Insecurity and Health Care Expenditures in the United States, 2011–2013." *Health Services Research* 53(3): 1600–1620. https://doi.org/10.1111/1475-6773.12730.

Berkowitz, Seth A., and Deepak Palakshappa. 2024. "Expanded Child Tax Credit and Food Insecurity." *JAMA Internal Medicine* 184(10): 1260–62. https://doi.org/10.1001/jamainternmed.2024.3972.

Berkowitz, Seth A., Hilary K. Seligman, and Niteesh K. Choudhry. 2014. "Treat or Eat: Food Insecurity, Cost-Related Medication Underuse, and Unmet Needs."

American Journal of Medicine 127(4): 303–310.e3. https://doi.org/10.1016/j.amjmed.2014.01.002.

Berkowitz, Seth A., Hilary K. Seligman, Joseph Rigdon, James B. Meigs, and Sanjay Basu. 2017. "Supplemental Nutrition Assistance Program (SNAP) Participation and Health Care Expenditures Among Low-Income Adults." *JAMA Internal Medicine* 117(11): 1642–49. https://doi.org/10.1001/jamainternmed.2017.4841.

Bermúdez-Millán, Angela, Julie A. Wagner, Richard S. Feinn, et al. 2019. "Inflammation and Stress Biomarkers Mediate the Association Between Household Food Insecurity and Insulin Resistance Among Latinos with Type 2 Diabetes." *Journal of Nutrition* 149(6): 982–88. https://doi.org/10.1093/jn/nxz021.

Bernard, H. Russell, Amber Wutich, and Gery W. Ryan. 2016. *Analyzing Qualitative Data: Systematic Approaches*. SAGE Publications.

Berry, William D., Evan J. Ringquist, Richard C. Fording, and Russell L. Hanson. 1998. "Measuring Citizen and Government Ideology in the American States, 1960–1993." *American Journal of Political Science* 42(1): 327–48. https://www.jstor.org/stable/2991759.

Bhargava, Vibha, and Jung Sun Lee. 2017. "Food Insecurity and Health Care Utilization Among Older Adults." *Journal of Applied Gerontology* 36(12): 1415–32. https://doi.org/10.1177/0733464815625835.

Bickel, Gary, Mark Nord, Cristofer Price, William Hamilton, and John Cook. 2000. *Guide to Measuring Household Food Security, Revised 2000*. U.S. Department of Agriculture, Food and Nutrition Service.

Billioux, Alexander, Katherine Verlander, Susan Anthony, and Dawn Alley. 2017. "Standardized Screening for Health-Related Social Needs in Clinical Settings: The Accountable Health Communities Screening Tool." *National Academy of Medicine Perspectives*, discussion paper. Washington, DC: National Academy of Medicine. https://nam.edu/standardized-screening-for-health-related-social-needs-in-clinical-settings-the-accountable-health-communities-screening-tool/.

Bitler, Marianne. 2015. "The Health and Nutrition Effects of SNAP: Selection into the Program and a Review of the Literature on its Effects." In *SNAP Matters: How Food Stamps Affect Health and Well-Being*, edited by Judith Bartfeld, Craig Gundersen, Timothy M. Smeeding, and James P. Ziliak. Stanford University Press.

Board of Governors of the Federal Reserve System. 2019. "Survey of Consumer Finances." Database, Federal Reserve Board, Washington, DC. Accessed October 14, 2024. https://www.federalreserve.gov/econres/scf_2019.htm.

Board of Governors of the Federal Reserve System. 2023. *Economic Well-Being of U.S. Households in 2022*. https://www.federalreserve.gov/publications/files/2022-report-economic-well-being-us-households-202305.pdf.

Boersma, Peter, Lindsey I. Black, and Brian W. Ward. 2020. "Prevalence of Multiple Chronic Conditions Among U.S. Adults, 2018." Centers for Disease Control and Prevention. https://www.cdc.gov/pcd/issues/2020/20_0130.htm.

Bohr, Jeremiah, and Anna McCreery. 2020. "Do Energy Burdens Contribute to Economic Poverty in the United States? A Panel Analysis." *Social Forces* 99(1): 155–77. https://doi.org/10.1093/sf/soz131.

Bovell-Ammon, Allison, Nicole C. McCann, Martha Mulugeta, Stephanie Ettinger de Cuba, Julia Raifman, and Paul Shafer. 2022. "Association of the Expiration of Child Tax Credit Advance Payments with Food Insufficiency in US Households." *JAMA Network Open*: 5(10): e2234438. https://doi.org/10.1001/jamanetworkopen.2022.34438.

Braveman, Paula, and Colleen Barclay. 2009. "Health Disparities Beginning in Childhood: A Life-Course Perspective." *Pediatrics* 124(Suppl 3): S163–S175. https://doi.org/10.1542/peds.2009-1100D.

Brostow, Diana P., Elise Gunzburger, and Kali S. Thomas. 2017. "Food Insecurity Among Veterans: Findings from the Health and Retirement Study." *Journal of Nutrition Health and Aging* 21(10): 1358–64. https://doi.org/10.1007/s12603-017-0910-7.

Brown, Adrianne, and Wendy Manning. 2021. "Relationship Status Trends According to Age and Gender, 2019–2021." Bowling Green State University, National Center for Family & Marriage Research, Family Profile No. 25.

Brown, Jennifer Erin, Nari Rhee, Joelle Saad-Lessler, and Diane Oakley. 2016. *Shortchanged in Retirement: Continuing Challenges to Women's Financial Future*. National Institute on Retirement Security. https://laborcenter.berkeley.edu/pdf/2016/NIRS-Women-In-Retirement.pdf.

Brown, Perry S., Dixie Durham, Rick D. Tivis, et al. 2018. "Evaluation of Food Insecurity in Adults and Children with Cystic Fibrosis: Community Case Study." *Frontiers in Public Health* 6: 348. https://doi.org/10.3389/fpubh.2018.00348.

Brucker, Debra L. 2016. "Food Insecurity Among Young Adults with Disabilities in the United States: Findings from the National Health Interview Survey." *Disability and Health Journal* 9(2): 298–305. https://doi.org/10.1016/j.dhjo.2015.11.005.

Brucker, Debra L., and Alisha Coleman-Jensen. 2017. "Food Insecurity Across the Adult Life Span for Persons with Disabilities." *Journal of Disability Policy Studies* 28(2): 109–18. https://doi.org/10.1177/1044207317710701.

Brucker, Debra L., Katie Jajtner, and Sophie Mitra. 2022. "Does Social Security Promote Food Security? Evidence for Older Households." *Applied Economic Perspectives and Policy* 44(2): 671–86. https://doi.org/10.1002/aepp.13218.

Brucker, Debra L., and Derek Nord. 2016. "Food Insecurity Among Young Adults with Intellectual and Developmental Disabilities in the United States: Evidence from the National Health Interview Survey." *American Journal on Intellectual and Developmental Disabilities* 121(6): 520–32.

Burke, Michael P., Sonya J. Jones, Edward A. Frongillo, Maryah S. Fram, Christine E. Blake, and Darcy A. Freedman. 2018. "Severity of Household Food Insecurity and Lifetime Racial Discrimination Among African-American Households in South Carolina." *Ethnicity & Health* 23(3): 276–92. https://doi.org/10.1080/13557858.2016.1263286.

Burris, Mecca, Laura Kihlstrom, Karen Serrano Arce, et al. 2019. "Food Insecurity, Loneliness, and Social Support Among Older Adults." *Journal of Hunger & Environmental Nutrition* 16(1): 29–44. https://doi.org/10.1080/19320248.2019.1595253.

Burtless, Gary. 2015. "Trends in the Well-Being of the Aged and Their Prospects Through 2030." *Forum for Health Economics and Policy* 18(2): 97–118. https://doi.org/10.1515/fhep-2015-0039.

Butcher, Kristin F., Lucie Schmidt, Lara Shore-Sheppard, and Tara Watson. 2023. "Living with Children and Food Insecurity in Seniors." *Applied Economic Perspectives and Policy* 45(1): 234–61. https://doi.org/10.1002/aepp.13333.

Canning, Patrick, and Brian Stacy. 2019. *The Supplemental Nutrition Assistance Program (SNAP) and the Economy: New Estimates of the SNAP Multiplier*. Economic Research Report No. 265. U.S. Department of Agriculture, Economic Research Service. https://www.ers.usda.gov/webdocs/publications/93529/err-265.pdf?v=8132.4.

Cao, Xingqi, Chao Ma, Zhoutao Zheng, et al. 2022. "Contribution of Life Course Circumstances to the Acceleration of Phenotypic and Functional Aging: A Retrospective Study." *EClinicalMedicine* 51: 101548. https://doi.org/10.1016/j.eclinm.2022.101548.

Carequest Institute for Dental Health. 2024. "Medicaid Dental Coverage by State." Accessed October 15, 2024. https://www.carequest.org/Medicaid-Adult-Dental-Coverage-Checker.

Carlson, Steven, and Brynne Keith-Jennings. 2018. *SNAP Is Linked with Improved Nutritional Outcomes and Lower Health Care Costs*. Center on Budget and Policy Priorities, January 17. https://www.cbpp.org/sites/default/files/atoms/files/1-17-18fa.pdf.

Carr, Deborah. 2023. *Aging in America*. University of California Press.

Carter, Julie. 2023. "Many Older Adults Face Unpaid Medical Bills Despite Insurance Coverage." Medicare Rights Center, June 1. https://www.medicarerights.org/medicare-watch/2023/06/01/many-older-adults-face-unpaid-medical-bills-despite-insurance-coverage.

Carvajal-Aldaz, Diana, Gabriela Cucalon, and Carlos Ordonez. 2022. "Food Insecurity as a Risk Factor for Obesity: A Review." *Frontiers in Nutrition* 9: 1012734. https://doi.org/10.3389/fnut.2022.1012734.

Castillo, Maria, and Joe Daniel. 2022. "By the Numbers: Low-Income Energy Assistance." Rocky Mountain Institute, August 22. https://rmi.org/by-the-numbers-low-income-energy-assistance.

Castner, Laura, Breanna Wakar, Kathy Wroblewska, Carole Trippe, and Nancy Cole. 2020. *Benefit Redemption Patterns in the Supplemental Nutrition Assistance Program in Fiscal Year 2017, Final Report.* Insight Policy Research. https://fns-prod.azureedge.us/sites/default/files/resource-files/SNAPEBT-BenefitRedemption.pdf.

Castwell, Julie A., and Ann L. Yaktine, eds. 2013. "Supplemental Nutritional Assistance Program: Examining the Evidence to Define Benefit Adequacy." Committee on Examination of the Adequacy of Food Resources and SNAP Allotments. Washington, DC: National Academies Press, 2013. https://doi.org/10.17226/13485.

Cayuga County. 2025. "Congregate Meals." Accessed February 8, 2025. https://www.cayugacounty.us/584/Congregate-Meals.

Center for Health Care Strategies. 2019. *Medicaid Adult Dental Benefits Coverage by State.* Accessed October 15, 2024. https://www.chcs.org/media/Medicaid-Adult-Dental-Benefits-Overview-Appendix_091519.pdf.

Center on Budget and Policy Priorities. 2024a. "A Quick Guide to Calculating SNAP Benefits and Eligibility." Last modified March 3, 2023. https://www.cbpp.org/research/food-assistance/a-quick-guide-to-snap-eligibility-and-benefits.

Center on Budget and Policy Priorities. 2024b. "Policy Basics: Supplemental Security Income." Last modified February 21, 2023. https://www.cbpp.org/research/social-security/supplemental-security-income.

Centers for Disease Control and Prevention. 2023a. "Older Adults and Extreme Heat." https://www.cdc.gov/aging/emergency-preparedness/older-adults-extreme-heat/index.html.

Centers for Disease Control and Prevention. 2023b. "QuickStats: Percentage of Adults Aged ≥18 Years in Fair or Poor Health, by Family Income and Age Group—National Health Interview Survey, United States, 2021." March 31. https://www.cdc.gov/mmwr/volumes/72/wr/mm7213a6.htm.

Centers for Disease Control and Prevention. 2024. "CDC Data Shows over 70 Million U.S. Adults Reported Having a Disability." https://www.cdc.gov/media/releases/2024/s0716-Adult-disability.html.

Center for Nutrition and Health Impact. 2025. "Nutrition Security and Related Measures: Nutrition Security, Healthfulness Choice and Dietary Choice." Accessed January 28, 2025. https://www.centerfornutrition.org/nutrition-security.

Chan, Sewin, and Ingrid Gould Ellen. 2017. "Housing for an Aging Population." *Housing Policy Debate* 27(2): 1–26. https://nlihc.org/sites/default/files/Housing_for_an_Aging_Population.pdf.

Choi, Shinae, Debrah Carr, and Eun Ha Namkung. 2021. "Physical Disability and Older Adults' Perceived Food and Economic Insecurity During the COVID-19 Pandemic." *Journals of Gerontology: Series B* 77(7): e123–e133. https://doi.org/10.1093/geronb/gbab162.

Christensen, Gigi, and Erin Todd Bronchetti. 2020. "Local Food Prices and the Purchasing Power of SNAP Benefits." *Food Policy* 95: 101937. https://doi.org/10.1016/j.foodpol.2020.101937.

Cody, Scott, Laura Castner, James Mabli, and Julie Sykes. 2007. *Dynamics of Food Stamp Program Participation, 2001–2003*. Mathematica Policy Research.

Colello, Kristen. 2020. *Senior Nutrition Programs' Response to COVID-19*. Congressional Research Service. Last modified April 1, 2020. https://crsreports.congress.gov/product/pdf/IN/IN11266.

Coleman-Jensen, Alisha. 2020. "U.S. Food Insecurity and Population Trends with a Focus on Adults with Disabilities." *Physiology & Behavior* 220: 112865. https://doi.org/10.1016/j.physbeh.2020.112865.

Coleman-Jensen, Alisha, Christian Gregory, and Matthew Rabbitt. 2020. *Definitions of Food Security*. U.S. Department of Agriculture.

Coleman-Jensen, Alisha, and Mark Nord. 2013. *Food Insecurity Among Households with Working-Age Adults with Disabilities*. U.S. Department of Agriculture.

Coleman-Jensen, Alisha, Matthew P. Rabbitt, Christian A. Gregory, and Anita Singh. 2021. *Household Food Security in the United States in 2020*. Economic Research Report No. 298, U.S. Department of Agriculture, Economic Research Service.

Coleman-Jensen, Alisha, Matthew P. Rabbitt, Christian A. Gregory, and Anita Singh. 2022. *Household Food Security in the United States in 2021*. Economic Research Report No. 309, U.S. Department of Agriculture, Economic Research Service.

Consumer Financial Protection Bureau, Office of Older Americans. 2023. "Medical Billing and Collections Among Older Americans." May 30. https://www

.consumerfinance.gov/data-research/research-reports/issue-spotlight-medical-billing-and-collections-among-older-americans/.

Congressional Research Service. 2023. *The Emergency Food Assistance Program (TEFAP): Background and Funding.* https://crsreports.congress.gov/product/pdf/R/R45408.

Cooper, Robin. 2022. "Climate Change and Older Adults: Planning Ahead to Protect Your Health." National Council on Aging, April 21. https://www.ncoa.org/article/climate-change-and-older-adults-planning-ahead-to-protect-your-health.

Costanzo, Chris. 2022. "More Food Banks Lift Wages, Setting an Example." Food Bank News, May 10. https://foodbanknews.org/more-food-banks-lift-wages-setting-an-example.

Creamer, John, Emily A. Shrider, Kalee Burns, and Frances Chen. 2022. *Poverty in the United States: 2021.* U.S. Census Bureau, U.S. Department of Commerce, Current Population Reports No. P60-277. U.S. Government Publishing Office. https://www.census.gov/library/publications/2022/demo/p60-277.html.

Cronquist, Kathryn. 2021. *Characteristics of Supplemental Nutrition Assistance Program Households: Fiscal Year 2019.* U.S. Department of Agriculture, Food and Nutrition Service, Office of Policy Support. https://www.fns.usda.gov/snap/characteristics-snap-households-fy-2019.

Cunnyngham, Karen. 2023a. *Reaching Those in Need: Estimates of State Supplemental Nutrition Assistance Program Participation Rates in 2020.* Prepared by Mathematica for the U.S. Department of Agriculture, Food and Nutrition Service. https://fns-prod.azureedge.us/sites/default/files/resource-files/snap-participation-2020-final-report.pdf.

Cunnyngham, Karen. 2023b. *Empirical Bayes Shrinkage Estimates of State Supplemental Nutrition Assistance Program Participation Rates in Fiscal Year 2017 to Fiscal Year 2019 for All Eligible People and Working Poor People.* Prepared by Mathematica. U.S. Department of Agriculture, Food and Nutrition Service, Office of Policy Support. https://fns-prod.azureedge.us/sites/default/files/resource-files/snap-tech-partrate2017-2019.pdf.

Daponte, Beth O., and Shannon Bade. 2006. "How the Private Food Assistance Network Evolved: Interactions Between Public and Private Responses to Hunger." *Nonprofit and Voluntary Sector Quarterly* 35(4): 668–90. https://doi.org/10.1177/0899764006289771.

Decker, Sandra L., Salam Abdus, and Brandy J. Lipton. 2022. "Eligibility for and Enrollment in Medicaid Among Nonelderly Adults After Implementation of the Affordable Care Act." *Medical Care Research and Review* 79(1): 125–32. https://doi.org/10.1177/10775587211027944.

DeLuca, Stefanie. 2022. "Sample Selection Matters: Moving Toward Empirically Sound Qualitative Research." *Sociological Methods & Research* 52(2): 1–13. https://doi.org/10.1177/00491241221140425.

Deokrye, Baek. 2016. "The Effect of Public Transportation Accessibility on Food Insecurity." *Eastern Economic Journal* 42: 104–34. https://doi.org/10.1057/eej.2014.62.

Desilva, Dana, and Dennis Anderson-Villaluz. 2021. "Nutrition as We Age: Healthy Eating with the Dietary Guidelines." Office of Disease Prevention and Health Promotion, U.S. Department of Health and Human Services. Last modified July 20, 2021. https://health.gov/news/202107/nutrition-we-age-healthy-eating-dietary-guidelines.

Dickert-Conlin, Stacy, Katie Fitzpatrick, Laura Tiehen, and Brian Stacy. 2016. "The Downs and Ups of the SNAP Caseload: What Matters?" Social Science Research Network, December 1. https://papers.ssrn.com/sol3/papers.cfm?abstract_id=3052570.

Dickinson, Maggie. 2020. *Feeding the Crisis: Care and Abandonment in America's Food Safety Net.* University of California Press.

DiMaria-Ghalili, Rose A., Kathryn N. Porter, Judith Haber, Carole Ann Palmer, and Michele J. Saunders. 2020. *Interrelationships Between Nutrition and Oral Health in Older Adults.* Gerontological Society of America. https://www.geron.org/images/gsa/documents/whatshotnutritionoralhealth.pdf.

Dorn, Stan, Sarah Minton, and Erika Huber. 2014. *Examples of Promising Practices for Integrating and Coordinating Eligibility, Enrollment, and Retention: Human Services and Health Programs Under the Affordable Care Act.* Urban Institute. https://www.urban.org/sites/default/files/publication/22961/413231-Examples-of-Promising-Practices-for-Integrating-and-Coordinating-Eligibility-Enrollment-and-Retention-Human-Services-and-Health-Programs-Under-the-Affordable-Care-Act.PDF.

Dumas, Brianna L., Diane M. Harris, Jean M. McMahon, et al. 2021. "Prevalence of Municipal-Level Policies Dedicated to Transportation That Consider Food Access." *Preventing Chronic Disease* 18: 210193. https://doi.org/10.5888/pcd18.210193.

Dunifon, Rachel E., Kathleen M. Ziol-Guest, and Kimberley Kopko. 2014. "Grandparent Co-Residence and Family Well-Being: Implications for Research and Policy." *Annals of the American Academy of Political and Social Science* 654(1): 110–26. https://doi.org/10.1177/0002716214526530.

Dushi, Irena, Howard M. Iams, and Brad Trenkamp. 2017. "The Importance of Social Security Benefits to the Income of the Aged Population." *Social Security Bulletin* 77(2). https://www.ssa.gov/policy/docs/ssb/v77n2/v77n2p1.html.

Dutko, Paula, Michele Ver Ploeg, and Tracey Farrigan. 2012. *Characteristics and Influential Factors of Food Deserts*. U.S. Department of Agriculture, Economic Research Report No. 140. https://www.ers.usda.gov/webdocs/publications/45014/30940_err140.pdf.

Edin, Kathryn, and Laura Lein. 1997. *Making Ends Meet: How Single Mothers Survive Welfare and Low-Wage Work*. Russell Sage Foundation.

Elder, Glen H. 1998. "The Life Course as Developmental Theory." *Child Development* 69(1): 1–12. https://doi.org/10.2307/1132065.

Ellis, Renee R., and Tavia Simmons. 2014. *Coresident Grandparents and Their Grandchildren: 2012*. Population Characteristics No. P20-576. U.S. Census Bureau. https://www.census.gov/library/publications/2014/demo/p20-576.html.

Environmental Protection Agency. 2021. "Climate Change Indictors: Heat-Related Deaths." https://www.epa.gov/climate-indicators/climate-change-indicators-heat-related-deaths.

Environmental Protection Agency. 2024. "Climate-Change Indicators: Heat-Related Deaths." Accessed October 15, 2024. https://www.epa.gov/climate-indicators/climate-change-indicators-heat-related-deaths.

Fannin, William C., Colleen Heflin, and Leonard M. Lopoo. 2024. "The Effects of Waiving WIC Physical Presence Requirements on Program Caseloads." *Social Service Review* 98(3): 482–513.

Federal Communications Commission. 2023. "Lifeline Support for Affordable Communication." Accessed May 20, 2023. https://www.fcc.gov/lifeline-consumers.

Federal Communications Commission. 2024. "Lifeline Support for Affordable Communications." Accessed September 25, 2024. https://www.fcc.gov/lifeline-consumers.

Feeding America. 2022. "A Bold Aspiration." Accessed October 15, 2024. https://www.feedingamerica.org/about-us/financials/executive-summary/2022#2022-financial-report.

Feeding America. 2023. "Latest Food Bank Survey Finds Majority of Food Banks Reporting Increased Demand." May 2. https://www.feedingamerica.org/about-us/press-room/latest-food-bank-survey-finds-majority-food-banks-reporting-increased-demand.

Feeding America. 2024. *Annual Report 2024*. Accessed February 8, 2025. https://www.feedingamerica.org/sites/default/files/2024-12/FA_24AnnRep_d5_ONLINE.pdf.

Fellowes, Matthew C., and Gretchen Rowe. 2004. "Politics and the New American Welfare States." *American Journal of Political Science* 48(2): 362–73. https://doi.org/10.1111/j.0092-5853.2004.00075.x.

Finkelstein, Amy, and Matthew J. Notowidigdo. 2018. "Take-Up and Targeting: Experimental Evidence from SNAP." National Bureau of Economic Research Working Paper 24652. https://www.nber.org/papers/w24652.

Fiol, Olivia, Sofia Hinojosa, Julio Salas, Elaine Waxman, Emily Peiffer, and Rhiannon Newman. 2023. "An Illinois Food Bank's Move Toward Online Ordering and Grocery Delivery Is Removing Barriers to Healthy Food Access." Urban Institute. Accessed April 28, 2024. https://www.urban.org/storys/illinois-food-banks-move-toward-online-ordering-and-grocery-delivery-removing-barriers.

Fitzpatrick, Katie, Nadia Greenhalgh-Stanley, and Michele Ver Ploeg. 2015. "The Impact of Food Deserts on Food Insufficiency and SNAP Participation Among the Elderly." *American Journal of Agricultural Economics* 98(1): 19–40. https://doi.org/10.1093/ajae/aav044.

Flood, Sarah, Miriam King, Renae Rodgers, Steven Ruggles, J. Robert Warren, Daniel Backman, Annie Chen, Grace Cooper, Stephanie Richards, Megan Schouweiler, and Michael Westberry. 2024. *IPUMS CPS: Version 12.0* Food Security Supplement. Minneapolis, MN: IPUMS. https://doi.org/10.18128/D030.V12.0.

Food and Agriculture Organization of the United Nations. 2008. *An Introduction to the Basic Concepts of Food Insecurity.* Accessed October 15, 2024. https://www.fao.org/3/al936e/al936e00.pdf.

Food Research and Action Center. 2017. *A Guide to Supplemental Security Income/Supplemental Nutrition Assistance Program Combined Application Projects.* June 2017. https://frac.org/wp-content/uploads/guide-ssi-snap-combined-application-projects.pdf.

Fraker, Thomas M., Alberto P. Martini, James C. Ohls, and Michael Ponza. 1995. "The Effects of Cashing-Out Food Stamps on Household Food Use and the Cost of Issuing Benefits." *Journal of Policy Analysis and Management* 14(3): 372–92.

Freed, Meredith, Jeannie Fuglesten Biniek, Anthony Damico, and Tricia Neuman. 2024. "Medicare Advantage 2025 Spotlight: A First Look at Plan Premiums and Benefits." Kaiser Family Foundation, November 15. https://www.kff.org/medicare/issue-brief/medicare-advantage-2025-spotlight-a-first-look-at-plan-premiums-and-benefits/#:~:text=Medicare%20Advantage%202025%20Spotlight:%20A%20First%20Look%20at%20Plan%20Premiums%20and%20Benefits,-Meredith%20Freed%2C%20Jeannie&text=Note:%20This%20analysis%20was%20updated,describes%20trends%20in%20plan%20offerings.

Freed, Meredith, Tricia Neuman, and Gretchen Jacobson. 2019. "Drilling Down on Dental Coverage and Costs for Medicare Beneficiaries." Kaiser Family Foundation, March 13. https://www.kff.org/medicare/issue-brief/drilling-down-on-dental-coverage-and-costs-for-medicare-beneficiaries/view/footnotes/#footnote-395899-2.

Freed, Meredith, Nancy Ochieng, Nolan Sroczynski, Anthony Damico, and Krutika Amin. 2021. "Medicare and Dental Coverage: A Closer Look." Kaiser Family Foundation, July 28. https://www.kff.org/medicare/issue-brief/medicare-and-dental-coverage-a-closer-look.

Freedman, Vicki A., and Jennifer C. Cornman. 2023. "National Health and Aging Trends Study: Trends Dashboards." Michigan Center on the Demography of Aging, University of Michigan. https://micda.isr.umich.edu/research/nhats-trends-dashboards.

Freedman, Vicki A., Jennifer C. Cornman, and Judith D. Kasper. 2021. *National Health and Aging Trends Study Chart Book: Key Trends, Measures, and Detailed Tables*. https://micda.isr.umich.edu/wp-content/uploads/2022/03/NHATS-Companion-Chartbook-to-Trends-Dashboards-2020.pdf.

Fry, Richard, and Dana Braga. 2023. *Older Workers Are Growing in Number and Earning Higher Wages*. Pew Research Center, December 14. https://www.pewresearch.org/wp-content/uploads/sites/20/2023/12/ST_2023.12.14_Older-Workers_Report.pdf.

Fryar, Cheryl D., Yechiam Ostchega, Craig M. Hales, Guangyu Zhang, and Deanna Kruszon-Moran. 2017. "Hypertension Prevalence and Control Among Adults: United States, 2015–2016." *National Center for Health Statistics Data Brief* 289: 1–8. https://www.cdc.gov/nchs/data/databriefs/db289.pdf.

Ganong, Peter, and Jeffrey B. Liebman. 2018. "The Decline, Rebound, and Further Rise in SNAP Enrollment: Disentangling Business Cycle Fluctuations and Policy Changes." *American Economic Journal: Economic Policy* 10(4): 153–76.

Gavin, Kara. 2024. "Grandparents Help Grandkids in Many Ways—But the Reverse May Be True Too, U-M Poll Suggests." *University of Michigan News*, November 12. https://news.umich.edu/grandparents-help-grandkids-in-many-waysbut-the-reverse-may-be-true-too-u-m-poll-suggests/#:~:text=As%20many%20Americans%20prepare%20to,health%20and%20risk%20of%20loneliness.

Gearing, Maeve, Sujata Dixit-Joshi, and Laurie May. 2021. "Barriers That Constrain the Adequacy of Supplemental Nutrition Assistance Program (SNAP) Allotments: Survey Findings." Westat, U.S. Department of Agriculture, Food and Nutrition Service, June 2021.

Gearing, Maeve, Megan Lewis, Claire Wilson, Carla Bozzolo, and Dani Hansen. 2021. "Barriers That Constrain the Adequacy of Supplemental Nutrition Assistance Program (SNAP) Allotments: In-Depth Interview Findings." Westat, U.S. Department of Agriculture, Food and Nutrition Service, June 2021.

Geller, Daniel, Julia Isaacs, Breno Braga, and Borjan Zic. 2019. *Exploring the Causes of State Variation in SNAP Administrative Costs*. Prepared by Manhattan Strategy Group and the Urban Institute for the U.S. Department of Agriculture, Food and Nutrition Service. https://fns-prod.azureedge.us/sites/default/files/media/file/SNAP-State-Variation-Admin-Costs-Summary.pdf.

Generations United. 2023. *State of Grandfamilies: 2022. Together at the Table*. https://www.gu.org/app/uploads/2022/11/2022-Grandfamilies-Report-FINAL-R1-WEB.pdf.

George, Caroline, and Adie Tomer. 2022. "Delivering to Deserts: New Data Reveals the Geography of Digital Access to Food in the U.S." Brookings Institution, May 11. https://www.brookings.edu/articles/delivering-to-deserts-new-data-reveals-the-geography-of-digital-access-to-food-in-the-us.

Ghilarducci, T., Siavash Radpour, Bridget Fisher, and Joelle Saad-Lesser. 2015. *Inadequate Retirement Account Balances for Families Nearing Retirement*. Schwartz Center for Economic Policy Analysis and Department of Economics, New School for Social Research, Policy Note Series. https://www.economicpolicyresearch.org/images/docs/research/retirement_security/Inadequate_Retirement_Account_Balances_for_Families_Nearing_Retirement.pdf.

Giannarelli, Linda, Sarah Minton, Laura Wheaton, and Sarah Knowles. 2023. *A Safety-Net with 100 Percent Population: How Much Would Benefits Increase and Poverty Decline?* Urban Institute. https://www.urban.org/sites/default/files/2023-08/A%20Safety%20Net%20with%20100%20Percent%20Participation-%20How%20Much%20Would%20Benefits%20Increase%20and%20Poverty%20Decline_0.pdf.

Giannella, Eric, Tatiana Homonoff, Gwen Rino, and Jason Somerville. 2023. "Administrative Burden and Procedural Denials: Experimental Evidence from SNAP." *American Economic Journal: Economic Policy* 16(4): 316–40.

Giordono, Leanne, David W. Rothwell, Stephanie Grutzmacher, and Mark Edwards. 2022. "Understanding SNAP Use Patterns Among Older Adults." *Applied Economic Perspectives and Policy* 44(2): 609–34. https://doi.org/10.1002/aepp.13228.

Glaser, Barney G., and Anselm L. Strauss. 2017. *The Discovery of Grounded Theory: Strategies for Qualitative Research*. Routledge.

Goldberg, Shari L., and Barbara E. Mawn. 2015. "Predictors of Food Insecurity Among Older Adults in the United States." *Public Health Nursing* 32(5): 397–407. https://doi.org/10.1111/phn.12173.

Gonyea, Judith G., Arden E. O'Donnell, Alexandra Curley, and Vy Trieu. 2022. "Food Insecurity and Loneliness Amongst Older Urban Subsidized Housing Residents: The Importance of Social Connectedness." *Health & Social Care in the Community* 30: e5959–e5967. https://doi.org/10.1111/hsc.14027.

Government Accountability Office. 2019. *Nutrition Assistance Programs: Agencies Could Do More to Help Address the Nutritional Needs of Older Adults*. https://www.gao.gov/assets/gao-20-18.pdf.

Government Accountability Office. 2021. *COVID-19: Selected States Modified Meal Provision and Other Older Americans Act Services to Prioritize Safety*. Report No. 22-104425. Congressional Addresses. https://www.gao.gov/assets/gao-22-104425.pdf.

Government Accountability Office. 2022. *Comparison of Income, Wealth, and Survival in the United States with Selected Countries*. Report No. 22-103950. Committee on the Budget, U.S. Senate. https://www.gao.gov/assets/gao-22-103950.pdf.

Graff, Michelle, and Maureen Pirog. 2019. "Red Tape Is Not So Hot: Asset Tests Impact Participation in the Low-Income Home Energy Assistance Program." *Energy Policy* 129: 749–64. https://doi.org/10.1016/j.enpol.2019.02.042.

Gregory, Christian A., and Alisha Coleman-Jensen. 2013. "Do High Food Prices Increase Food Insecurity in the United States?" *Applied Economic Perspectives and Policy* 35(4): 679–707. https://doi.org/10.1093/aepp/ppt024.

Gregory, Christian A., Lisa Mancino, and Alisha Coleman-Jensen. 2019. *Food Security and Food Purchase Quality Among Low-Income Households: Findings from the National Household Food Acquisition and Purchase Survey (FoodAPS)*. Economic Research Report No. ERR-269, U.S. Department of Agriculture. https://www.ers.usda.gov/webdocs/publications/93725/err-269.pdf?v=3245.9.

Gregory, Christian A., Matthew Rabbitt, and David Ribar. 2015. "The Supplemental Nutrition Assistance Program and Food Insecurity." In *SNAP Matters: How Food Stamps Affect Health and Well-Being*, edited by Judith Bartfeld, Craig Gundersen, Timothy M. Smeeding, and James P. Ziliak. Stanford University Press.

Gregory, Christian A., and Travis A. Smith. 2019. "Salience, Food Security, and SNAP Receipt." *Journal of Policy Analysis and Management* 38: 124–54. https://doi.org/10.1002/pam.22093.

Gualtieri, Marie C., and Amy M. Donley. 2016. "Senior Hunger: The Importance of Quality Assessment Tools in Determining Need." *Journal of Applied Social Science* 10(1): 8–21. https://doi.org/10.1177/1936724414561258.

Gundersen, Craig, Emily E. Engelhard, Amy S. Crumbaugh, and Hilary K. Seligman. 2017. "Brief Assessment of Food Insecurity Accurately Identifies High-Risk

U.S. Adults." *Public Health Nutrition* 20(8): 1367–71. https://doi.org/10.1017/S1368980017000180.

Gundersen, Craig, and James P. Ziliak. 2015. "Food Insecurity and Health Outcomes." *Health Affairs* 34(11): 1830–39. https://doi.org/10.1377/hlthaff.2015.0645.

Gundersen, Craig, and James P. Ziliak. 2021. *The Health Consequences of Senior Hunger in the United States: Evidence from the 1999–2016 NHANES*. Feeding America, National Foundation to End Senior Hunger. https://www.feedingamerica.org/sites/default/files/2021-08/2021%20-%20Health%20Consequences%20of%20Senior%20Hunger%201999-2016.pdf.

Guthro, Andrew. 2021. "Enhanced SNAP Benefits Provided Better Food Security for Older Americans During the Pandemic." Mathematica, October 25. https://www.mathematica.org/blogs/snap-benefits-provided-food-security-for-older-americans-during-covid-19.

Haider, Steven J., Alison Jacknowitz, and Robert F. Schoeni. 2003. "Food Stamps and the Elderly: Why Is Participation So Low?" *Journal of Human Resources* 38: 1080–111. https://doi.org/10.2307/3558982.

Hake, Monica, and Sena Dawes. 2024. *Food Insecurity Among Seniors and Older Adults in 2022*. Feeding America. chrome-extension://efaidnbmnnnibpcajpcglclefindmkaj/https://www.feedingamerica.org/sites/default/files/2024-07/Food%20Insecurity%20Among%20Seniors%20and%20Older%20Adults%20in%202022.pdf.

Harrington Meyer, Madonna. 2014. *Grandmothers at Work: Juggling Families and Jobs*. New York University Press.

Harrington Meyer, Madonna, and Ynesse Abdul-Malak. 2020. *Grandparenting Children with Disabilities*. Springer.

Harrington Meyer, Madonna, Sarah Reilly, and Julia M. Finan. 2021. "The U.S. Should Expand Access to Dental Care for Older Adults." *Lerner Center for Public Health Promotion: Population Health Research Brief Series* 161. Syracuse University. https://surface.syr.edu/lerner/161.

Hastings, Justine, and Jesse M. Shapiro. 2018. "How Are SNAP Benefits Spent? Evidence from a Retail Panel." *American Economic Review* 108(12): 3493–540.

Heflin, Colleen M., Claire E. Altman, and Laura L. Rodriguez. 2019. "Food Insecurity and Disability in the United States." *Disability and Health Journal* 12(2): 220–26. https://doi.org/10.1016/j.dhjo.2018.09.006.

Heflin, Colleen M., Irma Arteaga, Leslie Hodges, Jean Felix Ndashiyme, and Matthew P. Rabbitt. 2019. "SNAP Benefits and Childhood Asthma." *Social Science & Medicine* 220: 203–11. https://doi.org/10.1016/j.socscimed.2018.11.001.

Heflin, Colleen M., Irma Arteaga, Jean Felix Ndashiyme, and Matthew Rabbitt. 2020. "Childhood Injuries and Food Stamp Benefits: An Examination of Administrative Data in One U.S. State." *BMC Pediatrics* 20: 297. https://doi.org/10.1186/s12887-020-02084-y.

Heflin, Colleen M., William Clay Fannin, and Leonard Lopoo. 2023. "Local Control, Discretion, and Administrative Burden: SNAP Interview Waivers and Caseloads During the COVID-19 Pandemic." *American Review of Public Administration* 53(7/8). https://doi.org/10.1177/02750740231186423.

Heflin, Colleen M., Leslie Hodges, Irma Arteaga, and Chinedum O. Ojinnaka. 2023. "Churn in the Older Adult SNAP Population." *Applied Economics Perspectives and Policy* 45(1): 350–71. https://doi.org/10.1002/aepp.13288.

Heflin, Colleen M., Leslie Hodges, and Chinedum Ojinnaka. 2020. "Administrative Churn in SNAP and Healthcare Utilization Patterns." *Medical Care* 58(1): 33–37. https://doi.org/10.1097/MLR.0000000000001235.

Heflin, Colleen M., Leslie Hodges, Chinedum Ojinnaka, and Irma Artega. 2022. "Hypertension, Diabetes, and Medication Adherence Among the Older Supplemental Nutritional Assistance Program Population (SNAP)." *Journal of Applied Gerontology* 14(3): 780–87. https://doi.org/10.1177/07334648211022493.

Heflin, Colleen M., Samuel Ingram, and James P. Ziliak. 2019. "The Effects of the Supplemental Nutrition Assistance Program on Mortality." *Health Affairs* 38(11): 1807–15. https://doi.org/10.1377/hlthaff.2019.00405.

Heflin, Colleen M., Jun Li, and Dongmei Zuo. 2022. "Changing Patterns of SNAP Take-Up and Participation and the Role of Out-of-Pocket Medical Expenses Among Older Adults." *Applied Economics Perspectives and Policy* 45(1): 336–49. https://doi.org/10.1002/aepp.13272.

Heflin, Colleen M., Andrew S. London, and Peter R. Mueser. 2012. "Clients' Perspectives on a Technology-Based Food Assistance Application System." *American Review of Public Administration* 43(6). https://doi.org/10.1177/0275074012455454.

Heflin, Colleen M., Leonard M. Lopoo, and Mattie Mackenzie-Liu. 2020. "When States Align Social Welfare Programs: Considering the Child Support Income Exclusion for SNAP." *Social Science Quarterly* 101(5): 2272–88. https://doi.org/10.1111/ssqu.12864.

Heflin, Colleen M., and Hannah Patnaik. 2022. "Material Hardship and the Living Arrangements of Older Adults." *Journal of Family and Economic Issues* 44(2): 267–84. https://doi.org/10.1007/s10834-022-09838-z.

Heflin, Colleen, and Ashley Price. 2019. "Food Pantry Assistance and the Great Recession." *Journal of Hunger & Environmental Nutrition* 14(1–2): 225–39. https://doi.org/10.1080/19320248.2018.1434099.

Heflin, Colleen M., John Sandberg, and Patrick Rafail. 2009. "The Structure of Material Hardship in U.S. Households: An Examination of the Coherence Behind Common Measures of Well-Being." *Social Problems* 56(4): 746–64. https://doi.org/10.1525/sp.2009.56.4.746.

Heflin, Colleen M., and James P. Ziliak. 2024. "Does the Reference Period Matter When Evaluating the Effect of SNAP on Food Insecurity?" *Applied Economic Perspectives and Policy.* January 25. https://doi.org/10.1002/aepp.13420.

Herd, Pamela, Melissa Favreault, Madonna Harrington Meyer, and Timothy M. Smeeding. 2018. "A Targeted Minimum Benefit Plan: A New Proposal to Reduce Poverty Among Older Social Security Recipients." *RSF: The Russell Sage Foundation Journal of the Social Sciences* 4(2): 74–90. https://doi.org/10.7758/rsf.2018.4.2.04.

Herd, Pamela, and Donald P. Moynihan. 2019. *Administrative Burden: Policymaking by Other Means.* Russell Sage Foundation.

Herman, Dena, Patience Afulani, Alisha Coleman-Jensen, and Gail G. Harrison. 2015. "Food Insecurity and Cost-Related Medication Underuse Among Nonelderly Adults in a Nationally Representative Sample." *American Journal of Public Health* 105(10): e48–59. https://doi.org/10.2105/AJPH.2015.302712.

Hernández, Diana. 2016. "Understanding 'Energy Insecurity' and Why It Matters to Health." *Social Science & Medicine* 167: 1–10. https://doi.org/10.1016/j.socscimed.2016.08.029.

Hill, Ronald Paul, and Debra L. Stephens. 1997. "Impoverished Consumers and Consumer Behavior: The Case of AFDC Mothers." *Journal of Macromarketing* 17(2): 32–48. https://doi.org/10.1177/027614679701700204.

Holben, David H., and Michelle Berger Marshall. 2017. "Position of the Academy of Nutrition and Dietetics: Food Insecurity in the United States." *Journal of the Academy of Nutrition and Dietetics* 117(12): 1991–2002. https://doi.org/10.1016/j.jand.2017.09.027.

Homonoff, Tatiana, and Jason Somerville. 2020. "Program Recertification Costs: Evidence from SNAP." National Bureau of Economic Research Working Paper 27311. https://doi.org/10.1257/pol.20190272.

Housing and Urban Development Office. 2017. "Housing for Seniors: Challenges and Solutions." U.S. Department of Housing and Urban Development. Accessed October 15, 2024. https://www.huduser.gov/portal/periodicals/em/summer17/highlight1.html.

Howe-Burris, Mecca, Stacey Giroux, Kurt Waldman, et al. 2022. "The Interactions of Food Security, Health, and Loneliness Among Rural Older Adults Before and After the Onset of COVID-19." *Nutrients* 14(23): 5076. https://doi.org/10.3390/nu14235076.

Hoynes, Hilary W., Leslie McGranahan, and Diane W. Schanzenbach. 2015. "SNAP and Food Consumption." In *SNAP Matters: How Food Stamps Affect Health and Well-Being*, edited by Judith Bartfeld, Craig Gundersen, Timothy Smeeding, and James P. Ziliak. Stanford University Press. https://doi.org/10.1515/9780804796873-007.

Hughes, Georgina, Kate M. Bennett, and Marion M. Hetherington. 2004. "Old and Alone: Barriers to Healthy Eating in Older Men Living on Their Own." *Appetite* 43(3): 269–76. https://doi.org/10.1016/j.appet.2004.06.002.

Iceland, John. 2013. *Poverty in America.* University of California Press.

Jackson, Jennifer A., Adam Branscum, Alice Tang, and Ellen Smit. 2019. "Food Insecurity and Physical Functioning Limitations Among Older U.S. Adults." *Preventive Medicine Reports* 14: 100829. https://doi.org/10.1016/j.pmedr.2019.100829.

Jih, Jane, Irena Stijacic-Cenzer, Hilary K. Seligman, W. John Boscardin, Tung T. Nguyen, and Christine S. Ritchie. 2018. "Chronic Disease Burden Predicts Food Insecurity Among Older Adults." *Public Health Nutrition* 21(9): 1737–42. https://doi.org/10.1017/S1368980017004062.

Johnson, Donna B., Sharon L. Beaudoin, Lynne T. Smith, Shirley A. A. Beresford, and James P. LoGerfo. 2003. "Increasing Fruit and Vegetable Intake in Homebound Elders: The Seattle Senior Farmers' Market Nutrition Pilot Program." *Preventing Chronic Disease* 1(1): A03. https://www.ncbi.nlm.nih.gov/pmc/articles/PMC544526/.

Joint Center for Housing Studies of Harvard University. 2016. *Projections & Implications for Housing a Growing Population: Older Households 2015–2035.* https://www.jchs.harvard.edu/sites/default/files/harvard_jchs_housing_growing_population_2016_1_0.pdf.

Joint Center for Housing Studies of Harvard University. 2023. *Housing America's Older Adults.* https://www.jchs.harvard.edu/housing-americas-older-adults-2023.

Jones, Jordan W. 2024. "SNAP Benefit Spending Varied with Changes to Maximum Benefit Amounts and Emergency Allotment from FY2020-2023." U.S. Department of Agriculture, Economic Research Service, Charts of Note, June 12. https://www.ers.usda.gov/data-products/chart-gallery/chart-detail?chartId=109295.

Jones, Jordan W., Charles Courtemanche, Augustine Denteh, James Marton, and Rusty Tchernis. 2022. "Do State Supplemental Nutrition Assistance Program Policies Influence Program Participation Among Seniors?" *Applied Economic Perspectives and Policy* 44(2): 1–18. https://doi.org/10.1002/aepp.13231.

Jones, Nancy L., Stephen E. Gilman, Tina L. Cheng, Stacy S. Drury, Carl V. Hill, and Arline T. Geronimus. 2019. "Life Course Approaches to the Causes of Health

Disparities." *American Journal of Public Health* 109(Suppl 1): S48–S55. https://doi.org/10.2105/AJPH.2018.304738.

Kaiser Family Foundation. 2024. "Medicaid 101." May 28. https://www.kff.org/health-policy-101-medicaid/.

Karpman, Michael, Elaine Maag, Stephen Zuckerman, and Doug Wissoker. 2022. *Child Tax Credit Recipients Experienced a Larger Decline in Food Insecurity and a Similar Change in Employment as Nonrecipients Between 2020 and 2021*. Tax Policy Center, Urban Institute and Brookings Institution. Accessed October 14, 2024. https://www.urban.org/sites/default/files/2022-05/CTC%20Recipients%20Experienced%20Larger%20Decline%20in%20Food%20Insecurity%20and%20Similar%20Change%20in%20Employment%20as%20Nonrecipients%20v2.pdf.

Katch, Hannah, and Paul Van De Water. 2020. *Medicaid and Medicare Enrollees Need Dental, Vision, and Hearing Benefits*. Center on Budget and Policy Priorities, December 8. https://www.cbpp.org/sites/default/files/atoms/files/12-8-20health.pdf.

Katz, Michael B. 1989. *The Undeserving Poor*. Oxford University Press.

Kaufman, Phillip, James M. Macdonald, Steve M. Lutz, and David Smallwood. 1997. *Do the Poor Pay More for Food? Item Selection and Price Differences Affect Low-Income Household Food Costs*. Report no. AER-759. U.S. Department of Agriculture, Economic Research Service. https://www.ers.usda.gov/webdocs/publications/40816/32372_aer759.pdf?v=1923.8.

Keenan, Teresa A., and Cheryl Lampkin. 2023. "Senior Hunger and Food Insecurity Are Growing Problems." AARP Research, February 28. https://doi.org/10.26419/res.00586.001.

Keller, Heather H., John J. M. Dwyer, Christine Senson, Vicki Edwards, and Gayle Edward. 2007. "A Social Ecological Perspective of the Influential Factors for Food Access Described by Low-Income Seniors." *Journal of Hunger & Environmental Nutrition* 1(3): 27–44. https://doi.org/10.1300/J477v01n03_03.

Kiszko, Kamila, Jonathan Cantor, Courtney Abrams, et al. 2015. "Corner Store Purchases in a Low-Income Urban Community in NYC." *Journal of Community Health* 40(6): 1084–90. https://doi.org/10.1007/s10900-015-0033-1.

Klerman, Jacob A., and Caroline Danielson. 2011. "The Transformation of the Supplemental Nutrition Assistance Program." *Journal of Policy Analysis and Management* 30(4): 863–88. https://www.jstor.org/stable/23019007.

Knight, Chadwick K., Janice C. Probst, Angela D. Liese, Erica Sercy, and Sonya J. Jones. 2016. "Household Food Insecurity and Medication 'Scrimping' Among U.S. Adults with Diabetes." *Preventive Medicine* 83: 41–45. https://doi.org/10.1016/j.ypmed.2015.11.031.

Kochhar, Rakesh, and Mohamad Moslimani. 2023. "Wealth Gaps Across Racial and Ethnic Groups." Pew Research Center, December 4. https://www.pewresearch.org/race-ethnicity/2023/12/04/wealth-gaps-across-racial-and-ethnic-groups.

Koma, Wyatt, Sarah True, Jeannie Fuglesten Biniek, Juliette Cubanski, Kendal Orgera, and Rachel Garfield. 2020. "One in Four Older Adults Report Anxiety or Depression Amid the COVID-19 Pandemic." Kaiser Family Foundation, October 9. https://www.kff.org/medicare/issue-brief/one-in-four-older-adults-report-anxiety-or-depression-amid-the-covid-19-pandemic/.

Kuh, Diana. 2019. "A Life Course Approach to Healthy Ageing." In *Prevention of Chronic Diseases and Age-Related Disability*, edited by Jean Pierre-Michel. Springer Cham.

Kuh, Diana, Sathya Karunananthan, Howard Bergman, and Rachel Cooper. 2014. "A Life-Course Approach to Healthy Ageing: Maintaining Physical Capability." *Proceedings of the Nutrition Society* 73(2): 237–48. https://www.cambridge.org/core/services/aop-cambridge-core/content/view/C57D67816B19489775D5E72DBEE6DC63/S0029665113003923a.pdf/a-life-course-approach-to-healthy-ageing-maintaining-physical-capability.pdf.

Kunkel, Mary Elizabeth, Barbara Luccia, and Archie C. Moore. 2003. "Evaluation of the South Carolina Seniors Farmers' Market Nutrition Education Program." *Journal of the Academy of Nutrition and Dietetics* 103(7): 880–83. https://www.jandonline.org/article/S0002-8223(03)00379-1/fulltext.

Lapham, Jessica, and Melissa L. Martinson. 2022. "The Intersection of Welfare Stigma, State Contexts, and Health Among Mothers Receiving Public Assistance Benefits." *SSM Population Health* 18: 101117. https://doi.org/10.1016/j.ssmph.2022.101117.

Laraia, Barbara A., Judith B. Borja, and Margaret E. Bentley. 2009. "Grandmothers, Fathers, and Depressive Symptoms Are Associated with Food Insecurity Among Low-Income First-Time African American Mothers in North Carolina." *Journal of the Academy of Nutrition and Dietetics* 109(6): 1042–47. https://doi.org/10.1016/j.jada.2009.03.005.

Lauffer, Sarah, and Alma Vigil. 2021. "Trends in Supplemental Nutrition Assistance Program Participation Rates: Fiscal Year 2016 to Fiscal Year 2018." Nutrition Assistance Program Report Series, U.S. Department of Agriculture.

Lecy, Jesse. 2024. *NCCS Core Series*. Urban Institute, National Center for Charitable Statistics. https://urbaninstitute.github.io/nccs/datasets/core/.

Lee, Jung S., Vibha Bhargava, Travis A. Smith, and Temitope Aiyejorun Walker. 2022. "The Effects of Aging Services and the Supplemental Nutrition Assistance Program on Food Insecurity Among Older Georgians: 2018–2020." *Applied Economic Perspectives and Policy* 44(2): 635–52. https://doi.org/10.1002/aepp.13230.

Lee, Jung S., and Edward A. Frongillo Jr. 2001a. "Factors Associated with Food Insecurity Among U.S. Elderly Persons: Importance of Functional Impairments." *Journal of Gerontology: Social Sciences* 56B(2): S94–S99. https://doi.org/10.1093/geronb/56.2.S94.

Lee, Jung S., and Edward A. Frongillo Jr. 2001b. "Nutritional and Health Consequences Are Associated with Food Insecurity Among U.S. Elderly Persons." *Journal of Nutrition* 131(5): 1503–09. https://doi.org/10.1093/jn/131.5.1503.

Lee, Soomi, Karley Deason, Diana Rancourt, and Heewon L. Gray. 2021. "Disentangling the Relationship Between Food Insecurity and Poor Sleep Health." *Ecology of Food and Nutrition* 60(5): 580–95. https://doi.org/10.1080/03670244.2021.1926245.

Lent, Megan D., Lindsay E. Petrovic, Josephine A. Swanson, and Christine M. Olson. 2009. "Maternal Mental Health and the Persistence of Food Insecurity in Poor Rural Families." *Journal of Health Care for the Poor and Underserved* 20(3): 645–61. https://pubmed.ncbi.nlm.nih.gov/19648695/.

Leung, Cindy W., Elissa S. Epel, Lorrene D. Ritchie, Patricia B. Crawford, and Barbara A. Laraia. 2014. "Food Insecurity Is Inversely Associated with Diet Quality of Lower-Income Adults." *Journal of the Academy of Nutrition and Dietetics* 114(12): 1943–53.e2. https://doi.org/10.1016/j.jand.2014.06.353.

Leung, Cindy W., Elissa S. Epel, Walter C. Willett, Eric B. Rimm, and Barbara A. Laraia. 2015. "Household Food Insecurity Is Positively Associated with Depression Among Low-Income Supplemental Nutrition Assistance Program Participants and Income-Eligible Nonparticipants." *Journal of Nutrition* 145(3): 622–27. https://doi.org/10.3945/jn.114.199414.

Leung, Cindy W., Jeffry T. Kullgren, Preeti N. Malani, et al. 2020. "Food Insecurity Is Associated with Multiple Chronic Conditions and Physical Health Status Among Older U.S. Adults." *Preventive Medicine Reports* 20: 101211. https://doi.org/10.1016/j.pmedr.2020.101211.

Leung, Cindy W., and June M. Tester. 2019. "The Association Between Food Insecurity and Diet Quality Varies by Race/Ethnicity: An Analysis of National Health and Nutrition Examination Survey 2011–2014 Results." *Journal of the Academy of Nutrition and Dietetics* 119(10): 1676–86. https://doi.org/10.1016/j.jand.2019.02.008.

Levin, Madeleine, Marian Negoita, Annelies Goger, et al. 2020. *Evaluation of Alternatives to Improve Elderly Access to SNAP*. Department of Agriculture, Food and

Nutrition Service, Mathematica Policy Research. https://fns-prod.azureedge.us/sites/default/files/resource-files/AlternativesImproveElderlyAccess.pdf.

Levy, Helen. 2022. "The Long-Run Prevalence of Food Insufficiency Among Older Americans." *Applied Economic Perspectives and Policy* 44(2): 575–90. https://doi.org/10.1002/aepp.13229.

Li, Jun, Dongmei Zuo, and Colleen M. Heflin. 2023. "Adoption of Standard Medical Deduction Increased SNAP Enrollment and Benefits in 21 Participating States." *Health Affairs* 42(8): 1173–81.

Li, Qingxiao, and Metin Çakir. 2024. "Estimating SNAP Purchasing Power and Its Effect on Participation." *American Journal of Agricultural Economics* 106(2): 779–804.

Li, Zhe. 2021. *Demographic and Socioeconomic Characteristics of Older Households with Debt: 2019*. Congressional Research Reports R46870. https://crsreports.congress.gov/product/pdf/R/R46870.

Linos, Elizabeth, Lisa T. Quan, and Elspeth Kirkman. 2020. "Nudging Early Reduces Administrative Burden: Three Field Experiments to Improve Code Enforcement." *Journal of Policy Analysis and Management* 39(1): 243–65. https://doi.org/10.1002/pam.22178.

Lipman, Micaela, and Elaine Waxman. 2017. "For Socially Isolated Seniors, Meals on Wheels Delivers More Than Food." Urban Wire, May 31. https://www.urban.org/urban-wire/socially-isolated-seniors-meals-wheels-delivers-more-food.

Livingston, Gretchen. 2019. "On Average, Older Adults Spend Over Half Their Waking Hours Alone." Pew Research Center, July 3. https://www.pewresearch.org/short-reads/2019/07/03/on-average-older-adults-spend-over-half-their-waking-hours-alone.

Loibl, Cäzilia, Alec P. Rhodes, Stephanie Moulton, Donald Haurin, and Chrisse Edmunds. 2022. "Food Insecurity Among Older Adults in the U.S.: The Role of Mortgage Borrowing." *Applied Economic Perspectives and Policy* 44(2): 549–74. https://doi.org/10.1002/aepp.13219.

Loo, Jaden, and Susan Brown. 2024. "Marital Status Distribution of U.S. Adults Aged 65 and Older, 1990–2022." Bowling Green State University, National Center for Family & Marriage Research, Family Profile No. 4.

Lopes, Lunna, Alex Montero, Marley Presiado, and Liz Hamel. 2024. "Americans' Challenges with Healthcare Costs." Kaiser Family Foundation, March 1. https://www.kff.org/health-costs/issue-brief/americans-challenges-with-health-care-costs.

Mabli, James. 2014. "SNAP Participation, Food Security, and Geographic Access to Food." U.S. Department of Agriculture, Food and Nutrition Service, Mathematica Policy Research, March 30. https://www.mathematica.org/publications/snap-participation-food-security-and-geographic-access-to-food.

Mabli, James, Elizabeth Gearan, Rhonda Cohen, et al. 2017. *Evaluation of the Effect of the Older Americans Act Title III-C Nutrition Services Program on Participants' Food Security, Socialization, and Diet Quality.* Mathematica Policy Research Report for the Center for Disability and Aging Policy, Administration for Community Living, U.S. Department of Health and Human Services. https://acl.gov/sites/default/files/programs/2017-07/AoA_outcomesevaluation_final.pdf.

Mabli, James, Stephen Tordella, Laura Castner, Thomas Godfrey, and Priscilla Foran. 2011. "Dynamics of Supplemental Nutrition Assistance Program Participation in the Mid-2000s." Arlington: Decision Demographics and Mathematica Policy Research. https://www.fns.usda.gov/research/snap/dynamics-supplemental-nutrition-assistance-program-participation-mid-2000s.

Marcos, Coral Murphy. 2021. "Dollar Tree Will Raise Prices to $1.25 by End of April." *New York Times,* November 23. https://www.nytimes.com/2021/11/23/business/dollar-tree-price-increase.html.

Masselot, Pierre, Malcolm Mistry, Jacopo Vanoli, et al. 2023. "Excess Mortality Attributed to Heat and Cold: A Health Impact Assessment Study in 854 Cities in Europe." *Lancet Planet Health* 7: e271–e281.

Mathers, Colin D., Gretchen A. Stevens, Ties Boerma, Richard A. White, and Martin I. Tobias. 2015. "Causes of International Increases in Older Age Life Expectancy." *Lancet* 385 (9967): 540-8. https://doi.org/10.1016/s0140-6736(14)60569-9.

Mayer, Susan E., and Christopher Jencks. 1989. "Poverty and the Distribution of Material Hardship." *Journal of Human Resources* 24(1): 88–114. https://doi.org/10.2307/145934.

McConnell, Casey, Lindsey Morgan, Catherine Benvie, et al. 2024. *State Options Report.* U.S. Department of Agriculture, Food and Nutrition Service. https://fns-prod.azureedge.us/sites/default/files/resource-files/snap-16th-state-options-report-june24.pdf.

McDonald, André J., Christine M. Wickens, Susan J. Bondy, et al. 2022. "Age Differences in the Association Between Loneliness and Anxiety Symptoms During the COVID-19 Pandemic." *Psychiatry Research* 30: 114446. https://www.ncbi.nlm.nih.gov/pmc/articles/PMC8842093/.

McDougall, Jean A., Shoshana A. Jaffe, Dolores D. Guest, et al. 2022. "Financial Hardship, Food Insecurity, and Forgone Medical Care." In *Advancing the Science of Cancer in Latinos,* edited by Amelie G. Ramirez and Edward J. Trapido. Springer. https://doi.org/10.1007/978-3-031-14436-3_11.

Meals on Wheels America. 2025a. *Final FY 2024 Federal Funding Levels for Key Programs Supporting Meals on Wheels and Older Adults.* https://www.mealsonwheels

america.org/docs/default-source/advocacy/final-fy-2024-federal-funding-levels-for-key-programs-supporting-meals-on-wheels-and-older-adults.pdf.

Meals on Wheels America. 2025b. *2025 National Snapshot.* https://www.mealsonwheelsamerica.org/docs/default-source/fact-sheets/2025/what-we-deliver_2025_national_snapshot_fact_sheet_feb25.pdf.

Melchior, Maria, Avshalom Caspi, Louise M. Howard, et al. 2009. "Mental Health Context of Food Insecurity: A Representative Cohort of Families with Young Children." *Pediatrics* 124(4): e564–e572. https://doi.org/10.1542/peds.2009-0583.

Meng, Ding, Margaret K. Keiley, Kimberly B. Garza, Patricia A. Duffy, and Claire A. Zizza. 2015. "Food Insecurity Is Associated with Poor Sleep Outcomes Among U.S. Adults." *Journal of Nutrition* 145(3): 615–21. https://doi.org/10.3945/jn.114.199919.

Meyer, Bruce D., and Wallace K. C. Mok. 2019. "Disability, Earnings, Income, and Consumption." *Journal of Public Economics* 171: 51–69. https://doi.org/10.1016/j.jpubeco.2018.06.011.

Meyer, Bruce D., and Derek Wu. 2018. "The Poverty Reduction of Social Security and Means-Tested Transfers." National Bureau of Economic Research Working Paper 24567. https://www.nber.org/papers/w24567.

Michener, Jamila. 2018. *Fragmented Democracy: Medicaid, Federalism, and Unequal Politics.* Cambridge University Press. https://ncoa.org/article/eating-better-on-a-fixed-income-what-you-can-buy-with-snap-benefits.

Middleton, Crystal, and Sylvia Smith. 2011. "Purchasing Habits of Senior Farmers' Market Shoppers: Utilizing the Theory of Planned Behavior." *Journal of Nutrition in Gerontology and Geriatrics* 30(3): 248–60. https://doi.org/10.1080/21551197.2011.591269.

Mills, Gregory, Tracy Vericker, Heather Koball, Kye Lippold, Laura Wheaton, and Sam Elkin. 2014. *Understanding the Rates, Causes, and Costs of Churning in the Supplemental Nutrition Assistance Program (SNAP) – Final Report.* Urban Institute, U.S. Department of Agriculture, Food and Nutrition Service. https://fns-prod.azureedge.us/sites/default/files/ops/SNAPChurning.pdf.

Miranda, Leticia. 2023. "When Delivery Costs More Than the Food You Ordered." *Washington Post,* May 26. https://www.washingtonpost.com/business/2023/05/26/when-delivery-fees-cost-more-than-the-food-you-ordered/93e69794-fbb4-11ed-bafc-bf50205661da_story.html.

Moffitt, Robert A. 2015. "The Deserving Poor, the Family, and the U.S. Welfare System." *Demography* 52(3): 729–49. https://doi.org/10.1007/s13524-015-0395-0.

Monkovic, Mia. 2024. *Characteristics of Supplemental Nutrition Assistance Program Households: Fiscal Year 2022.* U.S. Department of Agriculture, Food and Nutrition Service, Office of Policy Support.

Morello, Paul. 2021. "How Food Banks and Food Pantries Get Their Food." *Feeding America,* December 29. https://www.feedingamerica.org/hunger-blog/how-food-banks-and-food-pantries-get-their-food.

Morrissey, Monique. 2019. *The State of American Retirement Savings.* Economic Policy Institute. https://files.epi.org/pdf/136219.pdf.

Mozaffarian, Dariush, Heidi M. Blanck, Kathryn M. Garfield, Alissa Wassung, and Ruth Peterson. 2022. "A Food is Medicine Approach to Achieve Nutrition Security and Improve Health." *Nature Medicine* 28: 2238–40. https://doi.org/10.1038/s41591-022-02027-3.

Munnell, Alicia. 2013. "Social Security's Real Retirement Age Is 70." Center for Retirement Research at Boston College IB#13-15. Accessed October 9 2024. https://crr.bc.edu/briefs/social-security%E2%80%99s-real-retirement-age-is-70/.

Na, Muzi, Nan Dou, Monique J. Brown, Lenis P. Chen-Edinboro, Loretta R. Anderson, and Alexandra Wennberg. 2023. "Food Insufficiency, Supplemental Nutrition Assistance Program (SNAP) Status, and 9-Year Trajectory of Cognitive Function in Older Adults: The Longitudinal National Health and Aging Trends Study, 2012–2020." *Journal of Nutrition* 153(1): 312–21. https://doi.org/10.1016/j.tjnut.2022.12.012.

Nagata, Jason M., Kartika Palar, Holly C. Gooding, et al. 2019. "Food Insecurity Is Associated with Poorer Mental Health and Sleep Outcomes in Young Adults." *Journal of Adolescent Health* 65(6): 805–11. https://pubmed.ncbi.nlm.nih.gov/31587956/.

National Academies of Sciences, Engineering, and Medicine; Health and Medicine Division; Division of Behavioral and Social Sciences and Education; Board on Health Sciences Policy; Board on Behavioral, Cognitive, and Sensory Sciences; Committee on the Health and Medical Dimensions of Social Isolation and Loneliness in Older Adults. 2020. *Social Isolation and Loneliness in Older Adults: Opportunities for the Healthcare System.* National Academies Press. https://www.ncbi.nlm.nih.gov/books/NBK557972/.

National Agricultural Law Center. 2024. "Farm Commodity Programs: An Overview." Accessed October 15, 2024. https://nationalaglawcenter.org/overview/commodity-programs.

National Council on Aging. 2016. "Ending Stigma Around Receiving Benefits." June 1. https://www.ncoa.org/article/ending-stigma-around-receiving-benefits.

National Council on Aging. 2023. "Eating Better on a Fixed Income: What You Can Buy for $23 in SNAP Benefits." Last modified January 25, 2023. https://www.ncoa.org/article/eating-better-on-a-fixed-income-what-you-can-buy-with-snap-benefits/.

National Council on Aging. 2024a. "7 Facts about Older Adults and SNAP." Accessed November 16, 2024. https://www.ncoa.org/article/7-facts-about-older-adults-and-snap/.

National Council on Aging. 2024b. "What Are the Income Qualifications for LIHEAP?" January 29. https://www.ncoa.org/article/what-is-the-income-limit-for-liheap/.

National Institute on Aging. 2024. "Cold Weather Safety for Older Adults." Last modified January 3, 2024. https://www.nia.nih.gov/health/safety/cold-weather-safety-older-adults.

National Institute on Aging, National Institutes of Health, U.S. Department of Health and Human Services, and U.S. Department of State. 2007. *Why Population Aging Matters: A Global Perspective.* Publication No. 07-6134. https://www.nia.nih.gov/sites/default/files/2017-06/WPAM.pdf.

Neumark, David. 2018. "Experimental Research on Labor Market Discrimination." *Journal of Economic Literature* 56(3): 799–866. https://pubs.aeaweb.org/doi/pdfplus/10.1257/jel.20161309.

Niland, Katherine, Mary Kay Fox, and Elizabeth Gearan. 2017. *Nutritional Quality of Congregate and Home-Delivered Meals Offered in the Title III-C Nutrition Services Program: An Examination Utilizing the Healthy Eating Index Tool.* Administration for Community Living. https://acl.gov/sites/default/files/programs/2017-11/IB_NutritionServicesProgramEvaluation.pdf.

Nord, Mark, and Mark Prell. 2011. *Food Security Improved Following the 2009 ARRA Increase in SNAP Benefits.* Report No. ERR-116. U.S. Department of Agriculture, Economic Research Service. https://www.ers.usda.gov/webdocs/publications/44837/7469_err116.pdf?v=4037.8.

Obama Phone. 2023. "How to Get an Obama Phone." Accessed October 14, 2024. https://www.obamaphone.com/get-obama-phone.

Oberdorfer, Eric, and Keith Wiley. 2014. *Housing an Aging Rural America: Rural Seniors and Their Homes.* Housing Assistance Council. https://ruralhome.org/wp-content/uploads/storage/documents/publications/rrreports/ruralseniors2014.pdf.

Ochieng, Nancy, Juliette Cubanski, and Anthony Damico. 2024. "Medicare Households Spend More on Healthcare than Other Households." Kaiser Family Foundation, March 14. https://www.kff.org/medicare/issue-brief/medicare-households-spend-more-on-health-care-than-other-households.

Office of Disease Prevention and Health Promotion. 2023. "Food Insecurity." U.S. Department of Health and Human Services. Accessed June 1, 2023. https://health.gov/healthypeople/priority-areas/social-determinants-health/literature-summaries/food-insecurity.

Ohara, Yuki, Keiko Motokawa, Yutaka Watanabe, et al. 2020. "Association of Eating Alone with Oral Frailty Among Community-Dwelling Older Adults in Japan." *Archives of Gerontology and Geriatrics* 87: 104014. https://pubmed.ncbi.nlm.nih.gov/32000053.

Ohls, James C., Fazana Saleem-Ismail, Rhoda Cohen, Brenda Cox, and Laura Tiehen. 2002. *The Emergency Food Assistance System: Findings from the Provider Survey, Volume II: Final Report*. U.S. Department of Agriculture, Economic Research Service. https://www.ers.usda.gov/publications/pub-details/?pubid=46507.

Ojinnaka, Chinedum O., Irma Arteaga, Leslie Hodges, and Colleen Heflin. 2023. "Supplemental Nutrition Assistance Program Participation and Medication Adherence Among Medicaid-Insured Older Adults Living with Hypertension." *Journal of General Internal Medicine* 38: 1349–56. https://doi.org/10.1007/s11606-022-07994-4.

Onondaga County Aging Services. 2025. "Home Delivered Meals." Accessed February 8, 2025. http://www.ongov.net/aging/home-delivered-meals.html.

Organisation for Economic Co-operation and Development. 2023. *Pensions at a Glance 2023: OECD and G20 Indicators*. OECD. https://doi.org/10.1787/678055dd-en.

Ostchega, Yechiam, Cheryl D. Fryar, Tatiana Nwankwo, and Duong T. Nguyen. 2020. *Hypertension Prevalence Among Adults Aged 18 and Over: United States, 2017–2018*. NCHS Data Brief 364. National Center for Health Statistics. https://www.cdc.gov/nchs/data/databriefs/db364-h.pdf.

Palakshappa, Deepak, Arvin Garg, Alon Peltz, Charlene A. Wong, Rushina Cholera, and Seth A. Berkowitz. 2023. "Food Insecurity Was Associated with Greater Family Health Care Expenditures in the U.S., 2016–17." *Health Affairs* 42(1): 44–52. https://doi.org/10.1377/hlthaff.2022.00414.

Pew Research Center. 2024. "Internet/Broadband Fact Sheet." https://www.pewresearch.org/internet/fact-sheet/internet-broadband.

Pietropaoli, Davide, Rita Del Pinto, Claudio Ferri, et al. 2018. "Poor Oral Health and Blood Pressure Control Among U.S. Hypertensive Adults." *Hypertension* 72(6): 1365–73. https://doi.org/10.1161/HYPERTENSIONAHA.118.11528.

Pilkauskas, Natasha, Katherine Michelmore, Nicole Kovski, and H. Luke Shaefer. 2022. "The Effects of Income on the Economic Wellbeing of Families with Low Incomes: Evidence from the 2021 Expanded Child Tax Credit." National Bureau of Economic Research Working Paper 30533. https://www.nber.org/papers/w30533.

Pooler, Jennifer A., Heather Hartline-Grafton, Marydale DeBor, Rebecca L. Sudore, and Hilary K. Seligman. 2019. "Food Insecurity: A Key Social Determinant of Health for Older Adults." *Journal of the American Geriatrics Society* 67(3): 421–24. https://doi.org/10.1111/jgs.15736.

Pooler, Jennifer A., Vanessa A. Hoffman, and Fata J. Karva. 2018. "Primary Care Providers' Perspectives on Screening Older Adult Patients for Food Insecurity." *Journal of Aging & Social Policy* 30(1): 1–23. https://doi.org/10.1080/08959420.2017.1363577.

Pourmotabbed, Ali, Sajjad Moradi, Atefeh Babaei, et al. 2020. "Food Insecurity and Mental Health: A Systematic Review and Meta-Analysis." *Public Health Nutrition* 10(23): 1778–90. https://doi.org/10.1017/S136898001900390X.

Project Open Hand (home page). 2023. https://www.openhand.org.

Rabbitt, Matthew P., Laura J. Hales, Michael P. Burke, and Alisha Coleman-Jensen. 2023a. "Household Food Security in the United States in 2022." Economic Research Report No. (ERR-325). U.S. Department of Agriculture. https://www.ers.usda.gov/publications/pub-details/?pubid=107702.

Rabbitt, Matthew P., Laura J. Hales, Michael P. Burke, and Alisha Coleman-Jensen. 2023b. "Statistical Supplement to Household Food Security in the United States in 2022." Report no. AP-119. U.S. Department of Agriculture, Economic Research Service. https://www.ers.usda.gov/publications/pub-details/?pubid=107709.

Rabbitt, Matthew P., M. Reed-Jones, Laura J. Hales, and Michael P. Burke. 2024. *Household Food Security in the United States in 2023*. Report No. ERR-337. U.S. Department of Agriculture, Economic Research Service.

Rangarajan, Anu, and Philip M. Gleason. 2001. *Food Stamp Leavers in Illinois: How Are They Doing Two Years Later?* Mathematica Policy Research. https://www.ers.usda.gov/webdocs/publications/42929/51346_efan-01-002.pdf?v=42079.

Ratcliffe, Caroline, Signe-Mary McKernan, and Kenneth Finegold. 2008. "Effects of Food Stamp and TANF Policies on Food Stamp Receipt." *Social Service Review* 82(2): 291–334. https://www.jstor.org/stable/10.1086/589707.

Rector, Robert. 1999. *The Myth of Widespread American Poverty*. Heritage Foundation.

Rector, Robert, and Rachel Sheffield. 2011. "Understanding Poverty in the United States: Surprising Facts About America's Poor." *Backgrounder Report, Poverty and Inequality*, no. 2607. Heritage Foundation. https://www.heritage.org/poverty-and-inequality/commentary/understanding-poverty-the-us.

Reed-Jones, Madeline. 2024. *Prevalence of Food Insecurity Differs by Disability Status in 2023*. U.S. Department of Agriculture, Economic Research Service, Charts of Note. https://www.ers.usda.gov/data-products/charts-of-note/chart-detail?chartId =110370#:~:text=In%202023%2C%2033.9%20percent%20of,28.3%20percent %20were%20food%20insecure.

Ribar, David C., and Marilyn Edelhoch. 2008. "Earnings Volatility and the Reasons for Leaving the Food Stamp Program." In *Income Volatility and Food Assistance in the United States*, edited by Dean Jolliffe and James P. Ziliak. W. E. Upjohn Institute. https://doi.org/10.17848/9781435684126.ch4.

Richterman Aaron, Christina A. Roberto, and Harsha Thirumurthy. 2023. "Associations Between Ending Supplemental Nutrition Assistance Program Emergency Allotments and Food Insufficiency." *JAMA Health Forum* 4(8): e232511.

Rowlands, D. W., Mannan Donoghoe, and Andre M. Perry. 2023. "What the Lack of Premium Grocery Stores Says About Disinvestment in Black Neighborhoods." Brookings Institution, April 11. https://www.brookings.edu/articles/what-the-lack-of-premium-grocery-stores-says-about-disinvestment-in-black-neighborhoods.

Royer, Michael F., Nicolas Guerithault, B. Blair Braden, Melissa N. Laska, and Meg Bruening. 2021. "Food Insecurity Is Associated with Cognitive Function: A Systematic Review of Findings Across the Life Course." *International Journal of Translational Medicine* 1(3): 205–22. https://doi.org/10.3390/ijtm1030015.

Rudowitz, Robin, Alice Burns, Elizabeth Hinton, and Maiss Mohamed. 2023. "10 Things to Know About Medicaid." Kaiser Family Foundation, June 30. https://www.kff.org/mental-health/issue-brief/10-things-to-know-about-medicaid.

Sassine, AnnieBelle J., Matthew P. Rabbitt, Alisha Coleman-Jensen, Alanna J. Moshfegh, and Nadine R. Sahyoun. 2023. "Development and Validation of a Physical Food Security Tool for Older Adults." *Journal of Nutrition* 153(4): 1273–82. https://doi.org/10.1016/j.tjnut.2023.02.034.

Seligman, Hilary K., Barbara A. Laraia, and Margot B. Kushel. 2010. "Food Insecurity Is Associated with Chronic Disease Among Low-Income NHANES Participants." *Journal of Nutrition* 140(2): 304–10. https://doi.org/10.3945/jn.109.112573.

Sen, Amartya. 2000. *Development as Freedom*. Anchor Books.

Sen, Souvik, Lauren D. Giamberardino, Kevin Moss, et al. 2018. "Periodontal Disease, Regular Dental Care Use, and Incident Ischemic Stroke." *Stroke* 49(2): 355–62. https://pubmed.ncbi.nlm.nih.gov/29335336/.

Senior Living. 2023. *Older Adult Employment: 2021 Annual Report*. Accessed March 3, 2023. https:///www.seniorliving.org/finance/senior-employment-annual-report/.

Shafer, P. R., K. M. Gutiérrez, S. Ettinger de Cuba, A. Bovell-Ammon, and J. Raifman. 2022. "Association of the Implementation of Child Tax Credit Advance Payments with Food Insufficiency in US Households." *JAMA Network Open* 5(1): e2143296. https://jamanetwork.com/journals/jamanetworkopen/fullarticle/2788110.

Shanahan, Michael J. 2000. "Pathways to Adulthood in Changing Societies: Variability and Mechanisms in Life Course Perspective." *Annual Review of Sociology* 26(1): 667–92. https://doi.org/10.1146/annurev.soc.26.1.667.

She, Peiyun, and Gina A. Livermore. 2007. "Material Hardship, Poverty, and Disability Among Working-Age Adults." *Social Science Quarterly* 88(4): 970–89. https://www.jstor.org/stable/42956206.

Shenk, Marissa, and James Mabli. 2020. *The Title III-C Nutrition Services Program: Understanding Participants' Monetary Contributions*. Administration for Community Living. https://acl.gov/sites/default/files/programs/2020-09/AoA_participant_contributions.pdf.

Shipler, David. 2005. *The Working Poor: Invisible in America*. Alfred A. Knopf.

Shrider, Emily A. 2024. *Poverty in the United States: 2023*. Current Population Reports. U.S. Census Bureau. U.S. Government Publishing Office.

Shrider, Emily A., and John Creamer. 2023. *Poverty in the United States: 2022*. Current Population Reports, P60-280. U.S. Census Bureau. U.S. Government Publishing Office.

Shuman, Stephen, Paula K. Friedman, Michele J. Saunders, Xi Chen, Elisa M. Ghezzi, and Bei Wu. 2017. *Oral Health: An Essential Element of Healthy Aging*. Gerontological Society of America. https://www.geron.org/images/gsa/documents/oralhealth.pdf.

Siefert, Kristine, Colleen M. Heflin, Mary E. Corcoran, and David R. Williams. 2004. "Food Insufficiency and Physical and Mental Health in a Longitudinal Survey of Welfare Recipients." *Journal of Health and Social Behavior* 45(2): 171–86. https://doi.org/10.1177/002214650404500204.

Singhal, Astha, Peter Damiano, and Lindsay Sabik. 2017. "Medicaid Adult Dental Benefits Increase Use of Dental Care, but Impact of Expansion on Dental Services Use Was Mixed." *Health Affairs* 36(4): 723–32. https://doi.org/10.1377/hlthaff.2016.0877.

Singleton, Perry. 2023. "The Effect of Social Security Benefits on Food Insecurity at the Early Entitlement Age." *Applied Economic Perspectives and Policy* 45(1): 392–413. https://doi.org/10.1002/aepp.13312

Small, Mario Luis. 2011. "How to Conduct a Mixed Methods Study: Recent Trends in a Rapidly Growing Literature." *Annual Review of Sociology* 37: 57–86.

Small, Mario Luis, and Jessica McCrory Calarco. 2022. *Qualitative Literacy: A Guide to Evaluating Ethnographic and Interview Research*. University of California Press.

Smith, Mark A. 1997. "The Nature of Party Governance: Connecting Conceptualization and Measurement." *American Journal of Political Science* 41(3): 1042–56. https://www.jstor.org/stable/2111686.

Social Security Administration. 2008. *Strategic Plan: Fiscal Years 2008–2013*. Washington, DC: Office of Strategic Management.

Social Security Administration. 2020. *Annual Statistical Report on the Social Security Disability Insurance Program, 2020*. Office of Retirement and Disability Policy. https://www.ssa.gov/policy/docs/statcomps/di_asr/2020/sect04.html.

Social Security Administration. 2023a. *The 2023 OASDI Trustees Report*. https://www.ssa.gov/OACT/TR/2023/.

Social Security Administration. 2023b. *Social Security Administrative Expenses, 2023*. Accessed October 16, 2024. https://www.ssa.gov/oact/STATS/admin.html.

Social Security Administration. 2024a. *Never Beneficiaries, Aged 60 or Older, 2024*. May. https://www.ssa.gov/policy/docs/population-profiles/never-beneficiaries.html.

Social Security Administration. 2024b. *Social Security to Expand Access to SSI Program by Updating Definition of Public Assistance Household*. May 9. https://blog.ssa.gov/social-security-to-expand-access-to-ssi-program-by-updating-definition-of-a-public-assistance-household/.

Social Security Administration. 2024c. *Disability Benefits*. https://www.ssa.gov/pubs/EN-05-10029.pdf.

Song, Jintaek. 2022. "Propensity to Consume Food Out of SNAP and Its Welfare Implications." Social Science Research Network, November 15. https://ssrn.com/abstract=4293382.

Stacy, Brian, Laura Tiehen, and David Marquardt. 2018. "Using a Policy Index to Capture Trends and Differences in State Administration of USDA's SNAP." Report No. ERR-244. U.S. Department of Agriculture, Economic Research Service. https://www.ers.usda.gov/publications/pub-details/?pubid=87095.

Steiner, John F., Sandra H. Stenmark, Andrew T. Sterrett, Andrea R. Paolino, Matthew Stiefel, Wendolyn S. Gozansky, and Chan Zeng. 2018. "Food Insecurity in Older Adults in an Integrated Health Care System." *Journal of the American Geriatrics Society* 66(5): 1017–24. https://doi.org/10.1111/jgs.15285.

Stephens, Melvin. 2001. "The Long-Run Consumption Effects of Earnings Shocks." *Review of Economics and Statistics* 83(1): 28–36. https://doi.org/10.1162/003465301750160018.

Stone, Lyman. 2024. "1-in-3: A Record Share of Young Adults Will Never Marry." Institute for Family Studies, February 26. https://ifstudies.org/blog/1-in-3-a-record-share-of-young-adults-will-never-marry.

Strickhouser, Sara, James D. Wright, and Amy M. Donley. 2015. *Food Insecurity Among Older Adults*. AARP Foundation. https://www.aarp.org/content/dam/aarp/aarp_foundation/2015-PDFs/AF-Food-Insecurity-2015Update-Final-Report.pdf.

Sullivan, Briana, and Shomik Ghosh. 2024. *The Wealth of Households: 2022*. Current Population Reports, P70BR-202. U.S. Census Bureau.

Tani, Yukako, Naoki Kondo, Daisuke Takagi, et al. 2015. "Combined Effects of Eating Alone and Living Alone on Unhealthy Dietary Behaviors, Obesity and Underweight in Older Japanese Adults: Results of the JAGES." *Appetite* 95: 1–8. https://pubmed.ncbi.nlm.nih.gov/26116391.

Tarasuk, Valerie, Joyce Cheng, Claire de Oliveira, Naomi Dachner, Craig Gundersen, and Paul Kurdyak. 2015. "Association Between Household Food Insecurity and Annual Health Care Costs." *Canadian Medical Association Journal* 187(14): E429–E436. https://doi.org/10.1503/cmaj.150234.

Tavares, Jane L., Marc A. Cohen, Susan Silberman, and Lauren Popham. 2022. *Measuring Disease Cost Burden Among Older Adults in the U.S.: A Health and Retirement Study Analysis*. National Council on Aging and Leading Age LTSS Center at University of Massachusetts, Boston. National Council on Aging Research Brief. https://assets-us-01.kc-usercontent.com/ffacfe7d-10b6-0083-2632-604077fd4eca/34789367-444d-46d0-b38c-3c1348b1ea52/2022-Chronic_Inequities_Measuring_Burden.pdf.

Taylor, Paul, Jeffery Passel, Richard Fry, et al. 2010. "The Return of the Multi-Generational Family Household." Pew Research Center, March 18. https://www.pewresearch.org/social-trends/2010/03/18/the-return-of-the-multi-generational-family-household.

Todd, Jessica E. 2015. "Revisiting the Supplemental Nutrition Assistance Program Cycle of Food Intake: Investigating Heterogeneity, Diet Quality, and a Large Boost in Benefit Amounts." *Applied Economic Perspectives and Policy* 37: 437–58. https://doi.org/10.1093/aepp/ppu039.

Toossi, Saied, and Jordan W. Jones. 2023. *The Food and Nutrition Assistance Landscape: Fiscal Year 2022 Annual Report*. Report No. EIB-255. U.S. Department of Agriculture, Economic Research Service. https://doi.org/10.32747/2023.8054020.ers.

Toossi, Saied, Jordan W. Jones, and Leslie Hodges. 2021. *The Food and Nutrition Assistance Landscape: Fiscal Year 2020 Annual Report*. U.S. Department of Agriculture, Economic Research Service. EIB-227.

Trust for America's Health. 2021. "Public Transit Access to Full-Service Grocery Stores Will Help Address Country's Obesity Crisis." Accessed June 1, 2023. https://www.tfah.org/story/public-transit-access-full-service-grocery.

Tucher, Emma L., Tamra Keeney, Alicia J. Cohen, and Kali S. Thomas. 2021. "Conceptualizing Food Insecurity Among Older Adults: Development of a Summary Indicator in the National Health and Aging Trends Study." *Journal of Gerontology: Series B, Psychological Sciences and Social Sciences* 76(10): 2063–72. https://doi.org/10.1093/geronb/gbaa147.

Tufts University, Food is Medicine Institute. 2025. "Development and Validation of a Nutrition Security Screener." Accessed January, 28, 2025. https://tuftsfoodismedicine.org/project/nss/.

Umberson, Debra, Robert Crosnoe, and Corinne Reczek. 2010. "Social Relationships and Health Behavior Across the Life Course." *Annual Review of Sociology* 1(36): 139–57. https://www.ncbi.nlm.nih.gov/pmc/articles/PMC3171805/pdf/nihms313656.pdf.

Urban Institute. 2023. "Does SNAP Cover the Cost of a Meal in Your County?" July 13. https://www.urban.org/data-tools/does-snap-cover-cost-meal-your-county-2022.

U.S. Bureau of Labor Statistics. 2023. "12-Month Percentage Change. Consumer Price Index, Selected Categories (Past 20 Years)." Accessed April 25, 2024. https://www.bls.gov/charts/consumer-price-index/consumer-price-index-by-category-line-chart.htm.

U.S. Bureau of Labor Statistics. 2024a. "Current Population Survey: Design." Accessed April 25, 2024. https://www.bls.gov/opub/hom/cps/design.htm.

U.S. Bureau of Labor Statistics. 2024b. "Labor Force by Age Group, 2001, 2011, 2021, and Projected 2031." https://www.bls.gov/emp/graphics/labor-force-share-by-age-group.htm.

U.S. Census Bureau. 2024. "Current Population Survey, December 2023, Food Security File." Accessed February 11, 2025. https://www2.census.gov/programs-surveys/cps/datasets/2023/supp/dec23pub.zip.

U.S. Department of Agriculture. 2004. "Combined Application Projects." Food and Nutrition Service. Accessed April 1, 2022. https://www.fns.usda.gov/snap/combined-application-projects-0.

U.S. Department of Agriculture. 2012. *U.S. Household Food Security Survey Module: Three-Stage Design, With Screeners.* Economic Research Service. https://www.ers.usda.gov/sites/default/files/_laserfiche/DataFiles/50764/26621_hh2012.pdf?v=3672.4.

U.S. Department of Agriculture. 2019. *Commodity Supplemental Food Program.* Last modified July 2019. https://fns-prod.azureedge.us/sites/default/files/resource-files/csfp-program-fact-sheet-2019.pdf.

U.S. Department of Agriculture. 2021. "State Estimates of SNAP Participation Rates for Eligible Elderly Individuals, FY 2016–FY2018." Last modified May 2021. https://fns-prod.azureedge.us/sites/default/files/resource-files/SNAPElderlyPartRates_2016-2018.pdf.

U.S. Department of Agriculture. 2022a. "About the WIC Program." Last modified May 12, 2022. https://www.fns.usda.gov/wic/state-agency.

U.S. Department of Agriculture. 2022b. "Disability Status Can Affect Food Security Among U.S. Households." Economic Research Service. Last modified November 14, 2022. https://www.ers.usda.gov/data-products/chart-gallery/gallery/chart-detail/?chartId=105136.

U.S. Department of Agriculture. 2022c. "Food Access Research Atlas." Economic Research Service. Last modified July 3, 2023. https://www.ers.usda.gov/data-products/food-access-research-atlas/go-to-the-atlas.

U.S. Department of Agriculture. 2022d. "Food Distribution Program Tables." Last modified September 8, 2023. https://www.fns.usda.gov/pd/food-distribution-program-tables.

U.S. Department of Agriculture. 2022e. "USDA Actions on Nutrition Security." Accessed March 11, 2024. https://www.usda.gov/sites/default/files/documents/usda-actions-nutrition-security.pdf.

U.S. Department of Agriculture. 2023a. "Child Nutrition Tables." Last modified September 8, 2023. https://www.fns.usda.gov/pd/child-nutrition-tables.

U.S. Department of Agriculture. 2023b. "Definitions of Food Security." Economic Research Service. Accessed May 8, 2024. https://www.ers.usda.gov/topics/food-nutrition-assistance/food-security-in-the-u-s/definitions-of-food-security.

U.S. Department of Agriculture. 2023c. "Food Security and Nutrition Assistance." Last modified July 19, 2023. https://www.ers.usda.gov/data-products/ag-and-food-statistics-charting-the-essentials/food-security-and-nutrition-assistance.

U.S. Department of Agriculture. 2023d. "Recent Changes to SNAP Benefit Amounts." Food and Nutrition Service. Accessed May 8, 2024. https://fns-prod.azureedge.us/sites/default/files/resource-files/snap-sunset-ea-0223.pdf.

U.S. Department of Agriculture. 2023e. "Seniors Farmers Market Nutrition Program." https://fns-prod.azureedge.us/sites/default/files/resource-files/FY22-SFMNP-Fact-Sheet.pdf.

U.S. Department of Agriculture. 2023f. "Senior Farmers Market Nutrition Program (SFMNP) Profile Data." Accessed May 8, 2024. https://www.fns.usda.gov/sfmnp/sfmnp-profile-data.

U.S. Department of Agriculture. 2023g. "Special Supplemental Nutrition Program for Women, Infants and Children – 2023 FAQs." https://www.nifa.usda.gov/special-supplemental-nutrition-program-women-infants-children-2023-faqs.

U.S. Department of Agriculture. 2023h. "USDA Support for Food Banks and the Emergency Food System." Last modified November 8, 2023. https://www.fns.usda.gov/fact-sheet/usda-support-for-food-banks-emergency-food-system.

U.S. Department of Agriculture. 2023i. "What Can SNAP Buy?" Food and Nutrition Service. Last modified November 17, 2023. https://www.fns.usda.gov/snap/eligible-food-items.

U.S. Department of Agriculture. 2023j. "WIC Eligibility Requirements." Food and Nutrition Service. Last modified April 4, 2023. https://www.fns.usda.gov/wic/wic-eligibility-requirements.

U.S. Department of Agriculture, Food and Nutrition Service. 2023k. "USDA Celebrates SNAP Online Purchasing Now Available in All 50 States." June 9, 2023. https://www.fns.usda.gov/news-item/fns-010.23.

U.S. Department of Agriculture. 2024a. "A Short History of SNAP." Food and Nutrition Service. Last modified July 9, 2024. https://www.fns.usda.gov/snap/history.

U.S. Department of Agriculture. 2024b. "Measurement." Economic Research Service. Last modified November 4, 2024. https://www.ers.usda.gov/topics/food-nutrition-assistance/food-security-in-the-u-s/measurement.

U.S. Department of Agriculture. 2024c. "Official USDA Thrifty Food Plan: U.S. Average, January 2024." Accessed March 11, 2024. https://fns-prod.azureedge.us/sites/default/files/resource-files/Cost_Of_Food_Thrifty_Food_Plan_March_2024.pdf.

U.S. Department of Agriculture. 2024d. "SNAP COVID-19 Emergency Allotments Guidance." Last modified November 4, 2024. https://www.fns.usda.gov/snap/covid-19-emergency-allotments-guidance.

U.S. Department of Agriculture. 2024e. "SNAP – Fiscal Year 2025 Cost-of-Living Adjustments." https://fns-prod.azureedge.us/sites/default/files/resource-files/snap-cola-fy25.pdf.

U.S. Department of Agriculture. 2024f. "SNAP Special Rules for the Elderly or Disabled." Accessed May 8, 2024. https://www.fns.usda.gov/snap/eligibility/elderly-disabled-special-rules.

U.S. Department of Agriculture. 2024g. "TEFAP Factsheet." Food and Nutrition Service. Last modified October 30, 2024. https://www.fns.usda.gov/tefap/factsheet.

U.S. Department of Agriculture. 2024h. "Where Can I Use SNAP EBT?" Food and Nutrition Service. Last modified February 15, 2024. https://www.fns.usda.gov/snap/retailer-locator.

U.S. Department of Agriculture 2025a. "ABAWD Waivers." Last modified January 21, 2025. https://www.fns.usda.gov/snap/abawd/waivers.

U.S. Department of Agriculture. 2025b. "Retailer Management Year End Summary - Fiscal Year 2023." Last modified January 21, 2025. https://www.fns.usda.gov/data-research/data-visualization/snap-retailer-management-dashboard.

U.S. Department of Agriculture. 2025c. "Program Data Overview." Last modified February 14, 2025. https://www.fns.usda.gov/pd/overview.

U.S. Department of Agriculture. 2025d. "SNAP Data Tables." Last modified February 14, 2025. https://www.fns.usda.gov/pd/supplemental-nutrition-assistance-program-snap.

U.S. Department of Agriculture. 2025e. "Summary Findings: Food Price Outlook, 2024." https://www.ers.usda.gov/data-products/food-price-outlook/summary-findings.

U.S. Department of Agriculture. 2025f. "Supplemental Nutrition Assistance Program (SNAP): Status of State Able-Bodied Adult without Dependents (ABAWD) Time Limit Waivers Fiscal Year 2025 – 2nd Quarter." Food and Nutrition Service. January 1. https://fns-prod.azureedge.us/sites/default/files/resource-files/FY25-Quarter-2-ABAWD-Waiver-Status-Revised.pdf.

U.S. Department of Health and Human Services. 2023. "LIHEAP Fact Sheet." Accessed May 20, 2023. https://www.acf.hhs.gov/ocs/fact-sheet/liheap-fact-sheet.

U.S. Department of Health and Human Services. 2025. "Healthy People 2030: Reduce Household Food Insecurity and Hunger – NWS-01." Office of Disease Prevention and Health Promotion. Accessed February 9, 2025. https://odphp.health.gov/healthypeople/objectives-and-data/browse-objectives/nutrition-and-healthy-eating/reduce-household-food-insecurity-and-hunger-nws-01.

U.S. Department of the Treasury. 2023. "Racial Differences in Economic Security: Non-housing Assets." January 10. https://home.treasury.gov/news/featured-stories/racial-differences-in-economic-security-non-housing-assets.

U.S. Hunger. 2022. "It's Not Just Hunger: Transportation's Role in Food Insecurity." August 29. https://ushunger.org/blog/transportation-food-insecurity.

U.S. Senate. 2013. *Senior Hunger and the Older Americans Act: Hearing before the Subcommittee on Primary Health and Aging of the Committee on Health, Education, Labor, and Pensions, United States Senate, One Hundred Twelfth Congress, First Session on Examining Senior Hunger and the "Older Americans Act" June 21, 2011.* U.S. Government Printing Office. https://www.govinfo.gov/content/pkg/CHRG-113shrg99847/pdf/CHRG-113shrg99847.pdf.

Valliant, Julia C. D., Mecca E. Burris, Kamila Czebotar, et al. 2022. "Navigating Food Insecurity as a Rural Older Adult: The Importance of Congregate Meal Sites, Social Networks and Transportation Services." *Journal of Hunger & Environmental Nutrition* 17(5): 593–614. https://doi.org/10.1080/19320248.2021.1977208.

Van de Water, Paul N., and Kathleen Romig. 2023. "Social Security Benefits Are Modest." Center for Budget and Policy Priorities, last modified December 7, 2023. https://www.cbpp.org/research/social-security/social-security-benefits-are-modest.

Van Wormer, Jeffrey J., Amit Acharya, Robert T. Greenlee, and Francisco Javier Nieto. 2012. "Oral Hygiene and Cardiometabolic Disease Risk in the Survey of the Health of Wisconsin." *Community Dentistry and Oral Epidemiology* 41(4): 374–84. https://onlinelibrary.wiley.com/doi/10.1111/cdoe.12015.

Ver Ploeg, Michele, Vince Breneman, Tracey Farrigan, et al. 2009. *Access to Affordable and Nutritious Food: Measuring and Understanding Food Deserts and Their Consequences.* Administrative Publication No. 036, Economic Research Service. https://www.ers.usda.gov/publications/pub-details/?pubid=42729.

Ver Ploeg, Michele, and Chen Zhen. 2022. "Changes in SNAP Benefit Levels and Food Spending and Diet Quality: Simulations from the National Household Food Acquisition and Purchase Survey." Center for Budget and Policy Priorities. Last modified May 12, 2022. https://www.cbpp.org/research/food-assistance/changes-in-snap-benefit-levels-and-food-spending-and-diet-quality.

Vesnaver, Elisabeth, and Heather H. Keller. 2011. "Social Influences and Eating Behavior in Later Life: A Review." *Journal of Nutrition in Gerontology and Geriatrics* 30(1): 2–23. https://pubmed.ncbi.nlm.nih.gov/23286638.

Vespa, Jonathan. 2018. "The Greying of America: More Older Adults Than Kids by 2035." U.S. Census Bureau, March 13. https://www.census.gov/library/stories/2018/03/graying-america.html.

Vigil, Alma. 2019. *Trends in Supplemental Nutrition Assistance Program Participation Rates: Fiscal Year 2010 to Fiscal Year 2017.* Mathematica Policy Research. https://www.mathematica.org/publications/fy-2010-to-2017-trends-in-supplemental-nutrition-assistance-program-participation-rates.

Vigil, Alma, 2024. *Trends in Supplemental Nutrition Assistance Program Participation Rates: Fiscal Year 2020 and Fiscal Year 2022.* Prepared by Mathematica, U.S. Department of Agriculture, Food and Nutrition Service, Office of Policy Support. https://fns-prod.azureedge.us/sites/default/files/resource-files/ops-snap-trends-fy20fy22-summary.pdf.

Vigil, Alma, and Nima Rahimi. 2024. *Trends in Supplemental Nutrition Assistance Program Participation Rates: Fiscal Year 2020 and Fiscal Year 2022.* Full report. Prepared by Mathematica, Contract No. 12-3198-23-F-0047. U.S. Department of Agriculture, Food and Nutrition Service, Office of Policy Support, October.

Vilar-Compte, Mireya, Pablo Gaitán-Rossi, and Rafael Pérez-Escamilla. 2017. "Food Insecurity Measurement Among Older Adults: Implications for Policy and Food Security Governance." *Global Food Security* 14: 87–95. https://doi.org/10.1016/j.gfs.2017.05.003.

Wang, Xinyi, Wei Shen, Chunmei Wang, et al. 2016. "Association Between Eating Alone and Depressive Symptom in Elders: A Cross-Sectional Study." *BMC Geriatrics* 16: 19. https://bmcgeriatr.biomedcentral.com/articles/10.1186/s12877-016-0197-2.

Waxman, Elaine, and Poonam Gupta. 2023. *SNAP Fell Short in Helping Families Afford Rising Food Prices in 2022*. Urban Institute. Accessed March 24, 2024. https://www.urban.org/sites/default/files/2023-07/SNAP%20Fell%20Short%20in%20Helping%20Families%20Afford%20Rising%20Food%20Prices%20in%202022.pdf.

Waxman, Elaine, Poonam Gupta, Kassandra Martinchek, Paige Sonoda, and Noah Johnson. 2023. "Connecting People with Charitable Foods Through Home Delivery Partnerships: Insights from DoorDash's Project DASH." Urban Institute Research Report. Accessed September 13, 2023. https://www.urban.org/research/publication/connecting-people-charitable-food-through-new-home-delivery-partnerships.

Weinfield, Nancy S., Gregory Mills, Christine Borger, et al. 2014. *Hunger in America 2014: National Report Prepared for Feeding America*. https://www.feedingamerica.org/sites/default/files/2020-02/hunger-in-america-2014-full-report.pdf.

Wells, Whitney, Kaitlyn Jackson, Cindy W. Leung, and Rita Hamad. 2024. "Food Insufficiency Increased After the Expiration of COVID-19 Emergency Allotments for SNAP Benefits in 2023." *Health Affairs* 43(10). https://doi.org/10.1377/hlthaff.2023.01566.

White House. 2022. "Executive Summary: Biden-Harris Administration National Strategy on Hunger, Nutrition, and Health." Press release, September 27. https://www.whitehouse.gov/briefing-room/statements-releases/2022/09/27/executive-summary-biden-harris-administration-national-strategy-on-hunger-nutrition-and-health.

Whittle, Henry J., Lila A. Sheira, William R. Wolfe, et al. 2019. "Food Insecurity Is Associated with Anxiety, Stress, and Symptoms of Posttraumatic Stress Disorder in a Cohort of Women with or at Risk of HIV in the United States." *Journal of Nutrition* 149(8): 1393–1403. https://pubmed.ncbi.nlm.nih.gov/31127819.

Wiemers, Emily E. 2014. "The Effect of Unemployment on Household Composition and Doubling Up." *Demography* 51(6): 2155–78. https://doi.org/10.1007/s13524-014-0347-0.

Wilde, Parke E. 2018. *Food Policy in the United States: An Introduction.* 2nd ed. Routledge.

Wilmoth, Janet M., Andrew S. London, and Colleen M. Heflin. 2015. "The Use of VA Disability Compensation and Social Security Disability Insurance Among Working-Aged Veterans." *Disability and Health Journal* 8(3): 388–96. https://doi.org/10.1016/j.dhjo.2015.02.004.

Wolfe, Wendy S., Edward A. Frongillo, and Pascale Valois. 2003. "Understanding the Experience of Food Insecurity by Elders Suggests Ways to Improve Its Measurement." *Journal of Nutrition* 133(9): 2762–69. https://doi.org/10.1093/jn/133.9.2762.

Wolfson, Julia A., Travertine Garcia, and Cindy W. Leung. 2021. "Food Insecurity Is Associated with Depression, Anxiety, and Stress: Evidence from the Early Days of the COVID-19 Pandemic in the United States." *Health Equity* 5(1): 64–71. https://doi.org/10.1089/heq.2020.0059.

Wooldridge, Shannon. 2023. "Writing Respectfully: Person-First and Identity-First Language." National Institutes of Health, April 12. https://www.nih.gov/about-nih/what-we-do/science-health-public-trust/perspectives/writing-respectfully-person-first-identity-first-language.

Wright, Lauri, Lauren Vance, Christina Sudduth, and James B. Epps. 2015. "The Impact of a Home-Delivered Meal Program on Nutritional Risk, Dietary Intake, Food Security, Loneliness, and Social Well-Being." *Journal of Nutrition in Gerontology and Geriatrics* 34(2): 218–27. https://doi.org/10.1080/21551197.2015.1022681.

Xu, Jiaquan, Sherry L. Murphy, Kenneth D. Kochanek, and Brigham A. Bastian. 2016. "Deaths: Final Data for 2013." *National Vital Statistics Reports* 64(2): 1–119. https://pubmed.ncbi.nlm.nih.gov/26905861/.

Zhang, Chun-Qing, Pak-Kwong Chung, Ru Zhang, and Benjamin Schüz. 2019. "Socioeconomic Inequalities in Older Adults' Health: The Roles of Neighborhood and Individual-Level Psychosocial and Behavioral Resources." *Frontiers in Public Health* 7: 318. https://www.ncbi.nlm.nih.gov/pmc/articles/PMC6823619/pdf/fpubh-07-00318.pdf.

Ziliak, James P. 2015. "Why Are So Many Americans on Food Stamps? The Role of the Economy, Policy, and Demographics." In *SNAP Matters: How Food Stamps Affect Health and Wellbeing*, edited by Judith Bartfeld, Craig Gundersen, Timothy M. Smeeding, and James P. Ziliak. Stanford University Press. https://doi.org/10.1515/9780804796873-004.

Ziliak, James P. 2021. "Food Hardship During the COVID-19 Pandemic and Great Recession." *Applied Economic Perspectives and Policy* 43(1): 132–52. https://doi.org/10.1002/aepp.13099.

Ziliak, James P., and Craig Gundersen. 2016. "Multigenerational Families and Food Insecurity." *Southern Economic Journal* 82(4): 1147–66. https://doi.org/10.1002/soej.12082.

Ziliak, James P., and Craig Gundersen. 2019. *The State of Senior Hunger in America in 2017*. Feeding America. https://www.feedingamerica.org/sites/default/files/2019-06/The%20State%20of%20Senior%20Hunger%20in%202017_F2.pdf.

Ziliak, James P., and Craig Gundersen. 2020. *The State of Senior Hunger in America in 2018: An Annual Report*. Chicago: Feeding America. https://feedingamerica.org/sites/default/files/2020-05/2020-The%20State%20of%20Senior%20Hunger%20in%202018.pdf.

Ziliak, James P., and Craig Gundersen. 2023. *The State of Senior Hunger in America in 2021*. Feeding America. https://www.feedingamerica.org/sites/default/files/2023-04/State%20of%20Senior%20Hunger%20in%202021.pdf.

Ziliak, James P., Craig Gundersen, and Margaret Haist. 2015. *The Causes, Consequences, and Future of Senior Hunger in America*. Center for Poverty Research, University of Kentucky. https://nfesh.org/wp-content/uploads/2020/10/causes-consequences-senior-hunger-2008-full-report.pdf.

Zizza, Claire A., Patricia A. Duffy, and Shirley A. Gerrior. 2008. "Food Insecurity Is Not Associated with Lower Energy Intakes." *Obesity* 16(8): 1908–13. https://onlinelibrary.wiley.com/doi/epdf/10.1038/oby.2008.288.

Zuo, Dongmei, and Colleen Heflin. 2023. "Cognitive Impairment and Supplemental Nutrition Assistance Program Take-Up Among the Eligible Older Americans." *Journals of Gerontology: Series B* 78(1): 99–110. https://doi.org/10.1093/geronb/gbac111.

INDEX

Tables and figures are listed in **boldface**.

AARP (American Association for Retired People), 34–35, 47, 67, 80, 83, 87
Accountable Health Communities Screening Tool, 171
Administration on Aging (HHS), 131
adult care centers, 230*n*3, 231*n*25. *See also* senior centers
adults with disabilities: and community-based food programs, 129; and food insecurity, 12, 13–14, **25**, 26–28, 67–70, **68**, 72; and food preparation, 118; and housing accommodations, 72; and life course theory, 22–23; person-first language for, 217*n*9; rates of, 5, 68; as study participants, 35, **193**; and transportation issues, 84–85; and work-related injuries, 1, 44. *See also* chronic health conditions; Social Security Disability Insurance
age discrimination, 1–2, 8
Agriculture Improvement Act (2018), 116

American Association for Retired People (AARP), 34–35, 47, 67, 80, 83, 87
anxiety, 75–76, 78
arthritis, 60, 72, 86, 147
assistance programs: charitable organizations, 54, 58, 132; for phones, 63, 105; for subsidized housing, 53, 66, 77, 155, 177, **195**; for utility payment assistance, 57–58, 177, 180. *See also* community-based and subsidized food programs; Supplemental Nutrition Assistance Program
assisted living facilities, 103

Baby Boomers, 6, 29
Biden-Harris administration, 12, 36, 178, 181
Brookings Institution, 80
budget trade-offs: and debt management, 44, 46, 54; and food insecurity, 11; health impacts of, 6, 50–51; for housing, 53–54; interview questions on, 212–13; for medical

expenses, 2, 6, 41, 48–53, 82–83, 225*n*53; for personal and cleaning supplies, 3, 41, 60–63; for phone and internet bills, 63–64; rates of, 46–48, **46**, **48**, **194**; for transportation, 2, 42, 58–60; for utilities, 55–58
Bureau of Labor Statistics, 7, 44

Calarco, Jessica McCrory, 201
CAP (Combined Application Project), 121, 177
CARES Act (2020), 143
cash assistance programs, 178–79
Catholic Charities, 54
Centers for Disease Control and Prevention (CDC), 67–68
charitable organizations, 54, 58, 132
Child and Adult Care Food Program, **186**, 230*n*3, 231*n*25
children. *See* grandchildren
chronic health conditions: and diet and nutrition sensitivities, 5, 114, 145–48, 158; food insecurity resulting from, 67–69, 76, 89–90, 171, 225*n*53; and food preparation issues, 76, 118–19; and home-delivered meals, 147, 172; rates of, 5, 67–68; SNAP benefit gaps and medication underuse, 109. *See also* adults with disabilities
cleaning supplies. *See* personal and cleaning supplies
cognitive limitations, 69–70, 76, 82, 106
Combined Application Project (CAP), 121, 177
Committee on National Statistics of the National Academies, 20

Commodity Supplemental Food Program, **187**
community-based and subsidized food programs, 39, 125–66; congregate meals, 132–42, **134**, **136–37** (*see also* congregate meals); COVID-19 pandemic and closure of, 36–37; food banks and farmer's market coupons, 149–66, **150**, **152–53** (*see also* food banks); funding for, 10, 131–32; home-delivered meals, 142–49, **145–47** (*see also* home-delivered meals); lower participation rates among older adults, 11–12, 130; and transportation issues, 12, 23–24, 66, 127–28, 139; trends in, 129–31, **131**
computer use. *See* internet use
congregate meals: defined, 130; difficulty accessing programs, 138–39; funding for, 131; geographic variation in availability of, 135–38, **136–37**, 141; national numbers of, 130, **131**; and nutritional quality of food, 127–28, 137–38, 171–72; overview, 132–35, **185**; rate of use among older adults, 132–33, **134**; rate of use among study participants, **194**; soup kitchens, 139–42
Consumer Expenditure Survey, 45
Consumer Financial Protection Bureau, 49
COVID-19 pandemic: assistance programs during, 36–37, 54, 57, 179, 223*n*68; and community-based food programs, 126–27, 131, 133, 143–44, **145**, 151, 160, 162;

depression and anxiety during, 75, 78–79; food insecurity during and after, 15, **15**, 70; food insecurity measures during, 20; food prices during and after, 33; isolation and loneliness during, 78; policy change during, 11, 143; and public transportation, 59, 85, 225–26*n*60; and SNAP benefits, 39, 89–92, 94–95, 107, 116–17, 121–22, 174; and study participation, 35, 202–3

credit cards, 60, 74

Current Population Survey: on community-based and subsidized food programs, 133, 140, 230*nn*4–5; defined, **190**; excluding residents of group quarters, 30–31; on food bank usage rates, 150–51; on food insecurity, 20, 33–34, **34**; on food insecurity by age, 28–30, **29**, **183**; on food insecurity by characteristics, 24–28, **25**; Food Security Scale in, 19; on older adults and food insecurity, 9

debt: budget trade-offs for, 44, 46, 54; and car payments or repairs, 60; and chronic health conditions, 69–70; medical, 49–50, 89; of study respondents, 47

DeLuca, Stefanie, 201

demographic characteristics: food insecurity rates by age, 28–30, **29**; interview questions on, 207; and life expectancy rates, 6–8; and SNAP caseload, 94, 98–101, **99–101**; of study participants, **192**

dental care and dentures. *See* oral function and chewing

Department of Agriculture. *See* U.S. Department of Agriculture

Department of Health and Human Services (HHS), 58, 69, 131, 172

Department of Housing and Urban Development (HUD), 53, 180

depression: during COVID-19 pandemic, 78–79; and eating alone, 6; food insecurity, contributing to, 11, 75, 171; loss of teeth and social eating, 51–52

diabetes: budget trade-offs for medication, 50; and diet and nutrition sensitivities, 5, 114; and food insecurity, 171, 225*n*53; and home-delivered meals, 145; and SNAP benefits, 89–90, 109

Dietary Guidelines, 137, 146, 172

digital literacy, 12, 74, 96. *See also* internet use

disabilities. *See* adults with disabilities; chronic health conditions; Social Security Disability Insurance

Dollar Stores, 4, 33, 80

economic insecurity. *See* poverty and economic insecurity

education levels: and food bank usage rates, 151; and food insecurity, 12, 13–14, 66; and health issues, 69; and life expectancy rates, 8; and reduction in food insecurity, 7; and retirement ages, 7–8; of study participants, **192**

Elderly Simplified Application Project, 121

Elderly Simplified Reporting Program, 174, 176
Emergency Food Assistance Program, The (TEFAP), 132, 149
emergency food programs, 131–32, 171
employment: age discrimination in, 1–2, 8; and dental care, 53; food insecurity and reduction in, 7; health issues and limits on, 70; to increase household income, 44; interview questions on, 208; low wages and food insecurity, 67, **68**; and retirement age, 7, 8, 44; work-related injuries from, 1, 44
energy bills. *See* utilities
Environmental Protection Agency, 55

Families First Coronavirus Response Act (2020), 143
farmer's market coupons, 127–28, 163–66, **187**, **194**
Feeding America, 132
fixed incomes, 42–46. *See also* Social Security benefits
Food Access Research Atlas (USDA), 170
food banks: COVID-19 pandemic and closure of, 36–37; defined, 130; and difficulty accessing, 159–63; funding for, 132; geographic variation in availability of, 10, 152–56, **152–53**; medication, ability to pay for, 2; national numbers of, 130, **131**; nutritional quality of food at, 3, 66, 156–59; overview, 149–52, **187**; pickup and delivery options at, 172; rate of use by older adults, 150–51, **150**; rate of use by study participants, **194**; and running out of SNAP benefits, 17–18, 117; and stigma, 3
food deserts, 80–82, 170
food insecurity, 13–39; chronic health conditions and, 67–69, 76, 89–90, 171, 225*n*53; defined, 4; and food prices, 33–35, **34**; interview questions on, 211–12; life course perspective and social ecological model, 21–24, **21**; older adults and negative outcomes for, 5, 10; overview of measurement instruments, **190**; policy recommendations for, 168–70; poverty vs., 20–21; rates of, 4–5, 13–18, **15**, 46–47, **46**, 217*n*4; risk factors for, 13–14, 24–30, **25**, **29**; screening tools for, 171. *See also* Food Security Scale; study data
food preparation: and chronic health issues, 76, 118–19; and cooking skills, 118; and home-delivered meals, 146; and mobility issues, 5, 70, 73; and social networks, 77–78
food prices: and adequacy of SNAP benefits, 111–14, 116; and food bank use, 160; and food delivery services, 74; and food insecurity, measuring, 33–35, **34**, 67, **68**; increases in, 14, 33, 47; and mental health issues, 75–76
food security: defined, 4, 13, 219*n*3; levels of, 14–18, **15**; measuring (*see* Food Security Scale)
Food Security Scale (USDA): history of, 19–20; limitations of, 30–33, 168, 232*n*7; overview, 14–18, **15**, 219*n*9;

questionnaire, reprinted, 190–91; ratings of study participants, **193**
food stamps. *See* Supplemental Nutrition Assistance Program

GAO (Government Accountability Office), 171
gender: and employment, 8; and food insecurity, 12, 13, **25**, 26; and marital status, 45; and SNAP caseload, 98–99, **99**; and social isolation, 77; of study participants, 35, **192**
geographic location: and availability of nutritious food, 80; and congregate meals, 135–38, **136–37**, 141; and farmer's markets coupons, 164; and food banks, 10, 152–56, **152–53**; and food insecurity, **25**, 28, **183**; and home-delivered meals and groceries, 74, 144–45, **146–47**; and SNAP benefits, 111, 120–24, 173–74; of study participants, **192**, **195**. *See also* social ecological theory
Government Accountability Office (GAO), 171
grandchildren: and food insecurity, **25**, 26, 31–32, 65–66, 125, 232*n*7; providing childcare for, 31–32, 76; relationships with, 4; of study participants, **192**. *See also* multigenerational households
Great Depression, 91
Great Recession, 30, 91, 92, 153
grocery shopping: at Dollar Stores, 4, 33, 80; with family and friends, 77; and food deserts, 80–82, 170;

home-delivered groceries, 74, 174–75; physical health and mobility challenges, 69–73, 82; and transportation issues, 113, 225–26*n*60. *See also* food prices; Supplemental Nutrition Assistance Program
group meals. *See* congregate meals
group quarters, 30–31, 103, 232*n*7
Gundersen, Craig, 227*n*33

Haider, Steven, 101, 103
Harrington Meyer, Madonna, 31
Health and Retirement Study: on cognitive function and SNAP uptake rates, 106; defined, **190**; on food insecurity, 20, 217*n*4; on SNAP eligibility and uptake rates, 100–103, **101–2**, 227*n*33
health-care providers and settings, 171–72
health issues: budget trade-offs exacerbating, 6, 50–51; and dental care access, 51–53; and employment, 2; food banks, lack of nutritious food at, 3, 66; food insecurity, contributing to, 11, 67–74, 82–83, 225*n*53; heat- and cold-related issues, 55–57; interview questions on, 209–10; and life course theory, 22–23; mental health issues, 75–79; and nutrient requirements, 5, 75; policy recommendations and food security as health issue, 171–72; rates among study participants, **195**; retirement choices based on, 2, 8; SNAP benefit gaps and medication underuse, 109,

See also adults with disabilities; chronic health conditions; mobility issues
heat-related deaths, 55
Heflin, Colleen, 101, 109, 150, 225*n*53
home-delivered groceries, 74, 174–75
home-delivered meals: defined, 130; and difficulty accessing programs, 148–49; funding for, 131; geographic variation in availability of, 144–45, **146–47**; national numbers of, 130, **131**; nutritional quality of, 145–48, 171–72; overview, 142–43, **186**; rate of use among older adults, 144, **145**; rate of use among study participants, **194**
home health aides, 72, 73
Household PULSE Survey, 20, 55, **190**
housing: budget trade-offs for, 53–54; debt from, 44; eviction moratorium during COVID-19 pandemic, 54; inability to pay, rates of, 46–47, **46**; mobility issues and, 72; policy recommendations for, 180; subsidized, 53, 66, 77, 155, 177, **195**
hunger. *See* skipping meals
Hunger Vital Sign, 19, 171, **190**
hypertension, 5, 50–51, 109, 145, 171; and home-delivered-meal programs, 147

Instacart, 175
Institute of Medicine, 113, 116
insurance, 52–53. *See also* Medicaid; Medicare
internet use: digital literacy, 12, 74, 96; and home-delivered-grocery availability, 74; online retailers accepting SNAP payments, 122, 174–75; SNAP benefit applications, accessing, 96, 173; Zoom meals during COVID-19 pandemic, 133. *See also* phone and internet bills

Jones, Jordan, 101, 173

Kennedy, John F., 91

Li, Jun, 175
life course theory: and family, 45; food insecurity, measuring, 13, 21–24, **21**; and health issues, 27; and healthy diet, 123; and policy recommendations, 168, 178
Lifeline Program for phones, 63, 105
loneliness. *See* social life
Low-Income Home and Energy Assistance Program (LIHEAP), 57–58, 177, 180

marital status, **25**, 26, 35, 45, 151, **192**
Meals on Wheels, 10, 126–27, 142–43, 148. *See also* home-delivered meals
Medicaid: dental care through, 52, 172; Medically Tailored Meals, 143; SNAP enrollment and, 104; and social ecological factors, 49; of study participants, **193**; uptake rate of, 177
medical expenses: budget trade-offs for, 2, 6, 41, 48–53, 82–83, 225*n*53; debt from, 49–50; SNAP participation and standard medical deduction, 121, 175
Medically Tailored Groceries, 172
Medically Tailored Meals, 143, 172

INDEX

Medicare: dental care not covered by, 52–53, 172; eligibility for, 49; Medically Tailored Meals, 143; prescription medications not covered, 41; SNAP enrollment and, 104; of study participants, **193**

mental health issues, 75–79, **195**. *See also* depression

mobility issues: and arthritis, 60, 72, 86, 147; and food bank participation, 162; food insecurity, contributing to, 11, 169–70; and food preparation, 5, 70, 73; and grocery shopping, 69–73, 82; and home-delivered meals and groceries, 74, 147; and housing, 72; and public transportation use, 59–60, 86

multigenerational households, 12, **25**, 26, 45, 56. *See also* grandchildren

National Center for Charitable Statistics, 129–30, 231*n*25

National Health Interview Survey, 109

National Research Council, 113

National Strategy on Hunger, Nutrition and Health, 12

nonprofit organizations, 129–32, **131**, 135–36, **136**, 144, **146**. *See also* community-based and subsidized food programs

Nord, Mark, 19

nutritional quality of food: and chronic health conditions, 5, 114, 145–48, 158; and community-based and subsidized food programs, 127–29; at congregate meals, 127–28, 137–38, 171–72; at Dollar Stores, 4; and farmer's market coupons, 164; at food banks, 3, 66, 156–59; and food deserts, 80–82, 170; and home-delivered meals, 145–48, 171–72; nutrition security, defined, 169; and social determinants of health, 82–83; at soup kitchens, 140

obesity, 78–79, 83, 171

Older Americans Act (1964), 129, 130, 131–32, 139, 143

oral function and chewing, 5, 6, 51–53, 147, 172

overweight, 78–79, 83

people with disabilities. *See* adults with disabilities

personal and cleaning supplies: budget trade-offs for, 3, 41, 60–63; from food banks, 154–55; food vs., 3, 41; SNAP not covering, 119

Pew Research Center, 77

phone and internet bills, 63–64, 105

physical food insecurity scale, 169

policy recommendations, 39, 167–82; on cash assistance programs, 178–79; on food assistance programs, connecting with social welfare programs, 176–78; on food security as health issue, 171–72; on measuring food insecurity, 168–70; on other program expansions, 180; on SNAP, 173–76; on Social Security, SSI, and SSDI benefits, 179–80

poverty and economic insecurity, 38, 40–64; budgeting challenges for fixed incomes, 42–46; children, programs

for, 9–10; and congregate meal participation, 133, **134**; expense of social interactions, 79; food deserts and lack of access to groceries, 80; food insecurity vs., 20–21; and health issues, 69; and housing, 53–54; as indicator of food insecurity, **25**, 26; measures of, 9; Medicaid coverage and, 49; and medical expenses, 48–53; and personal and cleaning supplies, 60–63; phone and internet bills, 63–64; rates of, 43; Social Security benefits and reductions in, 8–9; and transportation issues, 58–60, 83; and utilities, 55–58. *See also* budget trade-offs; Supplemental Nutrition Assistance Program
prescription medications. *See* medical expenses
Prescription Produce, 172
Price, Ashley, 150
Project Open Hand, 140–41

race and ethnicity: and employment, 8; and food bank usage rates, 151; food deserts and lack of access to groceries, 80; and food insecurity, 12, 13, **25**, 26, 33; and health issues, 69; and heat-related deaths, 55; and housing burden, 53; inability to pay housing and utilities, rates of, 46–47, **46**; and SNAP caseload, 98–99, **99**; of study participants, 35, **192**; and wealth gap, 44
Reagan, Ronald, 149
rent. *See* housing

residential care facilities, 30–31, 103, 232*n*7
Restaurant Meals Program (RMP, USDA), 173, 174
retirement: early retirement and reduced Social Security payments, 43; education levels and age at, 7–8; and employment, 7, 8, 44; health issues forcing, 2, 8; savings for, 43–44
rural areas. *See* geographic location

Salvation Army, 54, 140–41
Sassine, AnnieBelle, 169
senior centers: accessing, 126–27, 138–39, 231*n*25; defined, 130; funding for, 230*n*3; national numbers of, 130, **131**; nutritional quality of meals at, 126–27, 171–72. *See also* congregate meals
Senior Farmers Market Nutrition Program (SFMNP), 163–64
shame. *See* stigma and shame
skipping meals, 16–18, 41, 65, 115, 125, 148
Small, Mario Luis, 201
SNAP. *See* Supplemental Nutrition Assistance Program
social determinants of health, 32, 69, 82–83, 171
social ecological theory: and community-based and subsidized food programs, 128; food insecurity, measuring, 13, 21–24, **21**; and Medicaid eligibility, 49; nutritious food, accessing, 80; and SNAP administrative burden, 106; and

transportation issues, 83. *See also* geographic location
social life: cost of, 4, 79; COVID-19 pandemic and, 37, 78, 126, 133; and dental health, 51–52; and eating alone, 6; and home-delivered meals, 142–43; interview questions on, 210; isolation and loneliness, 6, 11, 51–52, 75–78, 79, 143; and life course theory, 22. *See also* congregate meals; senior centers
Social Security benefits: effectiveness as anti-poverty program, 8–9; policy recommendations for, 179; shortfalls of, 8–9; and SNAP benefits, 98, **98**; of study participants, **193**; uptake rate of, 103, 176–77
Social Security Disability Insurance (SSDI), 1, 27–28, 177, 180, **193**
socioeconomic status. *See* poverty and economic insecurity
soup kitchens. *See* congregate meals
Special Supplemental Nutrition Program for Women, Infants, and Children (WIC), 9, **188**
stigma and shame, 3, 4, 103, 104, 163
study data: analysis of, 204–5; food insecurity by state, **183**; food insecurity measures, **190**; food programs, overview, **184–89**; Food Security Scale, reprinted, 190–91; interview guide for, 202, 206–14; participant characteristics, 35, **192–200**, 203–4; qualitative methods, 201–2; recruitment methods, 202–3, 206, 214–15

subsidized food programs. *See* community-based and subsidized food programs
Supplemental Nutrition Assistance Program (SNAP), 38–39, 88–124; accessing, 95–97; adequacy of, 110–24; administrative burden of, 3, 70, 88–89, 104–10, 121, 173, 176–77, 225*n*53, 228*n*52; average benefit amount, 33–34, 88, 178; and Combined Application Project, 121, 177; congregate meal participation and, 130; COVID-19 pandemic and, 36, 89–92, 94–95, 107, 116–17, 121–22, 174; farmer's markets accepting, 163–64; lower participation rates among older adults, 11–12, 103–24, 173, 177; minimum benefit, 97, 221*n*1; national participation rates, 88; older adults' participation in, 90–91, 97–103, **98–102**; overview of program, 91–95, **93**, **184**; policy recommendations for, 173–76; prioritizing food security through, 21; reduced funding for, 149; requirements for, 10, 120–21; running out of benefits, 17–18, 115, 225*n*53; study participants' rate of use among, **194**; uptake rates, local variations in, 120–24, **120**
Supplemental Poverty Measure, 9, 43
Supplemental Security Income (SSI): Combined Application Project and SNAP benefits, 121, 177; policy recommendations for, 179–80; and SNAP benefits, 98, **98**; of study

participants, **193**; success rate of applications, 28, 177
Survey of Consumer Finance, 44
Survey of Income and Program Participation (2018), 46, **190**

technology use. *See* internet use
TEFAP (The Emergency Food Assistance Program), 132, 149
Thrifty Food Plan (USDA): and adequacy of SNAP benefits, 111; on cost of older adult's monthly food, 98; revaluation of, 36, 95; SNAP benefits based on, 92, 97, 116, 174
transportation: budget trade-offs for, 2, 42, 58–60; car maintenance and gas costs, 2, 32–33, 59–60, 66, 85–86, 113; car ownership rates of study participants, **194**; community-based and subsidized food programs, accessing, 12, 23–24, 66, 127–28, 139; and farmer's market coupons, 164–65; and Food Access Research Atlas, 170; and food bank participation, 160–62; and food deserts, 80–82; food insecurity and lack of, 67, **68**, 83–87, 177; interview questions on, 209; medical transports, 59; public, availability and accessibility of, 37, 59, 66, 84–85, 125–26, 225–26*n*60
Trump, Donald, 12

unemployment, 44, 94, 123
United Nations Food and Agriculture Organization, 219*n*3
Urban Institute, 77, 176

U.S. Bureau of Labor Statistics, 7, 44
U.S. Department of Agriculture (USDA): Child and Adult Care Food Program, 230*n*3, 231*n*25; Emergency Food Assistance Program, 132, 149; Food Access Research Atlas, 170; on food deserts, 80, 170; food security, defined, 4, 13; funding for food programs, 131–32; on lower participation rates in SNAP among older adults, 103; on nutrition security, 169; Restaurant Meals Program, 173, 174; Senior Farmers Market Nutrition Program, 163–66; subsidized food programs, 10, **184–89**. *See also* Food Security Scale; Supplemental Nutrition Assistance Program; Thrifty Food Plan
U.S. Department of Health and Human Services (HHS), 58, 69, 131, 172
U.S. Department of Housing and Urban Development (HUD), 53, 180
utilities, 46–47, **46**, 55–58, 156, 177, 180

veterans' benefits, 7, **193**
Veteran's Health Administration, 19, 171
volunteers, 132, 141–42, 149, 151–52. *See also* community-based and subsidized food programs

wealth gap, 44
weight gain, 78–79, 83
World Food Summit (1996), 219*n*3

Ziliak, James, 94, 227*n*33
Zoom, 133